AUGUSTUS BALDWIN LONGSTREET

Reproduced from a copy of a line engraving in the University of Georgia Library.

Augustus Baldwin Longstreet

A Study of the Development of Culture in the South

BY
JOHN DONALD WADE

EDITED
WITH AN INTRODUCTION
AND A WADE BIBLIOGRAPHY
BY
M. THOMAS INGE

THE UNIVERSITY OF GEORGIA PRESS
ATHENS

Paperback edition, 2010
© 1969 by the University of Georgia Press
Athens, Georgia 30602
www.ugapress.org
All rights reserved
Printed digitally in the United States of America

The Library of Congress has cataloged the hardcover edition of
this book as follows:
Library of Congress Cataloging-in-Publication Data

Wade, John Donald, 1892–1963.
Augustus Baldwin Longstreet; a study of the development of culture in the South. Edited with an introd. and a Wade bibliography, by M. Thomas Inge.
xxxvi, 392 p. port. 25 cm.
Bibliography: p. 373–383.
1. Longstreet, Augustus Baldwin, 1790–1870.
I. Inge, M. Thomas, ed.
F213 .L85   1969
917.5'03'30924 B   70-83729

PAPERBACK ISBN-13: 978-0-8203-3480-6
ISBN-10: 0-8203-3480-4

To My
MOTHER

PREFACE

It is possible to write briefly about a subject of research if there is very little material to be had about it or if there is much more material than can be presented. In the case of Augustus Baldwin Longstreet, I have brought to light just enough information, perhaps, to make too ponderous a volume, but not quite enough, on the other hand, to justify any of its being permitted to sink back again out of memory. This book, then, tells about its subject nearly everything that I have been able to learn.

I wish to thank Professors William P. Trent, Carl Van Doren and George F. Krapp of Columbia University for their interest in my investigation. All of these gentlemen read the manuscript and gave me their valuable criticisms.

Professors E. L. Green and Yates Snowden of the University of South Carolina, Professor Mason Du Pré of Wofford College, Mr. Fitz R. Longstreet of Gainesville, Georgia, Mr. Duncan Burnet of the University of Georgia Library, Mr. Henry Beach Carrée of the Vanderbilt University Library, Professor David H. Bishop and Miss Gladys Short of the University of Mississippi, all gave me access to certain essential documents. I am very grateful to them.

Mrs. Lavinia Branham West and Mrs. Fannie Lamar Mayes of Jackson, Mississippi, and Mrs. Augusta Lamar Heiskell of Memphis, Tennessee, granddaughters of Longstreet, have very graciously given me personal reminiscences of their grandfather. I have had other such information from Mr. G. W. W. Stone, Mr. Harry Stone, and the Reverend Mr. W. R. Branham of Oxford, Georgia, and from Professor Charles W. Hutson of New Orleans.

Professors Willis H. Bocock and Preston Brooks of the University of Georgia kindly offered me their help and made some appreciated comments.

PREFACE

Professor Roosevelt Walker, of the University of Georgia, aided me throughout my work; he, Professors Merton Coulter, and Heyward Young, of the University of Georgia, and Mr. Aaron Blum Bernd of Macon, Georgia, read the manuscript and criticized it with an intelligence and sympathy that leave me deeply in the debt of all of them.

More deeply am I in the debt of Professor Robert Emory Park, also of the University of Georgia. He has helped me in ways too many to name. His sharply humorous though affectionate understanding of Longstreet's native state, his philosophic mind which remembers always that occurrences are but facets of universal life, his magnanimous heart which has endeared him to so many young Georgians—all of these I hope are, if but dimly, reflected in this book.

J. D. W.

University of Georgia.
May, 1923.

CONTENTS

	INTRODUCTION	xi
	JOHN DONALD WADE: A BIBLIOGRAPHY, 1922–1962	xxx
	EDITOR'S NOTE	xxxv
I	THE START	1
II	EDUCATION	23
III	A YOUNG LAWYER IN GEORGIA	48
IV	RELIGIOUS INTERESTS	100
V	AUGUSTA—AND POLITICS	117
VI	GEORGIA SCENES	143
VII	GEORGIA SCENES—ONE BY ONE	169
VIII	GENERAL LITERARY EFFORT IN GEORGIA	187
IX	UNCOLLECTED "SCENES"	199
X	THE MINISTRY	219
XI	EMORY COLLEGE	241
XII	ECCLESIASTICAL CONTROVERSY OVER SLAVERY	270
XIII	COLLEGES IN THE WEST	287
XIV	THE UNIVERSITY OF SOUTH CAROLINA	314
XV	THE WAR	339
XVI	HOME	351
	AUGUSTUS BALDWIN LONGSTREET: A BIBLIOGRAPHY	373
	INDEX	385

INTRODUCTION

Although the historical and critical study of what we have come to call the Southern literary renaissance is an activity which has elicited in recent years the participation of some of the best critical minds of this generation, very little direct attention has been paid to one of the minor genres in which the renaissance found expression—the biography. Many of the major figures felt the urge early or at the very beginning of their creative careers to turn to some historical figure and retell his life story in their own distinctive idioms. Thus Allen Tate published simultaneously with his first volume of collected poems a biographical study, *Stonewall Jackson: The Good Soldier* (1928), followed immediately by *Jefferson Davis: His Rise and Fall* (1929). He began research on a third biography —that of Robert E. Lee—which he finally abandoned. Robert Penn Warren initiated his literary career with a biography entitled *John Brown: The Making of a Martyr* (1929), which appeared six years before his first volume of poetry and ten years before his first novel. Likewise Andrew Nelson Lytle's first book was an account of *Bedford Forrest and his Critter Company* (1931). Why they all abandoned the biographical for the more creative poetical and fictional modes rather early we do not know, but an even more important question worth asking is why this was the first mode to attract the exercise of their considerable talents. Perhaps it has something to do with the fact that the Southern writer, as a Southerner, naturally engaged himself in a study of his region and its past, and the biography, a chronicle of the life of a shaper of that past, is a natural form for the expression of what he discovers. If the writer likes what he sees, what better way to commemorate than the biography, and if he dislikes his past, what better way to moralize over betrayed and lost opportunities? That the form is still viable and attractive for all these reasons is demonstrated by William Styron's recent *Confessions of Nat Turner* (1967).

The writer who may be said to have initiated this development in modern Southern literature is John Donald Wade.[1] While the *Fugitive* was just beginning publication in 1922 in Nashville, the point at which many feel the Southern literary renaissance properly began, Wade had already spent over three years in research that would result in his biography *Augustus Baldwin Longstreet: A Study of the Development of Culture in the South* (1924). Wade was later to merge forces with the core leaders of the Fugitive movement who also became proponents of an agrarian salvation for those members of society trapped in the belly of a collectivistic-industrial leviathan, but that was not to occur for a few years yet. How he came to write the study of Longstreet's life and times was related by Wade in 1960 in his retrospective essay on *Georgia Scenes*.[2]

When he was graduated from the University of Georgia in 1914, the presence of few doctoral degree-granting institutions in the South led him to enroll at Harvard. There he studied under Barrett Wendell, who offered the first course in American literature at Harvard and who wrote the early and quite eccentric *Literary History of America* (for which Fred Lewis Pattee proposed the alternative and more accurate title *A Literary History of Harvard University with Incidental Glimpses of the Minor Writers of America*).[3] When he learned that young Wade was interested in Southern literature, Wendell frankly recommended that he transfer to Columbia to work under a Virginian, William Peterfield Trent, founder of the

---

[1] For biographical accounts of Wade, see John O. Eidson, "John Donald Wade, 1892–1963: A Sketch of His Life," in *Selected Essays and Other Writings of John Donald Wade,* ed. Donald Davidson (Athens, 1966), pp. vii–ix; Virginia Rock, "The Twelve Southerners: Biographical Essays," in *I'll Take My Stand,* Harper Torchbook Edition (New York, 1962), pp. 380–381; and the latter author's biography of Wade in Appendix B to her dissertation "The Making and Meaning of *I'll Take My Stand:* A Study in Utopian-Conservatism, 1925–1939," University of Minnesota, 1961, pp. 547–554. The author is especially indebted to the last for many suggestions developed in this introduction. An important biographical and critical memoir is Donald Davidson's "Introduction: The Gardens of John Donald Wade" in his *Selected Essays and Other Writings of John Donald Wade,* pp. 1–20.

[2] *Georgia Review,* XIV (1960), 444–447. Reprinted in *Selected Essays,* pp. 165–168.

[3] Howard Mumford Jones, *The Theory of American Literature* (Ithaca, 1965), p. 100.

INTRODUCTION
xiii

Sewanee Review, a man who Professor Wendell said knew more about Southern literature than he did. Receiving his M. A. degree before his departure, Wade set out for New York to encounter the teacher whose advice gave him the sense of direction which would shape his career. Wade reports, with a light touch of the civilized irony which pervades his writing:

> I was from Georgia, said Professor Trent, and there was a subject cut out for me: Judge Longstreet, the author of *Georgia Scenes,* one of the really first "American books" in the Whitmanian sense of the phrase, the forerunner of many other notable books, even at last, most likely, of *Tom Sawyer* and *Huckleberry Finn.* The date, as I have remarked, was early, and the speaker was in consequence still able to name all these names standing rather than on his knees.[4]

When Wade had finished his study in 1924, after over four years of research, it proved to be a good deal more than the typical academic exercise required for the doctorate. He apparently had no trouble interesting the Macmillan Company, one of the more prestigious publishers, in the manuscript. Thus in 1924 he presented as dissertation copies special issues of *Augustus Baldwin Longstreet* fresh from the presses. While the biography retained the pedantic appendages of frequent footnotes and source citations, within the scholarly format Wade was able to enhance his study with a lively sense of style and dramatic interest. Note, for example, the comic skill demonstrated in leading up to the punch line in this typical anecdote from the book:

> Longstreet had one story of his law days that he used to tell with undiminished gusto. He and another man, a stranger to him, who had taken far too much to drink, were quartered together one night in a combination guest chamber and dining room. They were to leave early next morning at the same time for the same place. During the night, Longstreet heard his partner pottering stupidly around the room. Half asleep, he inquired as to the cause of disturbance. Hiccough—hiccough.—"I'm just looking for the window to see how the weather is, and how long it will be before daylight. . . . I can't find it though. . . . Here it is, if I can ever open it.

[4] *Selected Essays,* p. 166.

... Huh, now it's open." Silence. "Well, how does it look?" asked the judge. "Whew. Look! Good God, man, it looks like midnight, and stinks like hell!" He had opened the door of a cup-board and rammed his nose into an ancient cheese! (pp. 80–81)

It is perhaps a tribute to Trent's liberal forebearance as a thesis director that he permitted such episodes to stand, imagined dialogue and all, without citation of a source or authority, and it is the presence of such passages that brings the book into the realm of literature.

The study has its weaknesses, admittedly, some of them due to the rigid nature of the Germanic doctoral model, others due to immaturities in Wade's developing sense of style. To the latter account are due such rhetorical excesses as the occasional apostrophes—"Alas, that the day of giants has gone by!" (p. 30), or "What a man Mr. Calhoun was!" (p. 34)—and the infrequent sentence of twisted syntax, such as "what is down the fork of the road not taken one always must needs give up" (p. 52). The rather lengthy volume, too, could have benefited from some judicious pruning, as Wade intimated in his apology in the preface: "In the case of Augustus Baldwin Longstreet, I have brought to light just enough information to make too ponderous a volume, but not quite enough, on the other hand, to justify any of its being permitted to sink back again out of memory" (p. vii). But such defects are overshadowed by the preponderant originality and critical intelligence of the fledgling biographer.

In at least three ways *Augustus Baldwin Longstreet* was markedly ahead of its time. It was one of the earliest attempts to assess the backgrounds of Southern literature, an occupation that was to become increasingly important as a great groundswell of writers contemporary to Wade initiated the Southern literary renaissance (if this was the renaissance, the new birth, when did the original birth occur, they asked). Some critics have sought an explanation for the modern phenomenon in the literary past of the region, and such studies as Wade's help elucidate that past.

The book was also an early example of a kind of approach to understand our culture that we now call "American Studies," an attempt to combine the traditionally separate disciplines of history, literature, and social science to define the American experience more effectively. This is partly attributable to his theory of history which he expressed on the part of Longstreet although it is clearly his own as well:

> One intellectual inquiry his democratic soul could not get away from. It was concerned with history. Why does history, he wanted to know, say nothing except about the emperors and such like? Why does it not tell about the vast bulk of the population, the ordinary, every-day citizens? Could there be such a thing as social history? When we and our institutions live only in old records, for we shall all surely pass, what if someone should—would it not be enthrallingly interesting to find a document showing the Latin civilization as it existed for people in general, not just for the patricians? (p. 50)

Wade's own book, of course, is just such a document. His intent to produce an interdisciplinary study is evident in its subtitle, "A Study of the Development of Culture in the South," and in his statement at the beginning that he viewed Longstreet's life as "an epitome in some sense, of American civilization" (p. 2). He fulfills the roles of biographer, intellectual historian, and literary critic with equal ease. His refusal to confine himself to one discipline is evident, also, in his statement in a letter to Virginia Rock that as a teacher he "lived on a Bridge between American History and American Literature (both slanted south-wise), the Bridge supported by all that I can know or theorize about in any lines (the *main* line slanted toward History and Literature in general)."[5] In an age of the first academic specialists he was a refreshing generalist who tried to view his work as teacher and scholar in its broadest cultural context.

By writing on Longstreet, Wade also anticipated and initiated, as Donald Davidson observed, "the vogue, beginning joyously in the nineteen-twenties and lasting pretty well to the present day, of the 'humor of the Old Southwest,' as it used to be called, and of frontier humor in general."[6] He was, in fact,

[5] "The Making and Meaning of *I'll Take My Stand*," p. 549.
[6] *Selected Essays*, p. 4.

writing more than six years before the publication of Franklin J. Meine's *Tall Tales of the Southwest* (1930) and Constance Rourke's *American Humor* (1931), and more than thirteen years before Walter Blair's *Native American Humor* (1937), seminal works which gave critical interest in the Southwestern humorists a momentous push. Wade produced such a definitive assessment that nothing new or of consequence has been written about Longstreet or his work since then.[7] Another contribution to this school of scholarship was his essay "Southern Humor," prepared for W. T. Couch's anthology *Culture in the South* (1934). Unlike most theorists and anatomists of the nature of comedy and humor, Wade doesn't treat the subject with deadly seriousness and thereby kill it. The essay is a lively piece of cultural analysis which probes at the psychological origins of the peculiarly Southern kind of humor.

When *Augustus Baldwin Longstreet* appeared, it was greeted in the main by a chorus of critical superlatives, but tempered usually by a degree of fault-finding. Julia Collier Harris, the daughter-in-law of Joel Chandler Harris, wrote, "Mr. Wade's account of this full, attractive life is written in a style in keeping with its subject—picturesque, humorous, and suggestive of the homely, kindly spirit which is middle Georgia's best heritage from early days."[8] Edgar Legare Pennington found that "The book glides along like a romance, and yet it is all history."[9] With a greater precision in judgement and expression, the anonymous reviewer for the *Springfield Republican* noted, "This book combines the reliability derived from careful research with the animating force of a fresh, curious, humorous and impartial mind."[10] In a lengthy review for the *New York Times*, journalist Silas Bent felt that while Wade had done "a good, neat and workmanlike job," he failed to

---

[7] Except for a recent attempt to read one of the *Georgia Scenes* symbolically: Kenneth Silverman, "Longstreet's 'The Gander Pulling,'" *American Quarterly*, XVIII (1966), 548–549. Longstreet testified that the story was simply based on an actual occurrence with the names changed; see *Augustus Baldwin Longstreet*, p. 176.

[8] "A Middle-Georgia Pioneer," *Nation*, CXVIII (1924), 743.

[9] "The South in the Days of Poe," *Literary Digest International Book Review*, II (1924), 788–789.

[10] *Springfield Republican*, June 8, 1924, p. 7a.

INTRODUCTION

provide "an adequate picture of ante-bellum aristocracy in the South." He had, however, "given to the writing of American history a decided forward propulsion."[11] Historian Ulrich B. Phillips found the study "a clear, cogent, and illuminating treatment of significant themes," but called Wade's hand on his sense of geography and a few historical inaccuracies.[12] Robert Littell used the book as a source for an extensive sketch of Longstreet's life in the *New Republic* after designating it "a fascinating, if at times awkward and cluttered record of a very curious and lively character."[13]

Wade approached his study of the life and times of Longstreet with objectivity, without the preconceived intention of glorifying his milieu and making out a case for him as a neglected major literary figure. With candor and honesty he noted the fanatical egocentricities and occasional doubts and compromises of principle on the part of the Georgia lawyer, clergyman, college administrator, editor, and humorist, as well as the dilatoriness of Georgians in intellectual and literary pursuits up to the time of *Georgia Scenes* (1835). The negative nature of some of his findings predictably caused a few Southern readers to charge Wade with the defamation of his home region, a possibility George W. Johnson must have had in mind when he said in his review, "He has done a piece of work immensely creditable to the south, but one wonders if he will receive credit for it in the south."[14] One Southern reviewer, stirred to a passionate frenzy, castigated the book in this manner:

This is one of the most dangerous books that has appeared in the South in many a day. Not since Mr. Dickens and Mrs. Trollope visited our shores have American ideals and customs received as mean and petty a blow as is dealt them in this book—a book that was published by a supposedly reliable and trustworthy New York house

---

[11] "Augustus B. Longstreet, a Citizen of the South," *New York Times Book Review*, March 2, 1924, p. 9.

[12] *American Historical Review*, XXX (1924), 181–182.

[13] "Judge Longstreet of Georgia," *New Republic*, XXXIX (1924), 359–361; reprinted in Robert Littell, *Read America First* (New York, 1926), pp. 146–158. Other unsigned reviews appeared in *Outlook*, CXXXVII (June 25, 1924), 319–320; and the *Literary Review* of the New York *Evening Post*, July 19, 1924, p. 905.

[14] Greensboro (North Carolina) *Daily News*, April 27, 1924, p. 12.

(Macmillan) and which piously parades under the sub-title of "A Study of the Development of Culture in the South. . . ." Professor Wade takes a grand old antebellum character . . . a genuine gentleman of the old school, and builds up around him a pack of the most monstrous implications that have ever appeared between the covers of a book. What makes it all the more inexplicable is the fact that Professor Wade himself is a direct product of and is essentially identified with the Old South. He would have us believe that in those glorious old times there was not much civilization after all; that our brave and hardy ancestors were little more than uncouth, tobacco-chewing-and-spitting horse shoe pitchers, who, when they were not engaging in that sport, were lounging around the village or cross-roads tavern gorging themselves on whiskey bought in quart lots. . . . People of Georgia, Daughters of the American Revolution, Colonial Dames, United Daughters of the Confederacy, and ye stalwart sons and fair daughters of a glorious civilization, rise up and shake off such a slur as this! Shall we permit the untarnished name of this our grand old State to be traduced? Shall we permit the outside world to be told that our ancestors were rude, uncultured, uncouth people?[15]

The incredibly blind insensitivity of this patriot prevented him from seeing the loving regard for his region and the sane good humor which permeates Wade's honest gaze in his biography.[16]

Following the publication of *Augustus Baldwin Longstreet*, Wade went on to perfect the biographical art by beginning work on a biography of John Wesley and by working for one year as a member of the editorial staff of the *Dictionary of American Biography*. He wrote 117 biographical essays for the *Dictionary*, a record number of contributions equaled or exceeded by only seven of the other 2,250-odd contributors. Because of his experience and background, undoubtedly, Wade selected and

---

[15] Cited in Howard Odum, *An American Epoch: Southern Portraiture in the National Picture* (New York, 1930), pp. 106–107. Odum does not identify the author or source.

[16] Coincidentally, when his teacher, William Peterfield Trent, published his biography of William Gilmore Simms in 1892, Southern readers strongly objected to its criticism of slavery. Trent's strong criticism of Southern mores and customs, which concealed he felt an essentially primitive society, led Paul Buck to call it "the most devastating indictment of the intellectual life of the Old South ever written by an informed scholar" (*The Road to Reunion: 1865–1900*, Boston, 1937, pp. 218–219).

was assigned sixty-four distinguished Southern authors, politicians, educators, clergymen, lawyers, doctors, journalists, soldiers, philanthropists, and pioneers to write about. He prepared the sketches of several well known writers, such as William Alexander Caruthers, John William Fox, Jr., Johnson Jones Hooper, and the one figure on which he was the undisputed authority, Augustus Baldwin Longstreet. But his assignments were not exclusively Southern, as he also wrote on fifty-three notable people from all the other American regions, including Zerah Colburn, the Vermont prodigy and mathematical genius, William Ewing DuBois, the Philadelphia numismatist, and assorted other professionals, businessmen, poets, artists, and soldiers of fortune.

In the hands of a less-talented man, the preparation of these formula pieces could have become a dull routine task, but Wade utilized the opportunity to increase his skill by subtly achieving effects the chief editors may not even have noticed as the material passed across their desks. As Donald Davidson noted, "The experience of having to write with clipped terseness according to a prescribed pattern and within a strict work limit undoubtedly affected Wade's style. Among other things he learned how, in very few words, to make an apparently bald statement of fact carry with it a judgement, either through the vocabulary itself or by skillful placement of one factual item in juxtaposition with others. Thus he often secured a subtly ironic effect, perceptible to a close reader but not immediately evident to readers that take large eyefuls and run as they read."[17]

The essays contain many neat, quotable examples of what Davidson is talking about. For example, writing of Timothy Bloodworth, the eccentric North Carolina politician and senator, Wade concludes:

Almost all his life he stood against the main trend of history, and sixty years after his death even a newspaper editor in the North Carolina state capital was obliged to admit that he had never heard of him. (II, 385)

---

[17] *Selected Essays*, p. 6.

After suggesting that Chicago financier and philanthropist John Crerar was a man of geniality and imagination, and was "a civic force of great importance, lending his influence and resources to any cause that seemed to him at once sound of itself and conducive to the development of Chicago," Wade notes:

He lived quietly, in hotels, and when he was urged by his friend Jesup to engage in his lifetime in large-scale philanthropies, he demurred, saying, "I am satisfied and content." (IV, 537)

Note the touch of grim humor in his discussion of the main ideas in the sermons of Baptist clergyman Justin Dewey Fulton:

One of his clearest themes was that honesty and hard work, coupled with avoidance of whatever is not "useful," will inevitably lead to wealth and power; and he was always alert to denounce drinking, woman suffrage, and the drama. During the first part of his life the chief object of his condemnation was slavery, but after the Civil War, he finished off his concern with this matter by his adulatory sermon on the death of Lincoln (*Sermons Preached in Boston on the Death of Abraham Lincoln,* 1865), in which the sole error attributed to Lincoln is frequenting theatres. . . . (VII, 68)

This mordant irony is also evident in Wade's treatment of the career of Charles Henry Crandall, a minor Connecticut poet whose work, inspired by World War I, was ardently patriotic but patently pedestrian.

That theme stirred him most—the thrill of seeing one's flag unfurled, the superior bravery of the American military, the divine mission of America as guardian of her neighbors to the south, and as model for the governments of Europe. . . . When the United States went into the World War, Crandall's four sons entered the service of the government, one of them to be killed in action. The father's boundless enthusiasm was set forth in 1918 with vigor and sincerity—if without other merit—in his *Liberty Illumined* and *Songs for the Boys in Khaki.* The war was to him a holy and invincible crusade for everything that spiritual men most ardently and most rightfully desire, and at the conclusion of it, he believed, we should all be justly happy. One day, less than five years after the war ended, he killed himself with a pistol. (IV, 503)

INTRODUCTION   xxi

I daresay few biographical dictionaries, usually noted for their scholarly sobriety, contain the sort of witty surprises Wade gave to his share of entries in the *Dictionary of American Biography*. They may be read not only for information but for pleasure and profit as well.

Wade was invited in 1928 to come to Vanderbilt University to establish a graduate program in American literature. Under his tutelage the first graduate students followed the example of his work and began to prepare doctoral dissertations of a biographical type. Thus the first doctorate granted was awarded to Richmond Croom Beatty who wrote on William Byrd (1932), followed by Leota S. Driver on Fanny Kemble (1932), Linda Rhea on Hugh Swinton Legaré (1932), and Edd Winfield Parks on Mary N. Murfree (1932). Each was published and each remains today an important or definitive account of its subject.[18] Beatty, who spent much of his career writing further biographies, later filled Wade's position at Vanderbilt and continued to foster the writing of biographical dissertations, thus prolonging the Wade influence greatly to the benefit of modern scholarship.

With the *DAB* experience behind him and his book on John Wesley well under way, Wade was consciously breaking free of the carefully-documented approach used in the Longstreet study to develop a free-swinging style of his own. There is a story, reported by Davidson in his memoir of Richmond Croom Beatty, that in composing his Wesley biography Wade relied upon no card index or mechanically-gathered notes. Instead, "he sat at ease beside his famous revolving bookcase. With his right hand he wrote. With his left hand, as need arose, he twirled the bookcase to catch a brief reminding glimpse of the title and author on a back strip. A glimpse was all he needed; he knew the book's contents down to chapter and verse."[19] Davidson was not sure but what this was an affectionate fable

---

[18] Richmond Croom Beatty, *William Byrd of Westover* (Boston, 1932); Leota S. Driver, *Fanny Kemble* (Chapel Hill, 1933); Linda Rhea, *Hugh Swinton Legaré: A Charleston Intellectual* (Chapel Hill, 1934); Edd Winfield Parks, *Charles Egbert Craddock* (Chapel Hill, 1941).

[19] *Reality and Myth: Essays in American Literature in Memory of Richard Croom Beatty*, ed. William E. Walker and Robert L. Welker (Nashville, 1964), pp. 6–7.

of Wade's former students, and that may be. So radical, however, is the difference in style, structure, and content between the biographies of Longstreet and Wesley that this description would appear to be a fairly accurate one of his method of composition. While the Longstreet was highly detailed, compendious, and heavily annotated, the Wesley is selective in detail, rapidly paced, and entirely unacademic in its lack of documentation.

While the Longstreet attempted to take in a panoramic view of the psyche of an entire society through one representative figure, the Wesley attempts to analyze the psychological compulsions of a man, a saint finally, who not so much reflected the temper of his times as he profoundly influenced it. So narrow was Wade's focus that one reviewer complained, "it would have greatly increased the value of the book, I think, if he had told us more of the spiritual condition of Church and society in the England of that day."[20] For historians, perhaps, yes, but the high degree of selectivity and succinctness in this book greatly contribute to the striking creation of a singular character and provide for a pleasurable reading experience undisturbed by interesting but diverting historical circumstance.[21]

This is not to suggest that Wesley is portrayed with insufficient detail. Under the increasing skill of Wade's pen, John Wesley emerges as a multi-dimensional man, a marvelous combination of humility and ambition urged onward to private and public spiritual greatness by the strange and undeserved compliment of his father moments before death, "Now, you have done all," an utterance which served to point up the discrepancy between himself and the person his father saw him as. Finding himself among colleagues and superiors, none of whom appeared his intellectual or spiritual equals, only his brother Charles offered a challenge to his authority as he threateningly questioned the religious assumptions of his age. On his progress to sainthood, he faces the unnerving temptations of the world,

[20] W. L. Sullivan, in New York *Herald-Tribune Books*, December 4, 1930, p. 4.

[21] As one reviewer noted, "His work is modern without being iconoclastic, readable and vivid without being fiction, and full of human interest rather than theological controversy. It is a human document rather than an history of the times" (T. C. R., *Boston Transcript*, November 29, 1930, p. 4).

most of which he turns away without trouble, except for the prime villain of "Evil-Thoughts," or the "silken insinuation of Sex." Here is the paradox of a profoundly compassionate man who could, at the same moment that he sought God's guidance, turn impatiently to his sister Patty complaining over the death of her baby and say cruelly, "I believe that the death of your children is a great instance of the goodness of God toward you. You have often mentioned to me how much of your time they took up. Now that time is restored to you." Finally, we see Wesley as the paradox of a great spiritual leader and founder of a widely-influential protestant sect who to the last insisted, "I declare once more that I live and die a member of the Church of England, and that none who regards my judgement will ever separate from it."

Wade divides Wesley's life into twelve phases and devotes twelve chapters of an average twenty-three pages to each phase, or station of the cross so to speak. The chapter titles mark the progress: Creeper, Scholar, Monk, Bungler, Seeker, Preacher, Builder, Victim, Wrangler, Victor, Bishop, Saint. While the research Wade conducted in preparing to write this book must have been even more extensive than for his *Longstreet* (a grant from the Guggenheim Foundation partially helped support it), all documentation has been vigorously excluded, to the degree that quotations from letters and journals have been skillfully blended into the narrative without citation of source or even the use of quotation marks. None of the reviewers noticed this radical departure from scholarly technique, perhaps itself a suggestion of the extent of his success. The appearance of *John Wesley* in 1930 was a largely-unrecognized literary event of the first order.

Allen Tate gave the book deserved praise in a review entitled "Beautiful Prose":

Mr. Wade is doubtless the most remarkable stylist in biography we have had in America since the War. Considered sectionally, as a Southern writer, he is the only master of style who has ever taken up biography as a form. . . . There has been much talk of biography turning into art in Mr. Strachey's hand. Perhaps Mr. Wade is the first writer to make the talk good: he has an even mastery of tone in which never a false note appears, and a control of the material so lucid that the emphases invariably fall into the right place. . . . Strachey discovered that biographical style can be personal, and while Mr. Wade is indebted, as every one else is, to the discovery, he is indebted to no one for the perfection to which he has raised it.[22]

Most of the other reviewers had suspicions that the book was to be read with more literary appreciation than with historical interest, although none felt quite as enthusiastic as Tate.[23]

After the publication of *John Wesley* Wade carried the refinement of his art one step further by confining himself to the writing of briefer biographical essays where a concern with the superficial ephemeral facts could be altogether eliminated and he could come directly to grips with the motivating factors in his subjects' lives. There is a definite movement to be traced

---

[22] *New Republic,* LXV (December 10, 1930), 113. Tate goes on, however, to observe that he believes Wade's sensibility and style eventually overpower the subject: "At the end of the book—so remote is the subject matter—we can scarcely remember the high points of Wesley's life; the physical background of the narrative seldom comes out from the surface of comment. We are continually impressed with the singular purity of the author's style." The reviewer for the *New York Times* would appear to agree: "There does emerge dimly through the miasmic prose of Mr. Wade's study something like a portrait in tempera of the famous evangelist. . . . Perhaps the picture would be somewhat less in monotone if the comment were a little less personal and abundant. There are times indeed when one can hardly see the subject for the underbrush of abstract diction with which Mr. Wade feels it necessary to cloak even the simplest idea" (William Troy, "John Wesley, the Militant Founder of Methodism," *New York Times Book Review,* December 21, 1930, pp. 12–13).

[23] Gerald Sykes, *Bookman,* LXXII (1930), 321–322: "His life of Wesley represents a new phase of American scholarship, for although widely read in his subject he has treated it in a manner as steadfastly artistic, and even as playful, as that of Mr. Lytton Strachey might have been. His book bears no relation to the 'solid' academic biographies of the past; it is written in an impeccable style and reflects the most urbane tendencies of the day. Indeed, if it is open to reproach at all it is not for being ponderous or professional, but for hanging its portrait of the ascetic and earnest founder of Methodism in too precious a frame. . . . As a flight of style his book has a beauty of its own. It reduces the life of the great Arminian to a stream of unfaltering elegance. Every word is chosen with exquisite care. This is fastidious writing—even if it is not the best kind of biography." Stanley High, *Christian Science Monitor,* December 13, 1930, p. 6: "Mr. Wade has furnished refreshing proof that it is possible to write a great biography without muckracking; to portray for us a great personality with the lights not altogether darkened by the shadows." The reaction of the only review in a religious publication I have seen was surprisingly mild: "Yes, there's another life of Wesley. And a good one. . . . Dr. Wade has set nothing down in malice, but he has set down much that most Methodists, even the most loyal stripe, never heard about their spiritual father" (unsigned review, *Christian Century,* XLVII, October 29, 1930, 1315).

in his work from expansiveness, documentation, and detail towards conciseness, interpretation, and general significance. His studies of Joel Chandler Harris, Tom Watson, Henry W. Grady, and others, contributed during the 1930s to such publications as the *American Mercury,* the *American Review,* the *Virginia Quarterly Review,* and the *Southern Review,* are essentially studies in the human heart. He indicates how Joel Chandler Harris early came to a romantic conclusion about human relationships: "that if people make other people love them, the world will somehow hold together," and how this in turn led him to support a new way of life in the South destructive of the very humane principles in which he placed his faith.[24] Tom Watson is depicted as a man whose aim had been "to save the conditions that had made possible such a man as Lee," only to be rendered impotent by his attempts to play power politics.[25] Henry W. Grady emerges as a sentimental journalist and opportunist whose fatal flaw was simply that he loved everybody: "There were stupid people, whom one could certainly not blame; and malicious people, who were surely stupid if all were known of them; and misguided people, who were in a way stupid too, if that were not too ugly a word to brand them with. . . . He loved all of these people and a lot more, and they, unable to think of anything more appropriate under the circumstances, loved him very cordially in return."[26] Underlying these essays is a subtle irony that supports Wade's preference for the agrarian way of life over the industrial, and the life of a person like Harris becomes a kind of allegory of what was wrong with the "New South."

When Wade came to Vanderbilt in 1928, he arrived just in time to fall in with the group of young Southern intellectuals, led by John Crowe Ransom, Donald Davidson, and Allen Tate, who were formulating plans to oppose the encroachment of progressivism, scientism, and industrialism on the South. But Wade's agrarian convictions had already been formulated before he encountered this group, as he indicated in a letter to Grace Stone in 1938:

---

[24] *Selected Essays,* p. 94.
[25] *Ibid.,* p. 116.
[26] *Ibid.,* pp. 121–122.

My own conviction that a remedy lay in our own tradition rather than in socialism sprang chiefly, I suppose, from the work I did during 1927–1928 for the Dictionary of American Biography. I was in Washington at the time on the DAB staff, and it was my fortune to have to write sketches of a number of Americans of minor note who flourished in 1860–1900. There I picked up many notions. When I went to Vanderbilt to teach, I was interested to find some people who entertained notions like my own.[27]

The disillusionment Wade experienced in uncovering the egotistical and materialistic motivations of some of America's supposed angels of progress and enlightenment appears to have significantly influenced his thought, as one may witness in the thread of irony intricately woven in his sketches for the *Dictionary*.

When Wade was invited to contribute to the agrarian symposium, *I'll Take My Stand*, he preferred not to cast his contribution in the form of a prose polemic or rhetorical argument. Relying upon his highly-developed narrative skill and his tendency towards indirect ironical persuasion, he produced a semi-fictional biographical sketch, which has been classified by various critics as a paradigm, an *exemplum*, a profile, and a vignette, all of which terms apply but none of which precisely describe it. Instead of attempting to describe the virtues which Wade found admirable in the agrarian South and which creeping industrialism was threatening to destroy, he decided to illustrate them in the life of a fictional "Cousin Lucius," indirectly based on the career of his own Uncle Walter (Jack Walter Frederick, 1851–1928). Set in Georgia, the narrative traces the growth of Cousin Lucius from his early years in the Reconstruction era, through his education in the South's traditional society, his maturation as an ideal Southern gentleman, and his final tragedy as a man who finds it impossible to compromise with the depression-bound society of the twenties without sacrificing his personal integrity and individuality. The story is not only that of the observer-participant Cousin Lucius,

---

[27] Grace Stone, "Tennessee: Social and Economic Laboratory," *Sewanee Review*, XLVI (1938), 333.

INTRODUCTION

but as Davidson noted, "a dramatized history of John Wade's own beloved land of Peach and Macon counties in Middle Georgia from the days when the Fredericks, Rumphs, Murphs, Slappeys, and other still resident families migrated from Orangeburg County, South Carolina, up to the time when the boll weevil and automobile just about simultaneously invaded the cotton-growing parts of the South."[28]

The distinctive thing about this sketch is the talent it displays for effective fictional techniques. Wade adopted the third-person limited point of view, that of Cousin Lucius, and skillfully controlled it so as to win the reader over to his conviction that "the test of a society is the kind of men it produces."[29] A part of this control is the calculated use of physical detail. From the opening line, where Lucius recalls "the feel of the hot sand on his young feet on that midsummer day," to the conclusion when just before his sudden death he strides out in the morning air to luxuriate in the land he loves and lustily shout at the fluttering quail—the kind of shout "designed especially for sunsets and clean dogwood blossoms"—the story is richly permeated with sharp sensuous and physical details drawn from the kind of life lived closely in harmony with nature.[30] The only short narrative by any of Wade's contemporaries which uses this device more skilfully, also to make a point about the agrarian life, is Andrew Lytle's admirable short story "Jericho, Jericho, Jericho" (1936).

Wade tried this form of writing upon at least one other occasion, though without equal success, in the composition of a story called "The Dugonne Bust" for the *Georgia Review* in 1962. Like "The Life and Death of Cousin Lucius" it is restricted to the point of view of a narrator-participant, one Dugonne Truman V, and is intended, the narrator reports, as "not history purely, perhaps, nor yet fiction, purely—a commentary, I hope, upon the comparative value of what-is and what-one-thinks-is, in this world."[31] The dignified seriousness and con-

---

[28] *Selected Essays*, p. 11.
[29] *Ibid.*, p. 35.
[30] *Ibid.*, pp. 23, 45.
[31] *Ibid.*, p. 207.

trolled irony of Cousin Lucius' narrative is replaced by a warm comic spirit and *joie de vivre*. Dugonne is descended from a family highly conscious of its heroic founder, a Revolutionary War leader, whose familial and moral influence has profitably operated upon all branches of his descendants through a treasured bust said to portray him accurately. What Dugonne comes upon is evidence and reason to doubt the authenticity of the sculptured portrait, which appears to have been modelled rather after a grandson of the founder. But this revelation does not disturb Dugonne Truman V, because he realizes that, pragmatically, the influence of the bust is real, even though the likeness is not. Wade seems to be saying that what counts is the moral and intellectual influence a sense of tradition and the past exercises upon the present generation, not the actuality in every detail of what is believed to have existed in that past. Just as the handsome appearance and conduct of a grandson justified the grandfather, in serving as a model for the bust, so does the breeding and conduct of the narrator justify the entire family and all it has stood for. "I am not so much a breaker of images," says Dugonne, "as I am one who calls attention to how plainly useful images can be. . . ."[32]

Other facets of the career of John Donald Wade would reward further investigation. These include his exploration in several essays of agrarian principles, his accounts of local Georgia history, his critical essays (his contemporary reviews of the work of Thomas Wolfe and Erskine Caldwell remain superior to much that has subsequently been written about the two authors), his creation of the Marshallville Foundation to preserve in an effective, practical way the traditional elements in his local community that distinguish Southern culture, and, most importantly, his founding and editing of the *Georgia Review,* which has effected the most enduring tribute to his life by over twenty years of service as an outlet for some of the best creative writing and scholarship in the South and the nation.

The increasing number of scholars, critics, and literary historians who have been publishing books and essays about the Southern Agrarians have given scant if any attention to Wade,

---

[32] *Ibid.*

INTRODUCTION

and no appreciation whatever.[33] In neglecting Wade, they are overlooking one of the South's most intelligent and sensitive interpreters of its social and cultural values and a writer of praiseworthy talent and insight who carried the art of biography to a level of distinction seldom achieved in this country. Unlike John Crowe Ranson, Donald Davidson, Allen Tate, and Robert Penn Warren, Wade did not achieve the national attention they did as poets, literary and social critics, or novelists. But this is not to imply that his capabilities were limited, for his literary legacy, though relatively small in quantity, clearly indicates that Wade was a man whose fine mind, precise sense of style, and compassionate appreciation of human nature distinguish him as a writer worthy of the attention of posterity.

M. Thomas Inge

September 1968
Haslett, Michigan

---

[33] Two "definitive" studies of the Agrarians serve as typical examples. John Stewart in his *The Burden of Time: The Fugitives and Agrarians* (Princeton, 1965) mentioned Wade's name only five times in the 552 pages which compose the book, and in the only criticism offered dismisses "The Life and Death of Cousin Lucius" as "a maudlin and snobbish portrait of a Georgian Colonel Carter . . ." (p. 169). In *Tillers of a Myth: Southern Agrarians as Social and Literary Critics* (Madison, 1966), Alexander Karanikas mentions Wade three times, and calls the same essay "swiftly paced . . ." (p. 15). Excluded from this criticism is Virginia Rock's exhaustively-researched dissertation which in its revised form, presently underway, will undoubtedly prove to be the definitive work.

JOHN DONALD WADE
A BIBLIOGRAPHY, 1922–1962

I. BIOGRAPHIES.

Augustus Baldwin Longstreet: A Study of the Development of Culture in the South. New York: Macmillan Company, 1924.

"Judge Longstreet of Georgia," *Journal of Social Forces*, III (January 1925), 242–248. Reprinted as "Augustus Baldwin Longstreet: A Southern Cultural Type" in *Southern Pioneers in Social Interpretation*, ed. Howard W. Odum. Chapel Hill: University of North Carolina Press, 1925, pp. 119–140.

Contributions to the *Dictionary of American Biography*, ed. Allen Johnson and Dumas Malone. 21 volumes. New York: Charles Scribner's Sons, 1928–1937.

Samuel Ashe, I, 386–387; William S. Ashe, I, 387–388; William Waigstill Avery, I, 445–446; William Capers Bass, II, 36; Frances Courtenay Baylor, II, 76; William James Behan, II, 140–141; Elizabeth W. Croom Bellamy, II, 164–165; John Binns, II, 282–283; Mary Elizabeth McGrath Blake, II, 345; Timothy Bloodworth, II, 384–385; Lawrence Bohune, II, 412; Thomas Barbour Bryan, III, 190–191; Peter Bulkeley, III, 249–250; Henry Guy Carleton, III, 492; William Alexander Caruthers, III, 551; Absalom Harris Chappell, IV, 21–22; William Warland Clapp, IV, 118; Mary Bayard Devereux Clarke, IV, 158–159; Edward Henry Clement, IV, 198–199; Zerah Colburn, IV, 283–284; Alban Jasper Conant, IV, 333–334; Russell S. Cook, IV, 378–379; Ina Donna Coolbrith, IV, 390–391; James David Corrothers, IV, 452; Hiram Corson, IV, 453–454; Charles Henry Crandall, IV, 503; Anne Moncure Crane, IV, 504; John Martin Crawford, IV, 522; John Crerar, IV, 537–538; Gladys Louise Husted Cromwell, IV, 562–563; John Schuyler Crosby, IV, 568–569; James Oliver Curwood, IV, 622–623; Lizzie Petit Cutler, V, 12; Robert Lewis Dabney, V, 20–21; Virginius Dabney, V, 22; Frederick Dalcho, V, 32; Samuel Dale, V, 33–34; John Moncure Daniel, V, 67–68; James Wood Davidson, V, 93; Maria Thompson Daviess, V, 103; Jerome Dean Davis, V, 131–132; Mary Evelyn Moore Davis, V, 137–138; Noah Knowles Davis, V, 140–141; Charles Force Deems, V, 192–193; Felix Gregory De Fontaine, V, 196; Joseph Raphael De Lamar, V, 210–211; Amassa Delano, V, 217; Thomas Cooper De Leon, V, 224; Pierre Auguste Charles Bourgingnon Derbigny, V, 248–249; Regis Denis de Keredern De Trobriand, V, 258–259; Abby Morton Diaz, V, 284–285; Eugene Lenoine Didier, V, 307; Alexander Dimitry, V, 313–314; Charles Patton Dimitry, V, 314; John Disturnell, V, 319; George Leighton Ditson, V, 320–321; Eleanor Cecilia

Donnelly, V, 369; Julia Caroline Ripley Dorr, V, 381; Anna Hanson McKenney Dorsey, V, 384; Sarah Anne Ellis Dorsey, V, 386; Lorenzo Dow, V, 410 (reprinted in *Selected Essays,* pp. 161–162); Francis Samuel Drake, V, 430; Samuel Adams Drake, V, 432–433; John Christopher Drumgoole, V, 462–463; William Ewing Du Bois, V, 472; John Early, V, 597–598; Charles Elliott, VI, 95; William Elliott, VI, 101; Edward Sylvester Ellis, VI, 102–103; Alfred Langdon Elwyn, VI, 122–123; Joseph Estabrook, VI, 186; Augusta Jane Evans, VI, 255; Ignatius Alphonso Few, VI, 351–352; Roswell Martin Field, VI, 371; Sidney George Fisher, VI, 410–411; Amos Kidder Fiske, VI, 416–417; Oscar Penn Fitzgerald, VI, 436–437; Edmund Flagg, VI, 450–451; Patrick Ford, VI, 518; Justus Miles Forman, VI, 526; William Whitehead Fosdick, VI, 540; David Skaats Foster, VI, 545–546; John William Fox, VI, 570; Richard Fuller, VII, 62–63; Justin Dewey Fulton, VII, 68; James Clement Furman, VII, 75–76; Charles Betts Galloway, VII, 115–116; James Bruton Gambrell, VII, 121–122; Landon Cabell Garland, VII, 151–152; Joseph Henry Gilmore, VII, 311–312; John Lafayette Girardeau, VII, 322; Daniel Ayres Goodsell, VII, 405; Francis Robert Goulching, VII, 457–458; Henry Woodfin Grady, VII, 465–466; Charles Chapman Grafton, VII, 470–471; James Robinson Graves, VII, 507–508; John Temple Graves, VII, 508–509; Zuinglius Calvin Graves, VII, 510; Alexander Little Page Green, VII, 534–535; Miller Grieve, VII, 615–616; Absalom Carlisle Grimes, VII, 629–630; William McKendree Gwin, VIII, 64–65; Button Gwinnett, VIII, 65–66; William Nathaniel Harben, VIII, 238; Robert Kennon Hargrove, VIII, 265; Margaret Gaffney Haughery, VIII, 398; William Shakespeare Hays, VIII, 464; Henry Holcombe, IX, 133–134; Johnson Jones Hooper, IX, 202; James Barron Hope, IX, 205–206; Evan Park Howell, IX, 301–302; Charles William Hubner, IX, 335; Charles Colcock Jones, X, 165; Andrew Adgate Lipscomb, XI, 290; Augustus Baldwin Longstreet, XI, 390–391.

"Jefferson: New Style" [Tom Watson], *American Mercury,* XVIII (September–December 1929), 293–300. Reprinted in *Selected Essays and Other Writings of John Donald Wade,* ed. Donald Davidson. Athens: University of Georgia Press, 1966, pp. 106–119.

John Wesley. New York: Coward, McCann, Inc., 1930.

"Profits and Losses in the Life of Joel Chandler Harris," *The American Review,* I (April 1933), 17–35. Reprinted in *America Through the Essay: An Anthology for English Courses,* ed. A. Theodore Johnson and Allen Tate. Oxford: Oxford University Press, 1938, pp. 407–420. Reprinted in *Selected Essays,* pp. 93–105.

"Old Wine in a New Bottle" [Robert Lewis Dabney, Albert Taylor Bledsoe, Charles Colcock Jones, Henry Grady, and Walter Hines Page], *Virginia Quarterly Review,* XI (April 1935), 239–252. Reprinted in *Selected Essays,* pp. 149–160.

"Shakespeare—A Thumbnail Sketch," *Georgia Education Journal,* XXX (April 1938), 48–50. Reprinted in *Selected Essays,* pp. 224–227.

"Henry W. Grady," *Southern Review*, III, o. s. (Winter 1938), 479–509. Reprinted in *Selected Essays*, pp. 120–148.

II. ESSAYS AND NARRATIVES.

"College Life in the Old South," Nashville *Tennessean*, December 30, 1928.

"The Life and Death of Cousin Lucius," *I'll Take My Stand: The South and the Agrarian Tradition* by Twelve Southerners. New York: Harper and Brothers, 1930, pp. 265–301 (reprinted as a Harper Torchbook, 1962). Reprinted in *Selected Essays*, pp. 23–46.

"Southern Humor," *Culture in the South*, ed. W. T. Couch. Chapel Hill: University of North Carolina, 1934, pp. 616–628. Reprinted in *A Vanderbilt Miscellany*, ed. Richmond Croom Beatty. Nashville: Vanderbilt University Press, 1944, pp. 188–204, and in *Selected Essays*, pp. 47–60.

"Of the Mean and Sure Estate," *Who Owns America? A New Declaration of Independence*, ed. Herbert Agar and Allen Tate. Boston: Houghton Mifflin Company, 1936, pp. 251–263. Reprinted in *Selected Essays*, pp. 61–70.

"What the South Figured: 1865–1914," *Southern Review*, III, o. s. (Autumn 1937), 360–367. Reprinted in *Selected Essays*, pp. 82–89.

Editorials, *Georgia Review*, I (Spring-Winter 1947), 3–4, 139–141, 267–268, 391–393; II (Summer 1948), 127–128; III (Summer-Winter 1949), 127–128, 245–246, 351–352; IV (Summer 1950), 71–73. See also the editorials listed in next five entries under their titles.

"A Bet on the Bottom Man," *Georgia Review*, II (Spring 1948), 1–2. Reprinted in *Selected Essays*, pp. 80–81.

"All Will Be Well," *Georgia Review*, II (Fall 1948), 261–262. Reprinted in *Selected Essays*, pp. 76–77.

"A Broader Field of Usefulness," *Georgia Review*, II (Winter 1948), 375–377. Reprinted in *Selected Essays*, pp. 73–75.

"Cats and Queens," *Georgia Review*, III (Spring 1949), 1–2. Reprinted in *Selected Essays*, pp. 78–79.

"To Suit Your Quilt," *Georgia Review*, IV (Spring 1950), 1–2. Reprinted in *Selected Essays*, pp. 71–72.

"The Very Pulse . . . ," *Georgia Review*, VIII (Fall 1954), 281–289. [Short Story.]

"A Long Feud," *Georgia Review*, XI (Winter 1957), 427–439. [Memoir.]

"The Dugonne Bust," *Georgia Review*, XVI (Spring 1962), 3–16. Reprinted in *Selected Essays*, pp. 195–207.

III. LITERARY CRITICISM AND REVIEWS.

"The Authorship of David Crockett's 'Autobiography,'" *Georgia Historical Quarterly*, VI (September 1922), 265–268.

BIBLIOGRAPHY

"Exploits of a Rebel" (*A Gentleman Rebel* by John Hyde Preston), *Virginia Quarterly Review*, VI (July 1930), 427–429.

"The South in Its Fiction" (Seven novels about the South by Donald Joseph, William Faulkner, Charles Morrow Wilson, Fiswoode Tarleton, William Fitzgerald, Jr., Gerald W. Johnson, and Francis Griswald), *Virginia Quarterly Review*, VII (January 1931), 124–129.

"Joel Chandler Harris" (*Joel Chandler Harris, Editor and Essayist*, ed. Julia Collier Harris), *Virginia Quarterly Review*, VIII (January 1932), 124–127.

"Southern Fiction Catches Up" (Six novels about the South by Stanley Hopkins, Herbert Ravenel Sass, Caroline Miller, Rhys James, Roark Bradford, and Thames Williamson), *Virginia Quarterly Review*, X (January 1934), 140–145.

"Two Souths" (*Unfinished Cathedral* by T. S. Stribling and *So Red the Rose* by Stark Young), *Virginia Quarterly Review*, X (October 1934), 616–619.

"Prodigal" (*Look Homeward, Angel* and *Of Time and the River* by Thomas Wolfe), *Southern Review*, I, o. s. (July 1935), 192–198. Reprinted in *Selected Essays*, pp. 169–175.

"Romance Permitted" (*Gone With the Wind* by Margaret Mitchell), *Virginia Quarterly Review*, XII (October 1936), 618–620.

"Sweet Are the Uses of Degeneracy" (the early fiction of Erskine Caldwell), *Southern Review*, I, o. s. (Winter 1936), 449–466.

"The Flowering of New England" (*The Flowering of New England* by Van Wyck Brooks), *Southern Review*, II, o. s. (Spring 1937), 807–814.

"A Handsome Gift Indeed" (*All the King's Men* by Robert Penn Warren), *Virginia Quarterly Review*, XXIII (Winter 1947), 138–141.

Review of *The South in American Literature* by Jay B. Hubbell, *Georgia Review*, IX (Spring 1955), 114–116.

Review of *The Last Days of Pompeii* by Edward Bulwer-Lytton, *Georgia Review*, X (Fall 1956), 356–358.

Review of *The Little Shepherd of Kingdom Come* by John Fox, Jr., *Georgia Review*, XI (Summer 1957), 214–216.

Review of *Georgia Scenes* by A. B. Longstreet, *Georgia Review*, XIV (Winter 1960), 444–447. Reprinted in *Selected Essays*, pp. 165–168.

"Oasis" (*The Long Street* by Donald Davidson), *Sewanee Review*, LXX (Spring 1962), 208–212.

IV. MISCELLANEOUS.

Editor and Founder. *The Georgia Review*. Athens: University of Georgia Press, 1947–1950.

Editor, with Edwin M. Everett and Calvin S. Brown. *Masterworks of World Literature*. 2 volumes. New York: The Dryden Press, 1947. Revised edition, 1955.

The Marshallville Methodist Church from Its Beginnings to 1950. Marshallville, Georgia, 1952. Published in bound mimeograph form.

"On Jordan's April Banks," *Georgia Review*, VII (Winter 1953), 373–389. An excerpt from the above history. Reprinted in *Selected Essays*, pp. 208–223.

V. POEMS.

"Barber Shop Chord," *Vanderbilt Masquerader*, X (December 1933), 14. Reprinted in *Selected Essays*, p. 230.

"Initiation," *Vanderbilt Masquerader*, X (December 1933), 14. Reprinted in *Selected Essays*, p. 231.

"Brass Tacks," *Vanderbilt Masquerader*, X (December 1933), 14.

"The Lady Played," *Vanderbilt Masquerader*, X (December 1933), 14.

"Happy Birthday to You," *Georgia Review*, XI (Fall 1957), 264. Reprinted in *Selected Essays*, p. 228.

"M. B. F.," *Selected Essays*, p. 228.

"Mister Hugh," *Selected Essays*, p. 229.

"Sad Tidings," *Selected Essays*, p. 229.

"Axiom," *Selected Essays*, pp. 229–230.

"A True Friend," *Selected Essays*, pp. 230–231.

EDITOR'S NOTE

Since its appearance in 1924, John Donald Wade's *Augustus Baldwin Longstreet: A Study of the Development of Culture in the South* has remained a standard biography of one of America's earliest native humorists, as well as a perceptive assessment of life and letters in the antebellum South. It was issued by the Macmillian Company in only one edition, which contained about eighty errors, most of which are typographical or involve spelling and dates. The editor's intent has been to correct these errors and provide a more dependable text for the modern reader.

The substance of the study, however, has not been revised or altered in any way, although in a few places such changes might have been justified. For example, Wade assumed on the basis of evidence gathered in his own article on the authorship of David Crockett's *Autobiography* that Augustin S. Clayton wrote it (see p. 76). This evidence has been seriously questioned by James A. Shackford in his study of the historical Crockett in *David Crockett: the Man and the Legend* (1955). On page 194 Wades quotes Edgar Allan Poe from the *Southern Literary Messenger* of June 1838 which is incorrect since Poe edited the *Messenger* from December 1835 to January 1837 and was not writing for it in 1838. And Wade's summary of secession before the Civil War (see p. 339) contains incorrect dates, as Ulrich B. Phillips claimed in his review for the *American Historical Review*, XXX (October 1924), 181–182. Had Wade himself undertaken a revised edition, these matters would have doubtless been clarified or corrected.

The picture of Augustus Baldwin Longstreet facing the title page in this edition is reproduced from a copy of a line engraving held by the University of Georgia Library. The editor and the publisher consider it more suitable than the reproduction of Longstreet's portrait used in the 1924 edition as a frontispiece and mentioned by Wade in note 1 on page 53.

The editor wishes to express his gratitude to Mrs. John

Donald Wade and Mrs. Anne Wade Rittenberry for their permission for the University of Georgia Press to issue this edition. Mr. George Core has been very helpful and encouraging in the preparation of the book, and Mrs. Gay Post has provided invaluable secretarial assistance. Portions of the Introduction appeared in the *Georgia Review* for fall 1967 in another form, and the author is grateful for permission to use them here.

M. Thomas Inge

I
THE START

Vehemence, old and oldish men fall periodically to telling the world, counts for more than length of years in the matter of how much a man lives. Certainly there is no measure other than these two. Augustus Baldwin Longstreet satisfied both tests; he lived a very great while, always with the utmost intensity, not merely at one thing, or at two, but at things innumerable.

A person of considerable ability who turns his interests tirelessly into all sorts of directions often makes a more obvious impression on his time than does one who limits himself to a single line of activity. In the case of Longstreet, so great became the noise of his superlative faculties that before he died legend had taken hold of him and declared him to be of prodigious birth. He weighed twenty pounds from the start, and came into the world with a full set of teeth; such, at least, a friend of his, writing the year after his death, recorded as having always been the "report." All he lacked throughout his life, this friend says further, was a "concentration of talents."[1]

Now the time has gone—was never here, in fact—when one could pass absolute judgment upon this estimate. It is hardly likely that to his contemporaries a more nearly complete focusing of effort than he ever exhibited would have made the Judge (it was by this title that Longstreet was known for most of his life) seem much more remarkable than he seemed already. So far as they could tell, he was on the summit of achievement. Whether he was of the type of mind which if forced to work at one task uninterruptedly will work also

---
[1] George W. Williams, *Advice to Young Men* (Charleston, S. C., 1899), 107–8.

effectively, there is no way of determining. Never in his life, apparently, did he hammer continuously and exclusively at one problem for very long.

Almost everything that a landsman can find to do, Longstreet sooner or later tried his hand at; the sea only marked the limits of his contemplated dominion. The various capacities in which he served at some time in his life make of themselves a list fit for cataloguing: lawyer, politician, orator, judge, farmer, business man, patron of medical education, teacher, scholar, college-president, author, newspaper editor, preacher, musician, naturalist, carpenter, artisan, sportsman. . . . And whatever he did, he did well, not with the greatest distinction, to be sure, but with something far above mediocrity.

If Longstreet had kept himself to one kind of effort, the recognizable identity of his fame would unquestionably have proved more enduring, but one may question still whether his influence upon the arid world would have been more potent running in one channel and placarded as his than it has been seeping nearly everywhere diffused and nameless. Under necessity of skimming back over such wide spaces, humanity receives into its mind but few names from any one age, and most of these it eventually discards. And even those it does not discard—what shall the disciple of a faith despising eons and star-orbits for but shallow points in the lapses of eternity—what shall such a disciple, as Longstreet was, think, anyway, of human memory and of its awards?

A boy born in Augusta, Georgia, on the twenty-second of September, 1790, came upon a time and place that of themselves make his development interesting.[1] If his parents, representing Dutch, English, and French strains, had come to that frontier town from New Jersey only a few years before his birth, as indeed, in this case, they had, the history of the youngster becomes yet more engaging, an epitome in some sense, of American civilization.

Dirck Stoffels Langestraet came from the Netherlands to the New Netherlands in 1657, and soon afterwards married Catherina Van Lieuwen. These two became the ancestors,

---

[1] He was born on Reynolds Street.

four generations removed, of the little boy born over a hundred years later in Augusta. Dirck Stoffels had a son of the same name, who, like his father, retained throughout his life the old Dutch spelling of his surname, and who, like his father again, kept to the business of marrying among people whose ancestors he had known immemorially.[1] The third American Langestraet in line was a radical. He began calling himself Longstreet, and married a woman with the non-Dutch name of Abigail Wooley. Not for nothing had he been born as late as 1712 in a district settled by English Quakers as well as by the Dutch. He named his children, or suffered them to be named, Daniel, Gilbert, John, William, Mary, and Lydia.

Of these children, William was twenty-two years old when the father died in 1782. The father, and the mother also, who died some two years after her husband, William of course remembered throughout his life, and described to his own children as thrifty, worthy, and devout. As he was a sizable boy during the period of the American Revolution, and was living in Monmouth County, New Jersey, William could hardly have avoided partizan interest in the hostilities. There is no record, however, of his actual participation in the war, either in old books or in the statements about him made by his eminent son. If he fought, he did not afterwards talk much about his experiences, nor did he much like to think about them. He was a practical person who could not see why men should keep in mind, and be always discussing, matters already conclusively decided.

In 1784, or just about then,[2] William Longstreet married Hannah Randolph, whose parents lived not far from his. Hannah Randolph was the descendant, fifth in line, of James Fitz Randolph, who in 1630 came from Nottinghamshire, England, to New England and settled at Scituate, Plymouth Colony. James Fitz Randolph represented what even by European standards is ancient lineage, but it is doubtful whether the consciousness of this fact was very present with him during the raw years he passed in early Massa-

---

[1] Edward Mayes, *Genealogy of the Family of Longstreet* (privately printed), 21-2.
[2] Mayes, *Genealogy*, 22.

chusetts.[1] In the late 1690's, James's grandson, Benjamin Fitz Randolph, influenced probably by his wife, who was a New Jersey woman, removed from Massachusetts to Princeton. There he bought and lived on a tract of land which later became the campus of Princeton University.[2] Benjamin's son Isaac, and Isaac's son James, as the early American Longstreets had done, married women of their own ancestral nationality.

James Randolph, for with him the Fitz is dropped from the surname, was Hannah Longstreet's father. Born in 1730, he was during the Revolutionary War at the time of life at which convictions are surest. His were sure, without qualification, for the colonies. He became a soldier as soon as the war started, and refused to speak to those of his friends who, when the political issue became definite, decided for the Loyalists. The battles of Monmouth and Princeton, if no more, witnessed his services before he was captured by the British and permitted to die, the victim of prison abuses, in a British post in New York in 1781. James's two brothers, Daniel and Benjamin, were also active on the side of the Colonists. Benjamin got to be colonel, and Daniel went maimed to his grave as a result of injuries received in battle.

Hannah Randolph inherited from her father a considerable fortune, upon the receipt of which, doubtless, she and her husband decided during 1785 to join the numerous friends and neighbors of theirs who were migrating to Georgia. They were both of them descended from people always ready to change their residence on the chance of bettering their condition. So much money would go farther in Georgia than the same amount would go in New Jersey, and no one doubted that as soon as the colony—the state, it had become—had a little time on its side, it would be a very prosperous and delightful place to live in. Before the fall of 1786, William Longstreet, with his wife and their infant son James, had already settled in Augusta. Mr. Longstreet was about twenty-five years old when he made the trip, and his wife about a year younger.

---

[1] O. B. Leonard, *The Fitz Randolphs of Massachusetts and New Jersey* (privately printed).

[2] Mayes, *Genealogy*, 56–8.

THE START

Of the letters written by Mrs. Longstreet the few which are still in existence are worth some special notice.[1] On 10 May, 1787, she wrote from Augusta to her "dear and honoured" aunt, her mother's sister, Mrs. Rebekah Coward Hendrickson, in New Jersey. She has just learned, she says, of the death of her mother, on the thirteenth of the past February. This melancholy news, though, did not come to her as a complete surprise. She had had a premonition of the event on the fatal day itself, evil dreams about her mother all through the night, and on the next day, Valentine's day, she had expressed the fear that her mother had been overtaken by some great ill. She asks whether or not she was much in her mother's thoughts when death came. She directs that her uncle keep for her, until she calls for it, any little property she may inherit. Her mother's Bible and Psalm-book, both of which had been promised to her, she directs sent by Daniel Longstreet, who is soon to leave New Jersey for Georgia.

Her girlhood friends, she hears, are all of them moving away, some to Virginia, some to "Canetuck." "I wish," she says, "they would come to Georgia for I do believe they would do better hear than their." Her old home and friends are always in her heart. They are a long way off but she will keep up with them always as best she can. She is very tender. . . . Then, of a sudden, she is very sharp, incensed at the thought of the recent marriage of her brother, unable, she says, to "immagen what they think to doo with wives in their circumstances."

"I must now inform you," she continues, "what has happened to me since I wrote to you. In the first place I must tell you, I have got a fine Daughter. She was born the 9 of November, 1786, and I call her Rebekah after yourself. She is the finest child I ever had. . . . The time she was born Billy had lain for several weeks with the nervous fever that we expected every day and night almost would be the last. I could not get the mid-wife I spoke to for she lived above twenty miles from me so I was obliged to have an old woman that I did not like, and almost frightened me out of my senses the whole time. I was poorly indeed for a day and night before it was born, and

---

[1] Letters in the possession of Mrs. T. G. Bailie, Augusta, Ga.

had a most bitter time. . . . I had no warming pan so was put into a cold bed, and it was a violent stormy night. The room was wet from one end to the other where rain beat in. . . . I thought I could not live till morning. . . . We sent for the doctor and he gave me something that eased me but I slept none that night. The thought of home, my mother, my friends, the situation myself and family was in, and all among strangers, was quite as much as I could bear, threw me into histericks, and the women all went to sleep and I worryed the night out in the way you see.

"The nighbors came in and [have] done now and then, and I have great reason to be thankful to kind providence that my lot is cast among such kind good people as I am, for better I could not wish for." Then, "P.S. Little James remembers you all."

Eleven years later she was still keenly interested in old times and associations. She wrote during the first part of May, 1798, to this same aunt. It is twelve months, she says, since she wrote last, but she has had no reply. Perhaps there has been no way to send one. This letter "I shall send by one of my neighbors, a lady I have a very great esteem for, and one that will be sure to send my letters to you by a safe hand and take care of any you may think proper to send by her. If it should be convenient for you, I should be very glad that you would visit her and have her to stay a week or so amongst you. I should like her to visit you, Mrs. Morent, Mrs. Hendrickson, Mr. Smith's family, and any other of my acquaintances round you for a few days. Please assure all the kin of my continued love for them.

"We are all in good health, and no alteration in our family since I wrote to you, except the addition of a little boy. We call him William, as I am almost determined it shall be the last, for I am completely tir'd of nursing. I have grown very fat and hearty since I had this child and too clumsy and lazy to worry with it. I have never felt so well since I have been a married woman as I have for about six months."

Then there are some observations about another member of the family who has married contrary to her approval. "I hope you will all write," she concludes, "by Mrs. Forsyth (Mrs.

Forsyth's son was in school at Princeton), and that will furnish me with matter for my next letter."

A little later, 15 May, 1798, Mrs. Longstreet writes again. She has lately received letters from her aunt. Mrs. Forsyth, she hears, traveled from Augusta to Princeton in eight days, a fact which makes the distance seem not so appalling. She requests that her aunt send her some beet and cabbage seed, and some of the small white beans that used to be so plentiful, and were so good to eat. . . .

"You appear pleased," she says, "that I have declined sending Rebecca to Bethlehem,[1] but I assure you I am still very desirous to do so, for I know it would be a very great advantage to her, though I should not know how to spare her, for she is a great assistance to me now.

"You ask about little Augustus. Well, I must tell he is one of the finest boys you ever saw. He goes to school, reads and writes, and often makes observations that would surprise you for a child of his age,—was his father's Pett till William come, but now his nose is quite out of joint. Billy is very fond of his name-sake—has nursed him more than all the rest put together."

The baby has been ill for some time. "I shall take him in the country in about three days from now and stay two or three weeks. The Doctor says that will be of service to him, and Ellen Randolph is near lying in, and I hope my being with her will be of service to her so the advantage will be mutual.

"Gilbert is learning the hatter's trade, and James attends the cotton machine for his father. He is a very industrious lad.

"We have a very comfortable house and fine garden, and in a very agreeable neighborhood. . . . It is in a very retired part of the town, I feel like I was in the country."

She has heard from her brother James, who would, if he could get the funds, come to try his fortunes in Georgia. She is afraid though, she says, that she can be of no help; Billy finds need for all the money he can get hold of. If James could only get to Augusta she might be able to do something for him, and especially for his wife. "I could then help her to

---

[1] The Moravian Seminary and College for Women, founded in 1742, in Bethlehem, Pennsylvania, is still extant.

many things that would I know be very acceptable to her and the poor little children. They must be very indigent in their circumstances, which causes me many a painfull our, and I cannot have a face to mention to Billy that I would be glad if he could assist them, because Stephen [another brother] has lived so long upon us and you know it must make one feel disagreeable. . . .

"We can never expect to have much satisfaction in this life for if we are not eternally struggling with difficulties of our own th[ose] of our friends call forth the tear of sympathy; for what pleasure can the good things that this world affords give a person who possesses a feeling heart when we are sure that some of our nearest relatives have not the common necessarys of life. Happy would it be for us if we could learn that lesson so desirable and yet so hard; that is, to be contented in whatever situation it pleases Divine providence to place us. It appears to me at this time, I could be happy if I knew my friends were so, but while they are miserable, how can I be happy. Samuel's family, and John's wife in Jersey makes me often feel writched.

"I wish you would let Alice come and see us in the fall, when Mary Slaughter comes. I think it would be an agreeable trip for her and we shall all be so delighted to see her, and it would certainly be a great advantage to her. I apologize for not writing to Alice personally and will do this by the next opportunity.

"We all join in love to all of you and since we are deprived of seeing each other in this world, I hope and trust that we shall meet in a better to part no more. That we may all be prepared for that solemn period is the sincere wish and prayer of your affectionate niece.

"P.S. I forgot to mention that Miss Polly Cooper was married the 11th inst. to a Doctor Smelt of this place, a man of property and merit."

How could the son of a woman who turned with such ease from the solemn contemplation of Divine providence and its ways, to the shrewd perception of "property and merit," hope, even though a preacher, to keep his mind wholly riveted to the dealings of inscrutable Jehovah? How could one fail, being

THE START

her son, to manifest always traits of courage and sympathetic gentleness, of canny thrift and frank humor?

By 1816, Mrs. Longstreet had become a Directress of the Augusta Female Asylum, and was undertaking the education and support of an orphan who was not related to her.[1]

And there survives still another document of her writing. It is her Will, made in February, 1837. All of the characteristics shown by the letters written when she was a young woman are confirmed by this solemn testament of her great age. There is the old piety; "I have waited for thy salvation, O, Lord!" she directs shall be carved on her grave-stone. She is eminently just and shrewd. She has not forgotten her old tragic courage and self-sacrifice. Torn from her early home in New Jersey, she had lived in Georgia nearly fifty years, and yet she believed that the end of shifting westward had not come. "My sons," she states in this Will, "sometime speak of moving West or elsewhere from this country, and they may possibly wish to move, and it is my wish that they should remove to a land of better promise for them and their children, and I would do nothing to detain them here a moment longer than their own concerns detain them."[2]

William Longstreet was active and well-contented, and for the most part prosperous, throughout his life. He was always trying to invent something. An old letter of his preserved in the Georgia state archives testifies as to his inventive turn of mind:

"Augusta, Ga., Sept. 26, 1790.

"Sir:—I make no doubt but that you have often heard of my steamboat, and as often heard it laughed at. But in this I have only shared the fate of all the projectors, for it has uniformly been the custom of every country to ridicule even the greatest inventions until use has proved their utility.

"In not reducing my scheme to practice has been a little unfortunate for me, I confess (and perhaps the people in general), but until very lately I did not think that either artists or material could be had in this place sufficient.

"However, necessity—that grand source of invention—has furnished me with an idea of perfecting my plan, almost entirely with

---

[1] Richmond County Ordinary's Record, 8 January, 1816.
[2] Mayes, *Genealogy*, 23.

wooden materials, and by such workmen as may be gotten here; and, from a thorough confidence of its success, I propose to ask for your assistance and patronage.

"Should it proceed agreeably to my expectations, I hope I shall discover that sense of duty which such favors always merit, and should it not succeed, your reward must lay with other unlucky adventures.

"For me to mention to you all the advantages arising from such a machine would be tedious, and, indeed, unnecessary. Therefore I have taken the liberty just to state in this plain, humble manner, my wish and opinions, which I hope you will excuse, and I shall remain, either with or without your approbation,

"Your Excellency's most obedient and very humble servant,
"WILLIAM LONGSTREET.
"To His Excellency, William Telfair."[1]

When he lost hope that this bid for governmental aid would come to anything, the inventor finally mustered privately the funds requisite for his experiment, and in 1807, a few days after Fulton's successful test in New York, succeeded in moving his boat up current on the Savannah river at a speed of five miles an hour. The boat was propelled by long poles that pushed against the bottom of the river.[2]

William Longstreet was eternally about some new device. He invented something prophetic of the sewing machine,[3] and in his family there is still a tradition that he was the true inventor of the cotton-gin. He had been working on a contrivance of this sort since before 1790,[4] and people everywhere were talking about his efforts. During the period of his experiments, says the story, a lady came to his house asking the privilege of examining the new machine. Her request was granted, but when she had looked at it and was withdrawing from the premises, she fell down in such a way as to disclose the fact that after all she was a woman only by disguise. Shortly afterwards, Whitney's cotton-gin was an accomplishment.

---

[1] Mayes, *Genealogy*, 23.
[2] Lawton B. Evans, *History of Georgia* (New York, 1906), 167.
[3] Charles C. Jones and Salem Dutcher, *Memorial History of Augusta* (Syracuse, N. Y., 1911), 167.
[4] *Ibid.*

Longstreet did not surrender his field, however, to Whitney or to anybody else. In the Augusta newspaper for 24 December, 1796,[1] he advertised a gin "to be offered to the use of the citizens of Georgia upon the most liberal principles, as soon as I can procure my workmen, castings, etc." In an editorial in the same paper, eight gentlemen of local prominence were cited as collectively declaring that to them the machine seemed impossible of improvement. In the paper for 7 February, Robert Watkins averred that the gin which Longstreet was about to set in operation was in reality a copy of a gin invented by him. This charge Longstreet conclusively disproved. It was true, he admitted, that he had changed from bands to cogs as a means of transmitting power, but he had derived the idea of the cogs from some source not Watkins', indeed had considered cogs as early as 1792. Talk relative to the gin continued into July,[2] when it was announced over Longstreet's name: "This is the last time that I will pester the good people of Georgia upon the subject of cotton ginning." This "last-time" notice appeared then regularly in every issue of the paper through December, and at times even carried extra matter with it, such as inquiries as to who wanted to buy a few thousand weight of good cotton seed.

There was not much time for revising advertisements when one was so rushed with business. In June, 1797, the inventor wrote to his wife's uncle in New Jersey: "I should have wrote you much oftener than I have for sometime past, had it not been that I was so ingaged in the completion of a machine that will net me hereafter about twenty dollars per day, this I have effected after much trouble and expense."

Subsequently, William Longstreet established two gins successfully operated by steam, only to have both of them within one week destroyed by fire. And then he set up a steam mill near St. Mary's, Georgia, only (during the War of 1812) to have it destroyed by British soldiers.[3] His vitality already somewhat exhausted, Longstreet was never able after these disasters to take hold of life again in an effective manner.

[1] *Augusta Chronicle.*
[2] *Augusta Chronicle*, 22 July, 1797.
[3] Mayes, *Genealogy*, 24.

His old determination had been too violently and persistently assailed. He died in 1814.

While he lasted, however, he was a business man of an almost shocking degree of conformity to the later developments of that genus. Always he was trading, giving people power of attorney, buying a residence and selling it soon to some advantage, removing to another only to repeat the process, his money eye always wide open.

Nor was he averse to making money sometimes by means less highly esteemed than those of invention and petty bartering. With good company enough, it is true—General Wade Hampton, and others—he was influential in securing the passage by the Georgia Legislature of the infamous Yazoo Land Act.[1] By this act the Legislature of Georgia sold to a land-exploiting organization at a shamefully low price practically all of the land now comprising Alabama and Mississippi. Immediately the sale became a political issue of such burning interest that the state at large soon took the affair in hand and sent to the next legislative assemblage representatives who repudiated the whole transaction. The episode came to be regarded in Georgia as one so basely commercial and self-seeking in nature as to call down odium upon persons even remotely connected with it, but it was a degree of odium, in the case of the Longstreets, doubtless, who were prosperous and socially agreeable, that did not cause them any personal inconvenience.

William Longstreet managed always to keep his family in respectable circumstances. In 1797, he was a Justice of the Peace,[2] and when the City of Augusta was incorporated in 1798 he was one of its six commissioners.[3] A few years later he was President of the Augusta Association of Mechanics.[4]

He was the kind of man who could go to the theater and enjoy what he saw, or, if occasion demanded, intensely not enjoy it. One night an actor who had observed Longstreet's clumsy wooden-machinery boat then being put together on the

---

[1] W. H. Sparks, *Memories of Fifty Years* (Philadelphia, 1870), 30.
[2] *Augusta Chronicle*, 17 March, 1797.
[3] Jones, *Augusta*, 137.
[4] *Ibid.*, 167.

river, took it upon himself to surprise the audience with a song about its maker. And in the audience, it so happened, was the butt of the song:

> "Billy boy, Billy boy, can you steer the ship to land?
> Billy boy, Billy boy, can you steer the ship to land?
> Yes, I can steer the ship to land,
> Without a rudder in my hand.
> Billy boy, Billy boy, can you row that boat ashore?
> Billy boy, Billy boy, can you row that boat ashore?
> Yes, I can row that boat ashore
> Without a paddle or an oar."[1]

From the very start everybody craned to see Mr. Longstreet. He was wriggling with indignation. It was impossible to repress a titter. Soon everybody was shaking with laughter. In the midst of it all, says tradition, William rose from his seat, and "fixing on the merry son of Thespis a glance which caused the notes to die away in his throat, strode majestically out of the building."[2] "Strode majestically out"—it takes a degree of self-esteem on a man's part to fancy that an audience will be wilted by his withdrawal; but that quality William Longstreet had; and he passed it on to his son. Twice notably, as an old man, the son availed himself of this device; always through his long career he was talking about resigning, putting people on notice that all they had to do to get rid of him was to hint that he was no longer wanted.

William Longstreet took his children's doings much to heart. Young Gus Longstreet had a knavish way, when put on the dunce-stand at school, of getting the other school children vastly tickled. The side of his face towards the teacher he would keep very sober, while the other side he would contort in a manner wonderful to witness. To the teacher's mind, Gus simply exerted over the children a power not to be explained by ordinary means. Perhaps the boy was crazy. He was certain that this was the case, and so wrote to the boy's father, requesting that the culprit be withdrawn from school, and suggesting a lunatic asylum as the best place to put him

---

[1] Rebecca Latimer Felton, *Country Life in Georgia in the Days of My Youth* (Atlanta, 1919), 52.

[2] Jones, *Augusta*, 292.

in next. It was not long before "the news spread from Lower Market to Hawkes Gully that Gus Longstreet had gone stark crazy." The father was deeply mortified by this report, which he perhaps half-way believed, and let it crystallize his long-held design of turning farmer and removing to the country.[1] In 1800,[2] accordingly, or 1801, William Longstreet with all of his family went to live over in South Carolina, on a farm some fourteen miles from Augusta.[3] The head of this colony was clearly very proud and sensitive. Men do not usually permit themselves to be profoundly affected by what an irate young teacher says about the mental state of a twelve-year-old child.

In 1805,[4] the Longstreets came back to live in Augusta. Sensitiveness and pride are well enough in their place, but to a man of William Longstreet's temperament they are not to be listened to when they counsel one to continue living in isolation. And, besides, this man had enough humorous perception to let bygones be bygones without his constant effort to keep them alive. Everywhere his humorous outlook on life makes itself manifest. Frequently his own zealousness turns comic under his eyes. Even his tombstone attests to his blitheness of spirit. On it one finds engraved: "Sacred to the memory of William Longstreet, who departed this life Sept. 1, 1814, aged 54 years, 10 months and 26 days. 'All the days of the afflicted are evil, but he that is of a merry heart hath a continual feast.'"

* * * * * * *

In 1791, the year after Gus Longstreet's birth, Augusta had a population of eleven hundred persons; it had three warehouses with an aggregate capacity of ten thousand hogsheads of tobacco; it had a church, a courthouse, a stone jail, a government house for Federal and state officials, and an elegant, be-cupolaed academy, which, capable of accommodating 150, accommodated actually some eighty or ninety.[5] In this

---
[1] Williams, *Advice*, 108.
[2] Mayes, *Genealogy*, 24.
[3] Longstreet, "Valuable Suggestions" (in Frank Moore's *Rebellion Record*, New York, 1865), 436.
[4] Mayes (?) Manuscript.
[5] Jones, *Augusta*, 137–48.

building, President Washington himself, when visiting Augusta in May, 1791, had been tendered a grand ball, and here he had participated in an examination of the students, upon which he had been pleased to express himself handsomely.[1]

By 1800 there were on Broad street upwards of a hundred stores "filled with all the necessary manufactures of the Northern states, of Europe, the East and West Indies." And there was a Methodist meeting house.[2] The population had just been augmented by the arrival of a number of French colonists, refugees from late massacres in the West Indies. About the arrival of these people there was no end of talk, and no end of wonder, it can be guessed, to little ten-year-old Gus Longstreet.[3] Altogether there were in Augusta about six thousand people, half of them slaves, and in Richmond county about fifteen thousand, only a third of whom were slaves.

Everywhere there were evidences of a certain civic pride, and a certain desire to make life agreeable and safe. A fire company, with a regular engine, had been in existence since 1794, and on the fourth of July every year people who were lucky enough to have relatives belonging to the company met together with the organization and enjoyed a sumptuous meal and much sumptuous oratory.[4]

Professional actors had performed in the town since before 1790, and by 1798 there was a theater—in which brash young comedians were sometimes too free with their local references. The theater went up in fire in 1808, but by that time Richard Henry Wilde had come into maturity, and into influence enough, with his Thespian Society and Library Company, to get the place promptly rebuilt.

There was keen interest in horse-races. A little after 1800, the Gentleman's Driving Park Association and the Augusta Jockey Club both came into being, and opened their splendid

---
[1] Pleasant A. Stovall (with J. L. Maxwell and T. R. Gibson), *Handbook of Augusta* (Augusta, 1878), 64.
[2] Jones, *Augusta*, 148.
[3] George G. Smith, *History of Methodism in Georgia and Florida, 1785–1865* (Macon, 1877), 88.
[4] Jones, *Augusta*, 159.

courses, at which, from time to time, one might see races and the most entrancing tournaments.[1]

The town was full of great men, as great, a youngster might think, as one could see anywhere,—Governors, Generals, Admirals, Senators, Judges, poets. This was the first time in the history of the world, even the youngest boy could know that, in which the spirit of man had ever been quite untrammeled by despotism. In America autocracy was at an end forever, and it was on the way to being at an end everywhere. With selfish interests put aside, it was plain that the spirit of man, by nature good and aspiring, would soon rise to places theretofore scarcely hoped for. The more serious minded, contemplating this alluring possibility, could not see how any young man—Richard Henry Wilde, for instance—could waste time with an interest in dramatics, could not understand how later this particular young man brought himself to fritter away his years in scholarly research in Italy when he might have been in America, contributing, by his work in the processes of government, to the establishment of the Utopia always about to substitute itself for, or at least project itself into, the sovereign state of Georgia. Hope literally washed the heavens. Puritan Massachusetts, unable to rid itself of the idea of man's essential wickedness, could not as yet envision this earthly Paradise. Georgia, with fewer preconceptions, accepted Mr. Jefferson's ideas with less resistance, and believed to an amazing extent, it seems, that the world stood in fine way of becoming shortly a place of unvarying loveliness. Before this it had been kept unlovely only by the wicked dealings of a few people, and now it was too advanced to permit that sort of imposition any longer.

What a busy place Augusta was becoming! How rich people were getting! The stages going always to Savannah, going always to Charleston, seemed to pull the world in together. Early Saturday morning one could leave for Savannah in expectation of being there Monday for breakfast.[2] Everybody recognized the town's promise, and the worth of

---

[1] Jones, *Augusta*, 293; Moses Waddel, *Memoirs of the Life of Miss Caroline Elizabeth Smelt* (New York, 1919), 23–4.
[2] Jones, *Augusta*, 166.

the fine lands lying south and west of it. It seemed that half the people in Virginia and North Carolina came pouring through Augusta every day; and only a little later, everybody knew, they would commence hauling back into the Augusta warehouses the royal lint of cotton. (It was clear that the city must foster good roads for this traffic.) Little boys could run a mile down Broad street, they say, without ever getting down off the cotton bags.

All of this activity was duly reflected in the newspapers (*The Chronicle* already fifteen years old in 1800, and *The Herald* well established) and reflected too in the mind of Gus Longstreet.

In the latter case, the reflection was demoralizing. The boy persisted in doing everything except keeping his mind on his books. He was doubtless often reminded that he should be more in earnest, that his tuition alone cost his parents ten dollars a quarter, and that it was not every child who had opportunities equal to his for mastering "Latin, Greek, English, and the common, practical branches of mathematics."[1] He knew well enough that he was a disappointment to his people, had been crushed all too often by having pointed out for him the contrast between himself and the dutiful Mr. Augustus Baldwin, the first rector of the Academy, for whom, in fond hope, he had been named.[2]

Gus tried and tried to learn what the wretched books were driving at, but for the life of him could not. He had been held very bright as a young child, at eight, "could read and write and make surprising observations," but at ten,—it was very distressing. If his teachers could only explain the awful books, the boy thought he might do something. But they did not explain at all. They merely heard one's lessons and sent one to the dunce-stool. Occasionally Gus had to serve his turn on this eminence, and when he did he made a very ludicrous picture. He was a homely child, and his general appearance was made both ridiculous and pathetic by his high peaked cap. The little boy must have shifted uncomfortably under the scrutiny. How everybody stares at you when you are on a

---
[1] Stovall, *Handbook*, 44.
[2] Smith, "Some Overlooked Georgians" (detached newspaper clipping).

dunce-stool! What is one to do there? You know you can make the children laugh if you will only makes faces at them, that you can break their impertinent gazing, put them on your side, against the teacher.[1] The old Adam all too soon has his way with you.

It was the years Gus spent on his father's farm, following his eleventh or twelfth birthday, that brought him most happiness, and that most influenced his character. As his older brothers were there with him, he was straining and always straining to keep up with them. "My highest ambition," he wrote later, in speaking of this period of his life, "was to out-run, out-jump, out-shoot, throw down and whip, any man in the district, and I was giving fair promise of attaining my ends."[2] If Gus Longstreet once got you down in a wrestle you had as well say "calf-rope" and be done with it. There was no getting up until you did. The boy was renowned for his ability to shoot. He "won beef" at a shooting match, he says in one of the sketches written in his maturity, "when he was hardly old enough to hold a shot gun," and was thereupon by popular report declared a *"swinge* cat who had been born shooting and who had killed squirrels before he was weaned."[3]

The Longstreet family that went over into South Carolina to live consisted of the father and mother and their six children: James, Gilbert, Rebecca, Rachel, Augustus, and William, the children of ages from, say, seventeen down to six years. How much a boy could find there to entertain him! In Gus's case there were not only his brothers and sisters for him to occupy himself with, but all of the little slave children—the most delectable playmates; and there were a thousand acres of land to range over, almost the world, in fact, fourteen miles to Augusta and nearly twelve to Edgefield. There one could learn to ride horseback, and to drive wagons, could test whether or not an umbrella will buoy up, as a parachute will, a small boy leaping from a house-top. There one could hear

---

[1] Oscar Penn Fitzgerald, *Judge Longstreet, A Life Sketch* (Nashville, 1891), 14–15; Longstreet, "Old Things Become New," I (*Nineteenth Century Magazine*, Charleston, April, 1870).

[2] Longstreet, "Old Things Become New," I.

[3] Longstreet, *Georgia Scenes*, "The Shooting Match."

of groaning ghosts swinging their blue lights about the scenes of legendary murders, and could dispel those ghosts, finally, when properly steeled by a remembrance of high parental expectations.[1] There one could go hunting, of course, and could fish, could go occasionally to a corn-shucking or to some other "sociable," and, all other things failing, could always watch the wagons that went passing and passing towards Augusta and sometimes to far away Baltimore. It is incredible, old men say, how the wagons would pass. Loaded with cotton they would go down and loaded with provisions they would come back. Sometimes they would come back empty. Then how the drivers would crack their whips and how the mules would run! Could anybody conceive such a rattling as the wagons did make? Could anybody in the world resist catching hold of them at the back, and hanging on, or running along furiously to keep up?[2] So the days passed. The nights, for the most part, simply did not exist. Only when it was possible to go hunting or to attend some community festival did one think about the nights at all.

But how could such goings-on be to the advantage of a nearly grown boy, who at eight years old could read and write and make such surprising observations, and who, though eleven years old had found him accused of being insane, was giving now such evidence of normality as to be almost overwhelming?—How, Mrs. Longstreet wants to know of her husband, can this be to the child's advantage? Perhaps it is Mr. Longstreet who wants to know this of his wife; that part does not matter. It is evident that Gus will be a farmer, too, as James and Gilbert are going to be, unless we can get him educated. It is very hearty-sounding, and all of that, for children to grow up in a place called "The Game Cock District," and to get their poor smattering of education at a place called "The Hickory Gum Academy," but these simple surroundings are not the best dependence for teaching youngsters how to get along in a world of relative complexity. Heaven knows, two children are a plenty to have farmers. Mr. Longstreet, for his part, thinks one over-many. . . . In 1804, little Gus was bundled up

---
[1] Longstreet, "Valuable Suggestions," 436.
[2] Joseph L. Lamar, *Recollections of Pioneer Days in Georgia* (privately printed).

and sent back to Augusta, back to his "hated penitentiary," Richmond Academy.[1]

The boy knew nearly everybody in Augusta, had living there many relatives. The town had grown some during his absence, and become more important. But he still knew it through and through. Perhaps the chief difference he noticed was that he heard more talk now than he had heard before about the Methodists, a queer religious sect which people were somehow forced to think better of than they had formerly, on account of the admirable character and charming personality of the new Methodist preacher, a man named Lovick Pierce.[2]

Richmond Academy, the boy hoped, would have changed beyond his recognition. Alas! he found teachers and text books just as they had been before. Very soon it was plain to everybody that Gus's absence had not helped him. He was still a dunce, or worse, a person who had sense enough to learn and was too lazy to do it. He did well enough in some studies for his teachers to know that he could learn anything if he only would.[3] In all likelihood the boy was as greatly at fault as his teachers were, but he did not so regard himself, either then or sixty-five years later, when in setting down his reminiscences he still permitted himself to speak scathingly of the old Academy.[4]

In 1805, the Longstreet family came back to Augusta, financially at least none the better off for their sojourn in the country. Mrs. Longstreet opened a boarding house, "private at first but soon tolerably public,"[5] and in the house there was a store kept by a Mr. Meals. To this store came many people, each of whom must have done his part towards illustrating for Gus what people meant when they talked about "human nature."

One day Mr. Meals came in with an entirely new customer, a boy whom he had adopted, after a fashion, as raw a country-

---
[1] Mayes (?) Ms., Longstreet, "Old Things Become New," I.
[2] George G. Smith, *Life and Times of George Foster Pierce* (Sparta, Ga., 1888), 25.
[3] Longstreet, "Old Things Become New," I, 839.
[4] Longstreet, "Old Things Become New," I, 839.
[5] Mayes (?) Ms.

man as was ever seen, red-headed, of an age just about one with Gus Longstreet's, by name George McDuffie.[1] This boy was the son of some Scotch people who had immigrated to Georgia shortly after the Revolution and settled some miles northeast of Augusta. He had gone to a "district school" until he was twelve years old and made a good record as a "scholar," but at the time that Mr. Meals took charge of him he had been working for two years as a farm-laborer. It seemed to Mr. Meals that the boy's intelligence would serve him to better advantage in Augusta than it would in the country, and he felt sure that he could get him a position. A suitable job for the boy was found in the general merchandise store of Calhoun and Wilson, and a home for him at Mrs. Longstreet's boarding house. He and Gus were put into a room together in the attic.[2]

McDuffie knew superbly just the things that Gus had learned and learned to love during his happy years in the country. But he knew much else. This boy would actually read a newspaper as keenly as he would plan a hunting trip. Gus Longstreet had never seen anything stranger,—a normal boy like himself was here really taking interest in precisely those tiresome things that parents were eternally trumping up as fit topics for boy concern. George McDuffie really wanted so earnestly to learn that he persuaded Gus to teach him. He knew arithmetic, he said, and Gus knew some Latin. Why could they not exchange knowledge? Nothing would be simpler. He accordingly learned what Latin Gus could teach him, and insisted on getting into Gus's head a good deal of arithmetic. Gus was delighted to find the process not so unpleasant

---

[1] George McDuffie was born in Georgia in 1790 and died in South Carolina in 1857. In turn legislator, congressman, governor, and senator, he was throughout his life a most faithful and effective friend of higher education in South Carolina. At the beginning of his career, he favored a liberal interpretation of the Constitution, but, like Calhoun, he later became a strict constructionist. His oratorical powers are reported to have been dazzling; certainly his disposition to use slashing words was constantly demanding attention, and once it got him into a grave personal difficulty. In 1822, he fought a pistol-duel, and received a wound which, though not held serious at the time, finally, more than thirty years afterwards, caused him to die a piteous imbecile.

[2] Smith, "Overlooked Georgians."

as he had believed it.[1] Almost surreptitiously at first the young convert began reading.

As an old, old man Longstreet could remember the whole process of mental awakening stirred in him by his friendship and admiration for McDuffie. "The boy could only read at night," he wrote in his reminiscences, "but he devoured with greediness every book and newspaper he could lay his hands on. As I could not separate myself from him during his leisure hours, and as he seemed to regard it as a privilege and relish to have a boon companion to imbibe knowledge with him . . . he always read aloud. This, to me, was at first irksome, then tolerable, then delightful. Thus I acquired my first taste for reading, . . . but I derived a still greater benefit from my constant intercourse with this bright youth. I observed that when we read the same books and papers he always knew twice as much of their contents as I did. I determined to watch him if possible, and I commenced reading with care and in a measure studying what I read."[2]

Mrs. Longstreet saw, certainly, that some new interest had come into her son's life, saw him shifting the weight of his dissatisfaction with the world as he found it, away from external circumstances where it had reposed exclusively for so long, on to his own proper self. It was a happy sign. Gus was systematically going through a list of books got together by McDuffie.[3] Through 1805–07 this process continued. The boy was by then intellectually eager, but still prejudiced against the Academy and all of its works. On thinking of the place, he was constantly humiliated by the recognition of his past poor record there and by the fact that he was older than most of his classmates. He was in his mid-teens, restless, morose oftentimes in the face of what he had to do, discontented with himself, filled with a yearning, he supposed (never having known a life different from the one he was then living except the one he had known on the farm), for life in the country. This was the thing of all things that William Longstreet could not comprehend.

---

[1] Smith, "Overlooked Georgians."
[2] Fitzgerald, *Judge Longstreet*, 17–18; Longstreet, "Old Things Become New," I.
[3] Williams, *Advice*, 109.

II

EDUCATION

One day in 1808 somebody suggested that Gus might continue his education and enjoy country life at the same time if he could go to school to the Reverend Dr. Moses Waddel, at Willington, South Carolina, just across the Savannah river a few miles above Augusta.

Dr. Waddel was a Presbyterian minister, originally from North Carolina, but, since 1788, a resident of Georgia and South Carolina in the territory surrounding Augusta. He had begun teaching when fourteen years old, and had become a preacher at twenty-two. In 1794 he was sent to preach one Sunday at the Calhoun settlement in South Carolina. After the sermon, very naturally, everybody invited the young man to dinner, but, as Patrick Calhoun was the oldest member in the congregation, it was he who took the young lion off with him.[1] A year later, Waddel married Mr. Calhoun's daughter Catherine, and went with her to his home in Columbia County, Georgia.

This marriage served to identify the young minister with Augusta and particularly with the Longstreets. George McDuffie was working for Mr. James Calhoun, who was a brother of Mrs. Waddel's, and who, consequently, was in touch with the Waddel affairs. Before Gus decided to go to Willington, Mrs. Waddel, it is true, had died, and Waddel had remarried, but by 1804, the one-time son-in-law was living near his first wife's relatives, and was on very intimate terms with them. John Calhoun, after spending two years under Mr. Waddel's tutelage, had gone to Yale College in Connecticut, where he had stood at the top of his class, but he was now back at home, a most promising young lawyer. Besides, there were a num-

---

[1] John C. Calhoun, *Correspondence* (edited by J. F. Jameson, Washington, 1900), 70.

ber of prominent Augusta families who had sons at the Waddel School.[1] People said it was a place "of plain dressing, plain eating, hard working, close studying, close watching—and, when needful, good whipping,"[2] after all, not a place wholly unsuited to Gus's requirements.

In 1808 the boy's family sent him up to Willington. He found there, among people many of whom he already knew, a life exactly suited to his taste, and a degree of intellectual inspiration to which not even George McDuffie had been able to stir him. As an inspirational force, Dr. Waddel was phenomenal, and the influence of Mr. John Calhoun, whose family Gus boarded with,[3] with all of his fine looks and ways and power of demanding admiration, was a thing the boy could not get away from. From home, George McDuffie would write to him in terms that let him know how rich was his opportunity. His very being there created an item of expense not to be neglected in a large family. He knew, too, that he was there largely because of his dissatisfaction with the Academy, and because of his assurances, one can guess, that he would do better in the country. It would take complete absence of spirit in a boy of eighteen for him not to respond to such inducements to effort. In the place itself, however, and in the spirit of it and the man at the head of it, were the chief incentives that Gus found.

Dr. Waddel was an extremely successful teacher. He had to a remarkable degree the knack of getting work out of all the youngsters under his charge. His boys revered him and loved him. A short, stocky man, usually much on his dignity, he knew how upon occasion to let his tongue wag freely and entertainingly, and how to let his round Irish face indicate his merriment.[4] Nor did his sense of justice and propriety cause him to forget that he must always, insofar as practicable, see a thing from the students' viewpoint.

There are many traditionary incidents illustrating the

---

[1] Longstreet, *Master William Mitten* (Macon, 1889), 129.
[2] *Ibid.*, 129.
[3] Fitzgerald, *Judge Longstreet*, 20; Longstreet, "From Out the Fires," in *Nineteenth Century Magazine*, Charleston, Dec., 1869.
[4] Longstreet, *Mitten*, 108; Adiel Sherwood, *Gazetteer of the State of Georgia* (Washington, 1837), 128.

Doctor's methods. A boy swings under the noses of his classmates a cat, which, from appearances, had been several days dead. In defense of his act the boy urges that the weather has been so cold since the cat's death that there is no possibility of the body's having a foul odor. This process of reasoning strikes the Doctor as effective. He refuses to hold the boy accountable.[1]

At the University of Georgia, of which Dr. Waddel was President during the 1820's, it is told that the students used to sit in their windows in the dormitory and greet the Doctor as he was entering his workshop in the basement, by tilting a bucket of water out upon his head. The Doctor's retort, the story goes, was nothing more drastic than the procuring of an umbrella, which he always carried with him when bound for his workshop and raised just as he approached it. As long, however, as he conducted a preparatory school, he would regularly once a week hold court, and administer justice freely with a rod.

He knew thoroughly the subjects boys were taught, the old Tripos, and, besides, he was an excellent French scholar.[2] His methods of instruction permitted a wide range of individuality on the part of his students. A boy read as much Virgil for a lesson, for instance, as he cared to; 150 lines was a small amount for one day, and occasionally a good student read much more.[3] Studying where they would, out of doors under the trees when the weather was pleasant, the boys would "instantly repair to the common school or recitation room when called for by the name of the Homer, the Xenophon, the Cicero, the Horace, or Virgil class, or by the name of the author whose writings they were reading, class succeeding to class without the formality of definite hours for study or recreation."[4] It was a strange scheme, but, judged by the fair standard of results, it was a good one.

In fact, the more one learns about the Doctor's life the more one respects his unfailing instinct for making himself effective.

---

[1] Longstreet, *Mitten*, 117.
[2] John N. Waddel, *Memorials of Academic Life* (Richmond, 1891), 62.
[3] Longstreet, *Mitten*, 110.
[4] David Ramsay, *History of South Carolina* (Charleston, 1809), II, 370.

He took hold of the University of Georgia when it was impoverished and despised, and in a few years he put it in a position of prominence and influence. Students who had been under him could never have done talking about him and his ways, could never refrain from citing you the names of old Waddel boys who had achieved fame. Indeed, it is a formidable list: John C. Calhoun, William H. Crawford, Hugh S. Legaré, George R. Gilmer, James L. Petigru, and others,—congressmen, senators, governors, a straggling minister or so, an occasional teacher, but always, congressmen, senators and governors—always![1]

Longstreet throughout his life remembered Willington vividly and affectionately. "There was a street," he wrote, describing the school, "shaded by majestic oaks, and composed entirely of log huts varying in size from six to sixteen feet square. . . . This street was about forty yards wide and its length was perhaps double its width, and yet the houses on either side did not number more than ten or twelve; of course, therefore, they stood in very open order. They were all built by the students themselves or by architects of their hiring. They served for study houses in cold or rainy weather, though the students were allowed to study where they pleased within convenient reach of the monitors. The common price of a building on *front row*, water proof and easily chinked, was five dollars. The chinking was generally removed in Summer for ventilation. In the suburbs were several other buildings of the same kind, erected by literary recluses, we suppose, who could not endure the din of the city at play time—at *play time*, we say, for there was no din in it in study hours. At the head of the street, eastward, stood the Academy, differing in nothing from the other buildings but in size. . . . This was the recitation room of Mr. Waddel himself, the prayer room, court room, and general convocation room for all matters concerning the school. It was without seats, and just large enough to contain one hundred and fifty students standing erect, close pressed, and leave a circle of six feet diameter at the door for jiggs and cotillions at the teachers' *soirees* every Monday morning."[2]

---
[1] Longstreet, *Mitten*, 109, 150.
[2] Longstreet, *Mitten*, 100–102.

It seems that the small log huts were "offices" rather than "residences," made necessary by the fact that the school room was too small to accommodate all of the students at one time.[1] The students boarded, Longstreet says, "just where they pleased, among the neighbors around who nearly all took boarders and resided at different distances from the Academy, varying from a few hundred yards to three miles. As a rule, the boys would haul their own firewood and make their own fires. They might hire a servant to perform these tasks for them, if they would, or rather if they could, but, at every house there was at least a *truck wagon* and horse at the service of the students, and as wood was convenient and abundant, and to be had without stint or charge, they usually supplied themselves and made their own fires."[2] "For more than three years of my pupilage nearly all the fuel that was consumed upon my hearth was cut from the wood by my room-mate and myself and bourne a fatiguing distance to our door. . . . We often followed four hours' toil in this way by five hours' study on the same evening."[3]

At sunrise Dr. Waddel would blow his horn and presently someone in each of the boarding houses would answer. Soon, then, the boys would hustle off to prayers.[4]

The spectacle of this school, in a new country nearly two hundred miles from the sea coast, appealed mightily to the romantic sense of Doctor David Ramsay, who talks about it at some length in a history of South Carolina published by him in 1809. Here, he says, "the glowing periods of Cicero are read and admired. The melody and majesty of Homer delight the ear and charm the understanding in the very spot and under the identical trees which sixty years ago resounded with the war-whoop and horrid yellings of savage indians."[5]

One cannot help wondering if the proximity of the school to the horrid yellings of the savages did not, socially as well as historically, temper the place pleasantly for the students.

---

[1] Ramsay, *South Carolina*, II, 370.
[2] Longstreet, *Mitten*, 106.
[3] Fitzgerald, *Judge Longstreet*, 81–82.
[4] Calhoun, *Correspondence*, 79.
[5] Ramsay, *South Carolina*, II, 370–71.

Hardly at any time would such a location seem to a crowd of boys anything but agreeable, and in those days it was doubtless exceptionally to the boys' liking. The incident of the dead cat did not then seem unspeakably revolting. Bluffness was taken by many people as being identical with wit. An old man could tell a bride that her husband had made a mistake in marrying her, and refuse to admit that he was joking, and still be held as indulging in good-humored waggery.[1] "I remember," writes a survivor from that old time, "passing through Danielsville a long time ago, and seeing a crowd of men sitting under the shade of a tree. Stopping my buggy I asked Mr. Gabe Nash, an old lawyer I had met in Lexington, how far it was to Danielsville, and if he would be kind enough to direct me how to get there. 'You are right in Danielsville now,' replied my old friend, 'and if you have any doubts about it we have a callaboose for just such tramps as you passing through.' I stopped for a couple of hours and had an enjoyable time."[2]

All of this sort of thing Longstreet had been especially trained for in his hotel life of the last few years. He knew the give-and-take of it, and relished it. Here funny things were always happening, and one could always do things one's self. A box of shirts, all neatly embroidered "A. B. L.," was delivered to him. It turned out a week later, to the intense merriment of everybody, that the shirts belonged not to him but to a student named Augustus B. Linton. For a long time this was a hilarious memory.—There is a monitor who seems to Gus a little too "nosey." Behind that monitor all day long he goes with a Greek grammar in his hand "*Tupto tupteis, tuptei,* (of all the monitors) *tupteton, tupteton* (that I ever saw in my life) *tuptomen tuptete* (this monitor takes the lead) *tuptousi* (rather rousy)." How fine it was to see the Doctor when this "crime" was reported to him by the indignant monitor! "The Doctor's face," Longstreet wrote, "put on all sorts of expressions; to maintain the dignity of the monitor's character, it was of the first importance that he should hear him with the profoundest respect and gravity; and yet there

---

[1] *Georgia Scenes*, "Charming Creature."
[2] *Athens Banner*, 15 December, 1921.

was something so novel and farcical in this case [this is Longstreet himself speaking] that he could with difficulty suppress open laughter. He drew his eyebrows to their closest, pressed his lips forcibly together for a moment, and then passed judgment." Briefly the judgment was that this was a case involving a mixture of *idleness* and *study,* so novel in its nature that the first instance of it did not merit punishment.[1]

The year 1810 was marked in Gus's life by the failure of the firm of Calhoun and Wilson, for which George McDuffie was working in Augusta. Gus was concerned with this failure not only because of its bearing upon his friend George, but because of his liking for Mr. James Calhoun himself and for Mr. James Calhoun's brother, William, with whom he was then boarding. Mr. William Calhoun determined to go down and see what he could do for his city brother. "Find out, please sir," Gus must have asked him when he was leaving, "what is to become of George,—George McDuffie, you know, the boy who clerks for Mr. James, and who I told you is so smart."[2]

In Augusta, Mr. William looked after his business and his brother's as well as he could, and was ready to start home. "By the way," he said then, "is this young McDuffie Gus Longstreet talks of as wonderful a fellow as Gus makes him out?" "About as wonderful as anybody *could* make him out," says Mr. James. "He works all day faithfully, and then reads and studies, they tell me, half the night. A fine boy." The case was settled. Along with other of what he considered James's liabilities, William took over George McDuffie, and determined to see him through with at least a year or so under Dr. Waddel. It did not take George long to get ready. He put his clothes into his box, "a pine box [that] had a lid fastened with leather hinges, and a leather strap in front fastened over a nail,—and that was all there was to his preparations."[3]

---

[1] Longstreet, *Mitten,* 112–13.
[2] Longstreet, "Review of Perry's Article on Calhoun" (*Nineteenth Century,* January, 1870), 620.
[3] Benjamin F. Perry, *Biographical Sketches of Eminent American Statesmen* (Philadelphia, 1887), 668.

Gus Longstreet had by no means forgotten his friend, had, on the contrary, cherished his memory above almost everything; it seemed to him that George McDuffie was an example of what the American theory of politics held all men capable of. He thought everybody ought to know George. During 1809, one of Dr. Waddel's old students, James L. Petigru,[1] came down to Willington to visit the school. He had just finished his course at the South Carolina College and was planning soon to spend some time in Augusta. Young Longstreet came to know Petigru while he was at Willington, and soon grew to admire him. Immediately he wanted him to meet George McDuffie, and accordingly gave him a note of introduction to be delivered to George in Augusta. The meeting was effected, and years afterwards Mr. Petigru could remember how he and McDuffie took together "a stroll over the town of Augusta."[2] When McDuffie came to Willington, then, to live once more in the same house with Gus, both of the young friends were delighted.

George set straight to work, progressing so rapidly that the record of his achievement, set down by Longstreet some fifty years later, seems now incredibly prodigious. Alas, that the day of giants has gone by! This boy is reported to have mastered Latin grammar in ten days, and then to have rushed through Horace at the rate of 1212 lines a recitation. In his other studies, Longstreet says, he did as well. Certainly he was an extraordinary student, and certainly he and Gus were the closest of friends.[3]

Gus was getting out of his work now the most enthusiastic

---

[1] James Louis Petigru was born in Abbeville District, South Carolina, in 1789 and died in Charleston in 1863. After leaving college he began the practice of law in Charleston. In 1822, he succeeded Robert Y. Hayne in the attorney-generalship of the state, a position which he held until 1830, when his deliberate but passionate opposition to the Nullification movement cost him all possibility of further political advancement. Old age prevented his taking any effective part against secession, but his loyalty to the Union was a trait of character always more generally recognized in him, perhaps, than any other save those two of personal integrity and intellectual power which had so far won the confidence even of the "seceders" that in the bitter days just prior to the War, he was entrusted with the task of codifying the laws of his state. The Code was published the year before Petigru's death.

[2] Perry, *Biographical Sketches*, 668.

[3] Longstreet, *Mitten*, 110.

pleasure. He was familiar with the works of the English poets and was even speaking gratefully of the lines

> Tityre tu patulæ recubans sub tegmine fagi,
> Silvestrem tenui musam meditaris avena,

as being the passage that had first awakened in him a true appreciation of Latin poetry.[1] His literary ambition stirred him to write occasional sketches, one of which at least was published in an Augusta paper.[2]

The two boys were up to many pranks, the most famous of which got itself recorded years later in Longstreet's "The Debate." What the boys did was this: for discussion before a forensic society of which they were members they proposed the following high-sounding but altogether meaningless question, "Whether, at public elections, should the votes of faction predominate by internal suggestions, or the bias of jurisprudence?" Gravely, it is reported in the sketch, one member of the society after another arose and delivered his reflections upon this vexed subject. Did the two boys, one wonders now in reading the sketch, have any deeply ironical implication beneath their proposal of this fustian, did they mean to say that people after all, many of them, are influenced more by the sound of oratory than they are by the sense of it, more by the noise of life than by its reality, did they mean that it would be better to be more accurate and less grandiose, or did they mean merely to work a joke off on some fellow students? Ironical the episode is now, whether it was or was not intended as such by the youngsters who inaugurated it. In it, a group of intelligent young gentlemen have set before them for discussion a subject totally severed from reason, and they discuss it as seriously as they would have discussed daily bread. The episode shows indisputably that Gus Longstreet had at last set his keen head to working, and that he was bent upon indulging at any cost his insatiate love of fun. If thinking and jesting were what he wanted he was now in a place of unparalleled merit.

One thing, however, George and Gus were at a loss to follow.

---

[1] Longstreet, *Mitten*, 102.
[2] Williams, *Advice*, 112; Edward Mayes, *History of Education in Mississippi* (Washington, 1899), 206.

In spite of their admiration for Dr. Waddel they could not quite accept his idea about religion. Nor could Mr. William Calhoun, at whose house they lived, understand it any better than they could. As good a man as ever breathed, he somehow let the boys know without ever directly telling them, that this part of Dr. Waddel's character he, for one, could not sympathize with.[1] Here were two mentally alert youngsters, morally clean, and both of them by impulse generous and kind, but there was much in the religious business they could not grasp. A great revival came to the school. The Doctor preached and others preached. Certain boys, no better than Gus and George were, declared themselves changed, transformed, made clean over. Gus and George observed that for a few days these boys were sober-sided, perhaps, and then they were back at their tricks, it seemed to the spectators a hundred times more likable now that they were natural again.[2] Certain things that the Doctor was always telling from his pulpit seemed to Gus and George strange, and stranger still the more they pondered them. Later, Gus Longstreet found that he understood it all, but McDuffie never did grasp it, went to his grave in fact, broken, almost an imbecile, still wondering. Just before his death, Gus Longstreet came to him at his home to explain it all, but for all Gus could do, the matter was still vague to him, past any hope of his ever grasping it,—so vague that Gus, more concerned about this than about nearly anything else, could only hope for the best.[3]

Commencement at Willington was worth the attention of anybody. Longstreet remembered those occasions throughout his life, and eagerly took the opportunity to describe them fully in his book *William Mitten*.[4] "These exercises," he says, "continued for several days, and they were attended by multitudes. . . . The order was as follows: First the examination of all the classes; which was invariably conducted by the visitors, except when they declined the task, and this rarely occurred.

---

[1] Longstreet, "Review of Perry's Calhoun," 620.
[2] Waddel, *Memorials*, 54; Longstreet, "Old Things Become New," I (*Nineteenth Century Magazine*, April, 1870), 849.
[3] Waddel, *Memorials*, 215-6.
[4] Longstreet, *Mitten*, 186.

Then speaking, for which prizes were awarded. And lastly the performance of one or two dramatic pieces, usually a comedy and farce, but these were [finally] discontinued, and the reading of compositions was substituted for them. The speakers were divided into three classes, according to their age and advancement, the first class being composed generally of the oldest students in the school; the second, of those next in years; and the third, of the youngest, excluding those in the elementary studies."

Visiting parents, "all of the first respectability," would occupy, as a rule, their sons' living quarters, while the boys were packed off to sleep where they could. And how commencement did change things! All the year through the boys had uniformly dressed very simply, but at commencement there was a "complete metamorphosis." It was easy then "to distinguish the sons of the Patricians from those of the Plebs, though *turkey-red* and *indigo-blue* predominated largely over nankeen and gingham still.

"In the morning from seven o'clock till nine, people of all ranks, ages, sexes and sizes might be seen wending their way to the school house, or rather to the area in front of it—for the examination was conducted under the stately oaks of the campus. Some of the first men of the two States were there. At nine the examination commenced. The students with very few exceptions acquitted themselves admirably. . . . This day and the next were consumed in like manner. On the third day the speaking commenced."

A stage of rough plank was erected adjoining the school house. On this sat the Judges, of whom William H. Crawford, John Calhoun, and William W. Bibb were three. These hardly ever failed to attend the public exercises of Doctor Waddel's school.

"In front of the stage large logs were laid parallel to each other, on which planks were placed at convenient distances apart, for seats. The whole was covered with a brush-arbor. It was but a scant provision for the throng that attended upon this occasion, but what provision could accommodate all, when the number fell little, if any, short of two thousand people?

The ladies, several hundred in number, occupied all the seats, while the gentlemen stood wherever they could find room."

Mr. Calhoun, with a few complimentary words, presented the prizes, and the whole assembly applauded loudly and cordially. Pretty little girls, beautifully dressed, often quite forgot themselves, and kept on clapping after everybody else had done, to be stopped at last by their mothers, laughing most heartily. All the ladies, young and old, wanted to kiss the nice-looking little boys who had won the prizes, and all of the little girls fell in love with them. A thousand compliments saluted the ears of the boys' mothers, from lips that those ladies knew not. Everybody sought introductions to them, and everybody congratulated them upon the performances of their sons. Most.of the judges waited upon them and said flattering things to parents and offspring.

"Young sir," Mr. Calhoun would say, "the United States have an interest in you; and should I live to see you in the prime of life I shall be sorely disappointed if I do not see you the admiration of them all."[1]

What a man Mr. Calhoun was! When Dr. Waddel told George McDuffie and Gus Longstreet in 1811 that they were fit to enter the Junior class in college, it was Mr. Calhoun's example that the two boys turned to most adoringly. Having been graduated from Yale in 1804, and from the Reeves and Gould Law School in Litchfield, Connecticut, in 1806, Mr. Calhoun had returned to South Carolina to be elected to Congress in 1810, when he was only twenty-nine years of age. How proud Mr. William Calhoun was when his brother was at the house with him! How the boys listened to him, respectfully, as if he were a hundred years old and they mere youngsters, not with an assurance proclaiming that. after all he was only a little older than they were! The boys yearned to be at Yale, and at Litchfield.

Gus Longstreet's parents decided that they could send him, and were gratified beyond measure, doubtless, that he had abandoned the old shiftless way he followed at Richmond Academy. Mrs. Longstreet regretted perhaps that Gus did not

---

[1] Longstreet, *Mitten*, 186–92.

want to go to college at her old home, Princeton, which, besides being nearer than Yale, had the advantage of being already a sort of accepted destination for Augusta boys looking for more schooling than they could get in the South. But Gus was bent upon Yale.

George McDuffie also preferred Yale, but had to go instead to the South Carolina College at Columbia. Mr. John Calhoun was in politics, now, and it would not do for his brother's protégé to go elsewhere than to a "home" school. Of course, going to Yale was expensive, but it was not so much that the Calhouns begrudged the extra expense of sending George to Yale as it was that everybody knew that George had not the money himself to go there, and that if he did go it would be on Calhoun funds. At any rate the South Carolina College was as good as Yale, people were saying, doing course for course the same work. Gus Longstreet heard all of this reasoning and was duly convinced, but knew when it was all over that it was George's not having any money of his own that lay at the bottom of his bitter disappointment. And he wondered, as a youngster of twenty-one naturally would (and as an older man sometimes may), why it is that the plenitude or lack of so base and material a thing as money is, can, with such bludgeon finality, affect a thing as splendid and as ineffable and as rightfully far beyond the reach of money, as the human spirit. Here was a case in which a man's having merit on his side seemed to enter simply not at all into the matter of his getting what was due him. Could Gus dodge wondering?

The Southern boy going North to college in 1811, did not, it is likely, feel himself so violently transplanted as did the Southern boy going North in 1911,—this in spite of the facts that at the latter date the Civil War was largely forgotten and the railways had drawn the country infinitely closer together than it could ever have been in the time of stage-coaches and pony expresses. Economically the structure of Georgia and that of Connecticut were much nearer one in 1811 than they were a hundred years later. Politically this was true also. Josiah Meigs, a native of Connecticut, found his Jeffersonian politics so assailed in his own state in the early years of the nineteenth century that he was glad enough to leave a Professorship at Yale and accept the Presidency of the newly-organized University of Georgia. But in Georgia he found conditions little more to his liking. There, on account of his politics, he was after a short time practically expelled from his position. Georgia revered the central government almost unqualifiedly. It is true that the state had been defiant in the matter of the Yazoo fraud and thus put itself into the position of advocating extreme state rights, but the Yazoo unpleasantness had been somewhat forgotten by 1811, and even if it had not, it is natural to think that William Longstreet, the father of Gus Longstreet, as one of the promoters of the purchase, taught his son to feel that it was the Federal rather than the state government that held the right end of this staff.

Though Mr. John Calhoun was by no means a Federalist, he was as strongly and aggressively nationalist in his conceptions of government as anybody could have desired him. Young Longstreet, though, for his part, had heard much more talk about politics than he had let weigh upon him. He knew, indeed, that Mr. Calhoun was a "Republican," but had attached to that knowledge very little importance and comprehended it but vaguely.

How Gus Longstreet got to New Haven nobody can tell. In his book, *William Mitten,* he describes a young Georgian of about this period, 1810, going to Princeton by way of Savannah and the sea. Gus could have done this, or he could have gone by land. In either case, he might have stopped by Princeton to visit his relatives. But evidence on these questions is altogether lacking.

Yale College was not extremely dissimilar from the school conducted by Dr. Waddel. Grammar, Geography, and Arithmetic still occupied respectable places in the curriculum, and the teachers worked, not on the basis of subject matter, but on that of number of students.

F. A. P. Barnard, who was a Yale student a few years after Longstreet was, has left an account of his experiences at Yale in those early times. "The applicants for admission," he says, "were divided into squads of moderate numbers each. Mine consisted of eight victims besides myself. The examination was entirely oral and was completed at a single session. One officer conducted the examinations in all subjects, while another sat by and looked on. My examiner was Professor Silliman, who, though Professor of Chemistry, took us up on Virgil, Cicero, the Greek Testament, Graeca Minora, Xenophon, Geography and Arithmetic, all apparently with equal facility. . . . At least I was called up on Arithmetic, but to my great astonishment and relief, this important topic seemed to slip the mind of my examiner altogether. . . . At one time during the proceedings the President walked into the room and took a seat; but he made no remark, and though he looked dignified and grave, I could not but think that he looked a little bored also. When the whole ceremony was over we were requested to step into the corridor for a moment; but after a brief delay . . . we were recalled and informed that we had all been admitted.[1] . . . Every class at entrance was broken up into divisions of about forty students each, and the tutor assigned to each division remained its sole instructor in all branches of study whatsoever to the end of the junior year.[2]

The tone of Yale student life at this period was excellent. President Dwight, himself a man of great energy and prestige, had collected a number of superior teachers, most notable among whom, perhaps, were Jeremiah Day and Benjamin Silliman. Moreover, through his association with the Hartford wits and through his own literary compositions, the President brought a direct literary atmosphere to the whole college. Who did not know pleasantly Judge Trumbull's poem *McFingall?* Who could have failed to admire the *Conquest of Canaan,* or the vast *Columbiad* of Mr. Barlow? All of the students loved Professor Silliman. He had a fluent command of language, and "in his unwritten lectures on chemistry, mineralogy, and geology," the reports tell, "there were frequent bursts of genuine eloquence."[3] His power of using alliteration seemed to the boys almost miraculous; "omniscient, omnipresent, omnipotent Father," he would begin when called upon to pray of a morning in chapel.[4] Longstreet loved Silliman, as, he explains, he

---
[1] *Barnard Memoirs,* by John Fulton (New York, 1896), 32–3.
[2] *Ibid.,* 34.
[3] *Ibid.,* 35.
[4] Donald G. Mitchell, *American Lands and Letters.*

did all of his professors, but this man he loved most, Silliman being, in fact, the only one of the Yale teachers with whom he ever after his student time exchanged a letter.[1] These good teachers had established good traditions. "No man at Yale," writes Barnard, "who aspired to be ranked as a scholar was permitted by public opinion to obtain any assistance from any quarter whatever, even from his immediate tutor, in preparing himself for his daily scholastic exercises. A man's superiority was acknowledged because it was felt, not because he could point to a higher mark on the term record."[2]

The College rolls for the time of Longstreet's attendance at Yale include annually about thirty students from the South. In his class, the one of 1813, six of the seventy men graduated were from the South, but Longstreet was the only one registered as having had his preparation for college outside of a Northern preparatory school. In the class of 1814 there were three men from South Carolina and one from Savannah, in that of 1812 were two from South Carolina and one from Washington, Georgia.[3] With these boys and with boys not from his own section, young Mr. Longstreet undoubtedly struck up many friendships. With Ralph Ingersoll, the son of a prominent New Haven lawyer, he developed affectionate intimacy, visiting often in the Ingersoll home, and telling great tales about Georgia. These tales, they were always telling him, he really should put into a book.[4]

Some of the New Englanders' doings seemed to Gus very odd. He could not believe, for instance, in the defiance of the General Government shown by all of the agitation which led up to the Hartford Convention, but at the time he probably did not let this disturb him greatly. If there were bad elements in New England culture, there were countless good ones.

The mere antiquity of the civilization appealed to his romantic sensibilities. One day an incident occurred that he remembered always. He saw the workmen rebuilding the North Church, and with a crowd of boys bent over an old man

---

[1] Fitzgerald, *Judge Longstreet*, 26.
[2] *Barnard Memoirs*, 34.
[3] Yale Catalogue.
[4] *Records of Yale Alumni*.

named Nathan Beers who was showing a strip of wood which he, as a youngster, fifty years before, he told his audience, had put into the old church when it was being built. That incident Gus could never forget.[1] New Haven was on the whole delightful to him. Altogether he could conclude, even in the bitter year 1870, that the two years he passed at Yale were among the happiest of his life. "No graduate," he wrote, "left her halls with a warmer love for every member of her faculty than I had, or a tenderer regard for the people of New Haven. If parting tears never dried up, and he who shed them could always recognize them, I could point to many witnesses of this truth. The first gush of them was in the North Church while listening to the valedictorian of my class. The highest transport that I ever felt for vocal music was in this church. I loved all the Professors."[2] Throughout his life he was regretting his inability to renew old acquaintances, vexed that he had "no language to express the regret he felt at not being able to meet his classmates."[3]

When John C. Calhoun's relatives began urging him, as a boy, to train his recognizedly great mental powers, he had told them that if they would undertake to give him the best, the very best, legal training to be had in America, that he, for his part, would accede to their wishes, and undertake to put his education to such uses as he might. In pursuance of this program he had gone to Yale, and from Yale he had gone to Litchfield, Connecticut, to the law school conducted there by Judges Tapping Reeve and James Gould. Augustus Longstreet was following in Mr. Calhoun's path. There was not now at Yale any more of a law school than there was in the time of Calhoun. Truly there was a course of lectures in law, but this did not fit one for practice. Every year, therefore, upon being graduated from Yale, a great number of young men set out for Litchfield. Yale was Litchfield's chief "feeder," 150 of the 805 men who were graduated at Litchfield in the

---

[1] Longstreet, "Old Things Become New," I, 841-2.
[2] Longstreet, "Old Things Become New," I, 841-2; Fitzgerald, *Judge Longstreet*, 26.
[3] *Records of Yale Alumni.*

years 1798–1833 having been previously graduated from Yale.[1] The tradition in general, then, as well as the specific personal example left him by Calhoun, pointed young Longstreet to Litchfield. "Immediately," therefore, after his graduation from one school, the young man hastened to the other.[2]

Litchfield, like New Haven, was about five thousand in population, just the sort of town that Longstreet's acquaintance with Augusta made him feel most at home in. Just as in Augusta, the people there had their fine clothes for occasional dress, but went during most of the week dressed "so generally in home-spun that the exceptions might be fairly disregarded."[3] They played cards here, too, danced and even gambled, to an extent that one hardly expected among Puritans.[4] Gus was sorry to find little or no racing, but that was the only drawback. In the school was a large number of Southerners; when it finally discontinued its activities in 1833, nearly two hundred out of its approximately one thousand graduates were found to have been from the South.[5] In Longstreet's class of forty-six men, there were four from Georgia.[6]

Gus was a boy given to jokes. He was met with a joke on the very day that he got to his new home. "Here," a fellow-student had said to him, handing him a great ponderous knife, "Here, sir, is a knife given always to the ugliest student at the law school. Until now it has been mine, but beyond doubt, sir, since you are here, I have now no right to it any longer. Take it." Every age has its own idea as to what is funny, and it is probable that this greeting made Gus Longstreet, a true son of his age, feel better than he would have felt had the student given him some conventional welcome. He could not have been very homesick. Shortly after he arrived somebody showed him two elms planted by his friend Calhoun.

The whole routine of his new life Gus knew largely in ad-

---

[1] Emily Noyes Vanderpool and Elizabeth C. Barney, *Chronicles of a Pioneer School* (Cambridge, 1903), 337.
[2] Longstreet, "Old Things Become New," I, 840.
[3] Wilbert Lee Anderson, *The Country Town* (New York, 1913).
[4] Vanderpool, *Chronicles*.
[5] *Yale College*, II, 90.
[6] Dwight C. Kilbourne. *The Bench and Bar of Litchfield, 1709–1909* (Litchfield, 1909).

vance. Just as at Dr. Waddel's a man had been obliged to get himself board and lodging wherever he could, so it was necessary to do here. You paid for your room and bed, and beyond this you had to furnish everything, from "bellows to lamp wick," had to get everything else you needed, "wood, servants, carpets, lamp, oil, etc."

There were countless things that one could do socially. In the winter, kindly-disposed people asked you to go sleigh-riding,[1] and in the summer, what with attending to the parties, dramatic entertainments and recreative walks of the young ladies enrolled at Miss Pierce's School for Young Ladies, situated also in Litchfield, it was all that a young gentleman could do properly to get up his lessons. Mr. Calhoun in his time had largely eschewed activities of this kind, but Gus Longstreet liked talking for its own sake better than Mr. Calhoun did, and for him such a renunciation was harder. Sometimes he found staying in and studying quite out of the question. On fine days all of the young ladies in Miss Pierce's School would go walking for the exercise. Up and down the two long shaded streets to the music of flute and flageolet[2] passed the young ladies. And there were young gentlemen passing up and down also, young gentlemen dressed at times in pink gingham frock coats.[3] And then about once a week Miss Pierce's parlors were thrown open to the young gentlemen, and times were exhilarating indeed. The young ladies had a great fad of embroidering as they entertained their visitors. And what they were embroidering was crests. Somebody had procured a copy of Edmonson's *Complete Body of Heraldry*, a book which contained heraldic pictures charming enough to cause each young lady to select one of them as her own, and, having selected it, to embroider it and proclaim it forever thenceforth as her peculiar sign. Such was the merry comment of 1815 America upon the ancient devices of Europe.[4] But the most edifying diversion was to be found at Miss Pierce's dramatic performances. Written in blank verse and

---

[1] Calhoun, *Correspondence*, 102.
[2] Vanderpool, *Chronicles*, 150.
[3] *Ibid.*, 28.
[4] Vanderpool, *Chronicles*, 258.

based on Biblical episodes, these plays were the most engrossing and exemplary things conceivable.[1] On Sundays, of course, one went to church, generally to hear Dr. Beecher.

One day a great sensation was caused when Dr. Beecher openly reproved some of the law students for talking during his sermon. The boys were sitting as usual just to the right of the pulpit and the sermon was droning on as usual. Suddenly there was silence, and then, terribly, "I shall suspend my remarks," said the Doctor, looking around very grave and solemn, and finally letting his eyes rest fully upon the boys, "until those young gentlemen have finished their conversation."[2] To Gus Longstreet this, if he knew it, probably did not seem a tactful way of managing, and Dr. Beecher seemed because of it still less a proper object of admiration. But one of Dr. Beecher's daughters (not Harriet, he advises meticulously, but another, who was engaged to his friend Alexander Fisher) he did admire warmly.

Around Litchfield even more than around New Haven lingered the tradition of the Revolution. Colonel Benjamin Talmage, who had been a distinguished army officer and who was a close friend of Washington, was living now in Litchfield with little more to occupy him than the business of narrating his experiences. He it was who had performed, most romantically, since it was against his personal convictions, the task of getting Major André executed. He was old and garrulous and could talk indefinitely long about this adventure of his prime. He had visited Washington's home, and even remembered how Mrs. Washington, "less amiable than her husband, would at times sadly tax his patience. . . ." Colonel Burr he knew also, and Alexander Hamilton.[3] To Longstreet the opportunity of hearing talk of this kind was a privilege no more to be neglected than the opportunity of seeing planets leap on to the moon and back off again. Along with the rest of his world he knew that the American Revolution was the one great stupendous event of history. Politically (and in consequence, socially, of course) it was to remedy griefs and

---

[1] Vanderpool, *Chronicles*, 34.
[2] *Ibid.*, 149.
[3] Sparks, *Memories*, 184–91.

abuses which had weighed down the world since Adam, and which, had the Revolution failed, would probably have continued to weigh the world down forever. Young Mr. Longstreet felt himself, as an American citizen, standing above the rest of the world "on a lofty peak of moral elevation"; and from Colonel Talmage he could hear at first hand about the characters who had made this glorious new hope of the world no longer a fond dream but a practical reality.[1]

Judge Reeve himself was connected with the Revolutionary legend. A graduate of Princeton, he had in 1763 returned to his home in Connecticut, and with his brother-in-law, Aaron Burr, undertaken the study of law. Twenty years later he established a law school[2] which he thereafter conducted with such success that it soon became necessary for him to build near his office a sort of rustic class room.[3] In 1798, when, having been made a judge of the superior court, he needed help in conducting his school, he engaged for this purpose a young Mr. Gould just out of Yale. The two men worked together admirably. The older was genial and humorous, and the other dignified and severe, but they were both somewhat flamboyantly dominated in everything by the old idea of "Republican" simplicity. Though they long conducted the greatest law school in America, they were satisfied for fifty years to use as class rooms the temporary wooden shacks originally constructed as out-houses to their law offices.[4]

Something of the impression created by these men upon the students working under them may be learned from a speech by one C. H. Loring of the class of 1813, made in response to a toast of Chancellor Kent at the annual dinner, in 1851, of the Cambridge Law School: "In 1813, there were in the Litchfield Law School more than sixty students, every state then in the Union being represented. . . . We boys would pass along the shaded street . . . with our ink stands in our hands, and our portfolios under our arms, to the lecture room of Judge Gould—the last of the Romans, of Common-Law Lawyers, the

---
[1] *Augusta Chronicle*, 25 August, 1832.
[2] *Yale College*, II, 90.
[3] *Litchfield Enquirer*, 24 August, 1911.
[4] Vanderpool, *Chronicles*, 337.

impersonation of its spirit and genius. It was indeed in his eyes, the perfection of human reason, by which he measured every principle and rule of action, and almost every sentiment. Why, sirs, his highest vision of poetry seemed to be in the refinement of special pleadings [*Query: Was it from him that John C. Calhoun learned that "whereas" was a good word with which to begin a poem?*]; and to him a non-sequitur in logic was an offence deserving, at the least, fine and imprisonment, and a repetition of it, transportation for life. He was an admirable English scholar; every word was pure English, undefiled, and every sentence fell from his lips perfectly finished, as clear, transparent and penetrating as light, and every rule and principle as exactly defined and limited as the outline of a building against the sky. From him we obtained clear, well-defined and accurate knowledge of the common law, and learned that allegiance to it was the chief duty of man, and the power of enforcing it upon others, his highest attainment. . . . From his lecture room we passed to that of the venerable Judge Reeve, shaded by a venerable elm, fit emblem of himself. He was a most venerable man, in character and appearance, his thick gray hair parted and falling in profusion upon his shoulders, his voice only a loud whisper, but distinctly heard by his earnestly attentive pupils. He, too, was full of legal learning, but invested the law with all of the genial enthusiasm and generous feelings and noble sentiments of a large heart at the age of eighty, and descanted to us with a glowing eloquence upon the sacredness and majesty of the law. He was distinguished, sirs, by that appreciation of the gentler sex which never fails to mark the true man, and his teachings of the law in reference to their rights and the domestic relations, had great influence in elevating and refining the sentiments of the young men who were privileged to hear him. As illustrative of his feelings and manner upon this subject, allow me to give a specimen. He was discussing the legal relations of married women; he never called them, however, by so inexpressible a name, but always spoke of them as the better half of mankind, or in some equally just manner. When he came to the axiom that 'a married woman has no will of her own,' this, he said, was a maxim of great theoretic importance for

EDUCATION

the preservation of the sex against the undue influence or coercion of the husband; but although it was an inflexible maxim, in theory, experience taught us that practically it was found that they sometimes had wills of their own—*most happily for us*. We left his lecture room, sirs, the very knight errants of the law, burning to be defenders of the right and the avengers of the wrong; and he is no true son of the Litchfield School who has ever forgotten that lesson."[1]

A catalogue of the Law School published in 1828 describes as follows the methods of instruction practiced by the two Judges: "According to the plan pursued . . . the law is divided into forty-eight titles, which embrace all of its important branches, and which are treated in systematic details. These titles are the result of thirty years' severe and close application. They comprehend the whole of legal reading during that period, and continue moreover to be enlarged and improved by modern adjudications. The lectures which are delivered every day, and which usually occupy an hour and a half, embrace every principle and rule falling under the several divisions of the different titles."

Under these impressive men and these ominous forty-eight titles, Gus Longstreet fared well. Every day he went to school, and, according to the custom, took voluminous notes, which, rewritten, were to be turned later into books of reference. One of these note-books, still preserved in the Emory College Library, contains eighty-eight pages of such writing. In it one can see tabulated in a closely written hand and with the greatest possible neatness much legal matter relating to "Master and Servant" and to "Baron et Femme."

Symbolical of the life of Longstreet is the fact that by turning the book over and reading from the back towards the front one may find a series of sermons, written certainly some twenty-five years after the law notes. The handwriting of the boy is identical with that of the mature man. Scrupulously legible, neat, compact, it shows to the unimaginative, even, a disposition both systematic and orthodox. To James Wood Davidson, who evidently knew much of such matters, it indi-

---

[1] Kilbourne, *Bench and Bar*, 186–7.

cates, he says, "closeness, want of caution, naturalness, limited sympathies, and carelessness."[1] Certainly Longstreet vaunted himself somewhat upon the legibility of his writing, and condemned illegibility in the writing of others. In a letter to his young friend, George Pierce [Augusta, 4 November, 1839], he says, "I have received from you one of the most abominable (in penmanship, I mean), miserable, merciless, tantalizing epistles that ever was disgorged."[2]

But it is with Longstreet as a law student that one is as yet concerned primarily. The material of his note-book shows him to have been earnest, dutiful, and aspiring, eagerly concerned for his own future advancement. There is no idle sketching in it, no amazing flight of birds across the pages, no anything that would suggest that the boy occupied himself more divertingly while in class than by paying strict attention to his lectures.

The process of listening and absorbing and transcribing was officially broken every Saturday at Litchfield when the students were subjected to a formal examination. Somewhat less rigorous were the moot courts presided over by Judge Gould,[3] and the student debating societies which met regularly from six to nine o'clock every Monday evening.[4]

Nationally, great things were happening while Longstreet was in Connecticut. While the United States had been a second time engaged in war with England, the young Georgian had found himself in an atmosphere politically opposed to the ideas that he traditionally followed, among people who favored making light of a war that had just resulted in the ruthless destruction by the enemy of his father's chief means of livelihood, the mills at St. Marys, Georgia.[5] All through 1812–13–14 he had followed the newspapers, and winced under their fierce hostility to a national policy dictated by men identified with his section of the Union. The message which the Governor of Connecticut issued in 1813 seemed to him practically seditious,

---

[1] James Wood Davidson, *Living Writers of the South* (New York, 1869), 342.
[2] George G. Smith, *Pierce*, 100–3.
[3] Kilbourne, *Bench and Bar*, 194.
[4] *Ibid.*, 192.
[5] Mayes, *Genealogy*, 24.

and the agitation for a secession convention sickened the heart of the idealistic young man who regarded his nation as earth's sole hope of release and advancement. Did a man express himself freely in those days if he favored a war and yet definitely refused to take part in it, or did he preserve discreet silence? It is likely that he could express himself. Certainly there was some curious lapse of reason which permitted one to be violently in favor of war without having it borne in upon him that if able bodied, an advocate of war is duty bound himself to become a participant. The defection of the New England states from the general government, Gus Longstreet felt, was actuated by narrow and transient selfish interests, and, as such, he could only hold it ignoble, a thing to put rancors in the vessel of his otherwise pleasant memory of his life in New England.

Gus's father died in September, 1814, and in the late fall the young lawyer started home to Augusta. How he returned, whether by sea or land, one cannot tell, nor can one say, as Gus could have said, as he was going homeward, what he had done during his long vacations at Yale and at Litchfield, whether he had come home at all during his four years in the North, whether he had visited his relatives in New Jersey, or visited the Calhoun summer colony at Newport; all of these things have gone from human record forever. But the qualities of character that would have been augmented by such visits, an intense and self-conscious love of his native Georgia, an increasingly orthodox nineteenth century regard for the fetish of consanguinity, a personality of trained and yet spontaneous social charm almost hypnotic in its power,—all of these qualities had somehow become a part of the young man's individuality long before he left Connecticut.

III

A YOUNG LAWYER IN GEORGIA

When young Mr. Longstreet came home at about Christmas time, in 1814, his father was dead, but aside from the change caused by that loss he found his life in Augusta not much different from what it had been. How deep was his feeling of personal loss in this death no one can now say with great authority, but it is sure that no one who has gone through the various records he left and found in them no indication of any great tenderness or affection the boy held for his father,—it is sure that no such explorer can believe that the sense of affliction he experienced extended far beyond the bounds of conventional mourning. Even his mother seems somehow to have gone out of the young man's life. Other interests, other children, household cares, church and philanthropic work occupied her attention, one suspects, at a time when her son might easily have proved very susceptible to her influence. The bounds of convention, however, in matters of domestic affection, extended, in all conscience, far enough in 1815 to satisfy and even astonish a more cynical age. Young Mr. Longstreet would undoubtedly have been belligerently aggrieved at the suggestion that his love of his parents at this period of his life was more conventional than real, and it is, of course, entirely possible that what would certainly have been his own sure testimony as to his feelings should be accepted as of more weight than should the confessedly wavering impression of one who knows the man only through the fragmentary records of him now available.

It is time now to inquire into Longstreet's personality. So far as practical affairs went, he had, at this time, all of the established virtues, in one of them, thrift, going so far as to suggest parsimoniousness. But he was also impulsive and kindly, a man gifted with the ability to make friends, a person who liked people of all sorts and liked to be with them, a vehement person fond of active and competitive sports, hunting, for instance, and not fishing, wrestling, for instance, more than anything,—in all senses a mixer and a wholesome person, no recluse, no victim of morbidness and introspection. Neither now nor later does life seem to him to any great degree contradictory or intricate. The natural man he usually believed essentially good and capable of being kept so, if one would only take a little thought and "remove him from the temptations of vice."[1] Life to him was abundantly worth bothering with, and desperately to be held to. There was no question of his devotion to his wife, but it was equally unquestionable, in his mind, that it was she who was more to be congratulated on her longevity than it was anybody else; "I felicitated my wife," he wrote in 1870, with reference to an episode that occurred in 1856 when the two had been married nearly forty years and it seemed that they were at last about to settle to a fixed abode, "I felicitated my wife upon her having lived to see the end of my vagrant life."[2] Reasoning can very often, he thought, slip beyond the limits of sense. He could never follow, for instance, the fine-spun theory that slavery was worse on the masters than on the slaves.

Longstreet was enamored above all things else of good talk,—very frequently, it is to be feared, a love tainted with inability to discriminate between wit that is spontaneous and real, and those heavy slabs of wit, cut-and-dried jokes, paraded before the mind in lieu of the living flesh of it,—enamored though, nevertheless, of sparkling intelligence and clever phraseology. He was inimitable as a story teller. "No one," said a friend of his, "could resist the contagion of his humor. He was usually the center of a listening, laughing, admiring crowd. His tone, gesture, and play of features gave his narratives a peculiar zest and charm."[3]

His senses were keenly alive to beauty. The manifestations of nature often gave him the most tangible pleasure. He was also fond of music, had learned somewhere to play the flute

---

[1] William B. Sprague, *Annals of the American Pulpit* (New York, 1857), IV, 63–7.
[2] Fitzgerald, *Judge Longstreet*, 48.
[3] Fitzgerald, *Judge Longstreet*, 169–70.

and the piano. Out of these accomplishments he got enormous satisfaction. He could hear a piece of music and then play it off "by ear," and could even compose music, which, at times, after he became a preacher, he would connect with some familiar hymn, and deliver, solo-fashion, before his congregation.

One intellectual inquiry his democratic soul could not get away from. It was concerned with history. Why does history, he wanted to know, say nothing except about the emperors, and such like? Why does it not tell about the vast bulk of the population, the ordinary, every-day citizens? Could there be such a thing as social history? When we and our institutions live only in old records, for we shall all surely pass, what if someone should—would it not be enthrallingly interesting to find a document showing the Latin civilization as it existed for people in general, not just for the patricians?

Morally, the young man was orthodox. He saw no great harm, one can suppose, in drinking whiskey or in playing cards, but he was too canny, too thrifty of his own resources, to indulge in either of them to the extent of drunkenness or gambling. This instinctive thrift and caution, and, too, his natural predilection for the conventional and the respectable, dictated his actions as regards matters of sex. He admired the rigid morality of certain people he knew, but was aware of the existence in man of certain brutish-seeming implications. These things, in point of performance, he probably shunned, but touched upon, certainly, in point of contemplation and interest. He knew certain lewd songs that do not come to the acquaintance of persons not seeking them, and he believed all too badly of the motives little boys have in some of their enterprises; he was quite sure why a young man stands over a young lady in such a towering fashion when she is seated at the piano—in the evening. In short, he had a curiosity about sex that led him to accumulate a tawdry mass of information concerning it that remained in his mind embarrassingly long after he became a preacher. One of his characters, William Mitten, haunts the quarters of female servants, with no proper motives in his head; his young Squire Fisher is reported to have behaved himself with improper suggestiveness, in a way that Longstreet finds no trouble in explaining; one of his admirable girl characters says with mild regret that she doesn't believe there is a "pure" man in Georgia. One of the jingles published when he was over fifty years old and already several years in the ministry, shows Pan sporting through a preacher's mind in a dance not at all pietistic:

> "E'en lawyers 'legs and bodies' she
> Makes subject of her raillery,
> And in the midst of lady throngs
> Compares them to 'a pair of tongs.'
> I'd say to this sarcastic Miss
> She'd better mind her business
> Or she may find that tongs can pinch
> Enough to make a lady winch."[1]

In picking up ideas of this kind the young man was patently nothing worse than normal. It was his last idea that he would ever be a professional religionist. But he was too clear-thinking a person, even when at his blandest, to justify as a matter of theoretical righteousness, at least, the idea that men and women should be held to different codes of morality.

In religious matters also the young man was cautious and respectable. If asked about his convictions in this line he would probably have said curtly as John C. Calhoun said, "I am a believer in the Christian religion," and he would probably have felt in the matter as earnestly as Calhoun felt. As for the supernatural content of the Christian dogma, Gus Longstreet knew in his heart well enough that he believed every bit of it absurd folly; but he believed, too, that sentiments of that order could not be discreetly uttered by anybody, much less by a young man who was looking to popular confidence as his sole means of advancement. This much he had learned of the Calhouns.[2]

In addition to this canniness of outlook, for which it is possible either to praise or blame him, or to do both, he showed another trait which, though originating in a laudable motive, was in some cases pushed to the extent of accomplishing harm.

---

[1] Longstreet, "Gnatville Gem," *Magnolia*, June, 1843; *Stories Moral*, 31.
[2] Longstreet, "Review Perry's Calhoun," 620.

Except insofar as concerned matters of religious dogma, he detested above all things else the assumption of non-existent virtue. But he took to himself the authority of determining whether virtue really existed or did not exist, and in the exercise of this authority it must be confessed that he was often to a degree intolerant. Music, for instance, he would plead for as strongly as the next man, but the conglomeration of sound recently brought to this country as classical music, opera and so forth, was really not music at all, and could not therefore really appeal to the people who so loudly proclaimed their approval of it. Such people, that is, those whose profession of taste differed from his, were by this process of reasoning reduced to the position of lip worshippers merely, hypocrites, who pretend to admire a thing that they at heart detest. The trouble with Longstreet's method was that his denial of the validity of some appeals was based wholly on his own inability to hear them. But on the whole, his powers of sensuous enjoyment were more highly developed than were those of most of his contemporaries, and it is doubtful whether his jeers ever caused much undeserved flinching. Besides, if there were no intolerance there would not be much humor.

Up to this time the young man seems never to have done a thing out of the course of what seemed to him, and what in none too great flattery may be said would have seemed to any normal person, in the long run, easiest. Whatever course one takes, one is prevented thereby from taking some other course that offers allurements hard to abandon; what is down the fork of the road not taken one always must needs give up. There are to come times in Gus Longstreet's life when, in pursuit of some slight-seeming but to him commanding and supreme good he is to follow with magnificent faith down paths that to all appearances lead chiefly to wretchedness,—leaving paths that nearly every mortal instinct must have frantically bidden him keep. As yet he has given evidence of no such potentialities. As yet he is simply as able and as likable a young man as one often meets.

Certainly he must have attracted some attention in Augusta during the spring of 1815 while he was there studying law, with special reference to the laws of Georgia, in preparation for his

A YOUNG LAWYER IN GEORGIA

bar examination. He was tall and spare with an easy, graceful carriage, and though much has been said of his homeliness of countenance, he was of such magnetic personality that he was rather attractive than otherwise. He had fair complexion, brown hair, blue eyes, and a large, rather flexible mouth.[1]

William Longstreet had left enough property for each of his numerous heirs to inherit some three or four thousand dollars.[2] In addition to having this inheritance for a nest-egg, young Longstreet was a trained lawyer, and it was generally understood that any man who had brains to practice law, and would apply himself, was assured of both wealth and political distinction.

The Georgia into which Longstreet had determined to throw his life was now passing its transitory moment as the American frontier, a frontier relieved now of the very gravest danger of hostile attack, but none the less in most regards as typical a frontier as ever was. Practically the entire population in that section of the state which was known to Longstreet was made up of persons who for one reason or another had left Virginia and North Carolina, or, in a surprisingly large number of cases, had left New England and moved southward. In and about Savannah was a class of people that had come to feel itself ancestrally Georgian, but the inhabitants of the rich lands between Savannah and Augusta (Middle Georgia, as the section was called) were generally not of native birth. Even in Middle Georgia, however, there were two nuclei of settlement, Virginians and North Carolinians. Of these it was the practice of the old writers, most of whom belonged to the Virginia group and felt a very strong coherence among themselves,[3] to declare that the Virginians were characterized by most of the

---

[1] There are three pictures of Longstreet, each made at a different period of his life; (a) a portrait in the Library of the Emory University Academy, at Oxford, Georgia, which is reproduced at the front of this volume; (b) a daguerreotype reproduced in Green's *History of the University of South Carolina*, 70; (c) a photograph reproduced in Fitzgerald's *Judge Longstreet*,—Mitchell, *American Life and Letters*, II, 27,—Mayes, *L. Q. C. Lamar*, 38,—Buckle, *History of the Methodist Church*,—Northern, *Men of Mark in Georgia*, II, 264.

[2] Records Clerk Superior Court, 19 February, 1817.

[3] Garnett Andrews, *Reminiscences of an Old Georgia Lawyer* (Atlanta, 1870), 69–70.

social and personal virtues, while the North Carolinians were in a large measure morally and intellectually abandoned. If this was true, Georgia fared so much the worse. There were five or six times as many North Carolinians as there were Virginians.[1] The likelihood is that in general neither of these classes was aware of life's subtler refinements (the Virginians, one of the old chroniclers states, really had no more books than the North Carolinians[2]), but the certainty is that both of these classes were resourceful and determined, and as energetic as their prodigally productive section would spur them to be. They had come to Georgia at first with the idea of growing on the fresh unworn lands to the south of them the same old land-impoverishing tobacco crops that they had been accustomed to grow at home, but they had turned, when their advantage dictated their so doing, to the growing of cotton. As cotton became more and more profitable, the cotton industry, of course, became paramount, and the slave system, one of the corollaries of cotton, fixed itself, though not at the time recognizedly so, more and more banefully upon the economic order of the state.

There was in Georgia certainly, as in Virginia and the Carolinas, a growth of the great plantation system, but certain conditions in Georgia prevented the rise of it there to the extent to which it prevailed in other Southern States. Immediately to the north and south of Middle Georgia were districts too infertile to admit of a full development of great plantations, and immediately to the west, until a time later than is generally taken account of, there were Indians whose constancy and friendliness could not be fully enough relied upon to permit the settlers to live in great isolation.

The very character of the people, besides this, curtailed for a long time the development of great farms in Georgia. Very often the people who had come there were people who had not done well under the existing order in Virginia and the Carolinas, and were naturally unwilling to see established in their new home an order which they had found irksome in the old one. It may be taken for granted, too, that in any concerted

---

[1] U. S. Census, 1850, 1860.
[2] George W. Pascal, *Ninety-four Years* (Washington, 1871), 24.

migration there is generally among the immigrants a fair percentage of incompetents. Now an incompetent who can earn a livelihood on a small bit of ground, and exert only slight energy to do so, is very reasonably averse to pawning his sweet leisure and irresponsibility for the transitory and vain offerings of wealth; and he knows from within somehow, in addition, that he could not keep the grand pace even if he tried.

Virginia and South Carolina were settled at a time when people had definite ideas as to what constituted virtue in a man and what did not. A thriftless man was a poor citizen and that was all there was to him. When Georgia was being settled, however, Mr. Jefferson had suggested, partly by his own example but more potently by his popularization of French philosophy, that a thriftless man might be truly a "philosopher," and in many regards a better citizen than his successful neighbor to whom one could not always give unquestioned praise merely because he was well adapted to a world so likely to be evil. And in Georgia, in its most impressionable period of life, there were the New Englanders, missionaries then as always, but then, missionaries, and, as a rule, school-teachers combined. For their part, these people meant to live close to somebody, to constitute group settlements, or at least neighborhoods; and whenever possible they meant to proclaim the delights of this method of living, the advantages of the township, the allurements of the common, the convenience of concentration in matters of church-going and sending children to school, and in other ways that seemed to them countless. The influence of these people in the early development of Georgia was great, and has been lasting, though it has by now been long submerged and is no longer to be recognized as an entity.

In the old days, however, it was generally accepted. The fact that Liberty County, Georgia, had been settled by Massachusetts Puritans, gave grounds to the strictures made by those who found Georgia out of line with their concept of a good Southern state. William Gilmore Simms complains constantly that Georgia is a Yankee, and Richard Malcolm Johnston has Vermont school teachers dominating the lives of his early

Middle-Georgians. "Our old State," Johnston makes one of his characters say, in a letter written about Georgia, to his family in Vermont, "seems to be rather a favorite, so many have migrated thence, and done distinguished service, especially in the education of youth."[1] In actuality, it was New England men who shaped the University of Georgia up to the time of the Civil War. There was a distinct feeling among Georgians, who by absorption from the Virginians had got the old eighteenth century English idea of life, that school teaching was a low caste job,[2] and consequently most of the work of this sort that was done well was done by New England immigrants. And one New Englander was most prominent (Sherwood for the Baptists and Olin for the Methodists) in the early councils of each of the two leading churches of the state.

Alert travelers who come to Georgia and keen critics who write about it agree that the state is somehow different from the rest of the South. Old Niles, editor of the *Register*, of Baltimore, complains that to him its politics seem somehow contradictory. In 1783, it was impetuous to adopt the Federal Constitution, and in 1861, it was only by the slightest majority that it could adopt the Ordinance of Secession. There are numerous contemporary statements as to the Northerners who came South. Nearly everything the people in the interior of Georgia had during the War of 1812 was bought from the wagons of New England pedlars.[3] Longstreet makes Georgia say in a letter addressed to her sister Massachusetts that many of the children of Massachusetts had settled in Georgia's borders.[4] Many of the old notables were of New England origin. From their side, the home-keeping New Englanders did not look with favor upon the self-constituted outcasts. The New England people, says Fitz-Greene Halleck in his poem, *Connecticut*, are great home lovers,

---

[1] Richard Malcolm Johnston, *Old Mark Langston* (New York, 1884), 11, 201.

[2] Longstreet, *Mitten*, 291; Johnston, *Old Mark Langston*, 291; Longstreet, "Emory College Inaugural."

[3] Andrews, *Old Georgia Lawyer*, 14.

[4] Longstreet, *Voice from the South* (Baltimore, 1847), Letter 1.

All but a few apostates meddling
With merchandise, pounds, pense, and *peddling*,
   Or wandering through the Southern countries, teaching
The A. B. C., or Webster's spelling book,
   Gallant, and godly, making love and preaching,
And gaining by what they call "hook and crook"
   And what moralists call over-reaching,
A decent living. The Virginians look
Upon them with as favorable eyes
As Gabriel on the devil in paradise.

The census figures of 1850 and 1860 show that there were two or three times as many persons of Northern birth in Georgia as there were in either North or South Carolina, and that, even proportionately, there were almost twice as many.[1] The population of Alabama and Mississippi was still quite unsettled.

The Northern quality of thrift it has always been fashionable to attribute to Georgians. In one of Simms's books the reader is shown a group of people in a stage coach. They are all from different states. One man expresses his opinion one way about politics and another man another way. Of these the Georgian only presented an idea that had expediency for its sole inspiration.[2] Edward Mayes, in his *Life* of his father-in-law, L. Q. C. Lamar, speaks of Lamar's mother as "a typical Georgia lady, in the possession of these qualities of shrewd, practical, and strong common sense for which the people of that state, as a class, are noted."[3] "The Georgian," says Professor Trent, "has been called the Southern Yankee. . . . He has much of the native shrewdness and push that mark the genuine Down-Easter, and he has a considerable share of that worthy's moral earnestness. . . . The Georgian is the Southerner who comes nearest of all the inhabitants of his section to being a normal American. . . . The typical Georgian [is] energetic, shrewd, thrifty.[4] . . ." H. L.

---
[1] Census Charts prepared by Jos. A. Hill, Acting Director of Census, May, 1922.
[2] Simms, *As Good as a Comedy*, Proem.
[3] Edward Mayes, *L. Q. C. Lamar—His Life, Times, and Speeches* (Nashville, 1896), 33.
[4] William Peterfield Trent, *Southern Statesmen Old Régime* (New York, 1897), 199-200.

Mencken[1] declares that the "worst commercial bounderism of the Yankee" has been "borrowed and superimposed" upon Georgia culture. At one time in the early development of the railroads, Georgia had an amount of mileage far above that of most of the States in the entire Union. In 1860, the value of goods manufactured in Georgia was as great as that of the goods manufactured in both Alabama and Mississippi together, and about twice as great as that of goods manufactured in South Carolina. Proportionately there were in 1920 nearly four times as many Jews to the population of Georgia as there were in North Carolina, South Carolina, Alabama and Mississippi.

On the edges of civilization the necessity for looking out for oneself is urgent. Many people who come to a new country come fleeing from evil records left at home, and as a rule can bear watching in their new residences. David Crockett, in his book published during the thirties, records that "There exist throughout the extreme South, bodies of men who style themselves Lynchers."[2] But in Georgia they were called "Regulators." "What! you from Georgia," says an old Georgian to a young South Carolinian in Simms's *Guy Rivers,* "and never to hear tell of the regulators? Why that's the very place, I reckon, where the breed begun. The regilators are just then, you see, our own people. We hain't got much law and justice in these pairts, and when the rascals git too sassy and plentiful, we all turn out, few or many, and makes a business of cleaning out the stables. We all turn justices, and sheriffs, and lawyers, and settle scores with the growing sinners. . . . It's a regilar court, though we make it up ourselves, and app'ints our own judges and juries, and pass judgment 'cording to the case. Ef it's the first offence, or only a small one, we let's the old fellow off with only a taste of the hickory. Ef it's a tough case, and an old sinner, we gives him a belly-full. Ef the whole country's roused, then Judge Lynch puts on his black cap, and the rascal takes a hard ride on a rail, a duck in the pond, and a perfect seasoning of hickories, till thar ain't much left of him, or maybe, they don't stop to curry him, but

---
[1] *Prejudices*, II (New York, 1921), 141.
[2] David Crockett, *Autobiography* (Philadelphia, 1860), 310–311.

A YOUNG LAWYER IN GEORGIA

just halters him at once to the nearest swinging limb."[1] This sort of thing Longstreet probably never encountered, and if he had, he would, as a lawyer if not as a citizen, have condemned it.

The eagerness and rawness of frontier life obliterated to a great degree even the social barrier of race. The social judgment on "marriage" between the races was never favorable,[2] but distinguished lawyers, in the early days, in riding about the country and stopping at farm houses to meals, were sometimes set down to a table serving negro farm hands as well as themselves and the families of their host.[3] Negro veterans of the Revolutionary War were upon occasion eagerly received as guests by great gentlemen, who had come to be governors and senators.[4] Negro doctors were regularly patronized by people who could conceive that it would be better to be cured by a black man than suffered to let die by a white one.[5] This, of course, represents the extreme case. As soon as economic conditions resulted in the bringing into the state of a great number of negroes, the instinct of the whites, alive to the fact that their racial integrity would be destroyed unless definite lines of cleavage should be set up, did actually set these lines up to such a degree that it is scarcely possible for a subsequent time to realize how much more largely the whole phenomenon of race prejudice arises from questions of social expediency than from mere personal taboos.

The stronger the necessity for an infinitely great gap between the races, the greater became the urge for a denial of the existence of all other social distinctions. This compensating scale was recognized even by Southerners. "The *independent mass* . . . in the south are so accustomed," wrote a true member of the order,[6] "to making but two divisions in society—the republican freemen and the slaves— . . . that even our stage drivers [why 'even,' one wonders] feel a supe-

---

[1] Simms, *Guy Rivers* (New York, 1855), 70.
[2] John Melish, *Travels in the United States* (Philadelphia, 1812), I, 45.
[3] Stephen F. Miller, *Bench and Bar of Georgia* (Philadelphia, 1858), I, 332.
[4] George R. Gilmer, *Sketches of Some of the First Settlers of Upper Georgia* (New York, 1855), 214.
[5] Pascal, *Ninety-four Years*, 65.
[6] Anonymous, *Manolia*, 88-9.

riority over the pretensions" of the professed nobility of Europe. If a man was white, he was not to be questioned further. If he was black, there was an end of his aspiration. John Quincy Adams recorded in his diary an expression from John C. Calhoun as to how the South felt concerning social caste. Adams, it seems, had just made some public declaration of democratic principle. "Afterwards," he says, "I walked home with Calhoun, who said that the principles I had just avowed were just and noble; but that in the southern country whenever they were mentioned, they were always understood as applying only to white men. Domestic labor was confined to the blacks. . . . I said that this confounding of the ideas of servitude and labor was one of the bad effects of slavery, but he thought it attended with many excellent consequences. It did not apply to all kinds of labor, not, for example, to farming. He himself had often held the plough; so had his father. Manufacturing and mechanical labor was not degrading. It was only manual labor—the proper work of slaves. No white person could descend to that. And it was the best guarantee of equality among the whites. It produced an unvarying level among them. It not only did not excite but did not even admit of inequalities, by which one white man could domineer over another." [1]

Calhoun's ideal of society was patriarchal, Biblical, much as Longstreet's was. In writing of Calhoun, late in life, Longstreet said, "I believe that he regarded the government of the children of Israel in the wilderness, the most perfect that ever existed on earth. Be that as it may, he called my attention to it more than once as exactly the government ours ought to be, or was intended to be. 'There,' said he, 'each tribe had its place on the march and in the camp, each managed its own concerns in its own way, neither interfered in the slightest degree, with the private affairs of another, nor did their common head interfere with any of them in any matters, save such as were of equal interest to all, but unmanageable by them as separate and distinct communities.' " [2] To Longstreet rural life was always theoretically the life which was best and most

---
[1] Stedman-Hutchinson, *Library American Literature*, IV, 231–2.
[2] Longstreet, "Review Perry's Calhoun," 622–3.

normal; Dr. Waddel's students were good, he thought, because they were kept removed from cities—the city students who came to him were invariably disturbing elements.[1]

Recreations in early Georgia were of a nature crude enough to please the most red-blooded man conceivable. The social unit here as elsewhere in frontier communities was the trading post. Hear one of the contemporary writers: "There was a store near the hotel, where a general assortment of merchandise of every description, including many barrels of liquor, was kept and sold. The liquor was dealt out in quantities to suit the purchasers. Much of it was sold by the half-pint, and drank at the counter. The custom was for the neighboring-planters to meet at the store, wander in the beautiful groves, run quarter races, practice target-shooting, pitch quoits or silver dollars, talk . . . until some one felt thirsty, and ordered a "quart" or a "half-pint," which was socially imbibed at the counter.[2] . . . There were foot-races and wrestling matches.[3]

Occasionally there were formal celebrations, "public days," from which "no one thought so much or so meanly of himself as to be absent." There one might see racing and goose-pulling, witnessed by young men dressed in costumes similar to those lately worn by dukes in England, witnessed also by young ladies who prattled sentimentally by the hour, quoting from the poets. There was whiskey in abundance, complemented by ginger cakes, and cider with cold baked meats and barbecue. If the young ladies were not very careful they would be shocked by seeing scuffles and fights and hearing blasphemous language.[4] There were slaves running around everywhere. Poor whites and rich whites rubbed shoulders. Practically, classes did not exist.

In a melting-pot such as Georgia was in 1815 it is hardly possible that there was any rigid social stratification. Virginians whose parents had been friends even of Madam Washington herself knew that to attain political prominence it was

[1] Sprague, *Annals*, IV, 63–7.
[2] Pascal, *Ninety-four Years*, 99–100.
[3] Longstreet, *Mitten*, 223–4.
[4] Simms, *As Good as a Comedy*, 44–50.

necessary to have the votes of one's neighbors, and beside that, it is hard for the most stiff-necked aristocrat, who is in trouble, to repel the kindly advances of a man whose chief contamination lies in that he is ungrammatical in his speech and ignorant as to his ancestry.

If a neighbor had bad luck and got behind with his crop you went over and helped him plow it. If his barn was burned, you sent him a load of corn. If he wanted to build a house, or clear a piece of ground, you would help also. He would do as much for you. People were good-natured, simple, and, after the manner of frontiersmen, astonishingly credulous. Gilmer saw some people in Virginia get fleeced by a man who collected money from them on the ground that he was to buy for them from a factory in Ohio some spy-glasses that would enable them to see far into the earth.[1]

People were mutually dependent. When David Crockett went to New York, he could hardly bring himself, when he heard the cry "fire, fire," not to "jump on the first horse at hand, and ride full flight, barebacked to help put it out."[2] When a man wanted his corn shucked, he made a party for the community, putting the corn into two piles and giving each pile to a group of his guests. There was music at this sort of "entertainment," and much eating, and perhaps more drinking. Dances there were, and horse racing, and shooting matches with beeves for prizes, and school exhibitions, and withal, much marrying. It was a happy time, to be learned about nowhere probably so accurately and entertainingly as in Longstreet's own descriptions of it. Generosity and kindness of heart were the rule rather than the exception. Joel Chandler Harris, who grew up in Middle Georgia, under personal conditions not calculated to demand the most gracious treatment from his neighbors, held always very affectionate memories of his childhood. His lot when a boy, he wrote of himself, "was cast amongst the most democratic people the world has ever seen, and in a section where . . . the ideals of character and conduct are held in higher esteem than wealth or ancient lineage."[3]

---

[1] Gilmer, *Sketches*, 244.
[2] Crockett, *Autobiography*, 184–5.
[3] *Joel Chandler Harris, Life of*, by Julia Collier Harris (Boston, 1918), 8–9.

A YOUNG LAWYER IN GEORGIA 63

Living conditions were comfortable, as comfort went in those times, and rarely much more. Two rooms with an open hallway between them and a porch in front constituted the typical house. Occasionally two rooms were set above the two on the ground, and a couple of shed rooms, as they were called, were added on the rear. This got to be luxuriousness. If the porch across the front could be made a two-story affair instead of a single story one, the house was thought of as "rivaling the ancient corrupt splendors of Europe," or something else of the sort of equally naïve absurdity. One could not fret much over what happened to a house so poorly fit together that sandbags had to be used to keep the wind from rushing in under the front door. One could not find any emotion except one of amusement when the dogs chased a pig through the dining room of such a house and turned over tables and chairs and created general pandemonium. Only about a third of the white families owned slaves, and even those who did, and were consequently able to have house-servants, found these servants as a rule so shiftless and inherently filthy that if a house was to be kept in relative decency it was necessary either to give all of one's time to overseeing the servants, or to turn servant one's self. On the whole, fastidiousness was, by some rare coincidence, at once probably the least tolerable and the least manifest of all human qualities.

The men were as a rule strong and robust, given to out-of-door life and its enjoyments, careless, or dead, from inanition, of course, if from no other cause, to nearly all esthetic appeal. Oratory and religion indeed were the only avenue of such appeal open to a community knowing so few of the appurtenances of civilization.

Religion, more than anything else, gave some certain answer to the age-old yearning for beauty and for release from oppressive reality. In theory oftentimes narrow, crude, strict, pugnacious, the old denominations nevertheless kept constantly before the people's minds the ancient magical flame of righteousness and mystic contemplation, the sight of which, alone, can save from inanimate complacency, and lead to some indispensable, happy, cureless incertitude of one's own powers. In physical equipage bare, revolting, defiantly inimical to beauty, the old dogmas, nevertheless, in spite of themselves, served as glasses through which many a soul saw dimly visions of sheer rich loveliness that, learned of elsewhere than from the Bible, would have been accounted reprehensible. But the persons seeing thus far were few, and those who would dare acknowledge having caught such visions, even fewer.

In the rural districts, which constituted most of the state, the intellectual and esthetic elements of religion were largely absent,—whether through choice, or through the inability of a frontier community to command them. Heaven lay at the end of a trail blazed comprehensibly for ambulant and horseback pioneers.—Who could believe that there are many ways to Heaven? There are not more ways than one, to Augusta.— One of the contemporary editors, who had been out of Georgia and had some perspective, wrote about affairs very plainly: "We accompanied our host," he says, "to service at a meeting house . . . where our patience was wearied—despite our devotional feeling—by no less than three long-winded 'discourses,' as destitute of any ray of interest or reason, and as completely outrageous of every dictum of oratory, rhetoric, and even grammar, as they well could be. . . . 'Splendid sarmints,' commented our host, as we rode homewards. 'Which,' replied we, 'the first, second or third?' for, having service but once a month, it is a custom to sit out several long discourses, consecutively, like the famished tourist in the desert when his parched lips meet the cooling stream. 'Which,' we asked, 'do you admire so much? You certainly jest in praising the ranting of Mr. ——, the jargon of ——, or the rigmarole of ——.' . . . Our friend looked at us in astonishment. 'I'm afeard,' said he, 'that you have been to them minister making machines. Bretherin —— is powerful men —— powerful: they preach the gospel—the plain simple gospel; none of your new-fangled, high-flying preaching. . . . I don't want no edicated preachers about me. Larnin' only makes 'em proud and worldly.' The sermons were suited to the congregation."[1]

The music was little better. "We have," writes the same editor, "not unfrequently entered country or village sanctu-

---
[1] *Orion*, October, 1843, 89.

aries—for there is too little difference between them in regard to music—and while endeavoring to compose ourself to the sacredness of the place and the delightful solemnity of the service, have been startled and shocked out of all seriousness and propriety of feeling, by an outburst of sound, intended for singing, but which certainly resembled more nearly the midnight serenade with which a party of cats are wont to vex the dull ear of night, and the acute sensibilities of some sleepless victim. . . . We have heard the sound of 'bells, jangling and harsh, and out of tune,' and our teeth have been set on edge, by the grating of 'a wheel on a dry axle'; but these were streams of melody itself, compared with the torrents of discordant sounds which have overwhelmed us, oftentimes, in the house of worship, until we are fain to stop our ears.[1] . . ."
Practically, the social contribution of the churches was limited chiefly to their unequaled encouragement of morality, and to their offering unconsciously, as they had offered consciously in medieval times in Europe, a sort of center for social gatherings.

The schools also naturally contributed to the amalgamation of the people. Nothing perhaps is, however, more illuminative of the social crudeness of early Georgia than is the poor condition of its educational system. Primary education, especially in the rural districts, comes off well in being called nothing worse than farcical. Children went to school chiefly when there was nothing else for them to do.[2] Teachers were the last people one demanded. In 1831, out of the nearly three thousand inhabitants of the town of Macon, there was not one school-master.[3] And the worst part is that even when teachers were found, they were too often men of inferior attainments and no character, totally unable to command the respect of parents or pupils. One of them, the story goes, after he had been "turned out" of his school, "beaten, tied, and smeared with mud," surrendered and gave the school a "treat," a gallon of whiskey, which he drank with his "scholars."[4] These brutal and dishonest teachers held dominion over the chil-

---

[1] *Orion*, November, 1843, 134.
[2] Gilmer, *Sketches*, 154.
[3] Niles' *Register*, 27 August, 1831.
[4] George G. Smith, *Methodism in Georgia and Florida*, 205.

dren with little interference from the children's parents. Habitually half-drunk, boasting their ability to spell anything "from the point of a needle to the anchor of a ship," but in reality quite illiterate, these men were engaged, and paid, to sway the minds of little Georgians whither they would.

The people at large took the matter of education cavalierly. There is a story of how one of the "citizens," doubting the efficiency of the person applying for the teacher's position, proceeded as follows to examine him: " 'I ain't much of a speller, but I larnt to spell some words, right specially the things that's good to eat,—spell coffee.' The tramp began 'k-a-u-g-h-p-h-y, coffee.' 'Well, well,' said the citizen, 'he's got larning shore, for he's spelled it without usin' a letter that belongs to it. He'll do, don't want to ax any more questions.' "[1] It was nothing for a teacher to whip the blood from a boy as punishment for a bad lesson, and the phrase "nasty whelp" flew often from his lips during the course of the day.[2] In retaliation the little brutes could do nothing but hate their trainer with all the ardor at their command, and lock him out of his citadel, the only active measure tolerated by tradition, whenever occasion offered and they felt that they would like to.

The level of culture was as low as it is in most frontier countries. Though many of the women could speak with some attractiveness, most men felt it incumbent upon them consciously to affect an illiteracy of speech greater than they were held to by necessity.[3] But affectation, long continued, becomes second nature, and intimate exposure to noxious states of affairs, long continued, will finally victimize even the most resolute and apparently immune. It seems unlikely that the women of old Georgia upheld the ideal any more unsullied than the men did. The women in Longstreet stories, whom he admires, are always pious, and energetic, and thrifty, willing to sacrifice anything for people they love; but they are also inveterate gossips, delicate with a vapid delicacy which forbids their saying, for instance, "pig-tail," and, in addition, very frequently vulgar, superstitious, sentimental, and dishonest,

---

[1] J. D. Anthony, *Life and Times of Rev. J. D. Anthony* (Atlanta, 1896), 29-30.
[2] W. H. Sparks, *Memories*, 25.
[3] Richard Malcolm Johnston, *Mr. Absalom Billingslea* (New York, 1888), iv.

dishonest, that is, with a childish dishonesty which the men of that time thought rather admirable than otherwise in women if it was called forth by anything connected with their children, dishonest, too, in a sense which implies, incidentally, the existence of a certain unreasonableness and passionate temper on the part of the men.[1] This is not limited to Longstreet's women of the "lower class," who admittedly can talk about nothing but about how many chickens their hens hatched last spring, and what Mournin' Hoover's first husband's mother was named, but it extends to his grand ladies themselves. One lady grand enough to be the wife of a plantation magnate, and cultured enough to discuss abstract questions of pedagogy with her husband and somewhat abstruse questions of philology with her children, one such lady does not hesitate, when angry, as she very often becomes, to call her house-servant "black hussy," to threaten her children, to slap them indifferently, calling them by way of impressing her threat "vixens" or "impertinent brats."[2] Rich ladies who are devout members of the Presbyterian Church still persistently talk about "luck" with as crude an idea of fate as was ever held by a medieval ignoramus. The same ladies who shriek and faint away when they get the impression that they are believed guilty of lying do not hesitate to deceive by any means less palpable than that of direct speech.

Men found intelligence in women a quality that in general distressed more than it pleased. When they did not openly condemn it,[3] therefore, they treated it with insulting condescension.[4] The women proved marvelously adaptable to masculine demands. Though there was as near as Charleston, South Carolina, a hotel with a corps of white servants,[5] one Middle Georgia lady, a college graduate, had little enough imagination to refuse, by way of protest, to take a long anticipated trip to New York when she heard that white women, as maids, were

---
[1] Mrs. Mitten, William's mother, exemplifies nearly all of these traits, as does also the mother in "A Family Picture."
[2] "Family Picture," *Stories with a Moral*, 100-1.
[3] "Clara," "To the Gentlemen of Georgia," *Southern Ladies' Book*, August, 1840.
[4] *Southern Literary Gazette*, 2 December, 1848.
[5] *Orion*, February, 1848, 288.

expected to wash off the front steps of New York residences.[1] This lady had married a man who spat his tobacco juice so lustily as actually to extinguish the fire burning in the fireplace.

As for reading, there was very little done of one sort or another, beyond that involved by a disposition to follow the newspapers. These were of course read, with all of their shockingly detailed advertisements of various medicinal nostrums. Certainly there were few books; one old family of somewhat greater literary instinct than was common, owned copies of the Bible, *Pilgrim's Progress,* Baxter's *Call, Saint's Rest,* Fletcher's *Checks, The Spectator,* some of Johnson's works, Watts' *Psalms and Hymns,* and the book of Common Prayer, called then "The English Prayer Book,"—kept in every family, "not from any attachment to that church, but as a memento of the thraldom when there was an established church."[2] This family was Baptist. Even higher education seems to have been despaired of as not suited to Georgia conditions. The University of Georgia, chartered in 1785 as the first American State University and actually in successful operation for a decade following 1800, had by 1819 so sadly declined that it had to be started afresh almost by the President elected in that year.

Art, people as yet had no opportunity of knowing. Nomadic portrait painters were in the state sufficiently soon, and there were finally some magazines that carried, with endless boasts on the part of their editors, some atrocious colored pictures of Georgia scenery. Much later the Greek Slave was brought to Augusta for exhibition purposes. It was glowingly admired by the editor of one paper, and by the male population, one can suppose, in general. What the ladies thought of it must, since the ladies were required to view the masterpiece at a soirée for "ladies only," remain forever a secret.[3] That good Georgian, Major Jones, found the statuary adorning the Capitol at Washington a little more pornographic than he could well endure.[4]

---

[1] William T. Thompson, *Major Jones' Travels,* 28.
[2] Pascal, *Ninety-four Years,* 25.
[3] *Georgia Home Gazette,* 26 January, 1852.
[4] Thompson, *Travels,* Letter Six.

But in the early days of the United States art was no considerable item except insofar as concerns music. Even for that, John Adams thought, there was very little demand. "The Americans," he said, "had neither cultivated nor were much attached to music." He had wondered why this was true but "could not account for it otherwise than by supposing it owing to some particular construction of our fibres, that we were created without a strong devotion to music. . . . I pretend not to trace the cause," . . . he says, "but music is not an object of enthusiasm in America." Adams himself had "by dint of great pains . . . learned to blow very badly the flute."[1]

Music is easily reproduced, a fair degree of skill and a score being the only requisites, a fact which perhaps enables music to take such early hold on newly settled communities. In Georgia, a remarkably large number of people could play upon flutes and various stringed instruments, and there was a general appreciation of such effort. As soon as it was feasible to do so, people saw to it that pianos and music-teachers were brought into the schools, though, it is true, this was done over the heated protest of many good church people, to whom music was a vain thing, better suited to the devil and his coadjutors than to anyone else. Even good Methodists had to admit that "Mr. [Charles] Wesley, doubtless did greatly *err*, in giving *his sons* a knowledge of music." Lovick Pierce in speaking of music, drawing and painting, declared them all "worse than useless."[2]

So it goes. The moment a person digging into the past, as into the present, finds influences making for a more enlightened civilization, he encounters too often contrary influences emanating from a source that might in all reason have been relied upon to contribute to progress. The spirit of individualism, which so few had the courage to deny unlimited rights of development, forced contradiction and dissension into the closest councils.

But there was one counsel, as open as open could be, that heard speech overwhelmingly of one tenor. When Georgians

---

[1] Stedman-Hutchinson, *Library*, IV, 229.
[2] *Southern Christian Advocate*, 6 January, 1843.

talked about Georgia they talked about it glowingly. "The Georgian," says Professor Trent, "has an 'honest and hearty' pride in his state, and a sort of masonic affiliation with every person, animal, institution, custom—in short, *thing*—that can be called Georgian."[1] It is hard to believe that the united chorus of praise and ardent love that was always sounding in early nineteenth century Georgia was in any sense consciously insincere. The idea of nationalism, rapidly developing through those years, undoubtedly set an almost irresistible style of being patriotic, but no affectation could have actuated the complete lyricism and obviously deep sentiment of much of the old writing. One of the first governors of the state announced in dying that should his heart be removed after his death it would be found written over with the name Georgia. The poets could never be done talking about it.

> "The red old hills of Georgia!
>   O where upon the face
> Of earth, is freedom's spirit
>   More bright in any race?
> In Switzerland and Scotland
>   Each patriot breast it fills,
> But sure it blazes brighter yet
>   Among our Georgia hills!"

Again this laudation:

> "Ay! there are hearts within thy land
>   As warm and brave and pure and free
> As throbbed among the Spartan band
>   Of old Thermopylæ.
> And, like that band, should foes invade
>   To seek thy rights from thee to tear,
> Thy sons will lift the sheathless blade
>   And bid them come who dare.
>
> "As, clustered in the days of yore
>   Thy heroes 'neath the stripes and stars
> Unmindful of the sea of gore
>   And heedless of their scars,

---

[1] William P. Trent, *Southern Statesmen* (New York, 1897), 199-200.

> So ever more, that banner round,
>   In hours of peace, or days of strife
> Still be thy gallant children found
>   To guard it with their life."
>
> "O, may its stripes and spangled wreath
>   Be ne'er disgraced by sons of thine;
> Still may they cling its folds beneath
>   In one unbroken line!
> And still in ages yet untold
>   As brightly beam its glory's sheen
> As when it waved, with scanty fold,
>   Above the old thirteen!"[1]

And still again:

> "Where is a land on which a deeper blue
> Divinelier bends than that I proudly view,
>   Where broader rivers sweep to join the main
>   All brightly winding through their rich domain,
> Where prouder mountains look o'er softer dales
> Or greener forests wave to fresher gales?"[2]

"Imperial Georgia," says one of the poets, "count thy children's souls!"

There was a distinct sort of *naissance* here that stirred the imagination in a way that could not be forgotten. One of the men who had known these times gave an account of them years later in one of his books: "Striking, indeed," he writes, "was the spectacle as [Georgia's] fair, ample spaces presented themselves to view,—at the first, stretching out in all their unmarred primeval grandeur and beauty, a vast and towering woodland scene, nature's ancient, yet ever young blooming work—then, passing in turn one after another from the deep night of barbarism in which they had lain for unknown ages into the sudden light and life of high civilization. Elating to witness at the time, grateful to remember ever since, the successive expandings, the triumphal unfoldings of Georgia in this, her rich middle belt, her very zone of charms, as exulting she advanced

---
[1] Robert M. Charlton, *Poems* (Boston, 1842).
[2] Miller, *Bench and Bar*, II, 85.

by bound after bound from East to West, high-strung, hardy, laborious, 'disdaining little delicacies,' trampling down obstacles, disregarding hardships; subduing and transforming rude nature, forests falling before her, the wilderness budding and blossoming as the rose at her touch, rich crops springing up all around her called forth by her industry from the willing earth. It was the white man with the axe and the plow, the hammer and the saw, and in all the array and habiliments of civilization, superseding the Indian in his hunting shirt and moccasins. . . . It was Ceres with her garland of golden sheaves, her basket and hoe, and her divine gait and air putting an end to the reign of Pan and the Satyrs. And no metamorphosis the world ever saw, or fiction ever forged was more beautiful, picturesque and lovely than the change that was wrought, and wrought, too, with a magical ease and suddenness and on a largeness of scale that made the wonderful blend with the beautiful in the successive panoramas that were presented. It was a spectacle which will not occur again; it is one of those things that has been seen for the last time; it will never more be repeated!"[1]

The pageantry of this thing was too gorgeous to have escaped the notice of observant men, or to have failed of impressing them. Serious-minded people felt the responsibility of it and were eager to turn this stupendous new force into proper courses. "Can anyone blame the writer," inquired one of the poets of the time, "if he, looking over his own native soil and seeing so many towns and villages, that still, amid a forest dress of ever living, ever extending green, lift their glad countenances to the early notice of the world—can anyone blame him if he attempts to direct those brilliant forces to the road of real greatness and permanent utility?"[2]

Gradually the positive patriotism of the people absorbs their old negative self-consciousness. In the colonial days Georgia had won bad titles for herself by her unwillingness to enter into hostility against the British government. Certain bodies in South Carolina, in formal documents spoke of "that in-

---

[1] Absalom H. Chappell, *Miscellanies of Georgia* (Atlanta, 1874), 9-10.
[2] Samuel J. Cassels, *Providence and Other Poems* (Macon, 1838), 17.

famous colony of G—g—a."[1] The Yazoo frauds had, also, somewhat alienated the state from the rest of the nation. Her first senator declared her a "damn rascal," said he bought her and sold her and would buy her and sell her again when he pleased.[2] But patriotism thrives well upon a base of some old slight, becomes in the long run stronger from its springing from this rotten soil. There grows up a consciousness of difference from people without, and of oneness with people within. The old bitterness finally comes to be taken humorously, but it is none the less present and moving because of change of nature. The phenomenon of unreserved patriotism, then, was the chief exception in early Georgia to the eternal contradiction of frontier society, to the unending series of reminders that life was as yet totally unsettled.

Contributing greatly to the necessary stabilization, if not almost wholly accounting for it, was the presence and spirit of the legal profession. Possibly this profession throve on its difficulties; there is an old saw which says that things do that, and there was not much else, apparently, for it to thrive on. "It is more difficult to become a great man in middle Georgia," said Joseph Henry Lumpkin, "than in any country in the United States." "Judge Lumpkin merely meant," explains the man responsible for this statement, "that the country was without any great commercial mart; it was without a periodical press; had few mail facilities; no law reports; and the people were not a reading people. I speak now of that country in its prime, before the lands were so worn and its population so thinned by emigration. . . ."[3] Verbal speech was recognized as "the only way to instruct the great mass of voters."[4]

Certainly, though, great lawyers and statesmen did show themselves, and among these gentlemen, at last, one encounters some consistent evidence of sanity and smoothness and some willingness to abate for an occasional instant the high-headed

---

[1] Henry A. Scomp, *King Alcohol in the Realm of King Cotton, 1733–1887* (Blakely, Ga., 1888), 165.
[2] W. P. Trent, *William Gilmore Simms* (Boston, 1892), 182.
[3] Pascal, *Ninety-four Years*, 118.
[4] Andrews, *Old Georgia Lawyer*, 24.

whimsicality which so generally paraded the state under the colors of staunch Jeffersonian democracy.

It is a strange comment on human life that people will put up with poor everything else before they will with poor lawyers. In the category of professions, teachers, dealing largely with the future, like preachers, but laboring under the additional handicap of having no means of getting a livelihood out of society by scaring it out, are at the bottom of the list. Preachers are not greatly better off. Doctors, too, one pays largely as one pays insurance policies, against the chance of a collapse. When a person is assailed in his economic life by hostile circumstances as one is assailed in his physical life by disease, it is often necessary that a lawyer be retained to handle his case, but now, when economic health returns, it comes not directly out of the unknown to the patient, as it does after physical illness, but indirectly, through the hands of the lawyer. The lawyer can look out for himself as the money passes along. So it is that even in a community in which standards are none too scrupulously adhered to it is possible for lawyers to make headway and to prosper.

On Friday morning, 26 May, 1815, the following item was recorded in the Minute-Book of the Richmond County Superior Court: "Augustus B. Longstreet, Esquire, having petitioned this court to be admitted to plead and practice Law in the several Courts of Law and Equity in this State, and having accordingly been examined in open court, and being found well qualified, and he having taken the usual oath, he is therefore admitted to plead and practice Law in the several Courts of Law and Equity in this State, and his name ordered to be enrolled among the names of the attorneys and solicitors of this State."

As a lawyer, then, into the Georgia constituted as Georgia was in those times, Longstreet went out. It was an inspiring group of men whom he was associated with in Augusta and in the various villages to which his practice led him. Somehow there had developed in the state a group of attorneys whose native ability, careful training and indescribable raciness of mind would have gained them distinction anywhere. Particularly was this true of the middle circuit, the one with which

Longstreet was at first most intimately identified.[1] Richard Henry Wilde, William H. Crawford,, George Gilmer, John M. Berrien, John Forsyth, Oliver Hillhouse Prince, William C. Dawson, George M. Troup, Augustin S. Clayton, Duncan G. Campbell, John M. Dooley, and Edmund Bacon of South Carolina were among the men whom young Longstreet knew and associated with freely. Many of them he had known from his childhood, and the others he knew readily enough how to become acquainted with.

All of these men had marked intellectual power and personal aspirations. Conscious of their own conspicuous position as participating in the early councils of a new nation, they were sobered to such a degree officially that it is easy to understand how, when not officially occupied, they at times permitted themselves the very greatest hilarity and irresponsibility. They knew very well that to stand in the new competition of republican government it was necessary to work constantly and faithfully.

Richard Henry Wilde, in addition to being a good lawyer and a successful politician, had got into his head a decided love of pure literature; but Longstreet probably could not endorse this sort of love any too much. In the first place it was inspired by poets like Collins and Gray, to whom Mr. Pope, he held, was manifestly so superior; was inspired, too, by Italian poets of medieval times, by persons who believed, in spiritual matters even, as well as in temporal, in the principle of autocratic authority. In the second place, it was understood that Mr. Wilde considered the possibility of going to Europe and spending years, if necessary, in an effort to write a life of those long-dead papists—this in a time when the spirit of man was struggling, struggling to arise from the long stupor in which the very autocracy which Wilde found so attractive had for so long held it.

Mr. Clayton, too, had literary ambitions, his of a type which Longstreet found more admirable. Had he not as a boy received from George Washington himself a book given in token of Washington's appreciation of his marked ability as a

---

[1] Andrews, *Old Georgia Lawyer*, 68.

speaker? Had he not a thorough and elegant acquaintance with the Greek and Latin classics? Was he not contemplating a book to be called *The Mysterious Picture*, satirizing affectation and folly in his native Georgia just as sometime before Mr. Addison had done in England? This was constructive. And then, too, Mr. Clayton was such a wit, had such a keen appreciation of the ridiculous. He liked a large joke, as indeed he proved when he practically wrote the famous "autobiography" of Colonel David Crockett.[1]

And then there was Mr. Dooley, cherishing the story of the criminal who, when thundered at by the prosecuting attorney to the effect that it was blood the state wanted, suggested eagerly that if blood were all the state wanted, it should kill a "nigger"—Dooley, who encountering a peg-legged man in a duel, insisted that in fairness his own leg be run into a hollow stump. This man's pranks were innumerable. Once, while ill at an inn in Milledgeville, he had as his physician a dandy who had adopted the new style of wearing brass-heeled boots. One day the doctor came to see him. Dooley heard him coming down the long passage, his metallic heels clapping against the floor. "Drive in," he called as the doctor neared his room, "drive in, Doctor, and hitch your horse." Dooley's wit could even see through the very muddled business of what constituted an attack on a person's honor. Once just as he and a friend of his had been indiscreet enough to let an argument between them come to the point of blows, they were hastily interrupted by a group of onlookers. Dooley was greatly relieved. "I beg of you, gentlemen," he said, "look after my antagonist. One of you will be sufficient to hold me; the man you need to pacify is not Dooley." At another time, when he and his opponent were waiting for a pistol duel to be arranged, Dooley announced that since his opponent seemed to be bracing himself for battle against a mile-post, he, for his part, if there were no objection, would brace himself against the next mile-post.

Gamblers once had been giving him great trouble for a very long time. Heavy fines imposed upon them seemed to avail

---

[1] John D. Wade, "Authorship of the David Crockett Autobiography," *Georgia Historical Quarterly*, September, 1922.

nothing. One night after he had spent a good part of the afternoon in inveighing against gambling, he was so disturbed by the operation of a gambling contingent in the room next to his at his inn that he got up from bed and went to the room where the game was in progress. There was consternation at the Judge's presence. "Gentlemen," he said, "I have done what I could by regular means to break up your gaming and I seem to have failed. Will you not let me into your game?" With some misgivings, the gamesters admitted him. It was not long, the tale goes, before the Judge had completely emptied the pot.

Oliver Hillhouse Prince, also a wit, was for having his jest about everything. He had no teeth; he lost them, he used to say, by having them shaken out on the Georgia roads.

Longstreet came in for his share of the curious experiences incident to frontier life, and always hugely enjoyed telling them. Once he had reduced his jury to tears over the pitiable state of a client who was perfectly innocent, he said, but pursued and crushed by malign superior power. At this affecting juncture, the lawyer was unutterably disconcerted and his whole argument brought to ridicule, when, shouting with quivering voice, "Look at him, gentlemen, look at my client," he directed the attention of the whole court upon the prisoner, who at the moment, it turned out, was nearly choking from having eaten too greedily of gingerbread!

One of the men who experienced these times with Longstreet has set down an account of them better than could now be reconstructed: "Our circuit consisted of seven counties, and the ridings were spring and fall, occupying about two months each term. In each courthouse town was a tavern or two. These houses of entertainment were not then dignified with the sonorous title of hotel. The proprietors were usually jolly good fellows, or some staid matronly lady, in black gown and blue cap, and they all looked forward with anxious delight to the coming of court week. Every preparation was made for the judge and lawyers. Beds were aired and the bugs burned out. Saturday previous to the coming Monday was a busy day in setting all things to rights, and the scrubbing broom was heard in consonance with calls to the servants to be busy and careful, as Sally and Nancy sprang to their work with a will. With garments tucked up to their knees, they splashed the water and suds over the floors, strangers to the cleansing element until then, for months ago. A new supply of corn and fodder was arriving from the country; stables and stable lots were undergoing a scraping eminently required for the comfort of decent beasts, . . . The room usually appropriated to the Bench and Bar was a great vagabond hall, denominated the barroom, and for this purpose appropriated once or twice a year. Along the bare walls of this mighty dormitory were arranged beds, each usually occupied by a couple of the limbs of the law, and sometimes appropriated to three. If there was not a spare apartment a bed was provided here for the judge. And if there were no lawyers from Augusta, this one was distinguished by the greatest mountain of feathers in the house. Here assembled at night the rollicking boys of the Georgia Bar, who here indulged, without restraint, the convivialities for which they were so celebrated. Humor and wit, in anecdote and repartee, beguiled the hours. . . . [How fine it was to] enjoy a night in one of these old tumble-down rooms with A. S. Clayton, O. H. Prince, A. B. Longstreet and John M. Dooley . . . [all] chosen spirits of fun! Yes, that is the word—fun—for these [men] possessed a fund of mirth-exacting humor, combined with a biting wit. . . ." In these old inns,'when the landlord had "presided over the fried meat and eggs of this home for the weary and hungry, after a night of it, . . . all were huddled to bed like pigs in a sty."

One of the landlords, I remember, "was polite to all, but especially to an Augusta lawyer. Freeman Walker, of that ilk, usually attended this court, and was the great man of the week. . . . The choice seats, the choice bed, and choice bits at the table were ever for Major Walker." The landlord was "ever behind Major Walker's chair. He was first served. The choicest pieces of the pig were pointed out, cuts from the back and side bones and breast were hunted from the dish of fried chicken . . . for Major Walker. It was a great thing in those days in Georgia, to live in a little town of three thousand inhabitants, and wear *store clothes*. It was this and these which made a Georgia Major. . . ."

"When Newton County was first organized, the only tavern in the new town of Covington, was kept by a man of huge proportions . . . usually called Uncle Ned. . . . The location of the village and court house had been of recent selection, and Uncle Ned's tavern was one of those peculiar buildings improvised for temporary purposes—a log cabin designated in some parts of Georgia at that time, as a two-storied house, with both stories on the ground; in other words, a double penned cabin with passage between. Uncle Ned had made ample provision for the Bench and Bar. One pen of his house was appropriated to their use. There was a bed in each corner, and there were nine lawyers, including the judge. The interstices between the cabin poles were open, but there was no window and but one door, which had to be closed to avoid too close companionship with the dogs of the household. It was June, and Georgia June weather, sultry, warm, and still, especially at night. In the center there stood a deal table of respectable dimensions, and this served the double purpose of dining-table and bed-place for one. Uncled Ned was polite and exceedingly solicitous to please. He had scoured the country for supplies: it was too new for poultry or eggs, but acorns abounded and pigs were plenty. They had never experienced want, and consequently were well-grown and fat. Uncle Ned had found and secured one which weighed some two hundred pounds. This he divided into halves longitudinally, and had barbecued the half intended for the use of the Bar and Bench. At dinner, on Monday, it was introduced upon a large wooden tray as the center substantial dish for the dinner of the day. It was swimming in lard. There were side dishes of potatoes and cold meats, appellated in Georgia, collards, with quantities of cornbread, with two bowls of hash from the lungs and liver of the pig, all reeking with the fire and summer heat. A scanty meal was soon made, but the tray and contents remained untouched.

"The court continued three days, and was adjourned at noon of the fourth day, until the next term. Each day the tray and contents were punctual in their attendance. The depressed center of the tray was a lake of molten lard, beneath which hid a majority of the pig. After dinner of the last day, all were ready to leave. When the meal was concluded Judge Dooley, who was present, asked if all were done. 'Landlord,' said he, 'will you give us your attention?' Uncle Ned entered. 'Your will, Judge,' he asked. 'I wish you, sir, to discharge this hog on his own recognizance. We do not want any bail for his appearance at the next term.' The dinner concluded in a roar of laughter, in which Uncle Ned heartily joined."[1]

The inns were caravansaries of a degree of primitiveness that back-to-nature apostles would doubtless greatly revel in. One of the old Judges ordered a foot bath. The negro servant washed the Judge's feet and began drying them with his coattail. The gentleman explained that that was not the proper utensil. The negro apologized for not having a handkerchief. The Judge explained that it was a towel that was needed. "Now," comments the man responsible for this anecdote, "though the waiter did not know what *was* the right thing for the service, he knew it could not be a *towel*, for it could never be that a thing which was considered so great a luxury for the face, could be degraded to the ignoble service of the *feet*. . . . He commenced laughing at the strange conceit, at what he thought was the Judge's pleasantry, or 'funnin', as he called it, and went down with his chuckling laugh that 'this nigger couldn't be fooled that way; he didn't know much, but better raised than that, towel for de foot, yah! yah!! yah!!!—no sich fool as dat, yah! yah!!' "[2]

It was their experiences at these inns that the merry transients remembered best—like boys remembering their escapades in dormitories. Longstreet had one story of his law days that he used to tell with undiminished gusto. He and another man, a stranger to him, who had taken far too much to drink, were quartered together one night in a combination guest chamber and dining room. They were to leave early next morning at the same time for the same place. During the night, Longstreet heard his partner pottering stupidly around the room. Half asleep, he inquired as to the cause of disturbance. Hiccough—hiccough.—"I'm just looking for the window to see how the weather is, and how long it will be before

---
[1] Sparks, *Memories*, 482–5.
[2] Andrews, *Old Georgia Lawyer*, 25.

daylight. . . . I can't find it, though. . . . Here it is, if I can ever open it. . . . Huh, now it's open." Silence. "Well, how does it look?" asked the Judge. "Whew. Look! Good God, man, it looks like midnight, and stinks like hell!" He had opened the door of a cup-board and rammed his nose into an ancient cheese!

When Longstreet came to the Georgia bar, he found a system of superior and inferior courts already functioning, but there was no Supreme court until 1848, and as late as 1820, certainly, there was no digest of laws, and there were no rules of practice. "For want of the first, the lawyers had to go through all the statutes to make up an opinion on statute law; for want of the second, there were no precedents of adjudicated cases, by state courts, to be relied on as guides; and for want of the last, a lawyer was in the dark often how to conduct his pleadings or prepare his interrogatories. The consequence of this was that hardly half of the litigated cases were tried on their merits." This was due to the fact that a lawyer who had traveled the circuit and noted some unrecorded opinions given by the Judge as to the admission of interrogatories, evidence, or amendment of pleadings, as well as upon great common or statute law questions, could frequently throw out of court the most important cases without touching their merits.[1]

The superior courts of the several circuits constituted, then, the highest law tribunal in the state, and a Judge of this court was a person of very great consequence, charged with responsibilities and onerous duties, as they appear chronicled in the old records, almost too great for belief.[2]

Seven years after he was admitted to the bar young Mr. Longstreet had been made a Judge and was laboring under his hard task, but before that time much had happened to him. He had kept close to his work, and made friends everywhere, had been elected captain of the 398th district company of Georgia Militia,[3] a fact which shows that the young man's ability was being recognized, and which, incidentally, put him in way of appreciating to the highest degree, when it appeared

---
[1] Andrews, *Old Georgia Lawyer*, 19.
[2] Robert M. Charlton, *Reports of Decisions* (Savannah, 1838), iii–iv.
[3] Mayes, *Genealogy*, 29.

some years later, Mr. Prince's literary sketch, "Militia Drill." About the militia was centered much of the social and intellectual activity of the state. The old statute books have page after page about it; the old newspapers, announcement after announcement. It was an avenue to fame. One lawyer of the time, writing of his early friendship for another lawyer, feels that he should not neglect the attention they gave to the militia. Besides their legal ambitions, he says, he and his friends had tastes similar in the military line; for, "almost beardless as they were, one was Colonel of the County regiment and the other was [a] Major, appointments most gratifying to their ambition. . . . If peace continued, they were certain of glory at the bar . . . and should war come, what a pair of chiefs they would make! Yorktown and New Orleans would be eclipsed by their strategy."[1]

Through everything, young Longstreet worked full time his faculty of enjoyment. He enjoyed his work, enjoyed the good fellowship of his brother lawyers, enjoyed his long rides over the bad roads alone through the country from village to village, and above all things, enjoyed his flute. Once when he had engaged an Indian to row him across a stream, he heard the Indian whistling, and straight-way he so indelibly recorded the air in his mind, that as an old man, living far from this scene, he could still play that air upon his flute to his grandchildren, or play it to the young poet, Mr. Henry Timrod.[2]

Now he had ample opportunity for indulging his love of horses. As he would ride along, frequently he would drive his horse up to overtake someone sighted far ahead of him. If it turned out to be another lawyer, so much the better. They could talk to their hearts' content. Sometimes it was he who was overtaken. Anyway, talk was the outcome. There is one instance on record of how in February, 1821, riding from Greensboro to Washington, he fell in with young W. H. Sparks, like himself a former student at Litchfield. The two stopped by the road at a farmer's house for dinner, where they found that the farmer's wife was a friend of Longstreet's whom he had known when she was a little girl in Willington. The sight

---
[1] Miller, *Bench and Bar*, I, 318–9.
[2] Edwin L. Green, *History University of South Carolina* (Columbia, 1916), 358.

of her wakened in Longstreet many long-neglected memories, especially one of how she had whipped him around the legs once and caused him to take some nauseous medicine, and how he had got the joke back on her by nearly biting off her finger.[1]

At times he had to examine young men for the bar, and during these examinations he rolled off the Latin phrases with such unction that the law fledglings began to say that if you would quote much Latin, Mr. Longstreet would think you good enough to start practising.[2]

In Greensboro, Georgia, a village about seventy-five miles west of Augusta, there happened to Mr. Longstreet, a year or so after he had commenced practising, a thing that had not happened to him previously. He met a young lady whom from the first he knew that if possible he was going to marry. He could not have been much over twenty-five when they met and the lady was nine years younger, but her youth was not considered an obstacle. They were married 2 or 3 March, 1817.[3]

In a letter written in 1870, Longstreet says that while at the time of their marriage his wife had "a very handsome estate," he himself "did not have money enough to buy wedding clothes."[4] It is certain that he gave nothing as a fee to the officiating minister, who had been enough "of the world" to let himself rather hope for something.[5] On the other hand, the Superior Court Records of Richmond County attest that 19 February, 1817, Augustus Baldwin Longstreet, for the sum of $3000, made over to one of his brothers his share in the lot lately owned by their deceased father, William Longstreet. On April 10, James Longstreet made a similar disclaimer for $4000. Was Augustus a poor trader, then, as he soon learned not to be, was he trading hastily in anticipation of his marriage, or was he paying off old debts? At any rate, less than two weeks later, he says, he did not have money enough to buy his clothes. Perhaps an old man's memory is not to be trusted.

It is true that Longstreet was young, and that three or four

---

[1] *Atlanta Constitution*, 8 April, 18—, in Scrapbook of Clement A. Evans.
[2] Pascal, *Ninety-four Years*, 197–8.
[3] Fitzgerald, *Judge Longstreet*, 45; Mayes, *Genealogy, Family of Longstreet*.
[4] Fitzgerald, *Judge Longstreet*, 45.
[5] The Reverend Mr. J. V. M. Morris, Athens, Georgia.

thousand dollars, it is said, was a large income even for a lawyer of experience and reputation,[1] but in spite of that fact, it was generally understood that a rising young lawyer was a "good catch." But even if Mrs. Longstreet had been marrying for material advancement, which she plainly was not, she would hardly have refused Mr. Longstreet for a merchant. Nor would she have done this if the above figures had been vastly more favorable to the merchant than they were. To be a merchant of the very richest sort is not equal to being a lawyer of a sort altogether poorer. "Mercy on me, William," says a lady, impatient at her son who had expressed his determination to drop the study of law and become a merchant, "close up all your bright prospects—bury your brilliant talents among goods and groceries! No, my son, I never can consent to that."[2] "Dear me, dear me," says one of the boy's friends, "what a pity! Why, William, you were cut out for something greater than a counter-hopper . . . take an old man's advice; return to school, complete your education, study law . . . and by and by you'll never get done thanking me for stopping you in the course you are now pursuing."[3]

In other places there were probably numerous roads to distinction, but so far as Georgia goes, at least, said one of the

---

[1] Richard M. Johnston, *Autobiography* (Washington, 1901), 103; the 45 lawyers who settled in one of the old county cites, it was estimated (see Andrews, *Old Georgia Lawyer*, 92), prospered as follows:
    2 made fortunes of $100,000 to $150,000,
    9 made liberal support for their families,
    7 barely supported themselves,
    3 made fortunes of $20,000 to $50,000,
    A few slightly increased their property,
    24 did not make a living.
The physicians came out little better: of 28,
    5 made $20,000 to $50,000,
    8 scanty to liberal support for families,
    15 less than support, to nothing at all.
In the same period there were 116 grocers and merchants. Of these,
    7, beginning with capital, made $30,000 to $150,000,
    12, beginning with capital, made $10,000 to $30,000.
    28 had averaged an increase on capital,
    69 had failed.
[2] Longstreet, *Mitten*, 276.
[3] *Ibid.*, 286.

A YOUNG LAWYER IN GEORGIA 85

writers of that day, "there is only one—politics."[1] And lawyers, Longstreet thought, have as exclusive rights to political honors as blacksmiths have to such honors as can come from making plows.[2] A girl of eighteen even, could know this much, and could be duly glad if the young man who proved so attractive to her, and whom her parents so heartily approved of, and who could play a flute so superbly well, could have these possibilities to offer in addition. If she were an ambitious girl, as Eliza Parke was, she could know it so much the better.[3]

About the financial status of Mrs. Longstreet at the time of her marriage, there is no question. She owned about thirty slaves, from the rent of whom she got in yearly about $1500, and who were worth at that time from $800 to $900 each,[4] and she had about $2000 in cash.[5] Materially, in short, the young couple's prospects were very glowing.

Frances Eliza Parke was born 5 March, 1799, in Randolph County, North Carolina, but she had been reared in Greensboro, Georgia, by her mother and her step-father, Ebenezer Torrance. To make a living Torrance served as the Clerk of the Court of Greene County, but his business was to be a "scholar" and philosopher, and a lover of polite literature. A man of good intelligence, of religious impulses, and of invariable kindness and thoughtfulness for his entire family, he himself took charge of the education of his wife's daughter. This young lady was small, graceful, and exceptionally pretty, not only charming in manners and able to quote poetry to fit any occasion, but punctilious in the performance of every duty that her time, which demanded very much of a woman, taught her pertained to a housewife. It would be hard to overemphasize her personal loveliness. She had a quality, it seems, altogether apart from physical or mental implications, a quality of spirit that dominated her and everything about her, a certain quietness, a sort of devastating renunciation, a calmness and a high serenity of life which nothing could fail bowing to.

---
[1] William W. Turner, *Jack Hopeton* (New York, 1860), 76.
[2] Longstreet, "Darby Anvil" in *Stories with a Moral* (Philadelphia, 1912), 60.
[3] Fitzgerald, *Judge Longstreet*, 45.
[4] Ulrich B. Phillips, *American Negro Slavery* (New York, 1918), 370.
[5] Office of Ordinary, Greensboro, Georgia.

Even her equals in rank, says her husband, "seemed to regard her with a sort of queenly deference."[1] Canny people soon learned better than to cope with her. Without permitting her antagonist to experience sense of shock enough to keep him on his guard, or hardly herself recognizing the subtlety of her method, this lady had a way of receding from her position so easily that before her opponent knew it, almost, he found himself, following her, exactly where she desired him. And the best part of the affair was that she left him with some feeling of gratitude to her for her kindness, and with an unbounded admiration for her gentleness and lady-like non-aggressiveness.

Nor was her trick of such a nature as ever to make the burnt children shun it. The more intimately you knew her the more resplendent became her fascination. To her son-in-law, L. Q. C. Lamar, she embodied, he wrote, "an indescribable charm, a spirit of love, a subtle effluence of refinement, a piety and culture of character," not often met with. "To an eye not accustomed to analyze the indications of a female character," he granted, "she might appear too reserved, and even retiring, to possess those qualities that make up a heroine in the conflicts of life, but" he was sure that "her modesty, which like a sensitive plant shrank from rude familiarities, was sustained by a courage that never shrank from hardship, trial, and self-denial." For him "the gentleness of her manners, the grace of her motion, the reserve of her dignity, only served the better to set off the brightness that shone in her conversation and to disclose an intelligence that threw a charm over the modesty of her nature; she was the non-pareil of women, full of warmth and tenderness and depth of feeling, confiding, trustworthy, a lover of home, a true wife and mother, whose hand touched and beautified and sanctified all domestic relations."[2]

Immediately after Longstreet's marriage,[3] he removed from Augusta to Greensboro and took up his residence in the house with his wife and her parents. Though it had been established in 1786 and incorporated in 1803, Greensboro was still in 1817

---

[1] Fitzgerald, *Judge Longstreet*, 46.
[2] Mayes, *L. Q. C. Lamar*, 41.
[3] *Yale Biography and Annals, Sixth Series*, 580, is authority for saying he removed to Greensboro shortly *before* his marriage.

only a small village. It was the seat of government of a county which had a population of about 15,000 persons, two-thirds of whom were white, "a sprightly country town in the center of a populous and wealthy country. There was a fine moral tone in the society of the village, and a considerable amount of cultivation." The Presbyterian minister, a graduate of Washington College, was, with his wife, conducting a school by way of uplifting the young; and had organized a Moral and Polemic Debating Society by way of edifying the mature, and very possibly of arriving at some new truth. Augustus Longstreet was a member of this society. Its regular weekly meetings were marked by debates upon some subject of "general interest, sometimes religious, sometimes metaphysical, sometimes political." Once, certainly, it is recorded that Longstreet argued before it as to the existence of "innate ideas."[1] Among other forms of entertainment in the village there were always church services, prayer meetings, and even at times scholarly lectures of a theological nature, on, say, the importance of the Oriental Languages to a divinity student.[2] With the ordinary run of business, and such intellectual stimulus as could be had from the debating society and from the sermons which were offered to one in such overwhelming numbers, and with his books, Longstreet probably spent most of his time. He gave much attention to his family and social connections, much to his love of talk (which, since he had political aspirations, he fortunately could justify himself in indulging), and much to his passion for planting things and seeing them grow, a passion which he was now for the first time able freely to satisfy.

The men of Greensboro very frequently combined farming with some professional or mercantile activity. They rode out to their farms once or perhaps twice daily, and looked them over, and the rest of the time they were in town in front of the stores, talking. Those who lived on their farms knew how to coax necessity, and were able to be obliged to ride into town daily at about the time at which the feast of words was most savory. There was not much to break the long peace of the

---

[1] Smith, *Pierce*, 37–8.
[2] Longstreet, *Mitten*, 26.

days. There was a United States Senator in the town, perhaps, and there were numerous members of Congress, a Judge, a distinguished doctor, none of whom felt it out of order on account of their position to sit down in front of some store and while off the morning in conversation.

Away somewhere they could hear the whirr of a forge and the intermittent ringing of hammers against plows, outwardly the most enterprising manifestation in the community. Perhaps the blacksmith was advanced enough to display a sign. Longstreet knew one such advertisement well enough, "a flaming sign-board" hanging "high over the entrance of the smithery, made from a piece of iron work of crooks and convolutions unutterable." It was decorated on either side with appropriate designs. On one side was the smith in person, shoeing General Washington's horse. The smith said it was Washington's horse and the man who painted it said it was—certainly it was large enough for Washington's horse, the Judge thought, for, comparing its height to that of the smith, it could not have been less than five-and-twenty feet high. On the other side was a plow, with handles, nine feet long (by the same measure), studded with hoes and axes, staples and horseshoes.[1] How the acute and sophisticated relished a thing of this kind!

Sometimes an event occurred that struck people as humorous, and they talked about that event unendingly. Mr. Longstreet, for instance, when he was married did not give Dr. Pierce, the Methodist minister who performed the ceremony, a single cent in due token of the happy groom's appreciation. Dr. Pierce, it was learned, was in much chagrin but said nothing. Months later Dr. Pierce and Mr. Longstreet met each other on the street. "I say, Doctor," said Mr. Longstreet, "about that little marriage fee. I want to begin payment." Thereupon the Doctor was led into a haberdashery and fitted out complete in clothes—elegant hat, elegant coat, elegant waistcoat, elegant trousers, elegant boots. And do you know that about every six months since, Mr. Longstreet has fitted the Doctor out with some elegant new article of clothing? A story of this sort, once out, was, of course, too great not to be

---

[1] Longstreet, "Darby Anvil," *Stories with a Moral,* 51.

A YOUNG LAWYER IN GEORGIA

told constantly, was told by Dr. Pierce himself over fifty years later, and after fifty more years got itself told again to the writer of this book. And what, asked the present writer, when he heard it, with the useful innocence of little Peterkin, is the point of it? "The point," came the answer, "why, sir, the point is that Judge Longstreet was a unique character!"

When Court convened there was a decided break in the pervading peace of the village. Lawyers came in from distant villages or cities, and country people came in, in general, to see what they could learn; and professional gamblers came in to prey upon anybody. Among the lawyers was fierce wrangling in the court rooms and loud companionable laughter and much guzzling in the hotels. Among the visitors there was constant guzzling, constant gambling, and very occasionally a bloody fight. The village people, the residents, were in bib and tucker for the thing properly, giving occasional parties to which young ladies invited visiting lawyers (as Eliza Parke had not long before, perhaps, invited young Longstreet), and there were church services to which, the villagers noted as a deplorable circumstance, the lawyers would never come. It was whispered that lawyers were all of them atheists, anyway. Heaven knows they all drank whiskey, and none of them were church members. Mr. Longstreet, it was said, did not drink, but there were few people who held that he was "right" religiously.[1]

In the midst of all of this life, Mr. Longstreet kept to his work and rose steadily in public esteem. One thing, however, he gave his attention to without ever talking about it. Occasionally he would write poetry. This interest of his, his use of the pseudonym "Bob Short," and his later association with the Harpers in New York apparently connect him with a slight book of verse, *Patriotic Effusions by Bob Short*, published in New York in 1819. The pseudonym is indisputable. In the 1830's Longstreet's newspaper carried over a long period of time a series of comments by a Bob Short whose identity with the editor of the paper was generally acknowledged; later, while Longstreet was president of Emory College, it was a

---
[1] Miller, *Bench and Bar*, 176, 211.

humored joke in the college community to refer to him as Bob Short, it being vaguely believed to this day by one who can remember old times in Oxford (where Emory College was situated) that the President assumed this name on becoming a member of some secret society or other which required its members upon entering to give themselves new identifications.

But Edward Mayes, Longstreet's grandson-in-law and literary executor, was very definite in his feeling that Longstreet had no connection with the *Effusions;* never had the Judge mentioned to him any such work; in fact, the Judge had never, in his belief, written a single poem. But Mayes's last declaration largely invalidates his disavowal of the *Effusions;* Longstreet did write poetry frequently. Mayes, however, was still right. Longstreet's failure to mention the *Effusions* was probably due to the fact that he died in happy ignorance of that book's existence.

In 1823 there appeared in New York *The Olio,* a collection of verse similar in physical make-up, in spirit, and in technique to the *Effusions*—published, indeed, "By the author of *Patriotic Effusions.*" The author did not without purpose make his second book over twice as long as his first; here are many hints of autobiography. It is stated that some of the "pieces" in *The Olio* "were written on the other side of the Atlantic, *viz.*, in England and France whilst I was in those parts, and others since my arrival in this country, but I trust they will not be less interesting on that account." Longstreet did not see Europe until 1860.

It cannot be said, then, that he ever published a volume of poetry, but it is clear that he did not hesitate to essay verse any more than he hesitated to essay anything else, whenever he felt so disposed.

As a matter of fact, he continued to try his hand at poetry throughout his life, but he never wrote any verse that would add to his reputation. He wrote an epitaph for his friend Edmund Bacon,[1] a hymn of commonplace religious sentiment,[2] jingles whenever he needed them in his stories,[3] or for the

---
[1] *Southern Field and Fireside*, 12 November, 1859.
[2] Newspaper clipping, unidentified.
[3] Longstreet, *Stories with a Moral*, 29–30.

amusement of his friends,[1] metrical exercises for the joy of seeing what he could do, and late in life an elaborate parody of Longfellow's *Hiawatha*.[2]

The Bacon Epitaph consists of six heroic couplets, broken, not with the grateful breaks of a master, but with the forced breaks of an amateur. The style is a struggling after Pope's; the matter a mixture of Charles Wesley and Jonathan Edwards.

The hymn, "Glory," consists of eight four-line stanzas and a refrain. It is hackneyed in imagery and undignified in rhymes (glory is rhymed successively with *bore he, wore he, pour he*), but it expresses with some effectiveness the longing of the human soul for a world more endurable than this one, and the joy of the human soul on being persuaded that some such world exists. . . .

The jingles and the metrical experiments are far less decorous. Once, when the Longstreets were visiting some friends, the Judge hitched the entire household together in a sort of monstrous limerick:

>Miss Dutton
>Has swallowed a button,
>And Mrs. Longstreet
>Has scalded her feet,
>And Cousin Sallie Lewis
>All black and blue is,
>And Pa-pa and the Judge
>Ain't able to budge.

One of the Augusta newspapers published a strain of music and offered a prize for the best words submitted to suit the music. Longstreet simply knew he could do it. He wrote the verses but they turned out a little too undignified for an ex-Judge and minister, or near minister, to offer in the contest. In the family, however, they were prized enough for them to have come down intact, by word of mouth, to the fourth generation.

---

[1] Fitz R. Longstreet, Gainesville, Georgia; Miss Mary Linton, Athens, Georgia; Letter of Mrs. Bessie Mayes Eakin, Jackson, Miss., 10 January, 1922.

[2] *Ibid.;* letter of Mrs. Augusta Lamar Heiskell, Memphis, Tennessee, 12 January, 1922.

> Once there was a sailor
> Lived with a tailor
> Down upon Green Street.
> Neither was quite neat,
> Tailor nor sailor.
>
> Once when the sailor
> Had left the tailor
> Cutting a round coat,
> In came a big shoat
> To eat the tailor.
>
> But when the tailor saw
> The shoat with open jaw,
> His goose he back did draw
> To give him a frailer,
> When, much to his delight,
> There hove into sight
> His friend the sailor.

The young lawyer did not let his literary ambitions infringe too greatly upon his activities in his profession. In the spring of 1819, through the Augusta newspaper, he calls to the attention of his old friends the fact that though living in Greensboro and practicing in Greene, he would undertake practice in the counties of Hancock, Baldwin, Putnam, Jones, Jasper, Morgan, and Richmond.

And sometime about now he wrote and published *A Review of the Decision of the Supreme Court of the United States in the Case of McCullouch vs. the State of Maryland*. Since this document would, more than any other, throw light upon Longstreet's methods and ability as a lawyer, it is regrettable that it has completely disappeared. The decision in question sustained the act creating the second bank of the United States. It held that, "while it was true that the government of the United States was a government of specified powers only, it must nevertheless be deemed to be sovereign within the sphere assigned to it by the Constitution; that the powers granted to it must be taken to include every privilege incidental to their exercise, the choice of the means by which the ends of the government were to be reached lying in every case within the discretion of the Congress, and not being subject to be restrained by the Courts."[1] Longstreet himself stated specifically that he grew more and more strongly unionistic in his feelings until 1816, but that after that time he began gradually to turn towards strict construction, being driven thither by what he considered the undue encroachments of the Federal power. His mind was of a literal cast. The doctrine of implied powers became as little comprehensible to him as to Calhoun. He wanted some specific guide. Later he regarded the Bible with the same satisfaction and assumption of complete finality with which he here most likely regarded the Constitution. Sin lies only in the breaking of the law, but it is equally gross whether you break the law openly or with clever evasion and logical refinements. It is natural to suppose, then, that his review of the Court decision was a somewhat hostile one, dictated largely by his desire to warn the nation of what a further development of this "implied powers" theory might lead to. From the fact that it has been entirely lost, one can suppose that the *Review* never attained wide publicity, but its merit seems to be to some extent vouched for by the respectful mention made of it by Alexander Stephens.[2]

In 1821 Mr. Longstreet went down into Baldwin County for another purpose than merely to practice law. The capital of Georgia, Milledgeville, was in that county, and Longstreet was going there in pursuance of his duties as a newly-elected representative from Greene County to the State Assembly. A little later, as a member of the Agricultural and Internal Improvement Committee of that body, he was offering laws looking to certain road legislation,[3] and, as a member of the Judiciary Committee, occupying the Chair while the Legislature considered certain matters relative to Constitutional Amendments.[4]

In November, 1822, he was notified by the Governor, John Clarke, that on the eighth of that month he had, by joint ballot of the two branches of the General Assembly, been

---

[1] Woodrow Wilson, *Division and Reunion*, 71–2.
[2] Mayes, *Genealogy*, 32.
[3] Georgia, Journal House of Representatives, 1821, 401.
[4] *Ibid.*, 407.

elected for a period of three years Judge of the Superior Court of "Ocmalgee [sic] District," this in recognition of the confidence reposed by that body in Longstreet's "patriotism, judgment, abilities, and good conduct."

There were in Georgia at that time five Judicial Circuits, of which the Ocmulgee was next to the newest.[1] It comprised seven counties, Morgan, Jasper, Jones, Baldwin, Wilkinson, Putnam and Greene,[2] where Sessions were held as follows:

<blockquote>
Morgan......First Monday, February and August.
Greene ......Second Monday, February and August.
Putnam......Third Monday, February and August.
Baldwin .....Fourth Monday, February and August.
Jones........Second Monday, March and September.
Jasper.......Third Monday, March and September.
Wilkinson....Wednesday after first Monday in March, First Monday in September.[3]
</blockquote>

Anyone knowing the functions of a judge in those times can realize how busy the young man now was, but it is very hard even for an initiate to conceive of the diversity of conditions that such a judge had to encounter. In his own circuit, which had been founded in 1813 and which comprised a fertile and populous district, Longstreet most usually dealt with people of a fair degree of civilization, but when called upon to preside for his brother judges in some of the less fortunate circuits, he found conditions that must have taxed even his long-suffering patience with rawness, and his invariable good humor and tact.

There is a story to the effect that Longstreet held his first court in Swainsboro, a new town not in his circuit. Possibly he did this for the experience, since court conducted in Swainsboro would probably not expose his first term as presiding judge to such keen observation from so many distinguished lawyers, and it certainly would not expose it to the observation of so many of his friends. The country around Greensboro had been rapidly taking on the air of a more advanced civiliza-

---
[1] Miller, *Bench and Bar*, II, 369–73.
[2] L. Q. C. Lamar I, *Georgia Code*, 361.
[3] *Ibid.*, 366.

tion. The economic urge towards bigger farms was already beginning to drive away many of the whites and to bring in more negroes; but such whites as were left were of a higher grade socially, as a rule, than those who emigrated. Education and religious organization and polemical debating societies were taking hands in the game. There was a dawning show of culture—before long the town would produce a book of literary criticism!

But to return to Swainsboro. The courthouse there, along with all of the other houses, was made of logs, put together to form one large room. The principal citizen of the town, with whom Longstreet stayed, lived in a building consisting of four rooms, two on the ground floor and two above. Blankets, swung over the openings, took the place of doors. . . . "Soon after the court was opened there appeared in the doorway a tall, long-haired man, who, giving a whoop that might have been heard half a mile, yelled out, 'Mr. Judge, I'm a hoss.' The sheriff called order but the long-haired man, taking no notice of this, gave another whoop and yelled, 'Didn't you hear me, Mr. Judge? I'm a hoss, I say.' The Judge told the sheriff to take that 'hoss' and put him into the stable and collect a fine of ten dollars. Long-hair said: 'Are ye in arnest, Mr. Judge? If so ye need not be mealy mouthed, but make the fine fifty or a hundred dollars; I can pay it just as well.' 'Very well,' said the Judge; 'Mr. Sheriff, take that man to jail and keep him till he pays a hundred dollars.' The next day it was found that this man was a good citizen except when he was drunk, and he was let off for five dollars." But on the whole, drunkenness is one thing with which the Judge has small patience. He had resolved long ago, he often told his friends, that if he ever had opportunity he would do as much as he could to rid his country of this incubus.

Longstreet's relations with the Judges of the other circuits were most cordial. Though he was becoming more and more strongly a state rights man and was now definitely allied with that faction in politics, he knew, even as he knew years later when his political ideas had become more fixed and ardent, how to be friendly with anybody who would meet him halfway. During the years 1822–5 the northern circuit had as judge,

John M. Dooley, and the western circuit Augustin S. Clayton, both of whom Longstreet knew well and particularly admired. The Solicitor General of the Ocmulgee circuit, Yelverton P. King, with whom Longstreet was necessarily much associated, was likewise a man of unusual worth.[1]

Especially close was Longstreet's association with Clayton. In the fall of 1823 Clayton was in Greensboro during Longstreet's absence, in charge of the Greene County Court, and he was there again in the fall of 1824, presiding for a day, even though Longstreet was present.[2] At its August, 1823, commencement, the University of Georgia, of which Clayton was Secretary, conferred on Longstreet the honorary degree of Master of Arts.[3]

Everywhere the man was liked. One of his Grand Juries in 1824 included in their record concerning him: "In closing our business at this term we should do injustice to our feeling were we to fail in an expression of the pleasure with which we have witnessed the untiring perseverance of his honor, Judge Longstreet, in the discharge of the arduous duties of his office."[4]

But the spoils system was already alive in American Government. The Governor of Georgia was in 1824 for the first time elected by popular ballot. George M. Troup, representing the state rights faction politically and, to some extent, the aristocratic faction socially, and John Clarke, representing the opposing factions, were arrayed against each other for this position. Troup, on account of his late defiantly successful stand against the Federal Government in the matter of Georgia's attitude towards the Indians, was accused by his enemies of being pert and needlessly audacious; Clarke was accused by his enemies of being subservient and spineless. There was the greatest interest in the election. When it occurred in October, 1825, it was found that Troup had been put in as governor, but that the Clarke faction had won a majority in the Assembly. With the exception of one man, Judge

---
[1] Miller, *Bench and Bar*, II, 369–373.
[2] Records, Greene County, Georgia.
[3] Trustees University of Georgia, Minutes, 1818–34, 96.
[4] Morgan County, Georgia, Superior Court Records, March, 1824.

A YOUNG LAWYER IN GEORGIA

Wayne, this Clarke legislature refused to reelect to the judgeship any Troup man then serving. The result was that of the seven circuits only two retained their accustomed judges or solicitors.[1] In this avalanche, Longstreet, being a Troup man, went down with the rest.

In July, 1820, a son was born to the Longstreets, and was named Alfred Emsley, after Mrs. Longstreet's dead brother. This child and another, a girl, named Henrietta Augusta, born on Christmas Day, 1821, both died in infancy, but the first of them lived long enough to take very deep hold upon his father's affections. The next two children, Frances Eliza and Virginia Lafayette, born April, 1824, and June, 1826, lived to maturity and were throughout their parents' long lives as great sources of happiness and solace as it is possible for intelligent and generous children to be. The four other children all died in infancy: Ebenezer Torrance, named for Mrs. Longstreet's stepfather; George McDuffie, named for the old friend of his father; Fitz Randolph, named for—(Mr. Longstreet was becoming conscious of his distinguished ancestry); and Rebecca Lewis, named for her father's sister.[2] Mrs. Longstreet, it is said, always blamed herself for the delicacy of her children and felt somehow that her husband had just cause to censure her for not presenting him a son of vitality enough to live to manhood and carry on the family name. But this is getting on too far.

In the meantime, that is to say between the period of his marriage and his peremptory dismissal from the bench, Longstreet had been occupied with matters other than legal ones. In addition to having a rapidly increasing family, he, and his wife, too, had political aspirations of a very high order, and they both knew that large families and large political ambition demand money. With his law fees, then, he was as prudent as could be, and he soon determined to augment the income derived from these by operating a farm. Not a year elapsed after his marriage before he went largely in debt to buy some six hundred acres of land near Greensboro, for about $6000. To operate this farm he had, he says, "some thirty or more of

---

[1] Miller, *Bench and Bar*, II, 199.
[2] Mayes, *Genealogy*, 33.

the likeliest field hands I ever saw—last year hers [his wife's], this year mine. These remained to her after she had given nine like them to her mother. . . ."[1]

Knowing General Oglethorpe's aspirations in connection with introducing silk culture into Georgia, Longstreet investigated the matter and became in turn an enthusiast himself. But this did not avail anything with his neighbors, now thoroughly taken up with the business of cotton, nor did it avail much with him longer than the time it took him to learn that it would not pay. He had a penchant, though, for budding trees, and grafting, which he carried with him everywhere he went, leaving freak monuments of it everywhere—apple trees bearing nineteen different varieties of apples, and so forth. Another enthusiasm which remained with him always, but which first fully developed in this period, was a love of horses.

But none of these enterprises did he carry to the point of neglecting his law practice, or his determination to make money. He was in business matters both aggressive and scrupulously provident. He somehow got possession of houses to rent out. He would borrow money when necessary to buy real estate that he thought would increase in value,[2] and he was constantly lending out small sums of money ($37, say, and $31) at interest. If the debtor would not pay up promptly, Longstreet did not hesitate to bring suit for collection, asking of the court double what was due him, by way of compensation for his trouble. He was constantly at law in such small matters. And steadily he grew richer. The times were booming.

Presently it was understood that Judge Longstreet was running for Congress. This was through the spring and summer of 1824. He had everything to recommend him. A friend of everybody worth knowing, he was still recognized as a man of clear political convictions who at no time refused to declare himself concisely and definitely as to what he thought. It was one of the first articles of his political creed, he says, "never to go with any party farther than he believed it to be right, and never to support an inferior for office in preference

---
[1] Fitzgerald, *Judge Longstreet*, 45.
[2] Records, Greene County, Georgia, January, 1818.

A YOUNG LAWYER IN GEORGIA

to his superior." He held that it was the "bounden duty of a candidate openly to avow his sentiments, particularly those which are averse to the prevailing opinion of those to whom he offers himself."[1]

There is here for the present reader to contemplate a Judge Longstreet whom his contemporaries probably had known for what he was, but who is now for the first time expressing himself with such force that his sentiments persist with increasing virtue through the years. Here is the man choosing, at last, the way which seems least promising but which he wills from within himself must be the only right one.

---

[1] *Augusta Chronicle,* 1 September, 1832.

IV

RELIGIOUS INTERESTS

Summer passed on; fall came; the campaign tightened and tightened over the state. In some districts there was doubt as to who would be elected, but in Longstreet's district there was little doubt, or none. Longstreet had only to wait for the election to find himself in Congress.

He was at home during most of this time. Mrs. Longstreet was consumed with admiration for him, and, as he himself recorded, "much concerned in a harmless feminine way with the high renown her husband was to acquire in Congress and the happiness she was to enjoy in witnessing the growth of that renown amidst the gaieties and splendors of the capital."[1] She learned to write a hand precisely like her husband's, possibly with the idea of doing copying work for him, possibly out of the fullness of a heart that taught her her husband was the paragon of all earthly men. The two children occupied their father's affectionate attention. His home circle was delightful. Mrs. Longstreet's mother and stepfather were both of them engrossed in the happiness and progress of the young family. . . . Day by day they all awaited the election.

And then, just before the election, down went everything. In September Mrs. Longstreet's mother and the oldest Longstreet child, Alfred Emsley, both of them died within two days time. Judge Longstreet was overwhelmed, dazed; he misdoubted himself, gave up utterly, the very center of existence seeming to have fallen out. The thought of Congress he abandoned immediately, withdrawing his name from the candidacy. Protests availed nothing. He was almost blind now with intense, impotent rage and disappointment. He demanded some help in this thing, implored some help, and got no help. He became ill and it was necessary for him to have a doctor.

---

[1] Fitzgerald, *Judge Longstreet*, 45.

"Time," said this doctor, in reply to the stricken Judge's complaints, "Time, Judge, is the only physician who can do your disease any good."

Mr. Torrance, Mrs. Longstreet's step-father, himself broken with grief over the death of his wife, and profoundly moved with sympathy for the Longstreets, when asked how he had stood so resolute under affliction, spoke quietly but with deep feeling of a physician whom Longstreet had heard about much and believed in little.

But for Mr. Torrance, Longstreet had great affection and respect. "Morning and evening," he wrote very late in his life, "would my bereaved household friend go down on his knees and acknowledge our afflictions as sent from God, and pray for strength to bear them submissively, and that they might be sanctified to our souls' eternal good. I would give a thousand worlds, thought I, if I could believe the Scriptures as that man does; their fruits are lovely, to say the least of them. And may it not be that my unbelief is my own fault? I am very ignorant of the Scriptures, I never bestowed an hour's study on them with the honest aim of ascertaining their truth in all my life. I am resolved that I will seek religion and I will seek it in just the way that those who know most about religion tell me to seek it. I announced my resolution to my wife, and then announced it to her step-father, and told him that thenceforward I would share family prayer with him. Tears of joy now filled his eyes, and my tears of grief ceased to flow. I commenced studying the Scriptures in earnest, praying God if they really were true that I might be convinced of their truth. I had studied them not more than a fortnight before I began to find in them some wonderful evidences of their divine origin, which I wondered the world had never discovered before. . . . All my doubts soon vanished, and I became a thorough believer in Christianity."[1] Thus Longstreet entered upon "a religious course of living," and turned his thoughts from earth to heaven, though, to be sure, more to the idea of heaven's reunions than to heaven's blessings, "to a world in which happiness is less precarious, and affections

---
[1] Longstreet, *Old Things Become New*, I, 850.

are more indissoluble than they are in this." But he was still not spiritually "broken." He would seek religion "in a way of his own, without the help of churches."[1]

In the meantime life went on; the world will not stop because a little boy is dead. Not even can the little boy's own parents stop. Mrs. Longstreet bowed in joyful and almost grateful submission to whatever her husband determined upon. That God loves his children she would not doubt, but for her part she would approach Him only as a lady should, under the escort of her husband. Mr. Longstreet continued in his duties as judge, and after he was unseated from that office continued his activities in farming and in the practice of law. Children came into the family. But this place, Greensboro, was no longer to their father what it once was, before he had been so ruthlessly smitten.

There was certainly no dearth of encouragement for a man of this period, allured by the idea of religion. Everywhere the churches were extremely active, and the year 1827 seems to have been marked by a great wave of religious enthusiasm.

Within this rolling wave, however, there were unfortunately the fiercest cross-currents and eddies. A Methodist called upon to testify in court as to a neighbor's character, said that he knew of no fault in the man further than that he was a Baptist. An old Methodist lady who was urging her niece to listen favorably to the suit of one of her lovers, when the girl mischievously advanced the fact that the boy went to the Baptist Sunday School, replied, "Never you mind, my daughter, he was raised by a good Methodist mother. You marry him and he will stop his wild foolish ways." Good Methodist ladies knew people who were estimable gentlemen, though Baptists. A Baptist matriarch whose son actually carried out his threat (she had deemed it ill-timed teasing) and married a Methodist, found herself for once speechless. Drawing her chair up before a low fire she sat down and, putting one foot on one andiron and one on the other, remained there through the long night in abysmal silence, dumb before an affliction too stupendous for her conceiving.

---

[1] Longstreet, *Old Things Become New*, I, 845.

Certain buildings on the campus of the University of Georgia having been destroyed by fire, the state legislature, composed mostly of Methodists and Baptists, refused to rebuild them because, the tradition is, they said the institution had been sedulously kept in the hands of Presbyterians. One Methodist and one Baptist had to be elected to the faculty before the deadlock could be removed.

The world was edified by the publication of two books, one by the editor of the Tennessee *Baptist*,[1] called *The Great Iron Wheel, or Republicanism Backwards and Christianity Reversed in a Series of Letters Addressed to [a] Bishop of the Methodist Episcopal Church;* the other,[2] *The Great Iron Wheel Examined or Its False Spokes Extracted, and an Exhibition of . . . Its Builder.* The first of these books ran in five years to thirty editions. Each of them angrily attacked the judgment and sincerity of the church of which its author was not a member.

One of the old Methodist preachers, in conducting a series of meetings, made it his special duty to grind his sermons into a Baptist preacher who was doing him the compliment of coming to hear him. He enjoyed seeing his auditor squirm. Finally he went too far. Rising and shaking his finger at the preacher, the man in the congregation shrieked in a sort of frenzy, "Now don't you ever preach that doctrine again!" This earnestness gets to be frightful.[3] A Methodist preacher, invited as a guest to a certain baptising, listened as long as he could to the Baptist's protests that immersion is the only mode of real baptism, and then blared out: "I say, Brother, what about the jailer and his household?"

Preachers debated upon the relative merits of the Methodist and Baptist dogma. One Methodist preacher, upon being challenged to a formal debate, managed to have the debate broken by arranging for the defendant to speak one Sunday, and for his adversary to speak the next Sunday. In the course of the rebuttal, as it were, the Baptist quoted the Methodist as

---

[1] J. R. Graves.
[2] Wm. G. Brownlow.
[3] George G. Smith, *Life and Letters of James Osgood Andrew* (Nashville, 1883), 39.

having said that "a man might get religion today and lose it tomorrow." "Now," said he, "suppose a man should be converted today and go to the borough tomorrow and be overcome by the influence of his friends [which is to say, should take an enemy into his mouth to steal away his brains], and on his way home he should lie down and go to sleep, and a rattlesnake should bite him and kill him, what would become of him? I say, what would become of him?" A Methodist local preacher in the congregation replied that he would go to hell, because he would die drunk. The Baptist brother replied that he was in a free country and would not allow himself to be disturbed. The Methodist said that he had not interrupted, that he had only answered a plain question. Upon this the Baptist called him a liar. Then the Methodist advanced upon him. . . . The two brothers were led out, one by one door and one by the other.[1]

The Methodists were actually accused in the newspapers of having encouraged the commission of murder to further certain political schemes. This talk proceeded to such a degree that Jesse Mercer, the great leader of the Baptists in Georgia, perhaps from breadth of view, perhaps from unwillingness to see the Methodists so identified with one political group as to force all persons of that political complexion into the Methodist Church, officially stated his disbelief in any such report; he considered it, he said, "as gratuitous no doubt as it was false."[2]

Contention of this sort bred the greatest loyalty within the bodies contending. Nor were the two denominations beset only by each other, but by outsiders as well. Even an Episcopal rector, with a rather unusual amount of grieved detachment, feared, he said in a letter addressed to a Methodist acquaintance, that "there is something in the Methodist system that leads on to boasting and self satisfaction, right or wrong. It is a wildfire that always finds enough in a waste world to keep it burning and fretting for conquest."[3] For everybody the early Methodists were a fair mark. In Savannah, one of

---

[1] Simon Peter Richardson, *Lights and Shadows of Itinerant Life* (Nashville 1900), 34.
[2] *Augusta Chronicle*, 14 September, 1833.
[3] Anonymous, *Pamphlets for the People* (Philadelphia, 1854), Preface.

the preachers was the victim of mob violence to such an extent that he could do nothing.¹ In Columbia, South Carolina, the students turned a live goose into the meeting house and threatened the life of the preacher if he came on the campus to make complaint.²

Certainly the Methodists became extremely self-conscious. Preachers had to wear coats of a peculiar cut, and to brush their hair straight downwards, could not wear beards, had to abjure suspenders. These men were defiantly peculiar. Preaching on the average of once a day throughout the year,³ they had left enough vitality to stamp, scream, weep, threaten, invite, throughout their sermons.⁴ Sometimes it was more than nerves could bear. People fainted. Once, at a camp meeting, the preacher in his madness leaped suddenly over the low book-board of the altar, and rushed out of the house into the woods crying always that all who wanted religion should follow him. And into the woods, following him, actually tore the procession of his spell-bound listeners.⁵

Members of Methodist societies had to behave with the most virulent probity. The first Methodist church bell in the United States was in Augusta. Bishop Asbury was shocked when he heard of it. The bell was already cracked, and he hoped it would break.⁶ It was held that no church member should be worldly to the extent of buying at one time so much as a hundred pounds of brown sugar. Nor should a man fall into the vanity of having silver stirrups to his saddle.⁷ A certain Baptist congregation, which would yield nothing to the Methodists in point of strictness, was torn three successive times in one season; first, by the "bombast" involved in one of the girl members' owning a parasol; second, by the pride involved in one of the matrons' owning a gig; and third, by one of the preachers' having lapels to his coat.⁸ A Methodist

---

[1] White, *Statistics*, "Methodists," 100.
[2] Smith, *Methodism in Georgia and Florida*, 108.
[3] Smith, *Pierce*, 81.
[4] Smith, *Andrew*, 64.
[5] Smith, *Andrew*, 39.
[6] Smith, *Methodism in Georgia and Florida*, 422.
[7] Andrews, *Old Georgia Lawyer*, 16.
[8] *Ibid.*, 13.

who was three times absent from class, who was guilty of wearing a ribbon, a ruffle, or a ring could expect to have his name erased from the class book.[1]

Palpable immorality such as "drunkenness, cock-fighting, duelling, were not more objects of attack than the theatre, the public show, the powdered head, or the frills and ruffles of the young ladies."[2] One of the preachers attacked President Monroe in a public letter for attending the theatre in Charleston while on his visit South. It was held dangerous to care for music, other than that made by the human voice. Little towns of which the people were conceded "kind and hospitable" were nevertheless pronounced as "next to Sodom and Gomorrah, preeminent for wickedness and profanity."[3]

"When a man was converted he shouted; he expected to 'get happy' at every circuit preaching day, and every 'class,' and all through camp meeting. He expected to pray in public whenever he was called on, to pray three times a day in private and to abjure all the vanities of the world."[4] And above all, a church member had to shun the twin demons of heresy, Pelagianism and Socinianism.[5] All of this was what the life of a good Methodist demanded. The demand was not always adhered to. There were incidents of persons joining the church while under the influence of whiskey,[6] and of honest men who, joining, would not promise to limit themselves to less than a quart of whiskey a day; to do more they knew would have been stark suicide.[7]

There were indeed, however, hidden in this unlovely welter of morbid inhibitions and violent controversy, spiritual implications of a very noble and exhilarating sort. By joining the church, people meant to signify that they were in a vivid sense "born again," that they were citizens of a world other than the one they had been citizens of formerly, that their standard of values was no longer a material one. Bishop

---

[1] Smith, *Methodism in Georgia and Florida*, 73.
[2] *Ibid.*, 99.
[3] *Southwestern Christian Advocate*, 13 June, 1843.
[4] Smith, *Methodism in Georgia and Florida*, 157.
[5] *Ibid.*, 182.
[6] *Ibid.*, 211.
[7] Gilmer, *Sketches*, 165.]

Andrew could remember the deep piety of his father, who would, he says, "often take me as a boy with him at eventide to his place of secret prayer in the woods, and, leaving me some twenty yards behind him, kneel down and wrestle earnestly with God."[1] The Bishop was of a mould as heroic as any other. On being stoned by some "dandies," as he was preaching, he could with a sadly bruised and bleeding face order his congregation to join him in prayer for his persecutors.[2] He was in prayer so much that his knees were actually calloused. He believed that Methodists "must consider themselves God's ambassadors to a world of lost and helpless sinners."[3]

There was everywhere the greatest religious fervor. Even a school boy and a layman knew that a church member was not to act as men did commonly. One Methodist boy who was put into a Georgia school found that besides himself, he wrote, "not a single youth or young man in the school claimed membership in any church. They were a graceless, godless set, often spoke lightly of the Bible and religion, and took great delight in ridiculing my church relations. They applied epithets to me that were hard to bear, but I endured them all manfully for a season, and studied plans to win them to Christ. One morning I carried two large luscious muskmelons and hid them near the school house. After the afternoon recess I invited the boys and teacher to partake of them, and all accepted the invitation. I asked one of my worst enemies to carve the melons and distribute them among the party, which he did very nicely. Every one joined in praising my act of kindness, and all agreed that the melons were very fine. Just as all parties finished eating, a young man of twenty-three years of age, and who had been foremost in heaping abuse on my religion, cut a piece of the rind from which he had eaten the melon, stuck the point of his knife in the back of the rind, hawked and spat upon it, and stooping, dipped rind and spittle in the sand, then rising he stuck the dirt and spittle to my mouth. Quick as the lighting's flash I struck at the aggressor with all my might. . . . I poured out some fearful oaths upon

---

[1] Smith, *Andrew*, 29.
[2] Smith, *Andrew*, 62.
[3] *Ibid.*, 503.

him. Turning upon my persecutors I addressed them about as follows: 'You boys have tried me in every way possible. You have abused me, called me by all the names you could think of. Still I determined to do and live right. . . . Now one and all please understand that I am no longer a member of the church, and any of you who so desire can get a fight just when you wish it.' " This resistance, the writer lamented, was a great victory for the devil.[1]

Longstreet himself was to give in 1839 an example of what splendid faith and unselfishness and utter absorption in an ideal can lift men to. Moral heroism was as common among these people as it often gets to be on this earth. With so many persons as simply good as any reasonable demand would have humanity be, there evolved here, as there did elsewhere in the country, a naïve trust in the none too distant attainment of a state of affairs as glorious as the millennium, a faith augmented and supported by the old tragic trust in the world's political destiny now that it was to be guided by the irreproachable course of the new republic. One sane man believed as late almost as the middle of the last century that the "demon had well nigh been banished from these lands."[2]

In Greensboro, though the less delectable aspects of Methodism were present, they were probably present to a slighter degree than in most places in the state. The denomination around Greensboro was under the influences of that brilliant and cultivated gentleman, Lovick Pierce, whom Longstreet had known by sight years before in Augusta. In connection with his practice of medicine, a profession which he had studied in Philadelphia, he was an active preacher in the Methodist denomination, and, as such, had achieved much for his church. The Presbyterians had had a church in Greensboro since 1799, but the Methodists languished (only figuratively) in a log shack on the outskirts of the town until 1815, when Pierce, able to endure the obloquy no longer, himself caused a Methodist church to be constructed within the town.[3] He was not reimbursed for his zealous outlay of money until 1827,

---

[1] Anthony, *Autobiography*, 36–8.
[2] *Southern Christian Advocate*, 6 January, 1843.
[3] Smith, *Methodism in Georgia and Florida*, 238.

when the great revival occurred. The Pierces had as a frequent visitor one Stephen Olin from Vermont, a very earnest Methodist, but withal a man of charming and somewhat merry personality, brilliant intelligence, and extensive education.[1] And James O. Andrew also was in the town very often, sometimes officially, and sometimes on mere passing visits to his friends.[2]

All of these people Longstreet doubtless knew intimately. There is a disposition among frontier people everywhere, and among frontier people of the South more particularly, to know all comers. Colonel David Crockett, according to his book, encountered persons in his early travels in the Southwest who fairly burned with anxiety to know who he was and where he was going. In one of Longstreet's stories a Mr. Doolittle who comes to a country town and puts up at the inn refuses for so long (an entire day) to explain himself to the villagers that they inaugurate a movement to ride him out tarred and feathered on a rail. It has been explained to the present writer by an old man living in a town of some two thousand people that whenever he sees a stranger on the sidewalk he makes it his business to go up and speak to him and inquire as to his business. American curiosity was an accepted phenomenon. The *Southern Literary Gazette*, 3 February, 1849, published an article on that subject translated from the French. To some extent Longstreet must have had this instinct; certainly he had a disposition initially so expansive that even with a little endowment of curiosity—and his was a large one— he would have become acquainted with the Methodist visitors. He was one of the show characters of the village; and the Methodist visitors he would certainly have known, anyway, through that staunch Methodist, his father-in-law, Mr. Torrance, who did not fail to exhibit him to any such guests.

It remained a fact that the Methodists were still a people set apart. Sincerely interested ladies could not help inquiring as to why the Methodists shouted so, and when that question was answered (this episode occurs in one of Longstreet's

---

[1] Smith, *Pierce*, 46.
[2] Smith, *Andrew*, 40.

books) volubly enough, surely, one would think, to prevent any further question, the sincere lady would ask how it came about "that there is shouting in no other church in the world but the Methodist"?[1] By the time Longstreet wrote this book, 1849, he conceived of himself very likely as the Colonel who so militantly and conclusively answered the lady's queries, but in 1824-27 he was himself somewhat in the position of the questioner. Daily, however, he became more and more reconciled to what he believed the necessity for affiliating himself with some group of organized Christians; the Calvinistic dogma was intellectually repugnant to him; most of his friends were Methodists; and it was accordingly towards the Methodist denomination that he leaned instead of towards either the Baptist or the Presbyterian.

But if his study of the Scriptures taught him anything, it taught him that by baptism Jesus meant immersion, meant being taken down into the water and put under it. He believed that the ministers of the Baptist Church had all of them been immersed by ministers who in their turn had been immersed, through the generations, back to the time of Jesus. Accordingly, the once "proud infidel," though he had made up his mind now to join the Methodist Church, approached Baptist Brother Adiel Sherwood with the idea of getting that brother to immerse him. Brother Pierce, of course, of the Methodists, would immerse him cheerfully, but Brother Pierce was not somehow exactly in the succession. Brother Sherwood describes the entire episode. He says, "It was in 1827, while the religious excitement prevailed in Greensboro, that Judge A. B. Longstreet . . . desired me to baptize him. 'Dr. Pierce (Methodist) had baptized a few who requested it,' he observed, 'but I prefer that the ceremony should be performed for me by one who has been regularly baptized.' I was about to respond in the affirmative to his wishes, after he should have satisfied me of his fitness, though on that score I should not have required much, as I had conversed with him in his distress; but he observed that his friends were in the Methodist Church, and that as his predilections were with that denomi-

---

[1] Longstreet, *Mitten*, 215-18.

nation he would join no other. I then answered, 'I cannot perform the ordinance for you, as you have thus expressed your intention not to continue steadfastly in the apostles doctrine and fellowship.' (Acts II, 42.) I conceived union with our Methodist brethren to be unscriptural, and I could not administer baptism to an applicant who anticipated union with them. Judge Longstreet was finally baptized [surely, one supposes, *immersed* is meant] but he cherished no unkind feelings toward me."[1]

Longstreet later became, in general, the most conforming of all good denominationalists, and took occasion at times to speak with some suggestion of levity about people other than Methodists, but he was in some regards to his dying day inherently less Methodist than Baptist. He was a convinced Protestant, distrusting elaborate church organization ["I have always been afraid of our becoming over-organized"] and tradition, limiting his credence and his confidence in religious matters to what he could find in his Bible.[2]

When the Judge came into the church, his doing so was more the result of long determination than of sudden "conversion," but it is true that he did join the church in the conventional revival manner. The year 1827 witnessed a sort of minor "Great Awakening." In Milledgeville, at a series of meetings led by Andrew, Lovick Pierce, and Olin, there were "converts" at the rate of twenty-five a day. In Washington, a town noted for "wealth, hospitality, refinement, skepticism and wickedness," the same group, except for Andrew, accomplished things almost as remarkable. Athens had a great revival. Everywhere the flame went high. Some of the courts were opened with prayer by the presiding Judge. In Greensboro, too, the church people of the town determined to "storm the battlements" of sin, and began a campaign. At one of the meetings at which Adiel Sherwood preached and "warm" John Howard (of the Methodists) exhorted, Judge Longstreet came forward amongst the penitents, his wife with him,[3] and the two there

---
[1] *Memoir of Adiel Sherwood* (Philadelphia, 1884), 231.
[2] Methodist Episcopal Church, *Debates of the Conference of 1844*, 113.
[3] Fitzgerald, *Judge Longstreet*, 45.

gave their hands to the Methodist minister in token of their wish to join his church.[1] This was in the fall.

At about this time, Longstreet determined to put into execution another plan that he had long been contemplating. That was to remove to Augusta, "where," he believed, he says, with the implication that this was the sole reason, he "could have a more lucrative practice than in Greensboro."[2]

Life in Greensboro had been most pleasant. It was his wife's home, and he regarded it now, in great measure, as his own. He had suffered here a long spell of illness and had found the people so tenderly solicitous for his recovery that he came to look upon the whole town as his family. He had rambled with various friends over the entire county-side. Two of his children, he remembered in 1870 as one powerful reason for his regret at leaving, he had buried there. The most fundamental elements of his emotional nature were intimately associated with this place. Here he had met his wife, and had become a professed Christian; here, somehow, it seemed to him, since his patriotic efforts had here first been recognized and rewarded, the spirit of his state which he loved so actively seemed to hover in a sense in which it could not hover elsewhere.

His home life had been delightful. In this house he had had the pleasure of entertaining his old teacher, Dr. Waddel,[3] and from there he and Mrs. Longstreet had gone repeatedly to Athens to visit his many friends: the Waddels, the Claytons, and the Hulls.[4] He could remember years afterwards the joyous meeting that had taken place in his house when Adiel Sherwood had come there to find his sister, escorted at least part of her way from New England by Longstreet himself.[5]

It was while living in Greensboro also that he had given himself up to the national patriotic debauch over the visit of Lafayette. The present writer has found, it must be confessed, no direct evidence that Longstreet ever saw Lafayette,

---

[1] Smith, *Methodism in Georgia and Florida*, 237–8.
[2] Fitzgerald, *Judge Longstreet*, 46.
[3] Moses Waddel, Diary, Ms., July, 1825.
[4] *Ibid.*, 2 August, 1825.
[5] Fitzgerald, *Judge Longstreet*, 177.

but for his part he is quite sure that Longstreet did. In the
first place here was an intensely patriotic American citizen,
and in the second place it was at a hotel conducted by Longstreet's sister, Mrs. Rebecca Longstreet Camfield, that Lafayette stayed while in Augusta.[1] It is hardly likely that the
ambitious young Judge did not visit his sister at this time,
hardly likely that she could have failed to urge her distinguished jurist brother to be with her for the credit of the
family. And besides, it was from Longstreet that the Government of Georgia had bought the horse for Lafayette to ride on
while in that state.[2]

The festivities in connection with Lafayette's visit were
notable. The General arrived in Augusta from Savannah in
the latter part of March, 1825, and remained there for two
days. His visit put into transports, of course, every loyal
American, but to Longstreet it must have seemed peculiarly
a personal matter. Certainly, a daughter born to him in June,
1826, was named Virginia Lafayette, and certainly when
Lafayette died in 1834, Longstreet's newspaper announcing
the fact went into deep mourning, deeper than any other paper
in Georgia, and published a lyrical and mournfully exultant
editorial,—"Would that his remains were deposited by the
side of our own Washington, where thirteen millions of freemen would mingle their griefs o'er his tomb, and not a deceitful
tear be shed. . . . No man ever died more revered by the
pure and virtuous of all nations."[3]

As Lafayette's boat from Savannah approached Augusta,
two steamboats, crowded with a great many citizens of
Augusta, went down to meet it. "These boats joined us,"
writes Lafayette's secretary, "as we ascended the river. There
was something frightful in this contest; the three roaring
vessels seemed to fly in the midst of black clouds of smoke,
which prevented us from seeing each other."[4] Can anybody
dream that Judge Longstreet, his emotions already highly
wrought, did not have on that day some recollections of his

---

[1] Authority Mr. Paul E. Carmichael, Augusta, Georgia.
[2] State of Georgia, Minutes Executive Department, 1822-5, 511.
[3] *State Rights Sentinel*, 30 June, 1834.
[4] *Lafayette in America*, II, 65.

father, and his efforts with the old boats long ago, recollections that stirred him inexpressibly? When Lafayette left Augusta he gave one of the little girls of the Longstreet connection a gold coin, which, promptly beaten into a finger ring, got before long into the hands of the Judge to be kept by him proudly all of his life.

Conjectural is the idea that Longstreet accompanied Lafayette to Milledgeville, but there is every reason to accept it. The celebration to be held there was anticipated as an event of unsurpassed splendor, not to be missed if you could help yourself. Hardly would the Judge have stayed away. At any rate, he had gone often over those roads, which now, unfortunately, were everywhere in a bad condition and so much broken up that the members of Lafayette's party were obliged to travel a part of the way on horseback. A man who stuck to his carriage as the General did was subjected to receiving jolts so violent as to occasion vomiting. Possibly the Judge left the General when it became necessary for him to change his course and go to Greensboro instead of to Milledgeville, and possibly he continued on. All of this is guesswork. Surely, it may be taken, he participated with everything that was in him in the general acclamation, and since he lived in Greensboro at the time, always associated the entire episode with that residence.

"Judge," the title by which he was known until his death, through all of his vicissitudes in the ministry, in educational, and in agricultural endeavor, was a title that originated in Greensboro, and there officially came to an end. A Middle Georgia villager this man remained always in sentiment.

Georgianism was to Longstreet always a most palpable reality, and of this reality he probably felt himself a very definite personification. When he came, later in life, to publish his book, *Georgia Scenes*, he signed himself "A Native Georgian." Bishop Fitzgerald writes of Longstreet as "the most typical Georgian that ever made a speech, preached a sermon, or waged a controversial warfare. . . . He was a Georgian all over, all through, and all the time . . . the father of its humorists, a peculiar kind, unlike any other. . . . The typical Georgian! No one will dispute his title. He was typical of what was truest, highest and best in his people. If, while he typed their virtues, he was in any degree tinged with their failings, we need not be surprised."[1]

Professor Trent defines a Georgian so clearly that it is worth transcribing his definition here by way of showing the manner of man Longstreet was when at nearly forty years of age he went back to Augusta. "I think I can tell a Georgian," says Professor Trent, "when I see one. . . . He has much of the native shrewdness and push that mark the genuine Down-Easter, and he has a considerable share of that worthy's moral earnestness. In addition to this, he has a good deal of the Virginian's geniality and love of comfort, of the North Carolinian's unpretending democracy, and of the South Carolinian's tendency to exhibitions of fiery temper. But, over and above everything else, he has an honest and hearty and not unfounded pride in Georgia, and a sort of masonic affiliation with every person, animal, institution, custom—in short, *thing*—that can be called Georgian. He may not always stand for culture, but he does always stand for patriotism, state and national. He loves success, straight-forwardness, and the solid virtues generally, neither is he averse to showy ones; but above all, he loves virtue in action. Though possessed of a strong, clear intellect, he is more particularly a man of five senses, of which he makes as good use as he can. He may not always taste the sweetness or see the light of the highest civilization, but he has a good healthy appetite for life. In fine, the Georgian is the Southerner who comes the nearest of all the inhabitants of his section to being a normal American. The various elements that compose the population [of the state] seem to have fused . . . rather than to have preserved their individuality; and the result is the typical Georgian, energetic, shrewd, thrifty, brave, religious, patriotic, tending on the extremes of society to become narrow and hard, or self-assertive and pushing."[2]

With all of his Georgianism, Longstreet was a good thrifty American without any too great patience for sentiment in its

---

[1] Fitzgerald, *Judge Longstreet*, 11–12.
[2] Trent, *Southern Statesmen*, 119–200. The present writer believes that they are not completely fused, that there are in this one state certainly as many as two civilizations.

practical manifestations. It was well enough, he thought, to rhapsodize over General Lafayette, but it was not necessary in consequence to refuse the opportunity of making out of his visit $170, if you could do so by selling to the state a horse for him to ride upon. Greensboro, too, was a thousand things in his heart, but law practice would be more lucrative elsewhere, and elsewhere he would go.

And where else should a person go but to Augusta? Augusta, as the gateway to a frontier conceived of as inexhaustibly rich in possibilities of money making, was enjoying a season of unbounded prosperity. The cotton trade had just become securely established. "A traveller who made a zigzag journey from Charleston to St. Louis in the early months of 1827 found cotton 'a plague. . . .' At Augusta the thoroughfares were thronged with groaning wagons, the warehouses were glutted, the open places were stacked, and the steamboats and barges hidden by their loads. On the road beyond, migrating planters and slaves bound for the west, 'where the cotton land is not worn out,' met cotton laden wagons townward bound, whereupon the price of the staple was the chief theme of roadside conversation."[1] The city was rapidly becoming, in its way, a sort of capital, so much so that provincials in a little while would think of it as "the Philadelphia of the South," a metropolis in which one might have "such ample opportunities of acquiring polish and refinement."[2]

---
[1] Phillips, *American Negro Slavery*, 212.
[2] William T. Thompson, *Major Jones's Chronicles of Pineville* (Philadelphia, 1843), 31–2.

V

AUGUSTA—AND POLITICS

"Well," Longstreet wrote reminiscently as an old man, "we moved to Augusta." This was in the fall of 1827.[1] "I sold my possessions in Greensboro," his statement continues, "at a sacrifice, bought a plantation near the city, and commenced planting and lawing with high hopes. Alas, they were soon blasted. My practice increased, to be sure, but my expenses increased in duplicate ratio, and my troubles in an innumerable ratio. My crops barely paid the expenses of making them, my negroes became thieves, they stole my hogs, my corn, my bacon (by false keys) and everything they could sell. Security debts I had to pay by thousands; in short, you can hardly name a trouble to which I was not subjected. Throughout them all my wife was my counsellor, my comforter, my encourager. At length I told her I must do one of two things: I must sell my plantation and negroes, or I must quit the practice of law. These negroes had been bequeathed to her and her brother in early childhood by their grandfather, who had selected them to correspond in age with the age of the two children, that they might grow up together. Her brother soon died and they all fell to her. She was eighteen when I married her, and here were these negroes, between forty and fifty in number, with not an old one among them save their parents who had been bequeathed with them. She was now called upon to say whether she would part with the slaves in a body (save the house-servants and their families). . . . I don't know that she paused a moment before she answered: 'Husband, I leave the matter entirely with you, and will freely acquiesce in your choice.' Then, said I, we will sell them. She showed a little sadness but never the first sign of disapprobation. A purchaser soon appeared in a companion of

---
[1] *Yale Biographies and Annals*, VI, 580–83.

my boyhood, a pious man and, of course, a good master. I sold them at fair prices all round. This sale put me out of debt and left me a clever sum over, and relieved me of the eternal torment of negroes, overseers and creditors. Things now brightened about me greatly."[1]

The Judge was no farmer, but he could never make up his mind to leave farming utterly alone. All of his life he kept it up. He was, however, a lawyer, and a most capable one, but it would not do to estimate his ability in this profession by his success in keeping out of the court records. On those old books he is forever buying or selling or suing.

On returning to Augusta to live, Longstreet purchased a splendid residence beautifully located on a large tract of land not far from the city. It had been built originally by some of the Byrd connection of Virginia and was named Westover after the old Virginia estate. It was here that he lived from 1827 till 1839, when he again left Augusta. By the spring of 1834 the management of the slaves had become more than he could undertake, and he began to sell them. The following year he commenced getting rid of his farm also, piece by piece, but did not dispose of the dwelling, "Westover," until 1844.

The Judge soon formed a law partnership with William W. Mann, a person of literary aspirations and ability, who later, after spending many years as an American correspondent in Paris, became the first literary editor of the *Southern Field and Fireside*, an ambitious publication begun in Augusta in 1859. In January, 1832, the partnership was augmented by the entrance of Charles J. Jenkins,[2] afterwards the recipient of all of the political honors the state could offer. The law firm was from the first prosperous. Longstreet had the art of getting along with everybody. Even people whose viewpoints he detested were often in point of character most admirable to him. Once when he was having a newspaper controversy with a person who called himself Seneca, in the midst of the warmest part of the disagreement, he announced that personally he held Seneca as "an old and tried friend, whom I have ever esteemed for many years past, and most tenderly loved. The

---

[1] Fitzgerald, *Judge Longstreet*, 46–7.
[2] *Augusta Chronicle*, 5 January, 1833.

attachment which I feel for him must, I believe, remain unbroken, however widely we may differ in sentiment; for we are both alike incapable of wilful error, intentional misrepresentation, or personal reflections. In the absence of all of these, conflicting opinions may cause mutual pain and regret, but can never estrange friendship."[1] This tolerance was general. A certain paper, he says, "was edited by one of the shrewdest, most intelligent and satiric writers of his time. Honored be his memory, though I never agreed with him in politics."[2] James L. Petigru once wrote him a very warm letter denouncing a certain speech of Longstreet's as a "diatribe." In answering Petigru's letter Longstreet was not apologetic, but he took occasion to say "your opinion of the diatribe will not abate a scruple of my regard for you."[3] "Men may," he reminded Alexander H. Stephens in 1869, "be political opponents and personal friends."[4]

In Augusta, Longstreet was in a very stimulating atmosphere. The town was rich, and growing in culture as well as in population and material resources. There have survived several traces of Longstreet's activities as a lawyer during this period of his life. In 1829 he was counsel for one Hightower Davis who had been implicated in a slave insurrection.[5] The next year he was agent for the state in some matters concerned with the behavior of the Savannah River below Augusta.[6] A letter written to him from the state Capitol by Governor George R. Gilmer, 22 February, 1831, is indicative of some of Longstreet's legal opinions and ideas.

"It is not my purpose," the Governor says with some tartness, "to investigate at large the doctrine of contempts as practiced upon by the English courts. . . . I think you are mistaken in saying that the common law of England is the law of this State. It is the law only so far as it is consistent with the Constitution. . . . You say that the power to remit the order of imprisonment may be concurrent in the Court and

---
[1] *Augusta Chronicle*, 5 September, 1832.
[2] Longstreet, *Stories with a Moral*, 23, "Gnatville Gem."
[3] Fitzgerald, *Judge Longstreet*, 106.
[4] *Ibid.*, 195.
[5] State of Georgia, Governor's Letter Book, 1829–31, 9.
[6] *Ibid.*, 43.

Governor, and analogize it to the power of pardoning which in England may be exercised both by the King and the Parliament. . . . You conclude your letter by asking if a Judge should order a citizen to be crippled, branded, or put to death for contempt, whether I would not remit the sentence or respite. I answer without hesitation, No. I would no more pardon in such a case than I would if a Judge should whilst walking a street order a citizen to be incarcerated for life, for moving in his sunshine."[1]

Though Longstreet's reputation as a lawyer was unquestionably very broad, it seems that he was only once called upon to carry a case before the Supreme Court. That was in January, 1839, after his interests had largely shifted from law to divinity. An account of that case is here given in a footnote for the benefit of whoever may be interested.[2]

---

[1] State of Georgia, Governor's Letter Book, 22 February, 1831; also *Gilmer, Sketches*, 457–8.

[2] JANUARY TERM, 1839

William McElmoyle, for the use of Isaac S. Bailey, vs. John J. Cohen, Administrator of Levy Florence.

Mr. Longstreet for Plaintiff, Mr. King for Defendant.

Brought to the United States Supreme Court on a certificate of division between the judges of the sixth Circuit Court of the United States for the District of Georgia.

HISTORY OF THE CASE: William McElmoyle, citizen of South Carolina, suing for the use of Isaac S. Bailey, also a citizen of that State, presented a petition in 1835 to the United States Circuit Court for the District of Georgia, stating that Levy Florence had died intestate, and having before his death resided in the State of South Carolina, had obtained a judgment against him in the Court of Common Pleas for the City Charleston for $968.07 on a promissory note on February 10, 1822, which remains unsatisfied.

Defendant pleaded statute of limitations of Georgia, stating that Levy Florence had removed to Georgia seven years after judgment had been rendered; that there is no statute of limitations in South Carolina, but that the Georgia Legislature passed, December 7, 1805, a law providing that actions of debt on judgments obtained in Courts of other States, must be commenced within 5 years from rendition of such judgments; no suit was brought on judgment during the seven years Levy Florence was resident of Georgia, nor for two years after defendant, John J. Cohen, had been appointed administrator of Levy Florence.

The questions were:

1. Whether the statute of limitations of Georgia can be pleaded to an action in that State, founded upon a judgment rendered in the State of South Carolina.

2. Whether, in the administration of assets in Georgia, a judgment rendered in South Carolina, upon a promissory note against the intestate, when in life, should be paid in preference to simple contract debts.

Mr. Longstreet had argued the first question negatively and the second affirmatively.

It may be gathered that the Judge's interest in his profession was in no sense parochial. His outlook here was national and even more; he knew with some intimacy what was going on in England. If Lord Brougham "is not a debtor for his judicial reform bill to my native state," he wrote, "there is the most remarkable coincidence between the two systems that ever occurred since the world began."[1]

In those times, law went hand in hand with the pursuit of politics. In the case of Longstreet, the lawyer's mind was given an added interest in the courses of government by the man's friendship for Calhoun and McDuffie. It is doubtful, however, whether the diminution of his faith had had time to make itself clear to him until some years later. McDuffie was, as late as 1821, most ardently pro-union. In response to a series of articles called *Signs of the Times,* published in a Georgia newspaper in July, 1821, McDuffie had soon followed with his *Defense of a Liberal Construction of the Powers of Congress, by "One of the People."* In this paper he was bitter against the strict constructionists. He looks upon much of the defection from the central government as the result of unholy personal ambition. "Always," he says, "ambitious men of inferior talents finding they have no hope to be distinguished in the councils of the national government, wish to increase the power and consequence of the state governments, the theaters in which they hope to acquire distinction. . . . We have more cause of apprehension from the states than from the general government. . . . He must have read the lessons of history to little purpose who does not perceive that the people of particular states are liable to fall, occasionally, into a dangerous and morbid excitement upon particular subjects."[2]

As to the first question, the Court held (the opinion being delivered by Justice Wayne) "that the statute of limitations of Georgia can be pleaded to an action in that State, founded upon a judgment rendered in the State of South Carolina."

As to the second question the Court held: "In the payment of debts of a testator or intestate, in Georgia, that the judgment of another State, whatever may be the subject matter of the suit, cannot be put upon the footing of judgments rendered in that State, and that it can only rank for that purpose as a simple contract debt."

[1] *Martin R. Delaney, Life of,* by Frank A. Rollin (Boston, 1883), 108–15.

[2] George McDuffie, *Defence of a Liberal Construction of the Powers of Congress by One of the People* (Philadelphia, 1831).

By 1828, however, or shortly thereafter, McDuffie had radically shifted his position; and soon thereafter John C. Calhoun had followed him. The sharp assertion of state rights was, it seems, not a political ideal forced on the people by their leaders, but one forced on the leaders by the people.[1] Since Longstreet was politically, at least, more of the people than either Calhoun or McDuffie, it is likely that he preceded both of them in his advocacy of state rights.

It was with the tariff that Longstreet was concerned chiefly. The Tariff of 1816, though professedly in the nature of a war measure, was, so far as Longstreet could see, exactly what it turned out, the familiar entering wedge that served ever afterwards as a precedent for further tariff legislation. The efforts made by Southern representatives in Washington in connection with the Tariff of 1828 had sickened him. He knew that the South was making three-fourths of all of the agricultural exports of the country and nearly three-fifths of all the exports, and yet he saw the South about to enter under the operation of a law by which "she was to suffer almost in direct proportion as other sections of the country gained advantage."[2]

In the summer of 1828, Calhoun issued his famous Exposition, showing him at last as a strict constructionist, and showing, too, the yearning of the South for the end of the Adams administration and the accession of Jackson. But in April, 1830, Jackson so thoroughly smashed Southern hopes that he would support state rights theories, that Calhoun fell back upon the drastic plan of advising an actual trial of nullification. Time passed on, and good Southerners still hoped, but the tariff legislation of 1832 looked so little more favorable to the South than did that of the years past, that in November of that year a state convention in South Carolina actually declared null and void and without force, so far as the sovereign state of South Carolina was concerned, all the tariff legislation of the quadrennium preceding. As the 1832 law was not to go into effect until 3 March, 1833, there was a period of very tense waiting, which was relieved only on March 2 by a com-

---

[1] David Franklin Houston, *Study of Nullification in South Carolina* (New York, 1896).

[2] Wilson, *Division and Reunion*, 49–50.

promise measure sponsored by Henry Clay. Soon after Clay's measure was enacted, the South Carolina convention again went into session and on March 11 rescinded the tariff nullification laws they had passed in November; but the convention did not adjourn without nullifying, as a matter of principle, the Force Bill which President Jackson had put through Congress to empower him to force compliance with the now dead tariff legislation of 1832. The practical aspects of the question having been disposed of, it no longer existed except in the minds of enthusiasts. Longstreet was one of those enthusiasts.

Georgia's bumptious attitude towards the Federal Government in connection with the removal of the Indians had caused many persons to think that it was probably from Georgia that some tangible resistance would first be offered to the constantly growing tariff restrictions, but for a long time Georgia was taken up so largely with settling its newly gained western territory and with the animosities and contradictions of personal politics that it was unable to adjust itself to clear political thinking. Even in the matter of nullification, it was influenced by the fact that nullification stood for John C. Calhoun, who, in turn, stood for the rock on which Georgia's great political aspirations for the presidency, in the candidacy of William H. Crawford, had gone so utterly to pieces. But Longstreet, through his personal friendship for Calhoun, was becoming every day a keener "nullifier" than he had been before.

It is likely that the Judge was in South Carolina on law business a good deal during the nullification controversy of the early 1830's, that he attended the Charleston State Rights and Free Trade Association in February, the Hamburg dinner in May, 1832, and the Augusta dinner soon thereafter. Longstreet was hand in glove with the two leaders in South Carolina. Calhoun, he said, was "matchless," and McDuffie "hardly inferior to him in anything."[1] He and McDuffie were "as closely knit as David and Jonathan."[2] McDuffie kept him thoroughly informed "with every step of the progress of nullification in his state from its inception," commiserated with him over the lack of unanimity of political thinking in the South,

---
[1] Longstreet, "Review Perry's Calhoun," 621.
[2] *Ibid.*, 620.

prophesied dolefully that as a result "this thing would end in civil war."¹ Calhoun was, he thought, above William Pitt, or any other premier who ever lived before or since his day.² He could never forget his boyish worship of this giant. Though he was a preacher, and Calhoun had been suspected of being a free-thinker, Longstreet could not keep out of his mind, whenever he thought of Calhoun, even long after Calhoun's death, the lines based upon Burns's *Willie:*

> Beneath these stones
> Lie Calhoun's bones
>   Whom canting wretches blame.
> With such as he,
> Where'er he be
>   May I be saved or damned.³

Calhoun dominated Longstreet's political thinking. He could not deny Calhoun anything. At first he believed him wrong in championing the subtreasury system against Jackson, but, upon being in Washington and hearing Calhoun explain his position, he changed.⁴

Longstreet was in Athens, Georgia, in August, 1832, and attended there the meeting in the University Chapel in which his friend Augustin S. Clayton fairly took the meeting out of the hands of William H. Crawford, and made it, altogether contrary to the intent of the persons who had originally called it, a meeting endorsing nullification policies.⁵ "The Athens meeting severely condemned the tariff and called on the counties throughout the state to elect delegates to a convention to meet in Milledgeville in November and to invest them with full powers in behalf of the good people of Georgia to maintain, preserve and defend the rights and privileges of the free citizens of this state."⁶

Certainly, also, Longstreet was in attendance at the great

---

¹ Longstreet, "Review Perry's Calhoun," 627.
² *Ibid.*, 623.
³ *Ibid.*, 620.
⁴ *Ibid.*, 629; *Augusta Chronicle*, 2 November, 1837.
⁵ *Augusta Chronicle*, 1 September 1832; E. Merton Coulter, "Nullification Movement in Georgia" (in *Georgia Historical Quarterly*, March, 1921).
⁶ Coulter, "Nullification," 15–16.

dinner given in Lexington, Georgia, soon after the Athens meeting and in honor of the Georgia congressmen (all but two, Forsyth and Wayne) who had voted against the last Federal tariff laws. "It was estimated that more than a thousand persons attended. They passed resolutions bitterly criticizing the tariff, 'to which as free citizens of Georgia, *we ought not, cannot, will not, longer submit.*' . . ." Though in accord with what was said at these gatherings, he did not at either of them let himself be formally heard from; indeed, he went to the Lexington dinner "only," he said, "because business held him in this vicinity."[1]

The situation seemed to Longstreet nothing short of desperate. He had thought himself permanently out of politics, and was ready to stay out, but now he thought he was actually needed in Milledgeville. He would make the sacrifice, go to the legislature, if he could get elected, and do what he could to sway the state. He could not bear to see Georgia, which he loved passionately, do now, for the sake of a momentary advantage, a thing that would ultimately involve the Union, and, through the Union, back again, Georgia herself, in unending wretchedness. In August, he announced his candidacy for a seat in the representative branch of the state legislature,[2] having determined, however, he said, before entering the race, that he would never again offer for public office.[3] There were other matters calling him insistently. Religion spoke to him daily more and more imperatively.

Longstreet knew how to run for office like a gentleman, in a way that was magnanimous and altogether admirable. In these activities he was the Judge Longstreet whom even his enemies knew for a great man and were proud of as a fellow Georgian. He wanted the office violently, but before he was a candidate he was a Christian knight, and he would have the office only upon Christian and knightly terms. The sad commentary is that by so doing he always missed getting it altogether. Three times he had run for office, always on what he

---
[1] *Augusta Chronicle*, 1 September, 1832.
[2] *Augusta Chronicle*, 29 August, 1832.
[3] *Ibid.*, 25 August, 1832.

considered the call of a decided majority, and he had always been defeated.

Shortly after the meetings in Athens and Lexington there was one held in Augusta for the purpose of electing delegates to the Milledgeville convention in November. To this Longstreet went, but from it, as will be seen, finding it going in a way contrary to his ideas, he soon retired in high disgust. In the *Augusta Chronicle,* however, itself a fiery advocate of state rights, the disgruntled leader published a speech indicative of his entire course as a politician. It is preceded by the following letter, dated Augusta, 20 August, 1832, and signed duly by Longstreet.[1]

"A writer, of no ordinary ability, has favored us, . . . with a speech which he would have delivered at the Lexington dinner had he been there. Following his example, I send you the speech which I intended to have delivered at the Richmond meeting, of the 18th, had not the assembly assumed something of a tumultuous character before the vote was taken upon the Resolution offered—when I deemed it prudent to retire."

Then comes the speech. "It was not my design," it begins, "to have addressed this meeting when I entered this Hall. But, sir, the Resolutions first offered, and which, it is easy to perceive, will be adopted, seem to leave me no alternative. They address me so personally, and my principles so unsparingly that it would be a departure from the duty which I owe to myself, to my fellow citizens, and my country to be silent. . . . Sir, I am as warm a friend to the Union as ever trod its soil—I mean, sir, the Union as it came in its beauty and perfection from the hands of the mighty dead who formed it. . . . It recommended itself to the affections of my boyhood; and these affections grew with my growth, and strengthened with my strength, until the year 1816. From that time to this, the chords [*sic*]of my attachment to it have been gradually yielding, because, from that time to this, the Union has been rapidly changing its features. Still I cling to it, as to a sacred relic, and would gladly embrace any plan which can be devised, to preserve it in its primitive beauty. I came hither in hopes

---
[1] *Augusta Chronicle,* 25 August–1 September, 1832.

of hearing some such plan suggested, but I find with regret, that it is a meeting to denounce plans, not to form them . . . Equally ardent is my attachment to the form of our government, I have often dwelt upon it with kindling rapture. I have felt that I stood on a lofty peak of moral elevation, while I contemplated it, and remembered that I was an *American citizen*.

"But, sirs, if this government is doomed to fall, under the political excitement of the day,—if Georgia shall be crushed in its ruins, and I in the ruins of Georgia; with my latest breath, but with an unfaltering tongue, with all the earnestness of Macbeth, but without any of his remorse, I will say to our Northern brethren—'Thou canst not say we did it.' I have examined the doctrine of nullification in its most alarming features, and I am more than willing that my name should go down to posterity, identified with its worst issues."

The darkest possibility of nullification, he declares, would be civil war, but as Georgia and South Carolina would in that case be vanquished, only the moral issue would be remembered, and those two states would accordingly occupy the more enviable position before the world. But he does not believe there would be any forcible prevention of secession; that "would be a curious question of international law, but not a cause of war." Before a war could come the factories of New England would be in ruins and their influence at an end. At any rate, this is a time for action. In Washington, he says, he has seen things that demand it. "I saw the champions of the South defeated again and again, when they were defending axiomatic truths. I saw them driven by the noise of a letter from positions, which would have been impregnable to a nobler enemy. I witnessed such defeats until the Union lost its beauty in my eyes, and Civil War lost its deformity.

"It has been said that I was opposed to nullification. I am at this moment, sir, opposed to *Georgia* nullification. I believe the opinion of the Supreme Court to be constitutional, and right; and so believing, I fearlessly declare in all places, that I think it should be submitted to. My first impressions were against South Carolina nullification, because my first impressions were that the tariff laws were constitutional. . . . It may be that I would stake too much for the honor and privileges of the South. If so, I plead the example of our forefathers as an apology. It may be that my notions of liberty are too refined; and I know that I could live with less than I have, and that I have more than the subject of any other government on earth. If then, I am asked, 'Why I am not content with the liberty which I have,' I answer—because it is not the liberty I was born to. I was never taught to measure my rights by the sufferings of other nations. I want, sir, not the liberty of speaking in the councils of the nation, but the liberty of being heard also. Not the liberty of asking redress of grievance—but the liberty which exempts me from insult, mockery, and derision when I respectfully solicit it. Not the liberty of tilling my own soil—but of using its fruits as my own. Not the liberty of selling my own—but of selling it where I please. Not the liberty of buying—but of buying from whom I please. Not the liberty which clothes the North in purple, and the South in rags—but the liberty which spreads health and cheerfulness and equality, through the whole republic. In a word, the LIBERTY which enables me to walk abroad with the port and mien and majesty of an American citizen; and not the liberty which entails upon me the faltering step and cowering look of a mere suppliant for liberty.

"These are my sentiments, and if Richmond exile me for them, I know that I shall not have to quit my native land, to find a country which will receive and welcome me, with no other passport to her heart and affections than these very sentiments."[1]

Throughout his life, Longstreet was, like his father, endowed with an impression of his worth and abilities so favorable as to make him consider that the sternest rebuke he could administer to a group of people was for him to withdraw from them. He sets out in this undelivered speech by saying that the convention was altogether too uncivilized a gathering for him to remain a part of—when, in fact, it is known that he was a speaker able to demand a hearing anywhere—and he ends with the suggestion that if Georgia did not like him, he was ready

---

[1] *Augusta Chronicle*, 1 September, 1832.

to take up with South Carolina. This does not seem in character, because it involves the presence of an exaggerated dignity and a disposition to evade difficulties in a man who was superbly adapted to his social surroundings, and who was always thoroughly courageous. Alas for paradox, and for the bewilderment of a mind, struggling to march in column for capricious and discordant masters! This protest by withdrawal was Longstreet's choice way of manifesting intense indignation. He can be found at it repeatedly. All during his years as president of various educational institutions he is holding above his trustees' heads the threat that he will resign. On a mission once to London, as the representative of the United States Government, he found it necessary to fall back upon this supreme rebuke. Even in his own home, as a tottering old man, he thrums his fingers along the table, when he conceives that the need comes, and with magnificent dignity announces his departure. What was it that prompted this idea? Was it the impression of awe created years before when Gus Longstreet as a little boy, behind his incensed father, trotted out of the old theater in Augusta? About that, of course, nobody knows anything.

The Augusta nullification speech was delivered only through the newspapers and had no effect on the meeting itself, which was over before the speech was made public. There, upholding the unionistic congressmen, resolutions had been passed which seemed to Longstreet objectionable "in mass and in detail." The convention even elected as its delegates to the state convention the same John Forsyth whom the nullifiers had so openly snubbed at their Lexington dinner, and two other gentlemen, both of whom were presumably of Federal leanings.[1] Nullification was suspect, whether advocated in theory or practice. On September 5, seeing that the sentiment of the county was against him, Longstreet formally withdrew from the race for the legislature.[2]

"During the next months there was a more thorough searching of hearts and minds among Georgians than had been the case during any equal length of time since the foundation of

---
[1] Miller, *Bench and Bar*, I, 34.
[2] *Augusta Chronicle*, 5 September, 1832.

the State. The value of the Union was now being calculated with greater seriousness than ever before. The parting of the ways was at hand."[1] "The convention came together in Milledgeville on November 12th with 131 delegates present representing sixty counties out of the eighty [that existed] at that time. The State House of Representatives, which had already begun its session, after a sharp debate, agreed that the convention use its chamber. Many legislators opposed this action for fear it might mean the recognition of the convention. The political ability and statesmanship of the state were here gathered together. South Carolina, whose nullification convention had not yet met, was watching closely. Two South Carolina representatives, Chancellor Harper and David Johnson, representing the State Rights and Union parties respectively, were admitted to the floor."

"The strong state rights element captured the meeting at the start," but not without great disturbance. John Forsyth, with his unionist following, one of the strongest men in Georgia at the time, remained a part of the convention until he saw that he could accomplish nothing, and then after registering a dramatic protest, still further acclaimed his disapproval by withdrawing, *a la* Longstreet.[2] Then the state rights people were free for their work, a work which, though it occupied them until the seventeenth of the month, did not consist of anything more than an analysis of the political theory of their opponents. The Federalists, they declared, advocated the following principles, all of which were false and worthy of destruction: (1) that the state never had a separate existence; (2) that nullification is impossible; (3) that secession is impossible; (4) that the people of the different states are in reality one people; (5) that the representatives in Congress are representatives of the United States and not of their respective districts; (6) that the states have not retained their sovereignty; (7) that the allegiance of citizens is due more to the United States than to separate states.[3] By way of con-

---

[1] Coulter, "Nullification," 16–17.
[2] Coulter, "Nullification," 24–5.
[3] Miller, *Bench and Bar*, I, 28–30.

ciliation, however, they resolved "that the people of Georgia are sincerely attached to the Federal Constitution and to the Union of these states," that "they are willing that the reduction and equalization of duties which they ask should be prospective and gradual that, fearfully admonished as they have been by experience of the fallacy of their past hopes for relief from the evils under which they suffer, they will still look to the justice and patriotism of their brethren of the manufacturing states."[1]

This meeting, the center of feverish popular interest, had been lent some spectacular elements by the fact that on the night of the thirteenth, the first day on which the convention had actually transacted business, there was a meteoric shower of such surprising copiousness as to seem altogether out of the realm of the natural.[2] Much preaching had run many of the people half mad with constant watchfulness for the hand of God, and constant dread of the final judgment. One knowing and thrifty housewife of the time, it is said, refused, through all the panic of her children and her negro slaves, to be disconcerted. Like the others, she recognized from the star shower that the Last Judgment was upon her, but like a sensible woman she meant to make the best of it. Reckoning that the process would be long and tedious, and wishing her progeny to present a favorable appearance, she ordered a house-servant to put fresh clothes on all of them, to wash their faces and hands, and to put a biscuit into every apron pocket. A people whose interpretation of the natural was so largely in terms of the supernatural could hardly have failed to be impressed by the coincidence of the stars' falling on the first day of the great convention.

In spite of the excitement about it and the store that had been set on it by the nullification advocates, the convention came to very little except among its projectors, and with certain half-way brethren for whom it probably marked the high-water mark of nullification sentiment in Georgia. When the meeting was over, one of the newspapers commented sagely

---
[1] Coulter, "Nullification," 25–6.
[2] Miller, *Bench and Bar*, I, 27.

enough that a mountain had been in labor and that only a mouse had been brought forth.[1]

But Longstreet was among those not to be discouraged by the fact that the state had just elected a governor, in the person of Wilson Lumpkin, who took most earnestly the Unionist principles upon which he had gone into office. In August, 1833, at the University of Georgia commencement in Athens, like the redoubtable advocate he was, the Judge, along with fourteen other men "acting for many citizens of this state, now assembled in this place," invited George McDuffie to a grand dinner to be given on the day following.[2] They felt, they said, that since Mr. McDuffie was then in the town, they could not let slip the opportunity of doing honor to him both as a native son of Georgia and as one who on the floor of Congress had made such able defence of state rights and Southern interests. The explanation that McDuffie was a native Georgian and the explanation that he was in Athens primarily for the graduation of a kinsman did not, however, cause the Union people to be any less severe (with none too consistent logic) in their strictures against the hideous precedent of bringing aliens into the state to give it advice. This distrust of Georgia towards South Carolina must have grieved deeply a man who, as Longstreet did, felt himself half a native of that commonwealth.

He was not one whose zeal for a cause is tempered directly according to the position the cause may occupy in popular favor. When the elections in October, 1833, showed the state more strongly unionistic in feeling than it had been previously, he was driven from within to exert himself more strenuously than he had done theretofore. *The Augusta Chronicle*, one of the most influential newspapers in the state, had always consistently and ably championed the cause of state rights, but Longstreet felt it incumbent upon him, when opportunity to buy out a Federalist paper and convert it into a state rights one presented itself, to make this purchase and effect the transformation.

He named his new paper the *State Rights Sentinel*. In the first issue, 9 January, 1834, he declares that he is himself the

---
[1] Coulter, "Nullification," 25.
[2] *Augusta Chronicle*, 17 August, 1833.

sole proprietor and editor of the paper, and avows that as for the persons who had been subscribers to the predecessor of the *Sentinel,* the old Federalist *North American Gazette,* "we can promise them nothing of a political character which will be in unison with their sentiments, supposing them to agree in sentiments with the late Editor, but apart from politics, we hope to lay before them such as may continue with us, useful and interesting matter enough to repay them amply for the support they may give us."[1]

In a prospectus dated January 9, and published in the other Augusta papers,[2] it is declared that the *Sentinel* will stand for the principles of the Milledgeville Convention, "which are but a restatement of the Resolution of 1798." On the practical side of his venture the new editor solicits job work, in which, he says, since his printing materials are new and well selected, and his operatives skilled and plentiful, he feels that he can give satisfaction. He will publish the paper once weekly till February first and twice weekly thereafter. By paying in advance one may have the paper for three dollars a year, but otherwise it will cost four dollars. This is for the semi-weekly edition; the weekly edition will cost five dollars, paid in advance, and six, paid at the end of the year. Ready cash is always at a premium.

Apparently the only files of the *State Rights Sentinel* now available are in the Library of the Emory University Academy in Oxford, Georgia. The rarity of these files has worked disastrously for Longstreet's fame, since the students who have of late years curried through the ancient Southern periodicals, not having run upon the paper, very reasonably concluded that it did not therefore exist.

So far as can be told now, Longstreet's paper compared most favorably with others of its time, and had a wider circulation than its extreme political view-point might have led one to hope for it. Though the Methodists were in large measure against nullification they were all of them still personally so loyal to their denomination that the very fact of Longstreet's prominent church affiliations assured his paper some audience.

---

[1] *Augusta Chronicle,* 11 January, 1834.
[2] *Augusta Chronicle,* 11 January, 1834; *Augusta Constitutionalist,* 17 January, 1834.

Besides that, he made it the unofficial organ of the growing temperance cause in Georgia. He was himself popular and respected, and his *Georgia Scenes,* which soon began appearing in the *Sentinel,* were certainly the most popular newspaper-writing the state had ever had presented to it.

The nature of the *Sentinel* may perhaps be better learned from a detailed review of one of its issues than from any generalized estimate. This issue has four pages, seven columns to the page. About one-sixth of page one is devoted to an edifying essay on Neptune, and the rest of it is taken up with countless announcements and advertisements. Most notable among the advertisements are those of the book stores and of the druggists. Literary persons are told that *Friendship's Offering, Bryant's Poems,* Cooper's last novel, *The Headsman,* Sparks's *Washington,* and Colonel David Crockett's *Life* (a book just published), can be had at Hornsby's Store. Rheumatic invalids, and persons suffering from various pulmonary affections, are persistently called to health by druggists anxious to sell their efficacious Botanical drops. These drops are "especially good," the announcement goes, "for Scrofula, Salt Rheum, Leprosy, St. Anthony's Fire, Fever Sores, White Swellings, Scurvy, Foul and Obstinate Ulcers, Sore legs and eyes, Scald Head and Venereal Taint, Measles, Red Blotches, pimples on the face, festering eruptions and other diseases." Persons interested in stock breeding are advised as to how they can come at a fine stallion whose services will be put at their disposal—with many details.

Page two, after giving various announcements as to the terms of publication and subscription, and for advertising, offers, as from Catherine G. Wirt, the daughter of William Wirt, a long letter written from Washington, D. C., 22 February, 1834, to her aunt, Mrs. Eliza Carlton of Augusta. The letter is preceded by a short introduction written by Longstreet. Here he shows his familiarity with Wirt's writings; and states, with the air of one preventing an irreparable loss, that, but for the daughter's letter, the world would have no knowledge of her father's personality.

Page three has a section called "Latest from Europe;" and then, at the top of the third column, comes the paper's motto, the invariable quotation from Abraham Baldwin's 1801 speech before the Senate on the repeal of the Judiciary act: "My own opinion is that it is the nature of all delegated power to increase: it has been very aptly said to be like the screw in mechanics; it holds all it gains, and every turn gains a little more." There is some comment on other newspapers in the state, a eulogy upon General Blair of South Carolina, a recountal of a horrible catastrophe in which a father goes mad after, through his own carelessness, suffering his motherless children to be burnt to death. There is some notice of the formation of a new military company to be known as the "Augusta Guards," and there are more advertisements, this time chiefly of a Literary Journal to be edited in New York by Horace Greely.

Page four shows the prospectus of the *Christian Index*, a weekly newspaper to be published at Washington, Georgia, by the Reverend Jesse Mercer. The druggists are at work again summoning to their healing precincts nearly all people under Heaven, debilitated females and those who suffer from corns, skin diseases or syphilitic disorders. It is announced that one may join the Philadelphia Circulation library for five dollars a year. And there is a prospectus of the *Georgia Academician and Southern Journal of Education*, to be published soon from Scottsboro, in Baldwin County, Georgia.

The paper in general is made up much after this plan. If this topical account of one issue of Longstreet's paper fails properly to portray the impression of it that exists in the memory of one who has gone through its files, the failure is due to the fact that the advertisements somehow do not show up in their due prominence. These lucrative space-fillers were ubiquitous, and omnifarious in subject. Always there are announcements about run-away slaves, with little conventionalized pictures of black Sambo jogging along with his pack swung to a stick held over his shoulder. Frequently there are announcements of the pending exhibition of a wild beast, an elephant, or a lion, or occasionally of serpents, introduced in one case as being too well trained and docile to frighten even the most timid ladies.

In the early spring of 1834, the *Sentinel* commenced publishing *Georgia Scenes,* and a little later, the brief, pungent comments on life and affairs emanating from one "Bob Short."

There is nothing that escapes the comments of this wiseacre, Bob, but it is to politics that he gives most attention. "I have been asked," he announces one day, "when should a man marry. My reply is at twenty if he is a State Rights man, and at eighty-five if not. So will we have more States rights children in the community."[1] In the issue of 5 June, 1834, he observes aggrievedly that his contributions cannot be highly regarded; if they were, why, when people attribute them to Judge Longstreet, should he take such great pains to disclaim them? But Bob does not for that reason stop writing except when Judge Longstreet is away from the city. Then, suspiciously enough, he is silent. All during August, 1835, he says nothing. On the first day of September, the *Sentinel* inquires as follows: "Did our old friend and correspondent Bob Short take fright at the appearance of a new conductor of this paper in the absence of the editor and foreman? If so, his alarms were unnecessary as the very talented gentleman who kindly conducted our paper in our absence would have held his name as sacred as we do. If the fear of having his name or handwriting known to too many has been the cause of his long silence, it may now be dismissed, as the *Sentinel* is again under the exclusive care of his old confident [sic]. In our rambles we found many who were impatient to hear from him, and we hope he will not keep them another week in suspense." In the issue of September 4, Bob is again present.

Editorially, Longstreet wrote about politics at first with almost exclusive attention, but as the active hope of nullification subsided he became less interested in politics and more and more interested in life in general. Judge James Jackson could remember thirty-five years after the event, how he, as a boy, had winced under the fierce political scorn which Longstreet had in the mid-thirties heaped upon one of his uncles running for Congress on the Federal ticket.[2]

---
[1] *State Rights Sentinel*, 21 August, 1834.
[2] James Jackson, "Life and Character of Rev. Dr. A. B. Longstreet, An Address delivered at Oxford, Georgia, July 18, 1871" (in Willam T. Smithson [editor], *In Memoriam Andrew, Longstreet, Smith* (New York, 1871)), 24.

But the editor touched upon everything. He became greatly interested in railway projects and did all he could to advance them.¹ He tackled any abuse that came to his attention. Once he inquired editorially of a prominent citizen if it would be possible to hire as a wet-nurse one of the citizen's "two negro wives." This sort of thing, he protested, he disliked to publish, but believed in some cases necessary. A man who wants to be spared much publicity should behave himself. He understood that the gentleman in question had two negro wives, was sure, if that report were true (*if* is the word he uses), "no satire is too severe for him."² This is the method of a fanatic.

His interests in religion, and in law, and in publicity soon swept him into the triple-natured work of a public moralist. One of his principal activities in this regard was concerned with his enmity to the custom of duelling. If he even suspected people of intending a duel, he hastened to swear out warrants against them. Some most reputable people thought these activities impertinent. " 'Swear me,' one of the men so accused, no less a person than Governor Cumming, said to the magistrate. The Governor then stated that the affidavit of Judge Longstreet was false, and it was not the first time he had heard of the Judge making such affidavits in similar cases. The magistrate rebuked the Governor, who replied to him, 'I know what I say, sir; take down my testimony.' "³

Toward the latter part of his career as an editor, Longstreet was accused in the writings of his political opponents of having lost his old democratic faith and gone over with James Madison "against the people," this, by stating openly, "with either folly or independence, that the people are not fit to govern themselves." For proof, doubters were referred to the *State Rights Sentinel* and to the *Federalist*.⁴ In 1836, between 22 and 29 July, the *Sentinel* was sold to William E. Jones, since January, 1835, editor of the *Chronicle*. On 3 January, 1837, this editor merged his two papers, making them,

---

¹ *State Rights Sentinel*, May, 1836; Theodore D. Jervey, *Life Robert Y. Hayne* (New York, 1909), 469.

² *State Rights Sentinel*, 26 April, 1836.

³ Benjamin F. Perry, "Judge Longstreet and his Malignantly False Criticisms" (in *Nineteenth Century Magazine*, Charleston, February, 1870), 725.

⁴ *State Rights Sentinel*, 15 March, 1836.

as the *Daily Chronicle and Sentinel*, the first daily newspaper in Augusta.[1] Longstreet had gone into the newspaper business to effect a definite political end, and as soon as it became evident that that end could not be effected, he abandoned his means, with, he stated, "much loss of time, and some loss of money."[2] So far as he was concerned the paper had always been primarily a "political" one, taken charge of, he wrote in 1843, "in the hope of convincing the majority of this state at least, and all the candid readers of the United States, that the much-abused doctrine of Nullification was the true doctrine of our government."[3] But his interest in politics was not by any means dead. He was writing political articles all of his life, signing them sometimes with his own name and at other times with names that were assumed.[4]

In the late thirties, apparently upon the request of his friend Mirabeau Buonaparte Lamar, then President of Texas, Longstreet wrote Lamar a letter setting forth his opinion as to whether or not Texas should enter the Union. The tone of this letter reveals much. To the writer of it, nationalism is in no sense idealistic. Texas is to take all she can get from Mexico, and is to stay out of the Union until she can make a good trade for entering. There are, in fact, more advantages out than in. The North and the South are unalterably opposed to each other. One section, subsisting upon the other and totally dependent upon it, yet inexplicably manages to control it. The Constitution was set up as a safeguard against such an eventuality, but party government was not long in learning how to evade the provisions it disliked. Ours is worse than any monarchical despotism of the past; with us, no one person can be held to account for anything. A government should have a legislative assemblage to represent each of its large economic interests, one, say, agricultural, one manufacturing, one commercial. No bill not acceptable to all three of these assemblages should become a law. The final disadvantage of entering the Union is that she is already near an end, "cor-

---

[1] Jones, *Augusta*, 297.
[2] *Yale Records*, 10.
[3] *Ibid.*
[4] *Augusta Chronicle*, 2 November, 1837.

ruption from heart to extremities." From one cause or another, no republic endures long. In our case, collapse will be due to the national policy of immigration, of accepting the filth of the world, like rank poison, into the body politic. "Only persons born in this realm should be given a hand in our government. Let Texas save herself by remaining apart from a nation so near catastrophe." Keep to yourselves and very likely you will in time have many distracted states petitioning to be let into your confederacy.[1]

No one so despondent of the political organization he is a part of, can give it any great passionate concern. Indeed, at the time of his Lamar letter, Longstreet held the political outlook of the United States too inevitably bad any longer to command his chief interest. And besides, other matters of more subjective appeal were now engrossing him. He was absorbed in religion.

This emphasis went hand in hand with a desire for general moral uplift. As he looked about him he saw that unquestionably one of the most flagrant abuses in Georgia, as is likely to be the case in any undisciplined society, was the excessive use of alcoholic liquors. To meet this evil, there had sprung up a number of temperance societies, fostered at first chiefly by the Baptist denomination, the Methodists asserting that their being Methodists was of itself enough to assure everything that might be implied by their belonging to the strictest temperance society. It was estimated in 1830 that the per capita consumption of liquors in Georgia was about five gallons a year.[2] In the first part of 1829, what proved to be a very active temperance society was organized in Augusta, with Longstreet as one of its chief promoters. In November, 1832, Longstreet having gone as a delegate from the Augusta society to the state convention which met at Milledgeville, was elected to the state presidency, an office which he occupied as long as the state society existed. Adiel Sherwood, who in the old Greensboro days had refused to immerse Longstreet, was there, too, an active member of the organization, later to serve under Longstreet as state-secretary. Others of the state officers then

---
[1] Mirabeau Buonaparte Lamar, *Papers* (Austin, Texas, 1922), I, 1-5.
[2] Scomp, *King Alcohol*, 257.

elected were Joseph Henry Lumpkin, and William Turner, of Eatonton.[1] At these conventions, also, most probably Longstreet renewed his acquaintance with Josiah Flournoy of Eatonton, who, though the owner of vast business interests, was, in a few years now, to neglect all of them for many months while he literally canvassed the state in his buggy in behalf of temperance. These associations were to Longstreet matters of the keenest pleasure. He could remember all of the children, it seemed to him, of nearly every delegate present, and could inquire of their fathers about them, by name. He could feel sure that the children would be thoroughly glad to know he had inquired. Half the children in Middle Georgia, it seems, had sat on his knee and listened to him play his flute, and some of these he had tried to teach how to play the flute themselves.

The state society never did thrive. In the first place, its members were for moderation rather than for complete abstinence. Longstreet, indeed, as its President, became, somewhat ostentatiously, and not with the fullest Godspeed of his preacher brethren, a "Tee-Totaller;"[2] but long before the war he went back to taking an occasional taste of wine.[3] Furthermore, it was reported, or generally understood to be a part of the National Temperance Society, which people said was identified with abolitionism, the object of all suspicion. On this account, only three delegates attended the convention called in Milledgeville, November, 1835. These gentlemen took it upon themselves to disavow any connection with the American Temperance Society and hoped that, as a result of their action, slander would "shut its foul mouth."[4] But in spite of this rebuff, slander talked on; things went from bad to worse until, in August, 1837, the Augusta society, because of the suspension of the state society, had to be completely reorganized.

The meetings of the Augusta society were always marked by an "address." It is somewhat tragic to note the faith that those men had in the bare matter of talking. At the Univer-

---

[1] Scomp, *King Alcohol*, 261-2.
[2] *Southern Christian Advocate*, 6 January 1843.
[3] Charles Woodward Hutson, Letter, 5 November, 1921.
[4] Scomp, *King Alcohol*, 303-5.

sity of Georgia the same mental attitude made itself manifest. In an old diary, kept by one of the students there during the forties, there is a complete record of a college temperance society. So far as the diary shows, the chief activities of the society consisted in listening to addresses and marching impressively about the streets of Athens, under a silken banner which had been presented to the society by some fair young lady—wrought by her own hands.[1]

But Longstreet really did something. He was constantly writing articles condemning people who threaten violence to legislators favoring Temperance legislation,[2] publishing Temperance propaganda in his newspaper,[3]—long philosophical disquisitions on the subject, written by distinguished professors, brisk and persistent notices of society meetings, and so forth,—which kept the agitation always in the public mind.

In his temperance interests too, however, Longstreet gave evidence of a trait that was very marked in his character. Just as he had not let his rapture over Lafayette's visit prevent his turning the visit to good account financially, so would he not let his enthusiasm for temperance sweep away his sense of values. Since he was state president of the temperance societies in Georgia he was naturally somewhat condemned when he began printing conspicuously in his paper an illustrated advertisement of some manufacturer desiring to sell whiskey stills. The noise of this must have become pretty general. Longstreet would not evade. In a convenient issue of his paper, he simply made his puppet Bob Short voice the public consternation at his course. "Will the Editor of the *Sentinel*, alias the *President* of the *Georgia Temperance Society*," asks Bob, 8 March, 1836, "be good enough to state how long it will be necessary to adorn his columns with the picture of a still?" This question was answered in a note: "Just as long as it pays the printer's tariff. Bob will please notice that the still in our paper is a very small one; just fit for rose-water and peppermint—not whiskey." The idea of editorial re-

---

[1] Diary James Daniel Frederick [Ms. in possession Mrs. Oscar McKenzie, Montezuma, Georgia].
[2] *Southern Christian Advocate*, 2 August, 1839.
[3] *State Rights Sentinel*, 22 May, 1834.

sponsibility for matter advertised had not then developed, but in spite of that fact it is difficult to understand how Longstreet could so prostitute his official position in the society to his financial gain, as to make this inconsistency the matter of pleasant jests. To jest out was by all odds the easiest way to free himself.

VI

GEORGIA SCENES

When at Yale, Longstreet had frequently amused friends of his in New Haven by tales of Georgia and Georgians. At the time, there was over the entire existing country much national patriotism, and Georgia as the youngest and least understood of the colonies was, by consequence, an item of great interest to the communities that were more definitely established. And it is likely even that the circumstances of General Oglethorpe's philanthropic experiment still appealed to the romantic imagination of a nation steeped in philosophy about the merit of the natural man. Cooper, at least, of the writers of the period largely given over in American fiction to the "matter" of the Revolution, felt bound to recognize the existence of Georgians, but hardly knew how to characterize them. He finally hit upon the plan of making them rather intensified Virginians, one hundred per cent pure passion. Hawthorne, too, for some reason, introduces into one of his stories some Georgians, who, "having chilled their southern blood on the top of Mount Washington, descend to the inn, where they hold an album between them and favor the company with the few specimens of its contents, which they considered ridiculous enough to be worth hearing. One extract met with deserved applause."[1] Hawthorne knew by this time that a Georgian had simply got to be funny. But aside from their disposition to comedy, his Georgians are, for the most part, nobodies, mere persons from a long way off, who fail to indicate their nativity further than by mentioning perhaps something about a "nigger."

As a political entity the state had fared worse. Georgia has always occupied a unique, if not always a favorable, place in the national imagination. Franklin stigmatized it as settled

---

[1] Sketches from Memory in *Mosses from an Old Manse*; Cooper, *The Spy*.

"with broken shop keepers and other insolvent debtors, many of indolent and idle habits, taken out of the jails. . . ."[1] Later, Georgia's half-hearted participation in the pre-Revolutionary demonstrations against the British won universal distrust for her. The fire company of Charleston resolved that "no provision be shipped from this province in any pretence whatever to that infamous colony G—g—a, . . ."[2]

The first senator whom Georgia sent to the seat of the National government had testified concerning the state as follows: "The state of Georgia is a damned rascal. I bought her and sold her, and will buy her and sell her again when I please."[3] . . . Beverly Tucker was sure, for his part, that Georgia had her price. Virginia, he wrote Simms in 1851, had "sunk in the slough of democracy" and Georgia had "been bought."[4]

Longstreet's presentation of Georgia character and manners proved, when it came, so much more in accord with universal experience than anything that preceded it that the older traditions largely gave way like impostors until time and forgetfulness had made it again possible for them to walk abroad. But the romantic idea never perished wholly. In a book called *Waymarks in the Life of a Wanderer* (Philadelphia, 1851), one can learn that Georgia men were "tall, large, sunburnt and swarthy," that they had ebon locks, and that, even at the age of sixty, they did not lose from their "black, large and piercing eyes, any of the fire of early youth." Such men were likely to have as sisters ladies who sat the day out in huge armchairs of green velvet, with their feet resting on soft cushions. About these ladies there would be an eagle glancing of the large dark eyes, and a firm compression of the mouth that bespoke great imperiousness of character. Most likely they would have silver hair parted in the middle, and combed straight back, leaving to view a fine lofty brow. Dressed in deep mourning, only by a snowy white cap would they relieve the sableness of their attire. As you entered they would rise with all the grace of a

---
[1] Franklin, *Autobiography*.
[2] Scomp, *King Alcohol*, 165.
[3] Trent, *Simms*, 182.
[4] *Ibid.*, 186.

high-bred aristocrat and receive you with a winning smile, but when they addressed you their cold, measured tones would probably strike a chill to your heart, and make you recoil from them in spite of yourself.

But any honest soul can understand most of this for morbid falsehood. The author of the *Waymarks* has no more character than to tell approvingly at the close of her book how "the wicked Mary" (a beautiful mulatto slave who had been the mistress of one of the sub-heroes) with her son Jacob (this hero's son also) had been sold to a cotton grower in Louisiana, where, the writer reports triumphantly, "she has been placed at labor in the field, and is removed from the chance of harming Octave's young and lovely wife."

The creator of Mary and Octave was not herself a Georgian, but some Georgians, even, enjoyed the idea of presenting themselves as having a few years past (always, a few years past) been a race of philosophic spirits. Men of this race, one of the old Georgians could fancy, at times would retire from the world to bring up their children in mountain fastnesses (lest the children, one supposes, should become contaminated by the philosophic spirits making up the state's population). Sometimes they would live in great mansions situate along the bright rivers, upon the banks of which their young lady daughters, by name Iolia and Manolia, calling each other "fair nymph," walked in the early dawn gathering historical relics of the Indians. There is a book called *Manolia, or the Vale of Tallulah*,[1] that will portray for anyone interested all of this side of early Georgia life. In the Georgia inhabited by such gentlemen and such young ladies it seems that college students, named Rossius, Julius, Render, and Cassanio, were likely to fall desperately in love with hallucinations of the mist, and to debate angrily with one another in Latin, as to what was to be done when it became evident that one of them had gone stark mad on the subject of his love. At other times, they would have done as well to talk Latin. *Thou* and *thee* quite replace humble *you;* and one of the heroines of this book complains of not understanding certain "tripartite obligations," declaring

---
[1] Published Augusta, 1854.

that they "don't so well suit the genius of our republic—I prefer being left untrammeled, free to act in reference to emergencies and inclination as may be consistent,"[1] and so forth. A student lover, having mounted on a rope ladder to the window of his mist-maiden, who turns out after all to be real, explains in connection with his ardent proposal of marriage, "Philosophical explanation of thy presence was given—plausible enough in theory—they with one voice protested against my credulity."[2] A mountaineer, approached for information regarding the whereabouts of Rossius, says, from the door of his secluded cabin: "I have heard tell of no such youth. Them ravens you hear screaming over yon chasm can give you some account of him likely."[3] And, worst of all, comes this, "Thou appearest to be so well posted."[4]

To Longstreet, the intellectual outlook that produced this kind of talk must have seemed execrable. There were clearly two traditions, one valid and original, the other false and imitative. It was the valid and original one that compelled universal attention and made for Georgia a very special place in the national imagination. Curiosity about Georgia was rife everywhere. Longstreet himself had done his part in spreading it by telling tales about his state when he was at Litchfield, before student audiences often representative of the entire country.

As late as 1840, the *Southern Literary Messenger* was offering to its readers some sketches by an artist who had lately "made an extensive tour through the comparatively unknown territory of our Southern Sister." The artist himself was even more definite in the expression of his feeling that in going to Georgia he had accomplished a feat: "I have at length," he commences his first letter, published in connection with his sketches, "reached this utmost bourne of Georgia—a *terra*

---

[1] *Manolia*, 108.
[2] *Manolia*, 54.
[3] *Ibid.*, 114.
[4] *Ibid.*, 109.

(Among the things that the cruel processes of Reconstruction so effectually crushed in Georgia, the disposition to write books like *Manolia* unfortunately does not appear. From the very ashes of the war came *Antebellum Southern Life As It Was*, and soon thereafter came *St. Elmo*.)

incognita to the people of the United States. . . ." From Athens, he writes later, assuring his friend, the editor of the *Messenger*, who has evidently made anxious inquiries, that there is "nothing to apprehend for our health."[1]

Longstreet was aware of this curiosity about his state and of his ability to amuse people by anecdotes based on his local experiences. He was probably urged to set these stories into print,—his law partners and other friends in Augusta and in Georgia at large having developed for their state in particular a small edition of the desire then prevalent throughout the United States that this country develop a literary genius comparable to those of Europe. Longstreet had always had a knack of talking entertainingly, and a taste for writing. When little past his teens he had had several of his little "effusions" published in the newspapers.[2] The first of these was a letter purporting to come from two convicts, who, under sentence of death, had broken jail and escaped.[3] In New Haven, the Ingersolls had declared often that his stories should be published.[4] Possibly they were right; possibly he could do something now to further the interest of his state. At any rate, a man could try himself out.

If this particular Georgian had any intention to minimize by his book the sense of difference with which the nation at large regarded his state, he went very wide of his mark. His book really set Georgia apart more than it had ever been set apart previously—so far apart that fifty years after it was published, a young lady from South Carolina, visiting for the first time in her life relatives of hers who had long ago migrated into Georgia, could hardly reconcile herself to her failure to encounter everywhere scenes more graphically suggestive of those she had read about in Longstreet's book. On being taken from her train to the residence of her kinspeople, she passed a house which, after the good Southern fashion, had its front door wide open. "Oh," gasped the young lady, "look! why the people have portières in their houses!"

---
[1] *Southern Literary Messenger*, November, 1840, 775-7.
[2] Williams, *Advice*, 112.
[3] Mayes, *Education in Mississippi*, 206.
[4] *Yale Records*, 10.

When James Wood Davidson published in 1869 his *Living Writers of the South,* he could speak with the blandest unconsciousness of a book as being in its humor "coarse, broad, and Georgian."[1] Longstreet humorously accepted the dictum that Georgia was strange, alien, bizarre. He talks of the "Georgia language,"[2] of "Georgia humor,"[3] and so forth. No one was better aware of the state's reputation as a sort of lovable *enfant terrible* than were the Georgians themselves, and hardly anyone enjoyed humoring the joke any more than they did. Niles' *Register,* 2 July, 1831, reprinted an extract from a recent issue of *The Macon Telegraph* which shows that the appreciation of Georgia's difference was indigenous as well as foreign. "We should not have ventured," says Niles, "on the following witty, and yet good humored exhibit, had it not been the product of a Georgian." Then the quotation: "As warm weather comes on, and the bilious and bullying season approaches, the demand increases for Lee's pills and pocket pistols, and goggles and gun powder, black patches and dirk knives grow in demand. Sundry of the *beau monde* have mounted green spectacles, and a rise is expected in sword canes and epsoms. The superior courts in the different circuits are also in session, and a good deal of lawing and liquoring is going on, as well as fighting and physicking. Attorneys and physicians, it is presumed, have their hands full. We like to see all trades prosper, and in a *bil-ious* season, those of the lawyers and doctors are not the least useful. One unravels a tangled case, the other cases up a shattered limb—one dives into the bowels of a statute, the other into the state of the bowels. This bleeds a patient in the arm for the sake of his health, the other bleeds him in the pocket for the health of his estate. Gamboge and gambling are seen in the back rooms, and ginger bread jacks and judges in the public squares. Duns and dirk knives grow saucy during court week, and mayors and bailiffs feel ticklish. *Enemas* and endorsements are sought for by some, cocktails and characters sued for by others. Half-pints and hickories are flourished in these times, and teething and

---

[1] Davidson, *Living Writers,* 574.
[2] Longstreet, *Georgia Scenes,* 72.
[3] "Wax Works," *Georgia Scenes,* 200.

gouging tolerated—all for the honor of liberty and the encouragement of business."[1]

If anybody did not believe that Northerners regarded Georgians as different from other Southerners, he should reckon with the experience of one Georgian, who, going to New York, found that he was charged more for his room at his hotel as soon as the landlord found out the state of his residence.[2]

In 1830, Longstreet says, three years after he moved back to Augusta from Greensboro, he began writing his *Georgia Scenes*,[3] but the first of these scenes actually published was "The Dance," which appeared in a weekly newspaper, the Milledgeville, Georgia, *Southern Recorder*, 30 October, 1833: "The Song," "The Horse Swap," "The Turf," "The Fight," "The Turn Out," "The Character of a Native Georgian," and "The Gander Pulling" followed during the successive weeks through 15 January, 1834. Then, having commenced a paper of his own, Longstreet transferred his sketches to the *Sentinel*. The last sketch appearing in the Milledgeville paper was number VIII, and the first appearing in those issues of the *Sentinel* still in preservation, was number XI, "The Charming Creature as a Wife," the second half of which appeared 14 April, 1834, the first part, at some date prior to April 10. "Militia Drill," "The Mother and Her Child," "The Fox Hunt," "The Wax Works," "Dropping to Sleep" (a short sketch not included in the collected edition), "The Debating Society," and "A Sage Conversation" followed at irregular intervals, but consecutively so far as regards number, through 17 March, 1835. Between No. XIII, "The Mother and Her Child," and No. XIV, "The Fox Hunt," there was a silence from 2 June, 1834, to 12 February, 1835. Only two places, then, those of numbers IX and X, are left to be assigned to four sketches, "Georgia Theatrics," "The Ball," "An Interesting Interview," and "The Shooting Match." Just when these four sketches were first published has not been determined. Two of them, in all likelihood, filled the gap in the *Sentinel* in the early spring of 1834, but the other two probably appeared in some Augusta

---

[1] Niles, *Register*, 2 July, 1831, 310.
[2] *Orion*, January, 1843, 127.
[3] *Yale Records*, 10.

or Milledgeville paper before Longstreet had decided to write a series of sketches and give consecutive numbers to them.

Everybody who knew his Georgia pronounced the sketches authentic, and, with that good-humored acceptance of the primitive which campers have, decided that although they presented the state in a light less rosy than romance might sigh for, the "scenes" should be applauded. When they appeared in book form the only identification given as to their authorship was itself disarming,—"By a Native Georgian." When they had appeared in the newspapers the effort at mystification had been very elaborate, the purpose having been to make them seem the work of two different writers. All of the sketches with women as their chief characters were signed "Baldwin," and all of those with men as their chief characters were signed "Hall." Now Lyman Hall and Abraham Baldwin were two of the early Georgia patriots. Hall had signed the Declaration of Independence, while Baldwin had signed the Constitution, and also had been the state's first influential man in Congress. The Georgia origin of the whole series was too palpable not to be noticed, and it was this fact that largely propitiated Georgia critics.

It is probably true, anyway, that during a period beginning with about 1825 and extending to 1850, Georgia was in a sense less self-conscious, in a disagreeable meaning of the term, than it ever was before, or has been since. At that time Georgia held itself, and held itself justly, in many ways, as the equal of any state in the Union; and with the loss of its sense of inferiority it naturally developed a certain buoyant healthful lack of sensitiveness that permitted it for a brief period to indulge in a degree of self-criticism that came near developing, by the process of feeding on its own output, a remarkable civilization. Longstreet especially refused to surrender the privilege of attacking an evil force merely because it was in Georgia that the force existed.

The rule seems to have been that it was all right to make strictures provided you would promise better things for the future. "I wish it understood," said one of the old writers, "that I use this term, *Georgia Cracker*, with all due respect. It belongs to a class of good people with whom it has been my destiny to become intimately associated, and I know that there is much to admire and respect in their characters. . . . As a class, they are brave, generous, honest, and industrious, and withal, possessed of a sturdy patriotism. . . . In a few generations more, education will have made the mass a great people."[1]

In *Georgia Scenes*, the new day is represented as already having dawned. The author cleverly emphasized the fact that his "scenes" dealt with a Georgia that had passed, an evasion which was made much of by persons who would otherwise have felt offended. Sherwood in his "Chamber-of-Commerce" *Gazetteer* of 1837 says expressly that Longstreet's book "represents the customs and manners of former days—days when there was less refinement than now."[2]

The news of Longstreet's connection with the stories, in spite of all his ruses, was not long in leaking out. In the preface to his first edition, though still refusing to give his name, he speaks as though the mystification were then mostly a thing of the past. Two years later, Sherwood says in the most matter-of-fact way that the "scenes" are "ascribed to the pen of Judge Longstreet";[3] and the authorship is formally stated by Longstreet's friend, Thompson, in the *Southern Literary Messenger*, July, 1840. Before that, it can be gathered from Thompson's article, the secret was public property in Augusta.

It was in 1835, then, that the "scenes" first appeared in book form, issued from the office of the *State Rights Sentinel*, Longstreet's newspaper. "For the last six months," the author says in his preface, "I have been importuned by persons from all quarters of the state to give [these sketches] to the public in the present form." He apologizes for possible errors in printing, but takes it for granted, surely, that the world understands that this whole matter of literary effort is, in the life of a man as busy as he is, only an incident. Truly, his writing had been dictated by the serious object of presenting to future times an accurate account of an interesting phase of the world's history, and truly he had written with an eye to "recommend-

---
[1] William T. Thompson, *Major Jones' Chronicles of Pineville*, Preface.
[2] Sherwood, *Gazetteer*, 43, 84.
[3] *Ibid.*, 84.

ing" it to the possible readers, but after all the thing was only a slight passing episode.

In book form, the sketches immediately attained wide popularity. The Charleston *Southern Literary Journal*, January, 1836, declared extravagantly in favor of it. "The author of this work," the review said, "is a humorist, and paints nature to the life. . . . Each story has a peculiar interest attached to it—a grateful freshness and originality; so that attention never flags, but is kept fully awake from the beginning to the close of the book, which, though containing several hundred pages, will, we dare say, be generally read at a single sitting. We may make this assertion with perfect confidence as to all laughter-loving philosophers who are in search of the rare and golden ore of genuine wit. The irresistibility ludicrous in composition has seldom been attained in greater perfection than by this writer; and the scenes introduced would, in nearly every instance, form appropriate subjects for the pencil of Hogarth."[1] A year and a half later the same writer still thinks of the *Scenes* as surpassing the *Pickwick Papers* "in spirit, in originality, and in all the characteristics of genuine humor."[2]

Poe even was vastly pleased with the book that had so mysteriously reached him. (Longstreet was evidently proud of his work, after all, and wanted to know what the leading journal of the South would think of it.) The author, Poe says, "is a clever fellow, imbued with a spirit of the truest humor; and endowed moreover with an exquisitely discriminative and penetrating understanding of character in general, and of Southern character in particular. And we do not mean to speak of *human* character exclusively. To be sure, our Georgian is *au fait* here too—he is learned in all things appertaining to the biped without feathers. In regard especially to that class of Southwestern mammalia who come under the generic appellation 'savagerous wild cats,' he is a very Theophrastus in duo decimo. But he is not the less at home in other matters. Of geese and ganders he is the La Bruyère, and of good-for-nothing horses, the Rochefoucault.

---
[1] *Southern Literary Journal*, March, 1836.
[2] *Ibid.*, July, 1837.

"Seriously, if this book were printed in England it would make the fortune of its author. We positively mean what we say,—and are quite sure of being sustained in our opinion by all proper judges who may be so fortunate as to obtain a copy of the 'Georgia Scenes,' and who will be at the trouble of sifting their peculiar merits from amid the gaucheries of a Southern publication. Seldom—perhaps never in our lives— have we laughed as immoderately over any book as over the one now before us. If these scenes have produced such effect upon *our* cachinnatory nerves—upon *us* who are not 'of the merry mood' and moreover have not been unused to the perusal of somewhat similar things, we are at no loss to image what a hubbub they would occasion in the uninitiated regions of Cockaigne. And what would Christopher North say?—ah, what would Christopher North say? that is the question. Certainly not a word. But we can fancy the pursing up of his lips, and the long, loud, and jovial resonation of his wicked and uproarious ha ha's!"

After discussing the Preface, which he thinks speaks well for the "Georgian taste" in its declaration of the popularity of the *Scenes* in that state, Poe takes up the various sketches individually, bestowing high praise everywhere.[1]

"In style and subject matter," say the Duyckincks, "the *Georgia Scenes* are vivid, humorous descriptions, by a good story teller, who employs voice, manner, and a familiar knowledge of popular dialogue in their narration. They are quaint, hearty . . . genial."[2]

They were all, Longstreet's favorable critics, joining a unanimous chorus. James Jackson, a distinguished Georgia contemporary of Judge Longstreet, thought the author of *Georgia Scenes* the greatest, he said, "of those writers of the English tongue, who assaying to paint the manners and customs of the time in which they lived, have used the pencil of wit and the brush of humor." The characters are not of universal types and consequently will never be so widely known as are the characters of Shakespeare, he thought, yet, "wherever known

---
[1] *Southern Literary Messenger*, March, 1836.
[2] Duyckincks, *Cyclopedia*, II, 314.

they will live as long as Falstaff and Prince Hal."[1] Somebody, "Jo of Mississippi," sent to the *Southern Literary Messenger* in the forties, a sketch called "My First Frolic in School." Addressing the editor, the author, after saying that perhaps his sketch is too frivolous for the *Messenger,* urges "the high sanction of the great Longstreet in giving such chronicles of our youthful days." Jo's sketch was published, "although," an editorial note explained, "we cannot compliment Jo of Mississippi by saying that he yet equals 'the Great Longstreet.'"[2] Stephen F. Miller states in his *Bench and Bar* of Georgia that in trying to collect information about old times in Georgia to be included in his volumes, he had, by various persons to whom he had applied for information, been referred repeatedly to Judge Longstreet "as the only writer who can dress things up to perfection."

Learned professors of "Metaphysics, Logic and Rhetoric," like Maximilian Laborde of the University of South Carolina, spoke, too, of the book, with such enthusiasm as learned professors can muster: "It is probable," he thinks, "that no Southern book has had a larger circulation than the *Georgia Scenes,* and I am sure that to few works of the kind have been accorded greater merit. . . . The sketches are from nature and are given as few could give them. We have the highest skill of the artist, and we know not where to look for more complete delineations. His portraits are perfect, and thousands among us will bear witness to their exact fidelity, nor have we been without a personal observation which would give us some right to pass a judgment upon them. To us they seem to breathe and to speak, and without effort to rise up in all their fullness and proportion. . . . In this peculiar field of labor none among us have achieved a higher success."[3]

It was felt that a good way to popularize a magazine was to have it publish some of the *Scenes.*[4] Persons wishing to promote a periodical appealed to Longstreet for contributions,[5]

---
[1] Jackson, "Rev. Dr. Longstreet," 20.
[2] *Southern Literary Messenger,* February, 1845, 109–12.
[3] Laborde, *South Carolina College,* 462–4.
[4] *Southern Literary Messenger,* January, 1844, 43.
[5] Smith, *Pierce,* 100–3.

and took it as an occasion for considerable talk if they had made an effort even, "to procure some of his writings."[1] They recognized so well Longstreet's popularity that if they received a contribution from him just as an issue was ready to go to press, they would change the entire make-up of the number in order to include the new material. They recognized so well the sanctity of his writings as the output of a literary artist, that they would print anything he sent them, however poor it was and however much too long. "The privilege so liberally accorded by the writer of cutting and carving his tale at pleasure," one of the old magazines published as a footnote with a Longstreet sketch, "we have seen no sufficient reason to exercise."[2] Once the Judge was so gravely troubled with his eyes that it was reported he might lose his eyesight. This "calamity," says one of the editors in commenting upon the news, "heaven forfend, not only for the sake of himself and family, but for the sake of the whole South; aye, the whole country."[3] He became the sort of person to be mentioned in groups of distinguished writers, with Simms and others, as constituting "an unrivalled galaxy of talent."[4] Sober reviewers thought him capable of "elevating the standard of literary excellence and diffusing the principles of correct taste."[5]

The *Scenes* appealed to everybody. An established carpenter who had young men working for him, and boarding in his house, would sometimes read at night some of the *Scenes* to his assembled household. This was a great treat. One of the young carpenters could remember it fifty years afterwards,—how the other young carpenters and how everybody else would laugh and laugh till the tears came.

Poe complained that one of the characters in the *Scenes* was not peculiarly Georgian, with the air that all of the others were. But this could hardly have been true. The book was too wide in its appeal. It immediately became popular in the North as well as in the South. There, by 1840, the demand for a

---
[1] *Magnolia*, September, 1842.
[2] *Ibid*.
[3] *Magnolia*, December, 1842, 396.
[4] *Southern Field and Fireside Index*, Vol. 1, 2.
[5] A. W. Dillard, "William Gilmore Simms and A. B. Longstreet" (in *Nineteenth Century Magazine*, Charleston, October, 1870), p. 425.

new edition of it had become so urgent that the publishers would not delay printing any longer, in the hope, which had been held out to them, that the author would revise the work as first printed in Augusta.[1] The Harpers issued during the first half of 1840 an edition which they called "the second," out of deference to the 1835 publication in Augusta.

Now for the first time appeared the illustrations, done by E. H. Hyde. These pen and ink drawings are as curious and interesting as their age and their having been done by an unimaginative man not acquainted with his subject matter can make them, but they do not properly illustrate Longstreet's text, nor do they present the most striking episodes of the stories. This fact was noted and deprecated by Thompson when the volume appeared,[2] but the American audience in general was one hardened to all sorts of discrepancies.

On its appearance in the North the book was immediately recognized as authentic and worthy of serious attention. John C. Calhoun, thinking the time had arrived for doing his friend a good turn, suggested to the authorities at Yale that they give Longstreet some honorary degree. The suggestion seeming altogether to the point, the Trustees conferred the degree of Doctor of Laws upon him at the Commencement of 1841. "I am aware," wrote President Day, with some hit possibly at Harvard and its LL.D. for President Jackson, "I am aware that these academic honors are liable to a diminution of their intrinsic value by being distributed with too lavish a hand. But this college aims to make a selection of men of such distinguished merit as will *confer* honor rather than receive it by having their names enrolled in the list of favorites."[3] In the North, *Georgia Scenes* was an item that the knowing simply had to be familiar with.

Subsequent editions by the Harpers, all branded as the "second," appeared in New York in 1842, 1846, 1850, 1854, 1857, 1858, 1860, and 1884, and in 1897 there appeared another branded as "a new edition from new plates." An edition was also published in Atlanta, Ga., in 1894.

---

[1] Note by Publishers, *Edition* 1840, v.
[2] *Southern Literary Messenger*, July, 1840.
[3] Fitzgerald, *Judge Longstreet*, 200-1.

Bishop Fitzgerald, Longstreet's first biographer, personal friend of Longstreet's family, was a wise and sympathetic man, aware of life in many of its widest implications and familiar with many aspects of its racy parochialness. His opinion of Longstreet's book, written nearly sixty years after the book was published, is, then, worth a great deal. He practically endorses what had been said by the others.

"The fidelity of these sketches to nature," the Bishop says, "is recognized by every reader who has any knowledge of the people of whom and of which he wrote. . . . On their first appearance they were recognized as masterpieces of their kind, and thousands of Georgia homes re-echoed with the mirth they provoked. The sketches were written at an age when all enjoyment is most intense, and the intense zest of the writer is caught by the reader. In [some of the] sketches you almost hear the laughter of the crowd at the broader passages of coarse rollicking fun while you see the smile that plays over the features of the author in the lighter and subtler touches that now and then give a special charm to his page. True humor is never wholly separated from genuine pathos, and there are pathetic touches in *Georgia Scenes* that go straight to the heart.

"The dialect is perfectly rendered—a dialect that yet lingers in some parts of rural Georgia. The dialogue exhibits the perfect art that conceals art. The dramatic instinct was possessed by Judge Longstreet in no small degree. Every character he sketches is consistent with itself."[1]

The inevitable comparison to make for *Georgia Scenes* is with Addison's *Spectator* and perhaps to some less degree, in matters of style, with Wirt's *Letters of a British Spy*. Addison's "great and only end," he himself said, "was moral, to banish vice and ignorance out of the territories of Great Britain." Longstreet's professed aim was in the main historical, to give a realistic, comprehensive account of life as he knew it, to leave for the future[2] a record of the "ways of the

---
[1] Fitzgerald, *Judge Longstreet*, 88–9.
[2] Longstreet, *Georgia Scenes*, 178, 208.

common walks of life . . . during the first fifty years of our Republic."[1]

But in most ways the aim of *Georgia Scenes* was as moral as was that of the *Spectator*. Longstreet is always beatified in recording a transition from "vice and folly to virtue and holiness,"[2] expands properly on recording the father's declaration to his son that one is under no condition to "play the coward or the traitor to save his property."[3] At times he is unabashedly a preacher: "Whence comes this gibberish?" he asks in speaking of "baby talk."[4] Drunkenness is an all-destroying vice . . . which "I flatter myself if I should live to number ten years more, I shall see . . . driven entirely from the higher walks of life at least, if not from all grades of society."[5] The modern dances seem to him abominable. He is "happy to say," in passing, "that the waltz has met with very little encouragement in Georgia as yet; the gallopade with none." "Ye fair of my native land!" he continues, "ye daughters of a modest race! Blush them away from the soil which your mothers honored by their example, and consecrated with their ashes. Born to woman's loftiest destinies, it ill becomes you to stoop from your high estate to ape the indecencies of Europe's slaves." Humor, he writes, or at least publishes in his paper, is only valid when it is designed to promote the reader's improvement either in correcting certain propensities, or in leading him to reflect upon the proper course to be pursued as a member of social and public circles. There is no better way to whip a person into line than to laugh at him.[6]

Longstreet wanted his sketches to be interesting (let his tales "enliven the family fireside"),[7] but this part of his work was always subsidiary to their faithfulness as a record and to the likelihood of their being preserved. He "used some little art in order to recommend them to the reader of my own times," knowing that "the chance of their surviving the author

---

[1] Fitzgerald, *Judge Longstreet*, 164–5.
[2] Longstreet, *Georgia Scenes*, "Georgia Theatrics."
[3] *Georgia Scenes*, "Turn Out."
[4] *Georgia Scenes*, "Family Picture."
[5] *Georgia Scenes*, "Interesting Interview."
[6] Longstreet, *Mitten*, 185.
[7] *Georgia Scenes*, "Fox Hunt."

would be increased in proportion to their popularity upon their first appearance."[1]

Though he wrote with Addison as his model, Longstreet is in a way broader than the man he patterned on. He writes for a general audience, both as to time and space, while Addison looks chiefly to the British Isles in the eighteenth century. Longstreet always has in his mind people who do not live in Georgia, and do not know Georgia ways; he has numerous footnotes, in the newspaper versions just as in the book versions of his sketches, explaining various words and phrases, *Georgianisms*. And certainly he has most plainly stated his desire that the sketches reach into the future. He used to tell his friends of his desire that through his writings "we may be seen and heard by our posterity two hundred years hence just as we are."[2]

And, too, Longstreet will write of things that Addison's classical viewpoint would have rejected as unfit subject matter, a case in which perhaps narrowness serves Addison well. Addison wrote of a time more sophisticated and intrinsically more interesting than the one treated of by Longstreet—one more in accord with the likely subsequent developments of society. Leaving aside any questions as to the two men's ability, it is apparent that Addison had an advantage over Longstreet in that he could write about and for persons of some degree of intellectual subtlety, while Longstreet, in view of his own desire for accuracy, and of his recognition of the necessity for a certain mechanical contemporary popularity, was obliged to write about and for persons whose intellectual subtlety was slight.

In many ways, however, other than in their moral outlooks, the men are similar. Both of them wrote of real characters and real incidents in fanciful combinations. "The persons introduced in these papers," Dr. Johnson says of the *Spectator*, "were not merely ideal; they were then known and conspicuous in various stations."[3] This is exactly the case with *Georgia*

---

[1] Longstreet, *Georgia Scenes*, iii.
[2] *Southern Literary Messenger*, July, 1840.
[3] Johnson, *Lives of the Poets: Addison*.

Scenes.[1] Addison, like Longstreet, though to a less degree, had his eye on history. "There is no question," Addison wrote, as if giving an excuse for his writing, "but our great grandchildren will be very curious to know why. . . ."[2]

Both Addison and Longstreet are genial and kindly and practical—determined to put their effort only upon such ideals as are possible of attainment, only upon such abuses as can be annihilated. The hopeless yearning of men for things they comprehend but dimly, the grotesquely irremediable maladjustment of humanity to the conditions it must exist under, the vague poignant tragedy of human uncertainty as to its end, the maniacal fury of humanity to be away from its fixed impediments, all of the grand passions of life, both of these men simply dismissed, but dismissed in no mood of cynicism or despair. Confronted with these mighty matters, Longstreet and Addison both of them turned away to contemplate the goodness and majesty of God, and, after the immemorial habit of humanity, found themselves comforted. These more ponderous things in life, they held, God in his own time would shape more intelligibly, and in the meantime it behooves good men to do such patting of the sides of this plastic clay as they believe not too presumptuous. And this, after all, is the type of man who is most "respectable," most completely endorsed by his contemporaries. Since nobody is so ridiculous as to conceive of life as perfect, it is necessary to regard it in one of three ways: hopefully, as Addison did; despondently, as Swift did; or indifferently, as did Congreve. Longstreet is in this completely Addisonian.

Stylistically, as a literary artist, Longstreet follows Addison only at a very great distance. The writing of his sketches, undertaken only as an incident of his work as a lawyer and newspaper editor, was done at times when he was away from his regular place of residence, and subject, most probably, to countless interruptions. He wrote often without mapping out his work in advance, sometimes shifting his whole concept of

---

[1] Laborde, *University of South Carolina*, 463; Fitzgerald, *Judge Longstreet*, 165–6; Jones, *Augusta*, 169.
[2] John Dennis, *Age of Pope*, 128.

a *Scene,* if it was being published in instalments, while it was in process of publication.[1]

The literary style of *Georgia Scenes* shows certainly that the author wrote hastily, and either in ignorance or with little consistent self-criticism. Here are some of his rhetorical blunders: "The hymn is given out and sung by the congregation."[2] "He was much the most active of the two."[3] "Bill wanted the room which Bob's finger occupied for breathing."[4] "He sat Ned down emphatically."[5] The "caravan moved forward leaving poor Curt in loneliness, wifeless, childless, helpless, and in money penniless."[6] "Five sittings ended nearly in the same way to the utter amazement of the senior."[7] His constructions are very muddled: "After proposing to go round in either way without my approbation [my horse] at length raised his forefeet and threw them lazily over the log, coming down upon them as the white bear does in breaking ice, and stopped right astride of the log." "The roof was covered by clapboards also, and retained in their places by heavy clapboards placed on them."[8] An exaggerated disposition to italicize bespeaks a failure to arrange the sentences within themselves so that emphasis will naturally fall where desired.

But withal the writing is entertaining. The sentences are varied in structure and neither excessively long nor excessively short, averaging, except in the conversational portions of the book, about twenty words each. Two or three such sentences will make a paragraph. The style is simple and pleasing, "destitute," a contemporary Augusta criticism says, "of the false gloss and affected sentimentalism so lavishly employed by a certain school of modern writers" [whose sentences are crowded with] "redundant superlatives and words of original coinage." Nevertheless there were enough footnotes and

---

[1] *Southern Field and Fireside*, 8 October, 1859.
[2] *Georgia Scenes*, 48.
[3] *Georgia Scenes*, 57.
[4] *Georgia Scenes*, 67.
[5] Longstreet, *Mitten*, 121.
[6] *Ibid.*, 208.
[7] *Ibid.*, 357.
[8] *Southern Literary Messenger*, July, 1840.

quotations and literary allusions to give 1835 the idea that it was being edified as well as being amused.

Longstreet indulges little in description that does not make towards the point of the story; most of the adjectives tell how things strike the mind rather than how they strike the sense (if psychology will admit of the distinction); one hears of *kind, detestable, thrifty* more than of *pretty, green, glittering*. But when he has occasion to do so, the author describes things graphically. Witness Darby Anvil, a candidate for the Georgia Legislature. "When he mounted the rostrum his appearance was quite unparliamentary. He was dressed in a full suit of mud-colored homespun. . . . His pantaloons were supported only by his hips . . . and even with this advantage at the one extremity, they were full five inches too short at the other. They reached his socks only when he stood firm on both legs —that is, when they were suffered to hang in a right line— but as Darby rarely used both limbs at the same time, there was an alternate flashing of naked skin from either limb of the most agreeable and bewitching novelty. His vest was more uncourteous to his pantaloons than were his socks, for no portion of Darby's body could induce it to come within an inch of them. His undergarment acted as a mediator between them, and gracefully rolled out into the vacant space, seemingly to encircle the orator with a sash of coarse but clean white cloth . . ." and so forth, at length.[1]

Taine has said that a person writing English may know that he is writing for a sermon-loving people, and that he can therefore concentrate his abilities on some aim other than the one of not being tiresome. Addison, it seemed to Taine, availed himself of this knowledge. Longstreet is guilty of much sermonizing in his *Georgia Scenes,* but, though he may seem disgusting or insignificant, he will hardly prove tiresome to anyone who will accept the actuality of the characters (for the doing of which there is valid warrant in the testimony of Longstreet's contemporaries), and who can overlook his somewhat antiquated technique.

The principle of surprise, Longstreet thinks, he can push

---

[1] Longstreet, *Stories with a Moral,* 77-8.

only about half through his story; he takes occasion at due intervals to inform the reader as to the true state of affairs.[1] The principle of ending his stories when he has come to the conclusion of the episode upon which they are based, he deliberately avoided; some comment he will have, some epilogue, some sort of direction as to how to get back to reality. The principle of avoiding a too obtrusive didacticism he seems never to have considered. "Thanks to the Christian religion, to schools, to colleges, and benevolent associations," he blurts out at the end of the extremely robustious sketch, "The Fight," "such scenes of barbarism and cruelty as that which I have been just describing are now of rare occurrence, though they may still be met with in some of the new counties. Wherever they prevail they are a disgrace to that community. The peace-officers who countenance them deserve a place in the penitentiary." . . .

Though it is largely the incident that supplies the force of some of the best sketches, it is in the characterization that the humor of *Georgia Scenes* is most evident. The characters, which are no more slavishly consistent than those of a short sketch must be if they are to produce any impression, have in some cases attained the dignity of being typical. Ransy Sniffle is an almost final portrait of a man given to stirring up personal discord, and Uncle Tommy in the same degree represents the wiseacre, who, by ambiguous prophecies, manages always to come out on top. Ned Brace is the arch practical joker; the Charming Creature, in the eyes of the pre-feminists, at least, the arch fool wife.

In all humor are certain traits which are constant. Everywhere the corrective instinct in some guise or other (if only in that of preaching at the reader not to preach) makes itself manifest; everywhere the hand of the world is turned against people who function not humanly but mechanically; and humor has taken for its duty the business of holding up as an object-lesson all men who persistently move like automatons and puppets. Everywhere on this earthly stage, unsophisticated men—whether their unsophistication be social or moral—are

---

[1] *Georgia Scenes*, 44.

fit butts for the jeering interpretation of Punchinello. This is universal. Universal also are certain stock devices for provoking amusement. With Longstreet, for instance, proper names are squeezed dry of their possibilities in humor, a very talkative man being called Major Loquax, or some such name, boarding-house keepers being called Mrs. Bull, Mrs. Fish, or Mrs. Bacon; at times, very long personal names are of themselves offered as inducements to mirth; at times,—to illustrate further Longstreet's dependence upon the readier devices,— at times pregnancy is suggested, and when it is, there is always occasion for sly and witty glances.

Historically, *Georgia Scenes* is precisely what the author meant it for, a very valuable source-book of the social status of Georgia in the first fifty years of the Republic,—and incidentally, not of Georgia only. The author is determined to give an honest report. Clayton had given such a cross-section in his *Mysterious Picture,* but that book, somehow, had not had enough story interest to it, was not quite enough of the soil, was too much of a sermon. Longstreet would have his book entertaining as well as documentary, but, after all, primarily a document. "For the honor of my contemporaries," he says, "I would register none of [our country's] crimes or its follies; but in noticing the peculiarities of the age in which I live, candour constrains me[1] . . . I should certainly omit such expressions as this could I do so with historic fidelity; but the peculiarities of the times of which I am writing cannot be faithfully represented without them. In recording these things, *as they are, truth* requires me. . . ."[2]

From the standpoint of literary history, the importance of *Georgia Scenes* is even greater. Appearing almost as early as *Major Jack Downing,* it develops an aspect of American life— the frontier—that has been more productive of wit than has even the typical Yankee. Seba Smith's *Major Downing,* published at first in the newspapers just as *Georgia Scenes* was, was the preeminent representative of a more or less general literary tradition in New England. Both of these productions

---

[1] *Georgia Scenes,* 178.
[2] *Georgia Scenes,* 47.

are of portentous influence in the formation of the American type of humor.

Longstreet and *Major Downing* exhibit traits generally catalogued as peculiarly American. Surprise is evident in *Georgia Scenes* throughout; the main incident of the first sketch turns out to be a hoax; exaggeration finds voice in the author's protesting that to forget a disagreeable song he had heard he had been obliged to take sixty drops of laudanum;[1] the serious statement of trivial circumstance is apparent in Longstreet's explanation that "the custom of kissing, as practiced in these days by the *amiables,* is borrowed from the French and by them from the Judas."[2] Slang, too, in some degree is offered as a cause of laughter, and dialect in plenty; even bad spelling is given a place.[3]

The Yankee type and the Georgia type were in truth so nearly one as to be easily confused by contemporary Americans. In 1840 William Tappan Thompson, a member of the literary circle in Augusta, was shocked by having Longstreet present to him a story, "Little Ben," that was plainly akin in origin to one of "Mr. Mathews' popular Yankee stories." It turned out that Mr. Mathews had found the story just where and just as (so far as concerned manner of telling) Longstreet had left it in Litchfield, Connecticut, and had taken it up as fitting in perfectly with his ideas of a type Yankee. Thompson was greatly relieved by the explanation, since, though his knowledge of Longstreet precluded any suspicion of plagiarism, he had himself "so often heard [a similar story] related on the stage by the Zepheniah Tairall of our play-going days, Mr. Hill, in true Yankee style."[4]

Soon *Georgia Scenes* was widely imitated. In 1840 Thompson published in his Madison, Georgia, *Miscellany* a series of sketches called *Major Jones's Courtship.* These sketches were suggestive enough of *Georgia Scenes* to be attributed to Longstreet. "I see some feller in Charleston," Major Jones complains in a postscript to his letter 21, "is advertisin' for sale,

---

[1] *Georgia Scenes*, "The Song."
[2] *Georgia Scenes*, "The Dance."
[3] *Georgia Scenes*, "Gander Pulling."
[4] *Southern Literary Messenger*, July, 1840, 572.

'Major Jones' Courtship, by Judge Longstreet.' That's a monstrous bominable mistake, for the whether he feels flattered by havin' my writens attributed to him, but if he does, I am even with him, for I take it as a very grate compliment to myself."[1] "Major Jones" was prolific. Other publications of the same nature followed at intervals until 1860.

Thompson was born in 1812 in Ohio, but, having lost his parents while he was still young, he had gone to Philadelphia and commenced work with the Philadelphia *Chronicle*. Later he went to the Territory of Florida as secretary to the Governor, but by the early thirties he was in Augusta, associated with Longstreet in editing the *Sentinel*. He admired Longstreet enormously, and would talk with him whenever he had a chance. *Georgia Scenes*, it seemed to him, abounded in "beauty, sentiment, and eloquence of style."[2] He thought Longstreet's type of work of very great value and regretted that he would not write more, since "few would be willing to follow him in the same path." When Longstreet gave up the *Sentinel*, Thompson soon (spring, 1838) commenced editing the *Augusta Mirror*, for which he procured Longstreet as a contributor.[3]

In time, Johnson J. Hooper took up the Longstreet literary tradition with his *Simon Suggs* (1845), Joseph G. Baldwin with his *Flush Times in Alabama and Mississippi* (1853), G. W. Harris with *Sut Lovingood* (1867), John B. Lamar in Georgia with *Polly Peablossom's Wedding* (1851), and *Blacksmith of the Mountain Pass*, admired by Dickens. Davidson, writing in 1869, knew that it was Longstreet who had established the tradition, and spoke of the *Scenes*, as compared with its descendants, as follows: "It compares favorably with most similar works, though I consider it less uniformly humorous than the *Adventures of Simon Suggs*, less racy though less rude generally than *Wild Western Scenes*, less ludicrously natural than *Major Jones's Courtship*, and less Western and therein less laughable than the *Big Bear of Arkansas;* but yet

---

[1] Thompson, *Major Jones's Courtship*, 143.
[2] *Southern Literary Messenger*, July, 1840.
[3] *Southern Literary Messenger*, June, 1838.

it has merits that none of these have in an equal degree."[1] The truth is that the *Scenes* exactly suited the taste of the country. Clayton knew the taste and so did Crockett when together they got up Crockett's *Life*. Minor imitators without number have faded into non-existence: "Jo of Mississippi," who wrote for the *Southern Literary Messenger* in 1845,[2] Abraham Goosequill, Esq., who wrote "The Coon Hunt" for the *Southern Literary Gazette* (Athens)[3] in 1845, and "Ned Brace," who in 1852 favored the *Georgia University Magazine* with four sketches which the student editors characterized as none too good: " 'The Serenade' and 'Turkey Supper,' they pronounce, are passable, but the 'Possum Hunt' is not so good, and the 'Pistol Scrape' is outrageous."[4] *Mississippi Scenes* was an item to be considered by anyone in 1860 who was interested in Mississippi literature,[5] and before the sixties Richard Malcolm Johnston had begun in Georgia the work soon to be published as Philemon Perch's *Georgia Sketches*.[6]

After the Civil War Johnston, Joel Chandler Harris, and many other persons of less note, all of them conscious of their indebtedness to Longstreet, kept alive what he had inaugurated. Between Harris and Longstreet there was almost actual contact. It was Thompson who in 1871 secured Harris's services for the *Savannah News,* Harris's articles in the *Forsyth Advertiser* having proved so much to his liking.[7] Could Colonel Thompson fail to tell the young man many anecdotes, lingering in his mind, of Middle Georgia and old Judge Longstreet? Somewhere, certainly, Harris learned his lesson. In December, 1893, he expressed himself as of the opinion that "Middle Georgia," on which subject he had "in mind two or three articles," "was and is the center of the most unique—the most individual—civilization the Republic has produced. 'Georgia Scenes,' 'Major Jones's Courtship,' and all that is racy in 'Simon Suggs' and Colonel John-

---

[1] Davidson, *Living Writers,* 339.
[2] *Southern Literary Messenger,* February, 1845, 109–12.
[3] *Southern Literary Gazette,* 25 November, 1848.
[4] *Georgia University Magazine,* November, 1852.
[5] *Southern Literary Messenger,* February 1860, 81–90.
[6] *Southern Field and Fireside,* 26 November, 1864.
[7] Harris, *Joel Chandler Harris,* 93–108.

ston's characters, all came out of Middle Georgia."[1] Perhaps the influence went even further; perhaps in California, where "Flush-Times" Baldwin later became a Judge of the Supreme Court, it reached Bret Harte and reinforced his determination to deal more or less faithfully with local incidents; perhaps through the southwest it reached Mark Twain and affected him also. Certainly Mark Twain had, when he was an old man, known the *Scenes* for a long, long time.[2]

---

[1] Harris, *Joel Chandler Harris*, 316-7.
[2] A. B. Paine, Letter, 25 January, 1922.

VII

GEORGIA SCENES—ONE BY ONE

The first of the *Scenes* in the 1835 collection is "Georgia Theatrics." In that sketch a man is riding through the country when, hearing what he takes to be the noise incident to a fight, he goes hurriedly in the direction from which it came. As he approached he heard one of the fighters shout with satisfaction something that led him to think that the victor had with his thumbs gouged out the victim's eyes. In spite of the fact that "gouging" was considered a legitimate method of warfare, the stranger took it upon himself to reprimand the two peace-breakers. It turned out that after all only one man had been engaged, that he had simply stopped from his ploughing long enough to rehearse a fight, and that his actual crime had been no greater than that involved in plunging his thumbs, not into the eye-sockets of an antagonist, but into the soft earth. If Longstreet meant this for allegory—for Don Quixote charging at the windmills—he did not plainly declare himself, but that fact has not kept the story from being allegorically construed. There is an account of how, after the Civil War, read once before Congress at an appropriate moment in the midst of heated sectional tirade by some bloody-shirt Republican, it had an effect that was most wholesome and quieting.[1] Longstreet's son-in-law, L. Q. C. Lamar, sitting in that august body, heard the old Judge's sketch read and was moved almost to tears, wishing the old gentlemen might have known how his words had confounded the enemies of the dear South.

But this *Scene* was held worthy from the start. In the 1830's it was incorporated in *Colonel Crockett's Exploits and Adventures in Texas* (1837), where it stands yet as Chapter

---

[1] Fitzgerald, *Judge Longstreet*, 88-9.

XXV of the *Life of Col. Crockett, Written by Himself* (1860). Whoever wrote these "exploits" took this sketch as allegory; to him it suggested Andrew Jackson's attack upon the United States Bank. Poe's comment in the *Southern Literary Messenger* was merely that "the whole anecdote is told with a raciness and vigor which would do favor to the pages of Blackwood."[1]

Of "The Dance," Poe says, "the oddities of a backwood reel are described with inimitable farce, fidelity, and picturesque effect."[2] The old dances are portrayed as much more delicate from the standpoint of morals than were any of the dances current when the sketch was written.

"The Horse Swap," to quote Poe further, "is a vivid narrative of an encounter between the wits of two Georgian horse-jockies. This is most excellent in every respect, but especially so in its delineation of Southern bravado, and the keen sense of the ludicrous evinced in the portraiture of the steeds. We think parts of this free and easy sketch . . . superior, in joint humor and verisimilitude to anything of the kind we have ever seen." Especially notable in its faithfulness, to one familiar with the etiquette of the frontier, is the silence maintained by all of the onlookers during the horse-trade. The Virginian, years later, in Owen Wister's book, knew how to keep his silence in the same manner, while Balaam was dickering with poor Shorty. To beat a man in a horse-trade, says Gilmer, was a matter of great pride.[3]

"The Character of a Native Georgian," in spite of Poe's branding it as inferior to the other *Scenes* and as concerning itself with a character neither original nor "appertaining exclusively to Georgia," has generally been considered the best of Longstreet's work.[4] It is concerned with the practical jokes of one Ned Brace, while on a visit to Savannah, to which city he and the writer are represented as having recently made a visit.

For years Ned Brace was supposed to be a literary portrait

---

[1] *Southern Literary Messenger*, March, 1836.
[2] *Southern Literary Messenger*, March, 1836.
[3] Gilmer, *Sketches*, 167.
[4] Jackson, *Rev. Dr. Longstreet*, 28.

of Judge Edmund Bacon, a highly accomplished and jovial older friend of Longstreet's who lived in Edgefield, South Carolina. Bacon was born in 1776 in Virginia, but he grew up in Georgia. As a student of the Richmond Academy he had in a formal speech welcomed President Washington to Augusta upon the occasion of the presidential visit in 1790. Later he had attended the Waddel Academy and the Litchfield Law School, and still later had become a very learned and distinguished lawyer (as what boy who had welcomed President Washington could miss doing?) and a sort of grand-scale gentleman to boot, with a fine home and library and rose gardens, and with countless slaves and vast acres of land to back them all up. He was deeply religious. "His slaves," his granddaughter says, "were taught to worship God on every Sabbath, and really they were given fine characteristics."[1] But Bacon could not be glum-faced. He was always cracking jokes, to the almost inextinguishable merriment of everybody.

In his rascally way he would, for instance, on overtaking a crowd of gentlemen in a stage-coach, suggest that he exchange his horse, he being on horseback, for one of the places in the stage-coach, so that both he and the gentlemen he was talking with might be rested by the change. Now one of the gentlemen, a friend of Bacon's, seeing indeed that the horse was both nick tail and sorrel, but having no way of knowing that it was as *"hard-going a racker"* as was ever seen, accepted the offer gladly. Presently the stage-coach struck good roads and began going on its way so rapidly that the man on horseback had to push his horse vigorously (and with extreme discomfort to himself because of the horse's rough gait) to keep up. Judge Bacon considered this episode most amusing, as everybody else did, and could not for a long time restrain himself from laughing when he thought of "the credulity of his friend."[2]

It was natural that a man of this kind, known as a close friend of Longstreet's, should be associated with Ned Brace. But this association was only half accurate. Longstreet began to write the sketch with his mind dominated by one Dredzel Pace, a resident of Augusta, whom he had known as a "very

---
[1] Mrs. Katherine Wigfield Cheatham, Letter, 10 December, 1921.
[2] *Southern Field and Fireside*, 21 January, 1860.

whimsical fellow,"[1] years before at Willington. Pace had the reputation of trying to imitate Judge Bacon, but was generally thought of as succeeding in duplicating only the more oafish aspects of Bacon's character. "It was . . . Pace," writes William W. Mann, Longstreet's one-time partner, "whom Judge Longstreet had in his eye, when he commenced his sketch . . . and he had proceeded about one-half through the sketch and sent what he had written . . . to the press when it occurred to him that the sketch would be enhanced by the substitution of the original for the imitation." As late as 1860, Longstreet was regretting this half-and-half creation, and planning, if he could get to it, to issue "a new, revised, and enlarged edition of the *Georgia Scenes,* in which, with other emendations, the discordant portions of the chapters devoted to 'The Character of a Native Georgian' would be harmonized, and made to form a congruous whole."[2]

"The Fight" tells how a degraded, dirt-eating character named Ransy Sniffle, abetted by Uncle Tommy Loggins, a village know-all, finally, after repeated failures, succeeds in pitting against each other, through bringing their wives at odds, two community strongmen who had each of them for a long time and with such happy effect adopted the policy of avoiding the other. The ensuing fight, watched by an army of spectators who conceived of it "fair, catch as catch can, rough and tumble, no man touch till one or the other halloos,"[3] resulted, besides in many bruises, in the loss between the combatants of an ear, a nose, and a finger. Poe described it, and very naturally, as "involving some horrible and disgusting details of Southern barbarity," but granted that as a sketch it was "unsurpassed in dramatic vigor, and in vivid truth to nature." Its characterization he thought unusually good; and, on the whole, he declared, what seems to have been the summit of praise with him, "this article [would] positively make the fortune of any British periodical."

"The Fight" is peculiarly interesting as throwing light on the manner of combat and on the perversion of dirt-eating. A

---
[1] Longstreet, *Mitten*, 100.
[2] *Southern Field and Fireside*, 8 October, 1859.
[3] *Georgia Scenes*, 65.

gentleman born in March, 1820, has corroborated for the writer of this book the impression which Longstreet gives of a fight. "Yes," this gentleman says in his letter, "I have seen men fight. They would scratch, bite and gouge, bite fingers, nose, ears, gouge out eyes, blat like goats. I witnessed a fight at a political gathering. There was a political secret organization that held secret meetings in outhouses. They called themselves Know Nothing Party. On one occasion the speaker of the Democratic Party said: 'the Know Nothings are like gophers or ground hogs that do all their work in the dark; they went in their holes and pulled the holes in with them.' When he got through with his speech a great big double-fisted *panther-jawed jolter-shouldered* fellow stepped up and demanded him to take back what he said and he told him *no*. The little speaker was too fast for the big fellow; he knocked his nose and the blood flew. *That* opened the fight. In two minutes the most of the crowd was clinched together down on the ground, gouging the eyes, biting nose, cheeks, ears, and fingers. After the fight you could pick up fingers, ears and pieces of *noses*. . . . Sometimes persons who were angry with each other would resort to ring fighting, like an amphitheater. If two men quarreled their friends would arrange for them to fight. They would make a circle about thirty feet in diameter, put a rope around the circle, and no one was allowed inside the circle but the two combatants. Each one had his seconds and their duty was to keep everybody outside of the rope and instruct the fighters how to take advantage of every weak point, and to separate them when one hollowed 'Take him off.' The two seconds would have a bucket of water, and each one with a dipper of water would wash them of blood. Then they would put on their shirts, shake hands, and take a drink of corn whiskey or peach brandy. They would laugh and tease each other and help each other, [but you can] look in our school history of Georgia if you want to know how kind and loving [sic] the common people were to each other."[1] A general court-house fight, Longstreet alludes to in his "Darby Anvil"; a dignified semilegalized man-and-

---

[1] A. F. Williams, Letter, 14 February, 1916.

man fight, Richard Malcolm Johnston describes in "King William and His Armies."

Dirt-eating is a depravity to which persons living in warm climates have always been subject, one which having long stirred the curiosity of investigators, proved at last to be a result of no more occult a cause than the hookworm disease.[1] But in Longstreet's time the perversion was one which constantly piqued interest. It was, as indeed it still is in a much less degree, apparent throughout the Southeast, and there were tales of its existence in the Tropics. In March, 1837, the Charleston *Southern Literary Journal* published about it a story as realistic and insistent in its descriptions of the vice as it is romantic in its general plot,—which is saying much. The author of this story deplores mankind's weakness in not being able to withstand so unnatural a temptation and suggests with a long eye for the "campaign" method of arresting vice, to be developed later, that since the perverse craving clearly arises from acidity in the stomach all could be set right by a little magnesia. The disease, this pleasant article says, "grows upon its victims more and more . . . their skins become first sallow, and at length yellow, their lips colorless, and their whole countenance assumes a cadaverous appearance. The fiend is visible in their looks. . . . In the brief space of a year's time, a delicate, perfect creature whom one might gaze on in admiration, would under this vice, exhibit a countenance of pale ghostliness; with lips, once so beautifully red, colorless and seeming to loath each other too much to deign to approach, while the gums, pale and dry. . . ."[2] Longstreet had the instinct for connecting his subjects with a topic already much in the public mind.

Ransy Sniffle is a typical dirt-eater. He is "a little fellow . . . who in his earlier days had fed copiously upon red clay and blackberries. This diet had given to Ransy a complexion that a corpse would have disdained to own, and an abdominal rotundity that was quite unprepossessing. Long spells of the fever and ague, too, in Ransy's youth, had conspired with clay

---
[1] C. W. Stiles, *Soil Pollution as cause of Ground Itch, Hookworm Disease and Dirt-eating. Publications Rockefeller Sanitary Commission, Washington*, 1910.
[2] *Southern Literary Journal*, Charleston, March, 1837.

and blackberries to throw him quite out of the order of nature. His shoulders were fleshless and elevated; his head large and flat; his neck slim and translucent; and his arms, hands, fingers and feet were lengthened out of all proportion to the rest of his frame. His joints were large and his limbs small; and as for flesh, he could not, with propriety, be said to have any. Those parts which nature usually supplies with the most of this article—the calves of the legs, for example—presented in him the appearance of so many well-drawn blisters. His height was just five feet nothing; and his average weight in blackberry season, ninety-five."[1]

"The Song" tells about a young lady who had just returned South from her school in Philadelphia where she had been taught to sing by Madam Piggisqueaki. Upon being requested by her friends to sing for them she is good enough to do so. She would have done better to be less accommodating. Because she attempted some music that seemed to one of the audience to be basely French or Italian in origin, and not gloriously (in an ascending scale) German, English, or Scotch, she is bitterly condemned by the writer as an affected fool. This sketch is a burlesque, based upon the singing of one of the voice teachers in the Taylor Select Female School of Sparta, Georgia.[2]

"The Turn Out" is the story of some boys' locking their teacher out of the school-house and getting themselves a holiday. It seems that if the teacher of his own will granted the holiday, he forfeited his salary, whereas if his benefice were forced from him, his salary was not affected. The teacher's efforts to gain an entrance, then, were no more earnest than it was necessary for them to be to sustain the farce. "It is," says Poe, with something that he would have called pedantry in anybody else, "like Miss Edgeworth's 'Barring Out.'"

"The Charming Creature as a Wife," according to Poe, "is a very striking narrative of the evils attendant upon an ill-arranged marriage." The story is about a young man of the higher grade of society, who marries a new-rich woman too silly to settle down to the homely virtues of thrift and routine

---
[1] *Georgia Scenes*, "The Fight."
[2] G. Gunby Jordan, Letter, 9 January, 1922.

living. He takes to drink as a means of escape from his insupportably miserable existence, and at length (somewhat with the extenuating sympathy of the author) dies a drunkard's death. Incidentally it shows the extremely narrow range of life granted women in early Georgia. Clearly the thing one had to do was to be a fainting, thoughtless imbecile before marriage, and a sturdy, calculating phenomenon of wit and wisdom after marriage. If you could not do these things you were badly off indeed. If you failed of the first you got no husband, and if you failed of the second you ran your husband crazy. But this was the ideal. Practically, a man was often thankful enough to have his wife behave herself decently. One of the old governors, at least, thought it not beside the point to compliment his wife for the fact, that, in spite of her passionate love for him, she never delayed or prevented his going from her, "wherever duty or business called him, but always urged him on and aided him in getting ready."[1]

"The Gander Pulling" describes how some citizens suspended a greased goose by the legs above a roadway and then passed under the goose at a dead run on horseback, seeking every time they passed to snatch the bird's head off. It is explicitly and accurately stated in the sketch that this *Scene* actually happened near Augusta. "It did occur," Longstreet wrote later, "at the very place where I locate it. The names of the persons who figure in it are such as were well known in Richmond County at that time, and the language which I put in the mouths of my actors was just such as was common at such exhibitions. The horses that were engaged differed in action and character as horses generally do; but to give the whole an interest which it would not otherwise have, I made one of the horses (of a disposition not very uncommon among horses) break from the ring and make for Augusta, pass tobacco rollers, which were common at the time, receive their greetings as the rider of such a horse would be certain to secure from such characters—and so on to the close of his course. This latter part is fanciful, and thrown in to give interest to a scene that would be very insipid in simple historical detail."[2]

---

[1] Gilmer, *Sketches*, 295.
[2] Fitzgerald, *Judge Longstreet*, 165-6; Laborde, *S. C. College*, 463.

Poe takes it upon himself in his review of the "Gander Pulling" to give a somewhat more detailed account of the sport than is offered by Longstreet, and William Gilmore Simms, in his *As Good as a Comedy* (1852) describes a goose-pulling episode with much zest and considerably more precision than is evident in *Georgia Scenes*.

"The Ball" embodies the writer's swelling dislike for "modern" dancing, and his disgust for the hypocritical pretensions of men in their attitude towards duelling. Though the characters are designated by such names as Miss Mushy, Misses Feedle and Deedle, Messrs. Boozle and Noozle, the impression produced is graphic. "Some passages," says Poe, "in which a certain species of sly humor, wherein intense observation of character is disguised by simplicity of relation, puts one forcibly in mind of the Spectator."

In "The Mother and Her Child" Longstreet attacks the "gibberish which is almost invariably used by mothers and nurses to infants." He introduces here a considerable amount of negro dialect. Mrs. Slang, the mother in the story, appears to have been a very coarse and vulgar woman. She angrily mocks a little unoffending negro nurse maid, grins at her derisively, and calls her a "good for nothing nasty hussy," all for the reason that young Slang continues crying after he should have quieted himself.

"The Debating Society"[1] is the story of two school boys, in this case Longstreet and McDuffie, at Willington. These boys propose for debate, and actually drive their friends to debate upon, a subject that has no vestige of sense to it. Poe says that this is the best of all the sketches, and indeed if the capability of being shifted into a sort of high homiletic implication is to be taken as any element of greatness, one can hardly regard any other of the *Scenes* as comparable to it. Here, if you are of such complexion, which Longstreet, it may be said, was most probably not, you may see shadowed forth the whole sad business of human inadequacy, and human folly in agitating itself so profoundly over the maliciously thrown bait of some superior but perverse intelligence. Poe knew, for his

---

[1] John B. Gordon, *Reminiscences of the Civil War* (New York, 1905), 92-3; Longstreet, *Mitten*, 103.

part, what he liked. This sketch, he says in his review of *Georgia Scenes,* is one of the best things he ever read; it has force and freedom without any evident straining for effect. He copies the sketch in its entirety.

"The Militia Company Drill," though only another of the innumerable descriptions of military musters, which, Poe says, were in the 1830's "so rife in the land," is, to quote him further, without "equal . . . in the matter of broad farce." This *Scene* Longstreet did not write. An author's note accompanying the sketch in *Georgia Scenes* states: "This is from the pen of a friend, who has kindly permitted me to place it among the 'Georgia Scenes.' It was taken from the life and published about twenty years ago."

There is a tradition[1] in Georgia at large, and a very definite family tradition among the descendants of Oliver Hillhouse Prince, that it was this gentleman who was the friend referred to. Born in Connecticut in 1787, Prince came to Georgia as a young man to join his uncle, David Porter Hillhouse, who, since 1800, had been editing the Washington, Georgia, *Monitor.* He was admitted to the Bar in 1806. After his uncle's death, though his aunt, who was a Georgia woman by birth, continued editing her dead husband's paper, Prince removed to Milledgeville and assumed the editorship of a newspaper called *The Federal Union.* He was versatile with a vengeance. Having in the course of his spacious days picked up the ability to do civil engineering as well as to conduct cases in court, and write countless witty articles, he was, in 1822, appointed on a commission to lay off the newly established city of Macon. In the same year he published an admirably prepared *Digest of Georgia Laws.* From December, 1828, to March, 1829, he was a member of the United States Senate. From Milledgeville, he removed to Macon, and from Macon in turn, as soon as his children grew old enough to remind him of the necessity for their going to college, he removed to Athens, the seat of the State University, where, the chroniclers state, obtained "the highest status of Georgia society, outside of Savannah and Augusta."[2] Here he became a trustee of the University, and

---
[1] Richard H. Clark, *Memoirs* (Atlanta, Ga., 1898), 237.
[2] Richard Malcolm Johnston, *Old Mark Langston,* 200.

in the capacity of distinguished advocate and grand gentleman of infinite wit and charm, continued to live till 1837 when he went North to look after the publication of the second edition of his *Digest*. On October 9, *The Home,* the vessel on which he and his wife were returning to Georgia, was lost at sea off the North Carolina coast, and both Mr. and Mrs. Prince perished.[1]

It is said that the sketch of Prince's used by Longstreet attained wide popularity and was translated into several languages. "Mr. Prince," says one of his contemporaries, "wrote *Captain Clodpole, or The Oglethorpe Muster*, which was republished throughout the United States and in some parts of Europe."[2] Certainly it was several times reprinted in English. Bound together in one volume with *"The Way to Wealth . . . by Dr. Franklin"* (dateless), and *The Cutter, in Five Lectures Upon the Art and Practice of Cutting Friends, Acquaintances and Relations* (date 1808), one copy of *The Militia Company Drill* with some curiously graphic drawings, has been seen by the present writer under the title (dateless) *The Ghost of Baron Steuben; or Fredonia in Arms! Being a Description of that most Bloody Campaign, Styled the Alexandro-Caesaro-Eugenio-Frederico-Bonapartic Campaign out Napoleonified, or a Georgia Training, In which most exquisite discipline, subordination, military knowledge, clearly exemplified and pathetically recommended to all who are convinced of the uselessness and mischief of a Standing Army."* The sketch is given here as a letter written to "dear Fugy."

The next considerable noise made about this sketch, apart from its appearance in the recurring editions of *Georgia Scenes,* was when it became known that Thomas Hardy had used a part of it in Chapter XXIII of his *Trumpet Major* (1880). Friends of Longstreet promptly rushed to the defense of their rights,[3] accusing Hardy of plagiarism, whereupon Hardy in the Preface to his 1895 edition of *The Trumpet Major* stated that

---

[1] Appleton's *Cyclopedia American Biography;* newspaper clipping, *Macon Telegraph,* December, 1913, article by James Calloway based on similar article by John A. Cobb; Cobb, Letter to Miss Baseline Prince, 9 December, 1913.

[2] Gov. George R. Gilmer, quoted in Miller, *Bench and Bar*, I, 342.

[3] Clark *Memoirs*, 235-42.

he had based the chapter in question upon [C. H.] Gifford's *History of the Wars of* [sic; *occasioned by* is correct] *the French Revolution* (London, 1817). And there indeed (II, 968–70) may be found almost identically the same sketch, presented as a satirical account of an American drill, picked up somewhere by the compiler. Was it the eight-page *Ghost of Baron von Steuben* that Gifford used as his source?

The Hardy episode has been endlessly talked about. Richard H. Clark in his *Memoirs* (1898) devotes an entire chapter to "Georgia Scenes and The Trumpet Major." To him, Hardy is an out-and-out plagiarist, as indeed, without Hardy's explanation, the portentous parallel passages might seem to prove. Clark says that the discovery of this similarity between the two books caused a great deal of discussion of Longstreet in both the English and American newspapers. The likeness has been discussed subsequently by W. P. Trent, in "A Retrospect of American Humor," *The Century Magazine* (November, 1901), 60–1, and in *Southern Writers* (1905), 122; by Lyndon Orr, in "Thomas Hardy and Longstreet," *The Bookman* (February, 1906), 635–6; by Mildred Lewis Rutherford in *The South in History and Literature* (1907), 159; and by John Erskine, *Chief American Novelists* (1910).

"Almost as amusing as the apparently plundered sketch," says Professor Trent, at the time himself unaware of Hardy's alibi, "is the fact that when the 'lifting' was exposed by the 'Critic' in parallel columns, a writer in the 'Daily News' . . . came to the rescue of the British novelist by pointing out how far the latter had improved upon the crude sketch of the American provincial. But alas! no sooner had this convincing proof of British superiority been given than the 'Critic' was forced to explain that by an unlucky [*sic*] mistake, the authors' names at the top of the columns had been transposed!"[1]

"The Turf" describes a race, and incidentally does something towards upsetting the idea that Longstreet deals only with the "lower" orders of society. It is the firmest conviction among the descendants of the people this man wrote about that he was certainly not daring enough to sketch anybody but the

---

[1] William Peterfield Trent, "Retrospect American Humor," *Century Magazine*, November, 1901, 60–1.

"crackers." He was. Eight of the eighteen stories in *Georgia Scenes* deal with what anybody would have called the upper element of Georgia Society.—Horse racing was one of the passions of the Southern nature. Every town that attained any size soon made itself a race-track. In Charleston, the Episcopal Convention of South Carolina met during race week so that it might have a quorum.[1] One young lady at least, probably of this religious group, of as fine "sensibilities," one would guess, as anybody, has left a record of her enjoyment of the sport. Though in some fear of being smiled at by those who doubt the morality of a horse race—who regard the sport as low and vulgar, or who had never seen a race, I must confess, she says, that when "papa's beautiful Psyche, darting like a sun-beam, pressing on unflagging and triumphant, bounded to the goal, I unconsciously stood up and shouted aloud, though unheard among the cheers; and tears started to my eyes."[2]

But there were other sects much less latitudinarian. Dr. Waddel of the Presbyterians, for one, recorded with the greatest zest how some years before a pious and right-thinking little girl of eight had in sheer mortification been obliged to be brought away from a race, "as pale as a little corpse." When asked why she had left, Waddel says, "she replied that she had seen nothing but a *frightful confusion*, and the poor horses *whipped* and *run* almost to *death;* that she had concealed her terror as much as possible for fear of interrupting the friends with whom she was; but at length two men got to fighting near the carriage in which she was seated, and she heard a loud exclamation of War! War! which alarmed her so exceedingly that she was near *fainting;* when her friend, seeing her situation, brought her away immediately."[3]

Longstreet was on the side of Waddel. He considered this record of Waddel's "highly interesting," and to show its popularity stated proudly that it went through three editions in the United States and two in England.[4] Though a lover of horses, he did not believe, evidently, with General Grubbs of his

---

[1] Trent, *Simms*, 26.
[2] Caroline Gilman, *Recollections of a Southern Matron* (New York, 1838), 113.
[3] Moses Waddel, *Caroline Elizabeth Smelt*, 23–4.
[4] Longstreet, "Waddel," in Sprague, *Annals*, IV, 63–7.

sketch, that "we shall never have a fine breed of horses until the turf is more patronized," or if he did believe so, he thought the price too dear. This sketch has some accurate negro dialect, which, according to Longstreet's custom, is always obligingly explained in parentheses; it has also some rapid conversation, and, paradoxically, an indication of Longstreet's immeasurable scorn of the negro "out of his place" and his corresponding scorn of people who deny the negro the common rights of human sympathy.

"An Interesing Interview" is, Poe says, "a specimen of exquisite dramatic talent," a matter-of-fact reproduction of the "speech, actions and *thoughts* of two drunken old men—and its air of truth is perfectly inimitable."

"The Fox Hunt" is perhaps the most "literary" of all the sketches in *Georgia Scenes*. In it, the author quotes at length from Somerville's poem "The Chase," quotes Horace, and, himself, becomes more eloquent than usual. "Truly," one passage goes, "it was a lovely morning for the season of the year; December never ushered in one more lovely: Like a sheet of snow the frost overspread the earth, as rich in beauty as ever met the gaze of mortal. Upon the western verge, in all his martial glory, stood Orion, his burnished epaulets and spangled sash with unusual brightness glowing. Capella glittered brighter still, and Castor, Procyon and Arcturus rivalled her in lustre. But Sirius reigned the monarch of the starry host, and countless myriads of lesser lights glowed and sparkled and twinkled o'er all the wide spread canopy."[1] How the old Georgians must have relished such an extract! How complete a vindication it must have seemed to them of the potentialities of Georgia literature! It was passages of this sort that won Longstreet his fame as a man of letters. "If there be anything defective in this style, if it be not really beautiful," wrote one of the contemporary reviewers after quoting the above description, "we confess that we are much wanting in taste."[2] The story of the "Fox Hunt" is one of a novice in that sport trying to keep up, and finally despairing of keeping up, with a band of adepts. The incident is said actually to

---
[1] *Georgia Scenes*, 187.
[2] *Southern Literary Messenger*, July, 1840, 573.

have happened some three or four miles south-west of Greensboro, Georgia.

"The Wax Works" is a story of some young men from Augusta, who, visiting in the neighboring town of Waynesboro for the period of the Waynesboro Races, decide to make some money for themselves by taking over the stand and the "goodwill" of a departing Down-Easter's wax-works exhibition. Having themselves undertaken to impersonate the wax impersonations of the Sleeping Beauty, General Washington, and other such celebrities, the young men are in the midst of their performance discovered in their trick and run out of town—all with the utmost good nature on the part of the flyers. This incident, it is almost needless to say, is very curiously suggestive of Mark Twain. Freeman Walker, an Augusta lawyer and friend of Longstreet's, who was in the United States Senate 1819–21, is said to have been the original of Freedom Lazenby of the sketch.[1]

"A Sage Conversation" tells of the exploits of Longstreet, "Baldwin," and his old friend "Ned Brace" with three "nice, tidy, aged matrons, the youngest of whom could not have been under sixty." At the house of one of these, in passing through the country, the two gentlemen found themselves obliged to put up for the night. The kindness and the piety of these ladies is shown as only exceeded by their silly credulity and extreme narrowness of interest.

"The Shooting Match" shows "Hall's" experiences at a "shooting match," which, he says, he attended "about a year ago." Led there by a "swarthy, bright-eyed, smirky little fellow" whom he had accidentally encountered, and with whom on the way he engaged in a very lively wit-duel, Hall, entirely by accident, but, according to his statement to the spectators, by a phenomenal ability in marksmanship, succeeds in outdoing all efforts to hit the bull's-eye. "Shooting matches were very common throughout the Southern States, though they are not as common," Longstreet says in his sketch, "as they were twenty-five or thirty years ago."[2]

Col. David Crockett in his *Life* favors his readers with a

---
[1] Jones, *Augusta*, 169.
[2] *Georgia Scenes*, 219.

full account of this to him splendid sport. "I will endeavor," he says, "to give a description of this western amusement:

"In the latter part of the summer our cattle get very fat, as the range is remarkably fine; and someone, desirous of raising money on one of his cattle, advertises that on a particular day, and at a given place a first-rate beef will be shot for.

"When the day comes, every marksman in the neighborhood will meet at the appointed place, with his gun. After the company has assembled, a subscription paper is handed round, with the following heading:

" 'A. B. offers a beef worth twenty dollars, to be shot for, at twenty-five cents a shot.' Then the names are put down by each person thus:

> D. C. puts in four shots........$1.00
> E. F. puts in eight shots........ 2.00
> G. H. puts in two shots........ .50

and thus it goes round, until the price is made up.

"Two persons are then selected who have not entered for shots to act as judges of the match. Every shooter gets a board, and makes a cross in the center of his target. The shot that drives the center, or comes nearest to it, gets the *hide and tallow*, which is considered the first choice. The next nearest gets his choice of the hind quarters; the third gets the other hind quarter; the fourth takes choice of the fore quarters; the fifth the remaining quarter; and the sixth gets the lead in the tree against which we shoot.

"The judges stand near the tree, and when a man fires they cry out, 'Who shot?' and the shooter gives his name; and so on, till all have shot. The judges then take all the boards and go off by themselves, and decide what quarter each man has won. Sometimes one will get nearly all."[1]

This form of sport Colonel Crockett found most engaging. Once he killed two birds with one stone, as it were, by going to see his girl, and stopping for a shooting match on the way over. As a result of his work in this match, he says: "I sold my part for five dollars in the real grit."[2] Once when re-

---
[1] David Crockett, *Life* (1860), 237-8.
[2] Crockett, *Life*, 48-9.

ferring to a shooting match, Davy moralizes: "This is one of our homely amusements—enjoyed as much by us, and perhaps more, than most of your refined entertainments. Here each man takes a part, if he pleases, and no one is excluded, unless his improper conduct renders him unfit as an associate."[1]

The repartee at the outset of "The Shooting Match" is very amusing, a sort of sharp, racy, low-brow version of Romeo-and-Mercutio, Gobbo - and - Lorenzo wit - snapping. "David Crockett" is enlightening on this matter also. On his way west, he stops at an inn, where he is fairly pillaged of information. "Good morning, mister," says the landlord, "I don't exactly recollect your name now."

"It's of no consequence," said I.

"I'm pretty sure I've seen you somewhere."

"Very likely you may, I've been there frequently."

"I was sure 'twas so, but strange I should forget your name," says he.

"It is indeed somewhat strange that you should forget what you never knew," says I.

"It is unaccountable strange. It's what I'm not often in the habit of, I assure you. I have for the most part a remarkable retentive memory. In the power of people that pass along this way, I've scarce ever made, as the doctors say, a *slapsus slinkum* of this kind afore."

"Eh-heh," I shouted while the critter continued.

"Travelling to the western country, I presume, mister?"

"Presume anything you please, sir," said I, "but don't trouble me with your presumptions. . . ."

"Do you practice law, mister, or farming, or mechanicals?"

"Perhaps so," says I.

"Ah, I judge so; I was pretty certain it must be the case. Well it's as good business as any there is followed, nowadays."

"Eh-heh," I shouted, and my lower jaw fell in amazement at his perseverance.[2]

One brief scene, "Dropping to Sleep," which was published as Number XVI in the *Sentinel*, 26 February, 1835, was omitted from the collected edition. As that edition contained

---
[1] Crockett, *Life*, 238.
[2] Crockett, *Life*, 286-90.

writings by Longstreet published in the *Sentinel* subsequent to the date at which "Dropping to Sleep" appeared, it is evident that the author considered this *Scene* either too brief, or too uninteresting otherwise, for inclusion in his book. The gist of this *Scene* is as follows: Old Major Loquax and old 'Squire Somnus are put into the same room at a country inn. The 'Squire, as one may guess, was sleepy, and the Major verbosely wakeful. After having persistently talked for a considerable time to a man who is half unconscious, Loquax perceives that he has somehow been rebuffed. "Why I'll swear point blank you're asleep," he complains, nudging his friend. "Well," growls Somnus, "spos'n I am; what's that to you?"

VIII

GENERAL LITERARY EFFORT IN GEORGIA

The publication of *Georgia Scenes* brought Longstreet into a degree of prominence that he had hardly known before, for, whatever were the merits of Georgia, and however exultant was its patriotism, it had not shown much better literary activity up to that time than might have been expected from the frontier community which it was.

From 1802-4 the Reverend Dr. Holcolm of Savannah had conducted a literary and religious review called the *Georgia Analytical Repository,* and in 1809 Thomas U. P. Charlton of the same city had published a *Life of General James Jackson.* McCall's *History of Georgia* appeared in 1816. In Augusta, Parson Weems had in 1806 put forth the first edition of his *Washington* that contained the story of the cherry tree and the hatchet,[1] and in Augusta, prior to 1817, had been printed three editions of the Reverend Mr. Jesse Mercer's *Cluster,* a book of hymns, original and selected.[2] In about 1815 was published anonymously, and without the author's knowledge, "My Life is Like the Summer Rose." In 1817 also, appeared Waddel's morbidly religiose *Memoir of Miss Caroline Elizabeth Smelt,* which proved popular enough to run through three editions in this country and as many as two in England.[3] And in Macon, in 1838 (the slight infringement in point of time justified by the fact that the book had been in preparation since 1826), appeared the Reverend Mr. Samuel J. Cassells' 350-page book of poems, named *Providence.*

In 1825, Clayton had published *The Mysterious Picture, by Wrangham-Fitz-Ramble, Esq.,* a book of two hundred pages "bound in the style of the *Quarterly Review.*" Its contents

---
[1] *Cambridge History American Literature.*
[2] C. D. Mallory, *Memoirs of Elder Jesse Mercer* (New York, 1844), 85.
[3] Sprague, *Annals,* IV, 63-7.

were "The Mysterious Picture," "Human Depravity," "Vanity," "The Illusions of Pleasure," "Pride and Love," "The Disappointed Author," "The Politician," "The Widow and the Widower," "Education," "The Negro's Dream." In this book, the supposed author is taken to a church in which he is permitted to see what is going on in the minds of all the people in the congregation. He observes "a cotton planter fixing up his crop for market, the best of his staple where it can be seen,— beside him a Yankee cotton buyer, with gimlet and samples in his pocket, contriving how to mix up the qualities so as to obtain an advantage in his classification and sale. He sees a horse-jockey, patching up eyes, smoothing over defects, and concealing bad qualities; debtors framing excuses for want of punctuality; tailors *cabbaging* remnants; millers heaping up toll; bank-directors contriving to serve themselves and friends liberally; clerks resorting to various stratagems; a flippant young man, bent upon pleasing the ladies, dashing through the streets with a fine switch-tailed horse, and an elegant new silver-tipped gig, managing to pass all the houses that were inhabited by fair damsels; sees young gentlemen "dressed in the highest *ton,* their bodies drawn to the shape of an inverted cone, well swaddled in a fresh and increased supply of cravats, standing upon brass-heeled stilts, behind a goodly bale of ruffles." . . . In short, he sees nearly everything (and one suspects more than) Georgia had to offer. The book has been lost; since its subject matter was of an original and entertaining nature, it may be concluded that its disappearance is due to its lack of charm in style and to its lack of plot.[1]

There was a fair number of newspapers, and in 1833 Mercer brought to Washington, Georgia, from its home in Philadelphia, the *Christian Index,* and published it there as a weekly paper devoted largely to acrimonious religious controversy (which, though unfortunate, says Mercer's biographer, finally settled a good many theological questions theretofore doubtful).[2]

Aside from the works enumerated, and from the bountiful number of newspapers, most of the publications in the state had dealt with such unesthetic and intensely practical matters

---
[1] Miller, *Bench and Bar*, I, 167–72.
[2] *Mercer*, 110–12.

as the way to cure fevers or to escape hell. The list of Georgia publications given in Sherwood's *Gazetteer* (1837) shows that almost the only people in Georgia with leisure enough to write, had been doctors, and preachers whose chief polemical curiosity lay in the method of baptism. 1837 was apologetic. "Look at our circumstances," says Sherwood. "Thirty years have not passed away since civilization crossed the Oconee westward. Our fathers and brothers have been compelled, while they have felled the trees and cleared our lands, to stand sentinel, the one for the other: they have labored, like the Jews in building the second Temple; with the hoe in one hand and the rifle in the other. Literary leisure has not been afforded them. But in no country is the spirit of education more roused up. . . . In about two years past, three colleges have been planned and over $100,000 secured for each."[1] Clearly there would be better things soon.

But it was not directly a dearth of leisure which caused the continuance of this lack of intellectual effort. Henry R. Jackson would accept no such excuse. "As compared with the North," he wrote, "there are with us more individuals of leisure not engaged in the busy avocations of life. They crowd the places of public resort in our cities, towns, and villages. They vainly attempt to chase the laggard hours by discussing the vexed questions of politics, or by retailing the petty news and scandal of the day. Nature has given them temperaments demanding strong excitement! Unaccustomed to seek it in the more ennobling pursuits of literature, they too often resort to the short-lived stimulus of the intoxicating cup. Fortune may have given them wealth. Instead of procuring with it a source of pure intellectual enjoyments, far too often around the gambling table, they seek a pastime and find their ruin. Turning from the town to the country, we meet with planters of wealth, many of education, some of great information on topics of general interest, and *all* of them cursed with hours of idleness."[2]

Southern backwardness in literary matters was probably due chiefly, on one count, to the general disposition to inactivity

---

[1] Sherwood, *Gazetteer*, 41-3.
[2] "Politics—Literature," in *Augusta Mirror*, 14 November, 1840.

that always evinces itself among a people living in a territory in which it is pleasant out of doors for much of the year, and, on another count, to a feeling among persons who were of the proper intellectual calibre to produce good literature, that as yet the time had not arrived for them to devote themselves to such pursuits. If the new game of getting rich had so early lost its fascination for them, surely it was still possible for a man to entertain himself in tending the policies of a government which was already acknowledgedly a beacon for the troubled earth.

A few men, perhaps, felt otherwise, and were discontented; there was Richard Henry Wilde, traveling into Italy and conducting researches about Tasso. But orthodox people knew what to think of such dilettantism even if their personal attitude towards Wilde was friendly. "The mission to which Mr. Wilde addressed his faculties and gave years of toil in Europe, was not," says one of his friends, "in harmony with his relative duties to mankind and with that position which his eminent talents and finished education had secured from the world. He was qualified for extensive practical usefulness as a jurist, scholar and statesman. That he should retire for a short period from his own country for relaxation amid the cities, establishments and relics of the Old World, was not surprising or extraordinary. All men of liberal views would do the same, other considerations permitting. But to remain seven years with no engagements more solid than glancing over antiquated documents from which no principles or systems could be educed beneficial to mankind, was a sacrifice of himself much regretted by many of his partial countrymen . . . [In Europe] there was delight for the senses, but mildew to the heart. The voluptuary, the man of fashion, the idler, were gratified; but the moral hero, the public benefactor, the man of enterprise and the scholar of a just ambition, desirous to leave a record of popular utility, would turn with generous self-denial from such enchantments."[1]

How was a man with any sensuous passion or any concept of God and the brooding futility of human effort, how was any

---

[1] Miller, *Bench and Bar*, II, 360.

artist, in short, to beguile himself in a world in which the best thought was so largely, so ingenuously, given to "quick-turnover" schemes for constructive uplift?

There was nothing that such a man could do, writes one of the old-school Southerners, a novelist (who, naturally enough, to be sure, when the pressure of external criticism became so great against his state in the late sixties, took occasion to withdraw his criticism), there was nothing that such a man could do except amuse himself and his friends as best he could, and experience some deep, keen regret; and of course he could complain to his friends.

"In this section of the United States," says this novelist, "however humiliating the confession is to me as a Southerner, it must be acknowledged that there is scarcely such a thing as literature. The profession which elsewhere furnishes employment, ample pecuniary remuneration, and gratifying fame to so many, is here unknown. There are one or two professed and successful authors in the Southern States; but this fact does not disprove my general proposition any more than the existence of the Siamese twins proves that men are generally born in pairs.

"There is not a publishing concern in all this region which can give currency to a book, save perhaps some religious houses and even these cannot bring a work into that general circulation which is gratifying to an author. No parallel of this case exists, or ever has existed, in the wide world. Nowhere else on the globe is there so extended a territory, or so large a population, ranking with enlightened nations, where such a thing as literature is almost unknown.

"Everywhere else there are numerous roads to distinction; here, there is only one—politics. All who have the least taste for this pursuit enter the broad road, which differs from the one mentioned in Holy Writ in this: that all those who start in it do not reach their goal, though they may strive for it during a long life.

"The way, then, is crowded, and all who do not choose it, and a great many who do—are necessarily consigned to oblivion. Many are the men of talent and polished education, calculated to stamp their impress on the age, who, disgusted with the 'wild hunt,' and the crowds engaged in it, refuse to participate; who, with the capacity and inclination to strive in the world of letters, make no effort to do so, because, for lack of facilities at home, they would be forced to leave their much-loved section to seek for those aids necessary to the accomplishment of their wishes.

"Such men, with tastes the most cultivated and refined, finding no literary society in which to gratify their love of letters, seek in various ways to kill the time which hangs heavily on their hands, and to destroy the consciousness that they are living, and destined to die in oblivion. Some retire to their plantations—I speak of those who are blessed with competency (did not the writer know that *all* antebellum Southerners were blessed with competency?)—and devote themselves to agriculture, and reading, without the first attempt at writing. Some travel. Some, alas! become wretchedly dissipated."[1]

"Here," says old Garnett Andrews, "politics being open to all and so captivating to the ambitious, nearly all the talent of the country is turned in that direction."[2] Even the poet Henry R. Jackson put himself on record as considering "legislation the noblest science which can be presented to try the powers of the mind, and the greatest man of a nation deservedly he, who ranks the first in her legislative halls."[3]

One of the preachers complained that whenever he spoke of wishing to write poetry his congregation would remonstrate with him somewhat as follows:

> 'Tis trifling work, may it please your Rever'nce,
> For Poet, is akin to dunce.

Don't rush into print for other reasons:

> It's costly—look,
> It's *several dollars* for *a book;*
> The times are hard—cotton's falling,
> And such expenses are appalling.

---

[1] Turner, *Jack Hopeton*, 75–7.
[2] Andrews, *Old Georgia Lawyer*, 23.
[3] *Augusta Mirror*, 14 November, 1840.

GENERAL LITERARY EFFORT IN GEORGIA 193

To a poet, the explanation of this esthetic unsensitiveness lay in a too great preoccupation with money.

> Your minds are on the markets plac'd,
> On cotton gains, and cotton waste,
> On Steamboats, Packets, and the Dray,
> And news of every passing day.

And then he speaks for his opponents:

> Oh what a world we'd shortly have,
> All filled with honest men—no knave;
> If every man would seek his gains,
> And ply to making cash his brains.
>
> It matters not if we've no schools,
> Such things are only fit for fools;
> Nor aught concerns us, able lore,
> We have enough, enough and more.
>
> Depart, depart, ye bookish drones,
> And leave us to our monied thrones;
> We love enjoyment and play,
> Not study—time so thrown away.
>
> We love the race grounds prancing steed,
> And city ponies of the Gilpin-breed,
> Rattling carriages and windows
> Rich in gold for highest bidders.
>
> Festivals we love and barbecues
> Rich puddings and fine stues;
> Glasses, too, deep filled with wine.

Already the present reader doubtless finds it hard enough to blame the incorrigible parishioners for protesting against work of which this is a specimen; the last blow kills all blame that might attach to them:

> "The tear of the widow fell cold from her eyelid,
> And orphans were crying for bread all exhausted."[1]

---
[1] Cassels, *Providence*, 43.

There was, then, by the forties, leisure enough among the cultivated classes for the production of any body of literature. In the books of the time, people are represented as making long visits to one another, or even such swings around the circle (Augusta, Charleston, New York, Saratoga, Cincinnati, New Orleans, Mobile) as would set a President thinking. The resorts of Georgia were liberally patronized. "Of all the watering places which are presenting their rival claims to the public in our state this summer (announces one of the magazines, September, 1843) commend us to 'Madison.' . . . The Springs are at this time crowded with visitors, and mirth and music add wings to the hours and days which the young, the gay, and the beautiful of our land, are passing amid their charms."[1] The truth is that many of these people wrote freely, and sent their work to such magazines as existed.

The trouble was, as many early Georgians themselves knew, that most persons of intellectual capacity were drawn into strident politics, and that the few intelligent and potential writers who were left, having no enlightened audience, fell into the habit of keeping quiet. The old magazines complain much about the quality of the work contributed to them, but they do not complain at all about the quantity. As long as people could write in a spirit of leisure pass-time and somewhat absurd romanticism they would write copiously, which, luckily, is not to say anything as to how they would be read.

Longstreet's writing was hailed as being the work of a person of intelligence, frankness, and some command of literary artistry, at least of a command of a style that could compass both the swiftly entertaining and occasionally the meditatively romantic. A hero of this sort would be persistently sought after by the magazines of the state. There were several magazines.

In the early summer of 1838 young W. T. Thompson, after having spent some time in the campaigns in Florida, had begun publishing a literary paper "neatly printed and well edited," Poe testifies, called the *Augusta Mirror*.[2] According to its prospectus, this publication was "a semi-monthly journal de-

---

[1] *Orion* (Penfield, Georgia, March, 1842–February, 1844), September, 1843, 41.
[2] *Southern Literary Messenger*, June, 1838.

voted to the development of our own domestic literature; containing contributions from many of the most popular writers of the South. Besides selections from the best English and American magazines. . . ." [It covers this, that] and "every other subject in the range of polite literature, the whole comprising at the end of the year a volume of 312 large quarto pages. . . . $3.00 per year."[1] The prospectus is truly grand in sound, but the actual issues of the *Mirror* (25 May, 1839–25 July, 1840, 19 September, 1840–14 December, 1841) which it has been the privilege of the present writer to examine, do not vibrate in the memory with any too musical a persistence. They contain a good deal of matter reminiscent of Thompson's experiences in the Florida campaigns, innumerable articles on Female Education (whether it is a good thing, after all), many commencement addresses, many reviews, many poems. There is a letter in the issue of 16 May, 1840, describing in detail, and quoting liberally from, the pageant given to celebrate May-Day in Waynesboro, Georgia. King Richard and Robin Hood and the rest spoke through this pageant with accustomed dreariness. The *Mirror* had an "operative," all right, Longstreet wrote in November, 1839, to his friend Pierce; what it wanted was editors.[2]

On the whole, the *Mirror* is tiresome. Nevertheless, it continued until the late spring of 1842, when Thompson merged his paper with *The Family Companion*, a publication of similar rank, then being edited in Macon by Mrs. Sarah Lawrence Griffin.[3] The new paper, known as *The Family Companion and Ladies' Mirror*, was discontinued in the beginning of 1843 for lack of patronage.[4] Thompson was not dismayed. He went to Madison, Georgia, and began editing the *Southern Miscellany*.[5] *The Miscellany* was subsequently moved to Atlanta.[6] In 1845 Thompson associated himself with Parke Benjamin in the editorship of the Baltimore *Western Conti-*

---
[1] *Athens Banner*, 13 August, 1841.
[2] Smith, *Pierce*, 103.
[3] Lamar, *Polly Peablossom's Wedding and Other Tales* (Philadelphia, 1851), 24.
[4] Lamar, *Polly Peablossom's Wedding*, 24; *Orion*, May, 1842, 126.
[5] *Orion*, November, 1843, 137.
[6] Mildred Rutherford, *South in History and Literature* (Atlanta, 1907), 838.

nent,[1] in which also he published his articles by "Major Jones." When Thompson next came to Georgia in 1850 it was to establish a newspaper. Of course Longstreet had to contribute to the *Mirror*. As a very young man Thompson had worked under him in Augusta, and of course, therefore, always commanded Longstreet's affectionate interest.[2]

Another young friend of Longstreet's, George F. Pierce, had literary ambitions. During the fall of 1839, this young man had written to the Judge asking about the possibility of securing contributions for a magazine which he and Philip C. Pendleton were about to organize in Macon as *The Southern Ladies' Book*.

The name, Longstreet wrote back, "will do, but I should have preferred something less commonplace. The plan is well conceived, will go into operation, progress twelve or eighteen months, and expire, because subscribers won't pay, though dunned from the first number to the last. It will start pretty fair, grow lamer and lamer at every step until it expires; simply because your long list of presidents won't write for it. Maybe Brother Jesse Mercer will give you a few lines *a la mode The Cluster*, but I doubt it. I question whether you ever get more from him than some didactics upon Babto and Babtizo. Your only hope of escape from these issues is the minimum which you have fixed for your subscription list, before you start. You have run up to five hundred so fast that you'll almost wish you had made three thousand the minimum—from five to seven hundred you'll begin to think surely the prospectus has not been half circulated, from seven hundred to one thousand you'll begin to fret at the want of public spirit in the South—and between one thousand and fifteen hundred it will gradually ease out of notice. It would have been more likely to succeed as a quarterly than as a monthly publication, because many will write by the quarter who will not per month, if it ever gets under way. I dare not promise to write for it because I know not that I will be able to do so without neglecting imperative duties; but I hope and think I shall. I have

---
[1] *Western Continent*, 17 July, 1847.
[2] Smith, *Pierce*, 100–3.

no grave 'Baldwin' or 'Hall' on hand finished but may have, or something else by the time you are ready for it."[1]

In spite of this warning, the magazine was begun in January, 1840, to be continued laggingly for ten months before it expired.[2] The subscribers evidently lost just one-sixth of the five dollar subscription which they had invariably been obliged to pay in advance. The only three numbers of the magazine which the present writer has seen, August–October, 1840, contain no reference to Longstreet further than the announcement of his name, along with those of William Gilmore Simms, Alonzo Church, J. P. Waddel, A. Means, I. A. Few, E. A. Nesbit, R. M. Charlton, J. H. Lumpkin, A. B. Meek, A. H. Stephens, W. T. Colquitt, and others, as prospective contributors. Commencement addresses—articles on the "General Superiority of the Ancients to the Moderns"—"Thoughts on a Journey to the Moon"—a poem "Home," by the author of *Guy Rivers*, signed W. G. S.—and similar articles fill the magazine. In the August issue, there is an article (signed "Clara," dated Newton County, 7 August, 1840, and addressed "To the Gentlemen of Georgia") the burden of which is that it is inexpedient for a Georgia woman to let it be known if she has any intelligence; if it were known, Clara says, people would call her a blue stocking. In the September issue, the editors expatiate at length on the text that whoever is really patriotic will set to work and help relieve his country of the worst stigma to which it is subject; that is, that it has no literature; clearly, writing is the only method known for producing a literature. "Why," they inquire, "are the strong energies of our masterminds asleep? Why does the flame of our literature flicker and flare—giving but a moment's steady light and an hour's shadowy and uncertain gloom?" . . . This sort of thing proceeds at considerable length through a mire of flowery language and archaic word forms, *cometh, goeth,* and so forth, and then breaks into militancy. Though we have licked the British in arms, they are now about to get the better of us in letters. . . . "Your own state has been the arena of more than one hundred sanguinary conflicts with the natives, be-

---
[1] Smith, *Pierce*, 100–3.
[2] *Ibid.*, 100.

sides many with the British and Spaniards. Through seas of blood did our fathers wade!" Decent sons, therefore, cannot do less than make a showing for their country in the field of letters.

When the *Southern Ladies' Book* was discontinued in the fall of 1840, Pierce's associate, Mr. Pendleton, went to Savannah and began editing a magazine called the *Magnolia, or Southern Monthly*. "In some way or other, hardly by large payments, he induced Simms to become first its main contributor, then its associate editor, and finally, after the publication office has been moved to Charleston in June, 1842, its editor-in-chief. Simms labored heroically and secured contributions from the best Southern writers, such as Carruthers, Longstreet, Meek, and Charleston's mild poetess of the L. E. L. type, Miss Mary E. Lee. But a year of that climate, so fatal to literary journals, withered the promising bud, and the *Magnolia* was decently buried in June, 1843."[1]

---

[1] Trent, *Simms*, 131.

IX

UNCOLLECTED SCENES

To both the *Mirror* and to the *Magnolia* Longstreet contributed with some frequency. "Little Ben" (comprising "The Squirrel Hunt"),[1] "The Family Picture" and "Darby Anvil"[2] were written by the spring of 1838, and appeared in *The Mirror* over a time beginning prior to June, 1838, and extending through 1839.[3] "Julia and Clarissa," "The Old Soldiers," and "The Gnatville Gem," drafted off during the late thirties and early forties, were published in the *Magnolia* respectively in September and October, 1842, in March, 1843, and in June, 1843; but two other sketches done at the same time, "John Bull's Trip to the Gold Mines," announced in the *Magnolia,* November, 1842, as about to appear in December, and the "India Rubber Story"[4] seem never to have been published, and have, so far as the present writer knows, been utterly lost. "John Bull's Trip to the Gold Mines" obviously dealt with the British who had come to North Georgia in search of gold, a section and a pursuit known thoroughly by Longstreet. "The India Rubber Story" had something to do with a rubber bag supposed to be inflated, and used as a cushion by persons riding in a buggy. This story was held a shade too improper, a bit too rakish ever to be given to the public. It was written, of course, in the most harmless spirit in the world, but there are always so many people bent upon making evil out of innocence that a preacher has to watch closely what he says.

Other stories, the existence of which is only traditional, or the authorship of which is only conjectural, are, of the first

---

[1] Jackson, "Reverend Dr. Longstreet," 29; Mayes, *Genealogy*, 32.
[2] *Southern Literary Messenger*, June, 1838.
[3] *Atlanta Constitution*, 11 Nov., 1923; *Savannah News*, 11 Nov., 1923. See Note 1, 200.
[4] Mayes, *Genealogy*, 32.

class, "The Corn Shucking" and "Climbing the Greasy Pole"; and, of the second class, "A Night at College" (in which the student is waked from a dream of Heaven by suddenly rolling off of his bed to the floor), "The Coquettes" (in which a young man introduces to each other two young ladies, each of whom, he has previously told the other, is deaf), and "The Snake Bite"[2] (in which a young man having taken refuge under a bed from the irate father of his beloved is there pecked so sharply by an old setting hen that, unable to contain himself any longer, he comes sprawling out, shouting, "I'm snake bit, and I don't care who knows it!").[3]

The lost sketches of course cannot be judged, and even those which, though not lost, existed for years only in relatively inaccessible form, can hardly now be satisfactorily appraised. It was so long before most of this latter group of stories became available that they have not caught the attention of many people besides historians. At the time at which they were written, however, some of them were "pronounced by good judges, fully equal if not superior to any of the whole series."[4] One, "The Old Soldiers," was declared by the editor of a prominent magazine to be among Longstreet's "happiest efforts."[5]

The passage of eighty years does not serve to disprove these old judgments. In some regards, the less known series can be said to be of more interest than the others. Representing more strictly than the earlier sketches the result of Longstreet's effort to carry his faithful delineation of real scenes and characters "through all grades of society," they deal with types that have proved persistent in American life. The author strives with great earnestness to give (barring always the matter of sex and its implications among unmarried people) a

---

[1] These two sketches have been lost. The mention of them here is made upon the authority of Mr. Fitz R. Longstreet, of Gainesville, Georgia, who himself either saw the sketches or talked with persons who remembered having seen them in print and having heard Longstreet acknowledge them. See Note 3, 199.
[2] My ascription.
[3] *State Rights Sentinel*, 14 April, 1834.
[4] *Southern Literary Messenger*, July, 1840.
[5] *Orion*, March–April, 1843, 368.

complete picture of village life as experienced by the ordinary, every-day, middle and upper-middle class American. One associates in these stories with families worth in cold cash from twenty to sixty thousand dollars[1] (a good sum for 1816!), with families who send their daughters off to school in the North and have pianos for the daughters to play upon when they come home. Longstreet is very definite as to what he is talking about. "I describe a Georgia family," he says at the beginning of "A Family Picture." "It is a fair specimen of Georgia families generally, at the heads of which are parents of good sense, morals, and well-improved minds."

Since in these stories the writer was frequently dealing with a more refined grade of life than he had dealt with in a majority of the sketches included in the collected *Scenes*, he was naturally forced to less obvious and downright means for producing humor. Even these are obvious enough.

But if the stories of the book, *Georgia Scenes*, give evidence of something that was either carelessness or ignorance, on the part of the author, of the commonest rules of English syntax, the uncollected sketches give evidence of something that was unquestionably simple carelessness. Longstreet knew they did. He was proud of his work, but, after all, his activities as a writer were quite incidental. It was hardly good form for writing to be anything more than incidental. "I wrote these sketches," Philemon Perch declares in the Preface to *Dukesborough Tales*, "in the evenings when I had nothing else to do." "I dare not promise to write for [your magazine]," Longstreet told Pierce,[2] "because I know not that I shall be able to do so without neglecting imperative duties." "My labors are excessive," he wrote later to the *Magnolia*, "and therefore I may not be able to furnish you more than one piece for every other number, oftener if I can." Somehow he had let himself be led by Mr. Pendleton to promise some material to the *Magnolia*, but through forgetfulness he had let the time slip up on him without his having anything ready. He saw that he must either disappoint the *Magnolia* and its patrons a second time or send "some uncorrected produc-

---
[1] "Julia and Clarissa."
[2] Smith, *Pierce*, 100–3.

tion of my pen already on hand. . . . I am willing to take the worst consequences of the mistake upon myself by putting forth a piece of less merit than I think I could give it, one of a number of manuscripts (mostly unfinished and all uncorrected) which I have long kept on hand because I could not gain my consent to destroy them or publish them."[1]

But this was not unusual. Longstreet had a way of shifting his responsibility, in a sense, by intimating that he recognized the shortcomings of his work, and would remedy them if he only had time. Even in a letter which he wrote upon request to his friend, Mirabeau Lamar, outlining for him, as President of the Republic of Texas, some policies of the very highest political consequence, he had the hardihood to advance this specious excuse: "I must stop," he concludes the letter, "I have thrown the foregoing together without order and without reflection. . . . If there be one random idea in it that can be of service to you, I shall feel myself amply repaid for the little trouble it has cost me."[2]

In reviewing the uncollected stories in mass it may be said that they differ from the others chiefly in that they deal, upon the whole, with a higher grade of society, and with village life as opposed to country life; and also in the fact that they are perhaps less carefully written.

"Little Ben," after being published in the *Mirror,* was copied out and published in the *Southern Literary Messenger,* June, 1838; and, as late as October,1855, published as "selected" in *The Georgia University Magazine.* To this story there is a very erudite introduction in which the author respectfully dedicates his work to persons "who delight in tales of torment, a class large enough, since everybody enjoys the discomfort of somebody else. That is why people who do not like Horace in general, are always attracted to his ninth satire, the one in which he describes his being discommoded by a too persistent friend. This story shows how its author, as well as Horace, became the victim of too much garrulity, how every week for about two years he had found it necessary to lay himself liable to his tormentor's torrential flow of words. The name of the

---

[1] *Magnolia* (Savannah, 1841–1842; Charleston, 1842–1843), September, 1842.
[2] *Papers, Mirabeau B. Lamar,* 5.

tormentor was Benjamin Grinnolds, called generally 'Little Ben' to distinguish him from an uncle of the same name."

"Little Ben," the reader is told, "never used his upper lip in talking; he transferred this office to his upper teeth. If he was not driven to this expedient from necessity, it was certainly a kindness to both lips; for his upper teeth protruded so far forward as to make it a positive labor for his lips to salute each other. Some of his friends used to say that he could not blow out a candle without dislocating his neck, or burning his chin; but I do not believe that.

"This little deformity had the effect of changing all the b's and p's in Ben's narrative to v's and f's: nevertheless Ben delivered himself with great fluency. His sentences were uniformly short and distinguished only by the semicolon pause, save when he recounted some wonderful achievement, or astounding witticism of his hero: then, indeed, he took a semibreve rest; during which, he assumed a look of self complaisance, an arch cut of the eye, and a veiled smile that would hardly have been tolerated in Bonaparte after the Battle of Lodi. He did not always, however, use his favorite stop to divide distinct sentences, but sometimes made it usurp the comma's place; and very often ran from sentence to sentence without any pause between them. All other stops were dismissed from his discourses. He almost invariably threw the emphasis upon the first word of a sentence, and upon no other word. His delivery was naturally quick; and either from this cause, or from an irrepressible desire to pass from story to story, he dealt largely in the ellipsis. The reader has doubtless often listened to drops of rain descending from the eaves of a house, upon a platform some twelve or fifteen feet long, just after a shower. One big drop, and four or five little ones, descend in rapid succession—then a momentary pause, and fifteen or twenty roll on the ear in like manner. So fell Little Ben's words and sentences."

After this description follow two very short stories, both spoken by Little Ben in the manner above indicated. They make very hard reading. In the first, Little Ben and his two dogs, Jowler and Touser, and Uncle Ben and his dog Trigger all go squirrel hunting. Uncle Ben shoots a squirrel which lodges in "the fork of the fofler" (poplar), and Little Ben undertakes, on being promised a reward, to get the squirrel down. The reward, Ben reported, did not appear, although he had seen his uncle several times since the hunt, once at "Muster," and once at the "Court House," and upon both occasions had reminded him of his promise. "But I never see Uncle Ben," concludes the speaker, "that I don't run him about that trifle, and I reckon he hates it the worst o' anything you ever seed."

In the second story, Ben tells how when he had caught a huge catfish and shown it to his Cousin John, he was put to the necessity, by Cousin John's incredulity, of catching another such fish just to prove his skill in the matter of angling. Cousin John, Ben thought, was unquestionably entitled to his doubt until he saw proof. Ben actually catches the fish. "And ever since then," he says, "I've had the run on Cousin John about that cat."[1]

It was chiefly as a thing to be spoken that this sketch originated; its being written down at all was only secondary. Even Longstreet's contemporaries could see that the merit of the piece could be brought out only by having it properly read. *"When read by the author,"* Thompson wrote of this sketch, "we have no hesitation in pronouncing [it] the most laughter provoking of all [the *Scenes*], but it loses almost all its interest on paper." It was nothing short of a "luxury," however, to hear the author read this story to his friends, all "in its proper cadence, tone, emphasis, and pronunciation."[2]

"Darby Anvil," after appearing first in Thompson's *Mirror*, was later republished in the *Southern Literary Messenger*, January, 1844; in Fitzgerald's *Judge Longstreet, A Life Sketch* (1891); and, as "Darby the Politician," in *Stories With a Moral* (1912).[3] Longstreet was now old enough to talk about how fine things had stood in his youth. That his mind went a very long way back may be gathered from the opening sentence of this sketch, "I well remember the first man who, without any qualifications for the place, was elected to the Legisla-

---

[1] *Southern Literary Messenger*, June, 1838, 404–6.
[2] *Ibid.*, July, 1840, 572.
[3] Fitz R. Longstreet, Editor.

ture of Georgia," and from another sentence which states that "the people of those days pretty generally harbored the superstitious notion that talents were indispensable to wholesome legislation." The story is told rapidly and with shrewd observation. The plot of it shows how a totally unqualified blacksmith, by working on the vitiated, sentimental class-sympathies of his acquaintances, gets himself elected to the legislature, over two men in every way more suited for the position than he is. Proof that Darby had been a "crook" of some sort in Virginia before he migrated to Georgia, is made public just before the election, but the electorate, represented throughout as whimsical and irresponsible, decide that in producing the evidence at so critical a time Darby's enemies were unjust to him, that Darby was an object of persecution, and that he ought therefore certainly to be elected. This story proclaims Longstreet's complete abandonment of any but the most conservative democracy.

Darby was of a class of *immigrés* common in the development of most new communities. "David Crockett" encountered numbers of the genus in Texas. "He told me," says David, telling about some man he had met in the West, "that he had set down to the breakfast table one morning, at an inn, and among the small party around the board were eleven who had fled from the States charged with having committed murder. . . . 'Indeed,' said he, 'it is very common to hear the inquiry made "What did he do that made him leave home?" or, "What have you come to Texas for?" intimating almost an assurance of one's being a criminal.' "[1]

"A Family Picture" was first published by Thompson in the *Mirror;* then in a condensed form by Robert A. Whyte in his *Georgia Home Gazette,* 26 January, 1853; once in an old unidentified magazine; and finally, broken into two sketches, "Family Government" and "A Family Picture," in *Stories with a Moral.* In it, a husband and wife discuss with the supposed author whether or not it is right to punish a child before it can distinguish as to what is good and what is evil. The husband says it is not right, and the wife says it is. Longstreet agrees with the husband. He sees later, however, that

[1] David Crockett, *Life*, 331.

the wife's position was correct, and determines that the next time an argument arises between his two friends he will agree with the wife. Opportunity comes soon enough. When asked by the husband, upon that occasion, what his reasons are for his decision, the author answers that he has no reasons further than the one that experience had taught him to agree with the wife. In the brief space of nine years, the wife in this story presented her husband with eight fine children. (With much slyness Longstreet sets forth this fecundity, with much light reference to the birth of the children as the parents' being "blessed.") The hilarious pranks of these youngsters in connection with the great festival of a country hog-killing, constitute the chief interest of the plot. There is a strong suggestion here of the bad-boy type later to become universally known, and there is also a concession to popular demand for a tearful mother,—though Longstreet could not make her anything but robust and healthful. The sketch is carelessly written; it lapses into dialogue form wherever that method of presentation became least troublesome.

As "Julia and Clarissa" was too long for one number of Simms's *Magnolia,* it was made to bridge two numbers, those for September and October, 1842. It may be seen now in *Stories with a Moral* under the title, "The Match Maker, Julia and Clarissa." "The piece," Longstreet wrote when he sent it on urgent request to the *Magnolia* for publication, "was originally struck out for a *book,* not for a periodical of the common size. . . . [It is a] crude, uncorrected production of my pen [which you may] cut, trim, concentrate, or exclude, as you think proper."[1]

This story concerns itself with the obsequious but artful machinations of a Mrs. Carp and her daughter, Julia, to marry off the young Carp boy, Osborn, to Julia Carp's friend, Clarissa Gage, daughter of a widowed mother, and heiress in her own right to $30,000. All that the Carps can do finally proves unavailing before the great admiration stirred in Clarissa Gage's heart for "Milton Fisher, Esq., a young barrister whose name had been a full year before him at the village." Fisher "had everything but wealth to recommend him to a young

---
[1] *Magnolia,* September, 1842.

lady, and so high was his professional reputation that all could see that he was within a few years of a handsome fortune."[1] When one learns that the scene of this story is supposed to be laid in 1816, it is hardly possible not to conceive of it as in a large degree autobiographical. A rich young girl, whose father is dead, marries in her village home, in 1816, or soon thereafter, a poor but promising, flute-playing young lawyer who had just come to the village from some distant city. This story is remarkable, too, for its depiction of life in a small town, for its suggestion of the presence of petty, insidious evil even in supposedly uncontaminate places, and for its close similarity to Longstreet's novel, *William Mitten*. The novel was not begun ostensibly until seven years after the sketch was published, but there are portions of the longer work that look like expansions or adaptations, in spirit, at least, of the shorter one. The sketch seems in some sense, then, after all, to have been used as part of a "book," just as Longstreet had originally planned.

"The Old Soldiers," after appearing in the *Magnolia* in March, 1843, was suffered to remain in oblivion until 1912 when it reappeared in *Stories with a Moral*. In this sketch, two Revolutionary soldiers, meeting accidentally long years after the war was over, discover suddenly that they had been members of the same military organization. The revelation is more than they can bear up under. "The old men embraced," says the concluding paragraph, "but their emotions were too powerful for their strength, and they sank together to the floor."[2]

"The Gnatville Gem," which appeared in the *Magnolia* for June, 1843, must likewise thank *Stories with a Moral* for its resuscitation, though indeed, it should be stated, the agency that brought it back to life, feeling that it should, in its new existence, be given a new name, now offers it to the world as "The Village Editor." This story concerns itself with the activities of a Connecticut gentleman named Doolittle, of the strongest Federalist principles in politics, who came to Georgia in about 1800 and established a newspaper in a Georgia village. As Mr. Doolittle was a time-server, his conscience did not pre-

[1] *Stories with a Moral*, 135.
[2] *Ibid.*, 49.

vent him from conducting his paper on staunch Republican principles. He had no tact, however, and was unable to use his pliancy in politics to any advantage. It was not long before he found it expedient to leave Gnatville between two suns. No wonder. He permitted to be published in his paper contributions that anybody ought to have known were of a nature too acrimonious and personal to be unresentfully borne in a community in which everybody immediately recognized, in every case, not only the allusions, but also the source from which the contribution had come. Here is a sample of his anonymous contributions:

"A Little Receipt for Making a Big Judge. Go down to Goose Creek—catch a gander—put a quill in his mouth—blow him up until his middle parts hide his thighs—pour a half pint of old jamaica into him—set him on the bench, and call him Potgut, and he will make an excellent judge." . . . And then, as a retort: "A Receipt for making a Jack-legged lawyer. Catch a polecat, stuff him with brass, and call him Cheater, and he will make an excellent lawyer." This sketch also contains some of the doggerel verse that Longstreet permitted himself to indulge in all of his life.[1]

But the *Mirror* and the *Family Companion*, the *Magnolia* and the *Southern Ladies' Book* were not the only magazines published in Georgia in those hopeful years in the early forties. In the winter of 1840–41, William Carey Richards, an Englishman by birth and education, then only twenty-two years of age, had, with his brother Thomas Addison Richards, an illustrator, begun publishing in Penfield, Georgia (as the good Baptists which they were should have done, Penfield being the seat of the newly organized Baptist Mercer University), a magazine called *Georgia Illustrated*.[2] This publication managed in the face of great difficulties to live out a year, but was discontinued in about that time to be succeeded, beginning March, 1842, by the *Orion*. The *Orion* was edited by the same Richards, and named by Thompson of the *Mirror* ("an esteemed brother of the corps editorial who is to stand godfather to the

---

[1] Mrs. L. B. West, Jackson, Mississippi; Mrs. A. L. Heiskell, Memphis, Tennessee.

[2] *Orion*, September, 1842, 400.

newly born"), after "the most magnificent constellation in the Southern hemisphere."[1] With exhortations to people to patronize Southern magazines, with lyric assertions that this was the only magazine in the country publishing pictures illustrating the noble grandeur of Southern scenery, with occasional specimens of negro dialect,[2] with entreaties that an indigenous literature be developed, with sometimes frenzied protests that there is native talent enough lying "buried throughout the mountains and savannas of our 'sunny south' to maintain a dozen works, and that with a hundred times more originality than nine-tenths of the Northern magazines present,"—with such declarations and boasts this magazine continued through February, 1844. Richards was evidently a man of great enterprise and fair willingness to acclaim his own merits. The *Orion's* linotints, which are of great beauty, the editor continually advises, are the first produced in the United States; and indeed it is true that his magazine, running forty-eight pages to the issue, presents to this day a most respectable appearance, bespeaking an editor of some urbanity and cosmopolitan breadth of outlook. In the first issue, knowing how hard it is, he says, to establish a popular and permanent magazine, he expresses his sympathy with his contemporaries in Georgia in their struggles "to secure and maintain an independent existence." "We hope that this editor does not desire to engross or monopolize the public favor—indeed we shall prove that we are not thus selfish. We wish to labor with them [our contemporary publications] and would be one of a fraternity toiling in a worthy cause, and regarding only the great object of our toil. *The Magnolia* may bloom in beauty, never so rare and attractive—we will admire and applaud. *The Companion* may be taken to every fireside in the 'region round about' as a favorite guest—we will greet it wherever we may, and shake hands warmly. *The Mirror* may be upon the toilet of every fair reader, and in the parlor of every well-furnished house in Georgia and its great vicinity, and we shall never say aught against its brightness; and what is more, shall not be unwilling to see ourselves reflected in it occasionally. To them, one

---

[1] *Orion*, March, 1842, 54.
[2] *Ibid.*, October, 1842, 96; January, 1844, 240.

and all, we most cordially extend the right hand of fellowship, and beg to be esteemed a true, if humble, co-laborer."[1]

Everything that Richards could do to keep the tone of his magazine sectional only in the better sense of that word, everything that he could do to keep it general and free in its interests, he did persistently. He would talk, he said, of "literature in the South, not Southern literature, for we have a decided distaste for such local expressions, as if literature were of different characters in the South and in the North. It is the same everywhere except in degree and tone." . . .[2]

He conceived of his magazine as an organ of rational criticism. "We beg leave," he wrote in one of his issues, "to say a word or two to the young men, who read our magazine, upon the subject of *Literary Associations*. We believe it to be vitally important to the interest and happiness of society at the South that the young men could organize means for their intellectual improvement. We have, in other pages, asserted our belief that the mental preeminence of the people of the North is mainly attributable to the existence of Lyceums and other Societies in almost every village and hamlet of their territory. But where in Georgia—where in the South—can we find such associations? We do not think we should err in saying there are not twenty Young Men's Literary Societies in the whole state. . . ."[3] Sermons in the rural churches of Georgia are almost invariably "ranting, jargon, or rigmarole."[4] The congregational music in the rural churches too often overwhelming "torrents of discordant sounds."[5]

In November, 1843, the *Orion* was decently regretful in stating, in connection with its announcement of the discontinuance of the *Magnolia*, "that of three literary magazines which within the same number of years have been commenced in Georgia, *Orion is the sole* survivor . . . the *Companion* has lost its sociability, the *Magnolia* its bloom and fragrance— *Orion* still glitters in the literary firmament with undiminished

---
[1] *Orion*, March, 1842, 63.
[2] *Ibid.*, March, 1842, 63.
[3] *Ibid.*, September, 1842, 398.
[4] *Ibid.*, October, 1843, 89.
[5] *Ibid.*, November, 1843, 134.

luster . . . *alone* in the department of *belles lettres* in the immediate South. The *Messenger* is too remote from us to be the sole or even the principal organ of our literature—the chief exponent of our principles and institutions, and the fit repository of those delineations of Nature among us, those scenes which have too long remained unpictured and unsung. From Virginia to the Gulf of Mexico there is no literary magazine besides *Orion*."[1]

But the *Orion* did not have easy sailing through its heavens. Its very *good* qualities were tortured often into objects of rebuke. It had "no local attachments," said the *Magnolia*, and was "cosmopolitan."[2] Indeed, there was something of a war between the *Orion* and the *Magnolia* from the very beginning, originating possibly in the fact that the *Magnolia* was in a way the successor of the *Southern Ladies' Book*, a Methodist organ, and that the *Orion* was unofficially a Baptist organ. So Longstreet probably regarded it. He never once contributed to the *Orion* or even promised to contribute. It was edited by one who in addition to being a Baptist and a man of foreign birth, had had the assurance to say things about conditions in Georgia that could come fittingly only from a native, a man who stated openly that the North was intellectually superior to the South, and, with revolting boldness, attacked certain manifestations of organized religion. A great many Georgians probably felt likewise.

Richards fretted under this misunderstanding, and concluded, when invited to do so by Simms, to try his fortunes in the more generous atmosphere of Charleston. Here with Simms' strenuous help the *Orion* continued for a year or two, and then faded out.[3] By May, 1848, Richards was back in Georgia, running a bookstore in Athens,[4] and editing the weekly *Southern Literary Gazette*,[5] and, beginning January, 1849, editing, in addition, *The Schoolfellow*, a monthly magazine for girls and boys.[6] By the early fifties he was again in

---
[1] *Orion*, November, 1843, 137.
[2] *Ibid*., November, 1842, 59.
[3] Trent, *Simms*, 133.
[4] *Southern Literary Gazette*, 27 January, 1849.
[5] Lamar, *Polly Peablossom's Wedding*, "Electricity and the Temperance Agent."
[6] *Southern Christian Advocate*, 26 May, 1848.

Charleston with his Gazette, this time aided by Hayne,[1] but in 1852 he gave up the South for a bad job and returned permanently to the North, becoming subsequently a minister in the Baptist Church and a sort of popular lecturer.

Until after the Civil War this is about the end of periodical literary effort in Georgia, though there continued, of course, to be occasional up-flaring of such endeavor. *The Georgia Academician and Southern Journal of Education*[2] (begun in the spring of 1834 at Scottsboro, Georgia), the *Georgia Home Gazette* (Athens, January, 1852), the *Southern Field and Fireside* (Augusta, December, 1859–November, 1864), and even *The Countryman*[3] (Turnwold, near Eatonton, Civil War Period), comprising, by its own announcement, "everything that can amuse, instruct, or be of use to the general reader," and aiming, the editor declared, to be as powerful in the formation of public opinion throughout the civilized world as the *Edinburgh Quarterly* or *Blackwoods*,[4]—all of these may be considered as of the general class of Richards' *Gazette*. With only one of them, *The Southern Field and Fireside*, did Longstreet have definite literary relations, and that was at a time much later than the one now under consideration.

"The Gnatville Gem" (*Magnolia*, June, 1843), was the last published of Longstreet's *Scenes*, but its publication does not mark the termination of the author's interest and pride in his work. In 1839, it is true, he became a minister of the Methodist Church, and discontinued, for a while as "too light and trifling for his new station and calling," nearly all active interest in his writing, discontinued entirely the old way he had of edifying his friends at times by actually reading to them from his compositions. Indeed, by more than one person his writing of the *Scenes* was "held up to view," Longstreet stated, "as a test of my fitness morally and intellectually for . . . sacred office and . . . responsible position."[5] Many people probably thought them unbecomingly light. Bishop Andrew had as his very shibboleth the phrase, "Be serious." Undoubt-

[1] Trent, *Simms*, 231.
[2] *State Rights Sentinel*, 10 April, 1834, Prospectus.
[3] Julia Collier Harris, *Joel Chandler Harris*, 29.
[4] *Southern Field and Fireside*, 19 May, 1860.
[5] Fitzgerald, *Judge Longstreet*, 117.

edly, whenever the Bishop began contemplating his friend Longstreet he had to think very hard about the historical value of the *Scenes* before he could quite reconcile himself to the idea of a Methodist preacher's being best known in the capacity of funny-man.

It was not a great while, however, after Longstreet became a minister, before, so far as concerned the matter of cold publication at least, he was back in the field of letters, enheartened by his own convictions and by his friends' entreaties that his writings should be esteemed because of their worth as history. The *Scenes* were no "mere fancy sketches," he was reminded, but actual transcripts from life, which obviously, if the author is to be truthful [preacher though he be], must include at times perhaps both the ludicrous and the profane. It is hoped, said one of the contemporary papers, that the Judge's "pious" friends will endeavor to persuade him to take up his sketches again, and do what they can to persuade him that no one could be "so fastidious as to censure him, or transfer to *him* the levity which appears in *his characters*." It was called to his attention that the stories are really little sermons. "The *moral* of the pieces when not professedly drawn by the author, as is frequently the case, is to be found in the delicate satire which runs through the whole descriptions and delineations."[1]

This was an argument which an already half-hearted opponent could not well resist. As history then, perhaps, from the author's viewpoint, but as highly entertaining and humorous stories from the viewpoint of the world, the second group of stories (that is, those not published by Longstreet in book form) continued to appear regularly from 1838 to 1843, extending over the first years of their author's life as a minister. At times, later, he was disturbed by what he considered the essentially frivolous nature of his sketches, and condemned them as "literary bagatelles, the amusement of idle hours";[2] but, on the whole, throughout his life he enjoyed vastly his character as humorist and litterateur. In 1840, he could never definitely dismiss from his mind the idea of revising the *Scenes* for publication by the Harpers. In 1844, he was reported by

---
[1] *Southern Literary Messenger*, July, 1840, 572-4.
[2] Fitzgerald, *Judge Longstreet*, 117.

one of his neighbors as "not unprepared to unfold a budget full of as good things as ever relieved the cares of Nestor, and led him in to hearty worship at the side rending shrine of Momus."[1] In 1859, he was contemplating "a new revised and enlarged edition . . . in which, with other emendations [various] discordant portions [were to] be harmonized and made to form a congruous whole." During the winter of 1862-3 he was helping wounded Confederate soldiers while away the time, relating to them with zest and "indescribably amusing mimicry" the various incidents of his book.[2] In 1864, he was proudly alluding in a letter to Alexander Stephens to Ransy Sniffle.[3] Till his death he told the stories to his grandchildren.[4] The statement that Longstreet was ashamed of his book, and that he tried to suppress it, writes his friend, George G. Smith, himself a Methodist preacher, is "absurd." "Nothing could be falser. He was as proud of this bantling as any other author ever was."[5]

Longstreet was undoubtedly gratified over his having contributed something to the progress of Southern literature. After all, the best way to remedy Southern unproductivity in letters was to set out and write something. How, in one's private thought, meantime, was one to explain this phenomenon? Indolence? Slavery? Complacency? Let one again (for the thousandth time!) run through one's mind the various hypotheses. There was so much complaint, but so little real counsel. The Reverend Mr. Cassels had expressed the matter definitely in 1835.

> Why mayn't our Southern clime the race of learning run?
> Is it because we're burnt beneath a scorching sun?
> Beneath those rays how rich our vegetations rise!
> And may not *mind* attain beneath to equal size?
> Was not the cradle laid, of science, in the South?
> Was it not cherished first in the fair land of Thoth?
> The Hebrew learning, too, in Southern Asia lived,

---

[1] *Southern Literary Messenger*, January, 1844, 43.
[2] Gordon, *Reminiscences*, 92-3.
[3] Fitzgerald, *Judge Longstreet*, 194.
[4] Mrs. L. B. West, Jackson, Mississippi.
[5] Smith, "Some Unrecognized Georgians."

And 'twas in Southern Europe Greeks and Romans thriv'd:
The North was then barbarian, cold, and wild, and dead,
While in the South fair Science raised her glorying head.
Let *us*, then, claim the mantle ancient sages left,
And prove ourselves the worthy heirs of such a gift:
Nor let a law, to eastern lands of old applied,
Be in this western sphere, in modern times denied.[1]

The magazines had fretted over the question; Mr. Simms in South Carolina had fretted over it; Mr. Turner in Georgia thought somewhat too sharply on the subject; Longstreet himself recognized the shortcomings of his section in matters of the intellect. As late as 1840 he was still having to hope that soon Georgia would "be no longer under the necessity of importing our preceptors, our engineers, our geologists, our everything that demands proficiency in science," hoping "that the day is not far distant when Georgia will contribute something to the vast store of literature with which Europe is astonishing, enlightening, and blessing the world."[2]

"I confess," he says, "that I have often felt my national pride stung by a comparison of the Old and New Worlds in point of intellectual advancement. And when I reduce the comparison to England, France, and Germany on the one hand, and the Southern States on the other, I have felt humbled under a sense of their vast superiority over us. True, they have advantages in their long-established and well-endowed universities, their extensive libraries, their ready access to the relics of ancient literature and art, their hereditary fortunes, their dense population, and their constant intercourse with all parts of the world, which must for centuries, if not forever, keep them ahead of us in many departments of science.

"But there are some in which they lead us wherein they derive no aid from those auxiliaries, and others wherein the advantage is on our side. We have no apology for the distance at which we are in the rear of them in the exact sciences in chemistry, botany, natural history, geology, and in works of imagination and taste. Some of these depend upon principles

---
[1] Cassels, *Providence*, 26.
[2] "Emory College Inaugural," in Fitzgerald, *Judge Longstreet*, 78.

accessible to all, and others upon nothing more than close attention to the great volume of nature that lies open before us. If all that is grand, beautiful, picturesque or curious in that spacious volume could have induced us to study it, the Southern States should have been among the foremost in some of those sciences, and Georgia should have been abreast of some of the foremost of the Southern States. But it is a lamentable truth that in the sixty years of her independence she has not shed a gleam of light upon any one of them.

"There is a still more lamentable truth in reserve, which it is no longer a virtue to conceal. It is that some of her sons (if *sons* they may be called) harbor a deadly hostility to all that savors of moral or mental improvement in the country. Our university, to which we are now indebted for nearly all that is valuable in the council of the State, creditable on the bench, or noble in enterprize, they would have strangled at its birth, and, having failed in their purpose, they would now perish it by withholding from it its needed sustenance."[1]

Longstreet wondered what could be the trouble. If he ever faintly suspected that it was due to the laxity of the American system of government, he was reassured on all hands by his desire to believe otherwise. Did not Mr. Meek, an Alabama gentleman, speaking in 1844 to a body of men at his Alma Mater, the University of Georgia, specifically deal with the possible disadvantages of the American system, and show clearly that the loosely confederated American states would actually do better in literary matters on account of their very independence? Literature, Mr. Meek had shown, not being concentrated in one capital, would thus be kept free always of the danger of being made "a vile pander to the bad passions of the enemies of free institutions"; would spring into life excited by the rivalry existing between the different states.[2] The only drawback to Mr. Meek's thesis was that he seemed content with achievement in the distant future. What Longstreet wanted and believed possible was achievement in the near future.

---
[1] Fitzgerald, *Judge Longstreet*, 78.
[2] Alexander B. Meek, *Americanism in Literature*, Speech, University of Georgia, 8 August, 1844.

The absurdest way of accounting for Southern backwardness, it seemed to Longstreet, was to say that the South was shackled by slavery. One representative Southerner declared himself upon this point explicitly: "The very existence of negro slavery we consider an influence in behalf of literature."—It makes for a leisured upper class.[1] Did not any novice in history know that it was as slave states that Greece and Rome had seen the best days that ever came to them? And yet there were people who persisted in attributing all of the Southern woes to this system. Most nettling! Josiah Meigs, for instance, President of the State University, as staunch a Democrat, too, as ever lived, had openly so declared himself. "I have little hope," he had told somebody, "of anything really clever in states which permit Slavery.[2] Where Slavery is admitted, literature and science will never flourish. The Muses hate the Lash and Whip; they are of gentle mind."[3] And there was an old rumor about a book-seller in Charleston, who had found his well-established business somehow suddenly vanishing from under him almost immediately after the passage of some laws permitting the reopening of the slave trade.[4] All of these things were, of course, erroneous on the face of them, or only accidentally true. . . . Nevertheless, it was good to offer contradiction to our traducers, and *Georgia Scenes* was in the nature of such a contradiction. Longstreet knew this, and thoughtful Georgians everywhere knew it. He was naturally proud of his work, even if it contributed only a little towards upholding his state's fame.

The Judge's interest in the purely diverting aspects of literature had always been secondary. It is all well enough to tell your jokes, and do your mimicry, but when one sits down to write, it is incumbent upon one to instruct and edify as well as to amuse. Incidentally, it is as well as not to make your writing bring you any little money that people will pay for it. "The stories I am sending you," he wrote to one of the magazines which had solicited some of his work, "are unfinished,

---

[1] H. R. Jackson, *Augusta Mirror*, 14 November, 1840.
[2] *Josiah Meigs, Life of*, by W. A. Meigs (Philadelphia, 1887), 101.
[3] *Ibid.*, 107.
[4] Phillips, *American Negro Slavery*, 137-8.

but I am letting them go anyway, remembering that I partly promised them to you, and more especially as your very liberal offer for them (i. e., for the first publication of them) will make me turn them over to very good account."[1]

It is well, indeed, to turn an honest dollar whenever you can find an opportunity. In Augusta, this man was everything almost that one can conceive of, but in the midst of his manifold activities, and most surprisingly, perhaps, in the midst of his high religious enthusiasm, he took time off to go up with the crowd into northwest Georgia when gold was discovered there, and buy himself what he judged to be a plot of land rich in gold deposits.[2] He continued trading in real estate, and he knew and practiced the art of charging adequately for his services at law. He wanted full value-received all of his life, was distinctly vexed as an old man at the high boat-fare from Liverpool to America,[3] spent much time in his last years plotting and drawing in his little book that told how rich he was.

---
[1] *Magnolia*, September, 1842.
[2] Williams, *Advice*, 107.
[3] *Life of Delany*, 103–5.

X

THE MINISTRY

As time went on Longstreet became less and less hopeful of the approaching establishment of a satisfying social order. Now that he saw completely discredited all that nullification had represented, saw statesmanship turned in many places into demagoguery, he began, now that he was discouraged by the torpid inaction of life's courses, to look more definitely whither he had previously been taught to look by what had seemed to him those courses' malign and impertinent obtrusion. Like Jefferson toppling to his grave with a weakened faith in the unremitting wisdom of his fellow countrymen, Longstreet, politically embittered, knew how to do a thing that Jefferson did not know at all. Perhaps he thought always that the nation's failure to accomplish an ideal government was due to the South's rejection of the nullification nostrum, perhaps he became doubtful as to the capacity of men to set up for themselves in a brief period, or at all, a government that will function in any way not calculated to rend the hearts of its own projectors. There are few men who do not grow in despondency even faster than in years. Merit, Longstreet knew, will have its reward in this life,—and yet. . . . At times the whole process of recompense seems hopelessly vague and bungling. Humanity unaided seems incapable of any valid achievement. Government without spirituality, it seems, can never come to anything. One's surest convictions at times go vanishing.

During the late 1830's Longstreet was rapidly abandoning his hope of remedying the world's ills by the swift method of politics and was determining that he must resort to devices less tangible but more basic.

The way to popularize yourself politically and get yourself elected to office in Georgia, he says, is to "attend every gathering in the county, treat liberally, ape dignity here, crack obscene jokes there, sing vulgar songs in one place, talk gravely in another, tell long, dry stories, give short mean toasts, jest with the women and play with the children, grow liberal in suretyships, pay promptly and dun nobody, and ask everybody to vote for you."[1] It is, of course, an overwhelmingly desirable qualification to have fought in a war.[2] The legislature of Georgia, thrown open by such artifices, to knaves and fools, have enacted measures, "which for extravagance and folly have no parallel in the codes of enlightened nations."[3] He would say more, he says, but "in charity to my native land I forbear. And yet I am not so sure but that such charity is treason to the State and allegiance to her most deadly foes. Presumptuous ignorance should be reprimanded with a fearless tongue, its sins should be proclaimed abroad in warning to the people, and all good men should unite their efforts to redeem a State entirely from such influence."[4] In 1835, the Judge had been very careful to appease persons who could not "distinguish between a simple narrative of an amusing interview, and ridicule of the parties to it";[5] a little later, writing about the same general times, he could talk of the populace with a mordant force that he evidently thought more the part of a minister than of a lawyer in politics. The characters of one of his stories of this later period, he says, "saw how much rum it took to elect a captain and a Justice of the Peace. He saw justice administered by magistrates in their shirt sleeves, and heard stiff quarrels between them and the suitors."[6]

Clearly political activity will no longer appease an honest man who has come so to regard it. "The Christian religion," he wrote, ". . . would supersede all human laws and all human governments. . . . We see why it is that all human laws and governments have ever failed and ever must fail of their ends. . . . They do not reach the seat of the disease they are designed to cure."[7] As early as November, 1828, Longstreet

---

[1] "Darby Anvil," *Stories with a Moral*, 70.
[2] *Ibid.*, 80.
[3] *Ibid.*, 86.
[4] *Ibid.*, 87.
[5] "Sage Conversation."
[6] *William Mitten*, 232.
[7] "Old Things Become New," I, 847.

had become a local preacher in the Methodist Church,[1] and it is certain that he was "in the habit of attending the meetings of every kind, of that denomination. . . ."[2] The church was to be for him a veritable place of sanctuary, or as fully such a place as it could be for a man as thoroughly in accord as Longstreet was with the demands for tangible efficiency made by his time. Wilde, in the face of political disappointment, had gone to Europe and stayed six years in literary pursuits; his plan had been to remain always, and when he returned it had been reluctantly.[3] William W. Mann, Longstreet's law partner, disdaining politics, was driven to retire from the practice of law, and became for years the Paris correspondent of the *National Intelligencer* and the *Southern Literary Messenger*. Later he returned to Augusta as literary editor of the *Southern Field and Fireside*,[4]—Among other activities, to reject certain poetry contributed to his publication, because, it was explained, some of the lines had six instead of the regulation ten syllables.[5] But Longstreet, even if he had not been genuinely religious and inwardly persuaded to go into the ministry, would have been prevented from devoting himself at this juncture to literary pursuits because of his temperamental desire for action and because the literature he knew was of a type that does not attract men to it as a spiritual solace. He knew the Latin poets, and the English Augustans and their interpretation of Shakespeare, without knowing the Augustans' passion for artistic perfection. And, in addition, as a religious book, not a literary one, he knew the Bible.

In 1830 and 1831, the Augusta Methodist Church was served by James Osgood Andrew, who, the year before he came to Augusta, had been in Greensboro.[6] Naturally his having so recently come from the Longstreets' old home gave him a basis of friendship with them which soon grew into affectionate intimacy. During the summer of 1831, Andrew conducted a revival so strenuous in its nature that immediately

---

[1] George G. Smith, *A Hundred Years of Methodism in Augusta* (Augusta,1898), 31.
[2] *State Rights Sentinel*, 8 May, 1834.
[3] *Orion*, January, 1843, 127.
[4] *Southern Field and Fireside*, 3 September, 1859.
[5] *Ibid.*, 10 December, 1859.
[6] Smith, *Andrew*, 200.

upon its conclusion he fell into a long illness with bilious fever. His weakness necessitated his being given an assistant, and this assistant proved to be George Pierce, a young man whom Longstreet had always regarded almost as one of his own family, the son of his dear friend, Dr. Lovick Pierce of Greensboro. Here, preaching before white and negro, Andrew and Pierce delivered four sermons a week, besides conducting prayer meetings and class meetings, and attending to their official duties. In May, 1832, upon being made a Bishop, Andrew, though continuing to live in Augusta,[1] passed the leadership of the Augusta church to Pierce.[2] It was a grave responsibility for a young man of twenty-four, who was married, and who was receiving only $700 a year salary. He preached three times every Sunday and held a meeting every night in the week.[3]

Between the Andrews and the Pierces, Longstreet's religious fervor could not possibly have waned. His wife and his sister, Mrs. Camfield, were now both active in church work, and among the most liberal contributors to the beneficent enterprises of the denomination.[4] His own religious interests fitted in nicely with his work with the Temperance Society. The whole current of his inward emotions and of his external surroundings bore him one way. That was towards entering the ministry.

"I had felt for some years," Longstreet wrote late in life, "that I was called of God to preach the gospel, but I had excused myself on the ground of my peculiar embarrassments. In the fall of 1838, this impression became so strong upon my mind that I actually feared to resist it. I unbosomed myself to my bosom friend upon this head upon this wise: 'My dear wife, I feel that I am under the last call of God to preach his gospel. So far as it concerns me personally, it will cause me no effort to obey it; but when I think of *you* I recoil from it. A man may be a lawyer and a true Christian, but I am satisfied that he cannot be a practicing attorney and an efficient preacher

---

[1] Smith, *Andrew*, 238
[2] *Ibid.*, 521–2.
[3] Smith, *Pierce*, 80–1.
[4] Smith, *A Hundred Years*, 22–4.

at the same time. If, therefore, I enter the ministry, I shall abandon the law. I shall seek no favors or indulgences from the Church that would not be readily granted to the poorest man or the poorest preacher in it. Nay, I shall endeavor to set an example to my brethren of prompt and cheerful obedience to the bishop's orders as to my sphere of labor. If he says go to the rice-fields of the sea-coast and preach to the negroes or to the higher latitudes and preach to the mountaineers, I will go. But what is to become of you? You have never enjoyed three months of unbroken health since I first knew you. [She had had eight children in seventeen years.] You must bid adieu to this spacious, peaceful country-seat, with all its sacred associations (we had buried two children near it) and its comfortable surroundings, to follow your husband to all places and all classes of people, where and with whom he may be ordered to work for God. How can you endure such a life, after the life of ease and affluence which you have always led?

" 'But after all, it may be that I am mistaken in telling my impressions for the indications of Providence. Let us, therefore, make it the subject of prayer for one week, asking God to give us some intimation of his will in this all important matter.' At the end of three days I inquired of her whether she had come to any conclusion upon the subject of our special petition. She said she had, and it was that I ought to preach. I replied: 'I am thoroughly convinced of it.' The next Sabbath found me in the pulpit, a licensed Methodist preacher. Here I announced that as soon as I had filled my obligations to my clients I would cease to practice law and devote myself exclusively to the service of God. The negroes, at least, gave audible signs of rejoicing, for I had endeared myself to them by having opened and conducted a Sabbath school for their children, which was really an improving institution."[1]

But common-sense people would not acquiesce so promptly. Older men than Longstreet had become "converted," turned into earnest church members or even local preachers. That much was all right. One could comprehend how Judge Clayton at fifty-five, after a life of sound morality but of professed

---
[1] Fitzgerald, *Judge Longstreet*, 59–61.

religious scepticism, found it in himself to join the church, "repenting of his past follies, embracing with unfeigned sincerity, the truth of the Christian religion, tottering down the long aisle before a church full of people to shake hands, with his trembling paralytic hand, with an enemy he had not spoken to for years."[1] But in Longstreet one had a man forty-eight years old, notably successful in law and literature, and an acknowledged force for all decency in the community, determining to devote himself to—and what was more, to take his wife with him into—a new and trying profession in which even the most eminent qualifications did not assure success. The lawyers at least said that he was clearly out of his head, and that in less than two years he would be stark crazy.[2] Even as a child, it was remembered, there had been strange reports about his being unbalanced.

In 1838,[3] the call became too strong for resistance, and in December of that year Longstreet, as one of a class of seventeen, was admitted into the ministry.[4] A preacher had to pass through these stages: the first year he was admitted on trial, the second year he remained on trial, and the third year he was admitted into full connection.[5] It was in January, 1843, at the conference held in Savannah, before Longstreet was "admitted into full connection," "ordained," and made a "deacon,"[6] and 1844, at Columbus, before he was made an elder.

The Methodists kept up considerable ado over whom they should admit into their priesthood and whom not. The present writer can remember one of the old-line members of the church telling him that whenever he saw a Methodist minister he felt a thrill of pride, knowing what that minister had had to pass through with in the way of intellectual and moral examination before he received the sanction of the conference. Indeed, there was prescribed for new ministers a regular four years' course of reading, including the Bible, and various Biblical commentaries and dictionaries, the Dis-

---

[1] Miller, *Bench and Bar*, I, 184–90.
[2] Longstreet, "Old Things Become New," I, 845.
[3] Smith, *Methodism in Georgia and Florida*, 334.
[4] Minutes, Methodist Episcopal Church, II, 607.
[5] Minutes, Methodist Episcopal Church, II, 520.
[6] *Ibid.*, III, 217–9, 430–2.

cipline and History of the Church, Orthography, Etymology and Syntax, Wesley's Sermons, Psychology, Ancient History, and Geography, and a book called *The Calvinist Controversy*.[1] Upon certain portions of this reading, candidates were examined for each of the four years that had to elapse before they could be made full-fledged ministers. All of this Longstreet, of course, went through. "The only adverse report against him was that he *tripped in his examination on English grammar*."[2]

This was assuredly great mirth-fodder for all of the brethren, who, despite Bishop Andrew's exhortations to them to "be serious," could not for the life of them refrain from much laughing. The great Judge and aristocrat and litterateur had fallen down on a grammar examination set in general for people of such intellectual naïveté as not to be able to tell why a group of ministers look shocked when a young candidate for the ministry explains to his examiners that in some case or other a man would be "in a devil of a fix!"[3]

The Conferences were great occasions, earnest religious discussion, glowing religious emotion, genial gathering of old long-separated friends, warm popular adulation provoking at times in the object of it a domineering gruffness, full and lavish provision for the demands of hungry and tired physical nature —fried chicken, lemon pie, feather beds. "For breakfast in those times," Simms says, "they had hominy, waffles, ricecakes and fritters, with corresponding variety of meats—a dish of broiled partridges, a stack of venison and a dish of boiled eggs."[4]

As for the preaching, there were certainly, at least, no sophisticated and hypercritical imitations set on how far a man might range in his efforts at forensics. In a group of relatively illiterate persons, the palm for oratory goes to the man who can swing together the most platitudes with the greatest number of trite and high-sounding phrases. How ecstatically delightful it is to have audiences hungry for just

---

[1] Minutes Mississippi Methodist Conference, 1839, 13–4.
[2] Smith, *Methodism in Georgia and Florida*, 334.
[3] *Anthony, Life of*, 76.
[4] *As Good as a Comedy* (New York, 1852), 29.

what it is easiest to give them! "It was not long after he started preaching," says some one, lauding one of the ministerial idols of his youth, "before he reached the skies, and with wonderful ease and grace stepped from planet to planet." Of another he says: "Born an orator, he seemed as much at home in cloud and sky as at evening's quiet twilight on earth. I saw him once when he placed one foot on the Alps and the other on the Andes, and swept the whole circle. . . . I have heard him preach when he looked as if he had just bathed in the river of the water of life, and was baptizing the congregation with the very dews of heaven."[1]

At all of these annual conferences, Longstreet was present, the object of some popular curiosity among the young men especially, as being, for all of his ecclesiastical newness, perhaps the most distinguished man there. Bishop Andrew, honoring this sentiment, would sometimes appoint the Judge to give the younger members a talk. Once the Bishop asked him to tell these neophytes "the proper way to read hymns and scripture lessons," giving him full latitude as to how he should treat his subject, "which," observes one of the youngsters who heard him, "as the sequel proved, was all the better for him. At the appointed time the Judge began his lecture. In a few words, and by a few examples, he showed us how to read hymns, where to throw the emphasis, etc., then, in two or three minutes more, how a text of scripture, as a foundation for a sermon, should be read. At length he seemed to have exhausted the subject. Finally, he said, 'My young brethren, the best guide to the proper reading of both hymns and texts is your own good common sense. If you have this essential, but I must say very rare gift, you will read both your hymns and texts correctly. But if you do not possess this important commodity, all I could say, were I to stand here an age, would not give it to you.' He then closed his remarks."

"The older brethren," the writer continues, "said the Judge was 'in the brush.' The younger ones felt disappointed and felt they had gained but little if anything by the lecture. The Bishop said, 'I hope the young brethren will act on Brother

---
[1] Richardson, *Lights and Shadows*, 3–4.

Longstreet's suggestions.'" The whole programme evidently fell flat, and yet one wonders what else was demanded. Did they want the Judge to turn elocution teacher and mouth the vowels for them? They were dealing with a man of dignity.

Longstreet's mind could not adjust itself to the cult that sonorousness and splendor of sound be developed at the expense of matter. If he had time he could prepare for you a speech the sentences of which would roll as majestically as you could wish, but when he was taken unawares, when he was swayed by such deep feeling as to be unconscious for the moment that he was a literary person, his speeches, judging by the old reports, were solid and sincere and convincing to a degree, giving them something of permanent validity. If you gave him time he would force himself into the recognized forms, would tell you about "an aspect as sublime as the eagle on the storm, that rides in proud defiance before the blast that he cannot resist and strikes with strong wing the tempest that hurries him away."[1] Unfortunately, he would come off the worse. If you let him feel that he was on exhibition he would never get his real stride.

In March, 1842, he was in Athens, preaching before a congregation largely composed of the faculty and students of the State University, many of whom, having known him previously only as a literary personage, had come largely with the idea of hearing the lion roar in his new capacity. "Yesterday for the first time," wrote young Linton Stephens to his brother, Alexander, "I heard a sermon from Judge Longstreet. In the pulpit to me he appeared awkward, and to come much below himself. In preaching he sometimes used Latin phrases and terms of expression unbecoming his place. In praying, for instance, I recollect his saying in a very cold conversational manner, 'Lord, we can hardly generalize our sins, much less specify them,' which, though used by a very devout man, seems to be very much opposed to that earnestness and dignity with which we should address ourselves to a very Superior Being. Though his manner is not suited to the pulpit, yet I think even there he shows he has genius."[2] As a matter of

---
[1] Fitzgerald, *Judge Longstreet*, 85.
[2] James D. Waddel, *Biographical Sketch of Linton Stephens* (Atlanta, 1877), 32-3.

fact, he had a way of citing authorities in his sermons, precisely in the manner of a lawyer citing a code.[1]

It is the general testimony that the man could not preach. The fact comes out even in Fitzgerald's biography. In a section of his book, in which the preaching of several of Longstreet's ministerial contemporaries is described in such glowing terms that the reader is puzzled to determine which of them is being presented as best, Bishop Fitzgerald discusses his old friend's preaching with a restraint and a disposition to abbreviate too surprising to spring altogether from an inverted consciousness reminding him that it is Longstreet primarily whom he is supposed to be writing about and should therefore not praise at the expense of the others. One feels always that they were all of them determined, those old brethren, to say about each other only such things as would make one feel good. Possibly it was a sort of unconscious turnabout-is-fair-play compact. At any rate that was Rule One in the by-laws. If a man is unconscionably tall, you must say that he is not a dwarf; if he is ugly, you are to express your detestation of men who are pretty. When they praise Longstreet's "logic," then, "cultivated by his long practice at the bar,"[2] and his "exegetical clearness and logical method in conducting his arguments,"[3] when they speak of him as "not unsuccessful as a revivalist," when they praise his singing as "often more impressive than the sermon," when they go through all of these motions prescribed in their unwritten Discipline, one knows then what one knows.

George G. Smith had a way of talking plainly. To him, Longstreet's preaching seemed as pedantic as it did to young Stephens. His sermons, Smith says, were "calm, dispassionate, argumentative, so much so that Uncle John, his old slave, used to say, 'Mars Gustus can't preach, he just gets up and laws it.'"[4] But in reality it is hardly fair to consider Longstreet as a preacher at all. He never had opportunity to preach, never gained any experience. Though he was a member of

---
[1] Longstreet, Ms. Notebook.
[2] Fitzgerald, *Judge Longstreet*, 69.
[3] *Ibid.*, 66.
[4] Smith, "Some Overlooked Georgians."

the Conference for eighteen years he was for only five months able to devote himself primarily to preaching.[1]

But when argument was called for, as it was at times, especially when he was a delegate to the General Conference of the Church in 1844, he acquitted himself admirably. And when he could relax and not feel himself greatly responsible, as it was possible for him to do during the forties, when, going out from a busy week as President of Emory College, he would preach on Sundays at the village churches in the surrounding territory,—at such times he could produce high feelings in his listeners that lingered with them always. James Jackson, speaking at the Memorial Services held for Longstreet at Emory College in 1871, testified how years before in the little vilage of Monroe, he had heard Longstreet "preach Jesus with that simplicity and power which so characterized the man; and often, at the close of the service, as was the habit of many Methodist preachers of that day, have I heard him sing alone, with melting harmony and tenderness, some sweet, sad, soul-inspiring hymn; . . . I still see his tall, lean form and striking, peculiarly striking, face; and the melody and music of the song . . . still thrills my soul."[2]

And certainly no one who heard him as a very old man preach to his friends and neighbors in Oxford, Mississippi, could ever forget the simple majesty of the gaunt old gentleman as he would plead so earnestly, argue so persuasively, with persons all of whom had long since fully accepted every conclusion of dogma he was seeking to bring home to them— as he would sing, with such tragically broken notes, hymns that were those people's most tangible hold on a God who was to release them at last from a world filled only with the cruel disappointment and devastation of defeat in war—as he would from weakness sit down to continue his sermon, presenting a picture to his congregation, all the while, as unconscious as they were of it, of the implacable cruelty that brings at length all power and all beauty into gruesome ineffectuality. But who shall say that the testimony of these last men is worth anything? Who under the conditions that such a Mississippi

---
[1] Fitzgerald, *Judge Longstreet*, 48.
[2] Jackson, "The Reverend Dr. Longstreet," 20.

congregation found itself under in 1865-70, could keep the circumstances of a sermon apart from the sermon itself, who among them could distinguish what the man had said from the thoughts that had come to them as they sat before him and reflected on the immemorial return of spring, proclaimed gaily to them through the high windows, and upon the flat definitive absence of most that had been dear to them?

However you esteemed the preacher you were bound to admire the man personally. He was independent. In full accord with his denomination about most things, even to its distrust of an educated ministry (the illiterates then in the ministry "did no harm," he said in 1844[1]), he nevertheless about other things held to his own mind. He knew his power, and meant about some things to have his own way; he was not to be stampeded into anything. On joining the church he had declared himself not in accord with certain practices[2] and policies[3] of his denomination. He would not give up his individuality. When he went off to conduct revivals, he did not feel under necessity of showing his conformity by either praying or eating all of the time he was not in the church. He could pick out tunes on the piano for the young people, and sing funny songs for them, and tell them stories about absent-minded people who hitch their horses and then walk off with the bridles. These stories he could make so ludicrous that little girls' mothers were obliged to tell them not to giggle so, and not to crowd so around Judge Longstreet's chair,—whereupon, of course, he must needs catch the little girls up to him by way of protection. . . .[4]

In the pulpit he would neither weep too much nor laugh too much. He would not turn showman for the people after the hazardous, reprehensible practice of certain well-meaning brethren then taking up this manner in Georgia.[5] If God were good enough to let him be the means of a conversion, he was, of course, supremely happy, but he would not therefore cheapen

---

[1] Methodist Episcopal Church, General Conference, 1844, *Debates*, 216.
[2] Sherwood, *Memoir*, 231.
[3] Methodist *Debates 1844*, 113.
[4] Mrs. Rebecca Latimer Felton, Letter, 7 February, 1922.
[5] Turner, *Jack Hopeton*, 36.

his dignity by standing on his head. "I'm so glad, my dear sir," he would say, stepping down to greet a young stripling of a boy come to the altar to profess conversion, "I'm so glad, how do you feel?"[1]

It was thought by some denominationalists that it was their business to underrate all secular education, and that they should cause the Legislature not to appropriate any more money to state educational institutions than to the denominational colleges. This seemed to Longstreet preposterous. He said so in his inaugural address at the Methodist institution, Emory. Here, after endorsing the state university fulsomely, he declared: "I cannot understand why that which is confessedly a state institution should be denied the assistance of the state upon such a ground—this is to cripple a friend because other friends are crippled."[2]

There was a certain wholesome tolerance in Longstreet not generally met with among his kind, a tolerance that spoke in free condemnation of its antithesis. "Religious sects," he states, "are the most uncompromising in their difficulties and the most incorrigible in their errors of any people under the sun." He sees every reason why the Protestants and the Roman Catholics should coöperate, certainly believes in this coöperation to the extent of thinking it desirable that they say *Amen* to the same prayer. After describing an instance in which such fraternization had not proved fatal to the suppliants, he says, "Now if there is a member of any Church of Christ who is not tenderly and pleasantly touched with this picture, he is out of his place and a disgrace to any place."[3] One could, he was sure, be equally as good a Christian in some other churches as one could in the Methodist.[4] Wherever there was littleness or finickiness he was into it a-tilt. Through the summer and fall of 1842 he was conducting a newspaper controversy, urbane on his part and brutal on his opponent's part, with one Allen Turner, a fellow preacher, as to whether

---
[1] Jackson, "The Reverend Dr. Longstreet," 21.
[2] Fitzgerald, *Judge Longstreet*, 78.
[3] *Ibid.*, 67–9; Longstreet, "Old Things Become New," I.
[4] Longstreet, *Mitten*, 214.

or not instrumental music was too inherently wicked to be used in Church Services.[1]

But he makes, too, concessions broader and more basic. Unless a thing were immoral, no church member, he thought, need refrain from doing it. "I cannot," he says, "think that the interest of religion is subserved by cutting off any one innocent enjoyment";[2] unless the Bible specifically condemns a thing, it is to be considered as sanctioned.[3] This is not to say that he is latitudinarian—Lord forbid!

This preacher had boundless courage. Having been stationed in Augusta for the first year of his ministry, so that, the Bishop thought, he might wind up his business affairs there before being sent elsewhere in the state, he found himself leader of a group already thoroughly well known to him. In his congregation were six hundred persons, nearly half of whom were negroes, and all of whom worshipped in the same church. In the state-at-large there were over 35,000 Methodists, one-fourth of whom were negroes. The denomination was flourishing, and nearly everywhere well thought of, though some of the old-timers were still taking occasion to cast slurs at the way the Methodists would shout, and at the way (even John Forsyth could do this) their ministers would exhort "Groan, brother, groan."[4] This kind of taunt Longstreet would resent fiercely by newspaper editorial or in any other writing he then had in hand. "There is nothing reprehensible about 'shouting' in church," he makes one of his characters explain to a timid lady of his family. "Why should you wish to keep from it? It is one of the means which Providence has appointed for relieving the overcharged heart, and I do not see why it should be repressed. I know why it is repressed very well. It is regarded by most people as very undignified—only, however, when *most people* are devoid of the feeling that provokes it." "But, brother," asks the lady, "how does it happen that there is shouting in no other church in the world but the Methodist?" "Just because," Brother replies, "the Methodist

---
[1] *Southern Christian Advocate*, 5 August–27 November, 1842.
[2] *Ibid.*, 28 July, 1842.
[3] *Ibid.*, 9 September, 1842.
[4] *State Rights Sentinel*, 8 May, 1834.

is (in one sense) the newest church in the world. . . . I know very well where they all began; it was in such a scene of excitement and clamor as amazed the lookers-on, and led them to mock, and to say that the converts were full of new wine."[1]

Towards the first of June, 1839, yellow fever, a scourge then romantic almost in its fearful implications, made its appearance in Augusta, and continued in its devastating course until late fall. Out of the 1500 to 2000 cases there were 240 deaths.[2] Immediately upon the plague's being recognized, all of those people who could get out of the city into the country, did so. There was general panic. Mr. Key, Longstreet's ministerial colleague, was away from town, but came back as soon as he heard of the epidemic and worked faithfully among the victims until he was attacked himself.[3] Longstreet was equally as assiduous in his ministrations to the sick. Located upon the sand-hills some distance from the city proper, his home became the refuge of all, apparently, who cared to avail themselves of it. "My house," he wrote, "was soon filled with fugitives from the city, who boarded me out of everything I had to eat." He gave up all activity except nursing; and in his sacrifice he found great satisfaction. "While administering every day to the sick, the dying and the dead for five dreary months, expecting every day to become a victim to the disease, O how my soul rejoiced as it found me serving God instead of serving clients."[4]

It was during this period that Longstreet formed his friendship for John Barry, later Bishop of the Roman Catholic Church. Born in Ireland in 1799, Barry had in 1825 become pastor of the Holy Trinity Church in Augusta. His congregation was made up chiefly of people who had refugeed to Augusta from the Santo Domingo riots, and of Irish people who had come to work on the railways. He was inured to pestilence. In 1832, he had served heroically during an epidemic of cholera, and now that a new scourge was upon the city he was not to be dismayed. Though Barry was an anti-

---

[1] Longstreet, *Mitten*, 217-8.
[2] Jones, *Augusta*, 261.
[3] Smith, *Methodism in Georgia and Florida*, 437.
[4] Fitzgerald, *Judge Longstreet*, 47.

nullifier, and a Romanist, Longstreet could not help admiring his bravery and perseverance, and loving his nobility of life and spirit. "Mr. Barry was untiring," Longstreet wrote of his plague experience, "in his attention to the sick, the dying and the dead, and I tried to be. Of course in our ministrations we met every day, if not every three hours of the day. At first we met with friendly salutations, then with a few words of conversation, then with warmer feelings and more prolonged conversations, and finally with mutual demonstrations of brotherly love which, I believe, were sincere on both sides. ... Mr. Barry, meeting me one day, said to me: 'There's one of your people brought to the hospital [this was Mr. Barry's home temporarily turned into a hospital]. Will you go and see him?' 'Yes,' said I, 'I will go right away,' and we went together. He conducted me to the bed of the sick man, and stood by me while I conversed with him. At the conclusion I asked the sick man if I should pray with him. He answered in the affirmative. I knelt, and Barry knelt with me, and at the conclusion of the prayer we sent our *Amens* to heaven together."[1]

During the year that he had served in Augusta as a minister, Longstreet had continued living in his own home, and, in accord with his announcement, had fulfilled his obligations to his clients. During the first of 1839 he had been in Washington as an attorney before the Supreme Court,[2] and during the latter part of the year, even after he had removed to Oxford, for one case he had received a law fee, rumor stated, of $10,000.[3]

In August, 1839, the Methodists appointed Longstreet head of Emory College, then recently established by the Methodist Church,[4] and in December the appointment was confirmed by the Conference which met in Augusta.[5] At the end of the year, then, Longstreet, something of a pilgrim by now, sold

---

[1] Fitzgerald, *Judge Longstreet*, 68-9; Longstreet, "Old Things Become New," I.
[2] United States Supreme Court Docket, January Term, 1839.
[3] Smith, "Some Overlooked Georgians"; *History of Georgia Methodism, 1786-1866* (Atlanta, 1913), 379.
[4] *Augusta Chronicle and Sentinel*, 6 August, 1839.
[5] Methodist Conference Minutes, III, 28-30.

his "dwelling[1] and land . . . at their full value," he specifies, "and was foot-loose."[2]

Once more he was about to quit Augusta. It must have cost him much in the way of severance of old affections to leave this place. How gracious life had been there! He had friends on all hands, and on all hands he was recognized as of surpassing worth. It was a joy to him to look back over the pleasant years that he had spent since 1827, when he had returned from Greensboro. He had renewed in his native home, as a man of whom all his family could be exceedingly proud, the happy domestic associations of his childhood. His mother had lived there until her death only a year or two previous; and his sisters, and some of his brothers, were there still. He must now have contemplated all of this fondly, must have had flitting, incoherent recollections of many trivial things and many grave ones, of the death of his mother, and of the birth of his children and of the death of them, recollections of how in 1835 he had seen the first railway train make its epochal approach to the city, reminding him, somehow, of his father's steamboats and of his own youth. And then, perhaps, he could remember how his wife coming home from church had lost her crescent-shaped brooch, the one with the hair in it, and how he had tried by advertising in the newspapers, and in every other way, to recover it. He could remember how people had received *Georgia Scenes,* and how often he had made his friends laugh with his mimicry. Soon all of these memories must be abandoned. In the meantime, one had to keep going.

If there was a party among the family connection, of course he had to be present, "with his wit, keeping them all merry."[3] In this connection, too, there were countless memories. How things will happen! Mr. Longstreet loved to tell jokes on himself. "I was at a lady's house once," one of his stories used to go, "who was very proud of the fact that she had oysters

---

[1] This is his statement made in 1870. The likelihood is that the dwelling was sold later.
[2] Fitzgerald, *Judge Longstreet,* 47.
[3] Emma Eve Smith, "Our Family History," Ms. in possession of Mr. Paul E. Carmichael, Augusta, Georgia.

for dinner. But in spite of oysters being a rare delicacy I could not abide eating them. In order not to hurt the lady's feelings, I carefully slipped the oysters off my plate into my handkerchief, but I worked too well, since, when she saw my plate empty she insisted on serving me again. This time I acted more judiciously, and left some oysters on the plate. The meal over, I slipped the handkerchief-full of oysters into the great pocket in my coat tail.—Do you know that it wasn't half an hour before, dunce that I was, for some silly reason or other, I pulled out my handkerchief and scattered oysters everywhere?"[1]

Outside of his domestic circle the Judge had been received with equal favor. In addition to his manifold activities as farmer, lawyer, churchman, temperance advocate, newspaper editor, and literary man, he had found time to serve as President of the Board of Trustees of the Medical Institute of Georgia.[2]

What had involved him in more work was his reputation for making occasional speeches. As a lawyer he could always think on his feet. You went to hear him "expecting to listen to the breathings of true eloquence," and you might be sure of not being disappointed.[3] A speech from him was certain to be "beautiful in conception and felicitous in language, pervaded by the purest religious spirit, and breathing the most amiable emotions."[4]

Every lawyer, of course, had to know how to talk. That was his trade. But in a frontier country, where so many people are too boorish to be able to frame an idea in words, and are therefore willing to deliver over to someone else all of their privilege of talking, and to be thankful for that person's statement, or approximate statement, of an idea so far as they can tell pretty nearly their own—in such a country, oratory comes to be held a paramount accomplishment. In old Georgia someone, as a rule someone who could think clearly but could

---

[1] Related by Miss O. D. Eve, Augusta, Georgia, who had heard it from her father, John Eve.
[2] *Augusta Chronicle*, 8 September, 1832.
[3] *Athens Banner*, 6 August, 1841.
[4] *Southern Christian Advocate*, 1 August, 1845.

not talk according to the convention, complained occasionally that oratory was too highly regarded, that where it was not narcotic in its effect, it was always bound to be sensational. Garnett Andrews abominated it, in his old age, thought it, and pretty fairly showed it to have been, so far as politics went, a "modern" innovation. Howell Cobb, in 1851, he remembered, was the first Georgia governor to take the stump. When writing about the gift of oratory, Andrews invariably wrote *gift* in quotation marks. Lawyers, he thought, were on the whole the best people to whom to intrust the direction of government, were it not for the emphasis which lawyers put upon oratory. He saw an incompatibility between the elements which make a popular orator and those which make for sound judgment. The oratorical fervor, he said, " 'which comes from the heart and goes to the heart,' unhinges the judgment, and the intensity of feeling and conviction which sends the words 'two feet into the ground' at every sentence sends everything with them 'into the ground.' . . . A statesman cannot afford to have passions—an orator cannot afford to be without them. . . . A cartload of manure, under all circumstances, is of positive benefit to a country; the most eloquent speech ever made may be—as many have been—a curse."[1] To Longstreet, though he could remember when it had been held bad form for candidates to extol their merits to the electorate,[2] this sort of talk would have seemed probably no more than the snarling of a fox who could not reach the high grapes of eloquence. Of course he knew that a speech must have sense to it, but to suggest that it should not also have inspiration, even lyrical qualities, was pure heresy. At the State University commencement of 1828 John M. Berrien and Longstreet's friend Clayton had respectively defended "Eloquence" and "Oratory" in speeches delivered before the University literary societies. "Such a literary feast," wrote one of their listeners, "had never been spread before an audience in Georgia; and it may be feared that its like will never be repeated." How admirably Clayton had expressed the sentiments that everybody must needs accede to! Oratory is no more to be shunned than fire; it is a bad master,

---
[1] Andrews, *Old Georgia Lawyer*, 22-4.
[2] Longstreet, "Darby Anvil," *Stories with a Moral*, 78-9.

to be sure, but the best of servants. "Oratory," he had said, "is the great moral agent that guides and controls all human passions. . . . It is to the moral what electricity is to the natural world. It is the great pervading, connecting, and upholding principle of all sensual inclination and all intellectual influence. . . . It is the subtle, active, quickening impulse, restless as air and rapid as lightning, that runs through all sense, gives edge to its desires and effect to its designs. It assumes all shapes, tries all forms and shines in all varieties. It sues in the cry of infancy, woos in the sigh of love, wails in the groan of pain, implores in the suffering of despair, supplicates in the wretchedness of sorrow, beseeches in the misery of want, persuades in truth, thunders in vengeance, and rages in distraction."[1] Longstreet himself would have been very proud to make such an encomium.

Most notable perhaps of all of Longstreet's speeches was the one made in Augusta at the Washington birthday celebration of 1832, one "equal to the occasion," the newspaper reports said, "and honorable to the 'head and heart' of the American patriot; one rightfully 'received by a large and admiring audience with peals of reiterated applause.'"[2] In the best of his speeches, the Judge was terribly in earnest; he had, and could show forth, inherent, swaying passion. He was one of a class, said one of his contemporaries, who, "deeply imbued with an earnest impetuous spirit and manner, can with their veriest commonplaces, striking 'the electric chain wherewith we are closely bound' send a thrill through our frames and stir our hearts to their inmost depths, while more finished pieces of declamation make no impression upon us beyond the feeling of admiration of the gorgeous rhetorical flowers with which it was adorned."[3]

In some senses, leaving Augusta did not distress the Judge at all. He loved the sort of life he had known in Greensboro and would know in Oxford, and the Presidency of Emory College was a position much to his liking. It fitted in perfectly with his desire to spare Mrs. Longstreet the hardships of

---
[1] Miller, *Bench and Bar*, II, 166, 51.
[2] *Augusta Chronicle*, 25 February, 1832.
[3] Dillard, "Simms and Longstreet," 425–30.

an itinerant life in the ministry. And over and above this, Longstreet was a person who did not have the strongest local attachments. His remote ancestors had come from England and Holland to America, and his remoter ones, some of them, from France to England. His parents had moved to Georgia from New Jersey. He himself, as all of his brothers were, was fascinated somehow by the general surge of population westward, and there was constant talk among the family of moving to Mississippi or to Texas. They had by inheritance the philosophy that if one place does not prove lucrative it should be abandoned for another. Old Mrs. Longstreet, upwards of seventy-five, approved of this project of moving westward, in her Will, even, going out of her way to sanction it.[1]

Indeed, by this time Augusta did seem to have gone into a sort of decline. All Middle Georgia had done likewise. This state was learning now what had made John Randolph in 1814 exclaim over the dismantlement and desolation of Virginia, deserted for "Kaintuck or the Mississip',"[2]—what had years before caused dispassionate South Carolinians to recognize that even their state was constantly losing ground.[3] All over Middle Georgia, level fields which the pioneers had thought inexhaustibly fertile, were turning into bald hills, through which deep washed gullies ran down into sickly bogs.[4] By 1846, persons who had removed from Georgia westward and were returning for brief visits, could find their old homes fallen "in ruins, the soil washed into gullies, the orchards almost wild, the fields covered with young pines, broom sedge, and 'brier patches' . . . the neighbors dead or moved away." They could not escape wondering what had gone with them all—the fresh virgin soil, the luxuriant fields, the wide cane-brakes, "the happy forest men," the people in general. Only a few slave-holders remained.[5]

Augusta itself could not prosper while her tributary land was constantly deteriorating. "Major Jones," writing in the for-

---

[1] Mayes, *Genealogy*, 177.
[2] Phillips, *American Negro Slavery*, 183.
[3] Trent, *Simms*, 22.
[4] *Georgia Scenes*, "The Turnout," 83.
[5] Pascal, *Ninety-four Years*, 290–1.

ties, bore witness to the fact that, though a "monstrous pretty city, it aint the place it used to was, not by a grate site. It seems like it was rottin off at both eends, and aint growin much in the middle; and the market houses what a few years ago you couldn't hardly see for the wagons, looks more like pretty considerable large martin-boxes standin in the middle of the grate wide street, than places of bisness. The peeple that laid out the city must have been monstous wide between the eyes, and made very large calculations for bisness, for they've got it stretched out over ground enough to make two or three sich towns, and Broad street, whar the stores is, is wide enuff for the merchants to charge exchange from one side to t'other. I see by the papers that they're gwine to dig a big canal, as they call it, and turn the river upstream into the common, so they can go into the mannyfacterin of cotton. That's a sort of bisness I don't know nothin about, and I can't say how it'll turn out, but there's one thing very certain, if the Augusty people don't do something to start bisness agoing again, all the houses in the city won't rent for enuff to feed 'em. The fact is, if the people of Georgia don't take to makin homespun and sich truck for themselves, and quit their everlastin fuss 'bout the tariff and free trade, the fust thing they'll know, the best part of their popilation will be gone to the new States, and what'll be left won't be able to raise cotton enuff to pay for what they'll have to buy from the North."[1]

---

[1] William T. Thompson, *Major Jones's Sketches of Travel* (Philadelphia, 1848), 37.

XI

EMORY COLLEGE

The town of Oxford, located near Covington, in one of the counties in which Longstreet had often had law cases, was entirely built around the Methodist College, Emory. It had been laid off by the Emory authorities during the spring of 1837, in such fashion that the streets converge upon the campus like the stays of a fan.[1] The name Oxford, which was suggested by Dr. Few, the President-elect of the then nonexistent college, was of course given the town in commemoration of the Alma Mater of John Wesley.

From the urban decline and the universal depression evident in Middle Georgia, Oxford was essentially a relief. Farming as a business, and the management of negro farm labor, had always bored Longstreet excessively, but he had continued to dabble in such matters because it was to pursuits of that kind that the conventional Southerner looked for a livelihood. In Oxford, the population was made up of boys, and of church people, and of people who, freed to a great extent of economic necessity, had removed to Oxford to get their sons educated.[2] To this day the place retains a degree of lovely unreality which the present writer has never met elsewhere, and now that the college has been moved away to a city, and the old buildings left to house only a preparatory school,—the impression of frustration and of the continued presence of departed things haunts one everywhere. The citizens remember instantly men who were graduated fifty years ago. One is saddened there and made pensive, and charmed inexpressibly.

The atmosphere, even in Longstreet's time, doubtless had taken on the ineffable ideality of a place divorced from prac-

---
[1] Smith, *Georgia Methodism*, 378.
[2] Mayes, *L. Q. C. Lamar*, 32.

tical life. "Imagine to yourself," wrote an enthusiastic visitor to the commencement of 1842, "a dense forest with only trees enough to make room for the dwellings which have rapidly sprung up since the place was started—with here and there a fine mansion, or beautiful cottage, embowered in a grove of forest oaks, adorned in front with a tastefully arranged flower garden, and you may have some notion of the place. The college buildings are at the extreme end of the village, and arranged more for convenience than show. . . . Of the citizens composing the population it is not my purpose to speak, only to say that I have never fallen among a people more after my own heart."[1]

Around the village of Oxford lay the great farms presided over by the more intelligent and more adaptable, more socially trained of the citizens whom Longstreet had come to know so intimately through his familiarity with their section as the field of much of his law practice. If you had told him during those days that he was becoming out of touch with his world, he would have pointed you to his many close friendships; if you had asked him to justify for you a white civilization that was day by day becoming, numerically at least, more and more predominantly black, he would have pointed out that the blacks were voiceless, and that it was better to have them, politically dumb, than to have a group of whites equal in ignorance but superior in potential influence.

For unquestionably the Middle Georgia that Longstreet knew now was different from the one he had known formerly. The percentage of large imposing houses now, for instance, if you would in orthodox Southern fashion not count negro houses, was certainly much greater than it had been in 1820; there were more fine houses, and fewer shabby ones, the poor whites having moved off, forced back towards the mountains or down towards the infertile lands of the southeast. This section was now harboring a society that was rich and in some ways sumptuous and curiously oriental. In many families, every child had his individual slave; great gentlemen almost openly kept their concubines; great ladies half-dozed through the long summer afternoons on their shaded piazzas,

---

[1] *Southern Christian Advocate*, 12 August, 1842.

mollified by the slow fanning of their black attendants, and by the laving of their feet in water periodically fetched anew from the spring-house.

But not all of the parvenus put their wealth to such sensual ends. Though 1820 had not seen much encouragement of idleness or immorality, it had not seen either many of the valid phenomena that 1840 knew for its own house-mates. On the whole, the level of culture now was vastly higher than it had been formerly,—than, say, among the people represented in *Georgia Scenes*. Many who were still left here had by now been subjected to educational processes, and most of those who could endure no such processes had moved off. Schools and colleges, even women's colleges, were springing up now everywhere, everywhere people were taking a new interest in intellectual affairs. Many of the complacently ignorant had abandoned the country to people who contemplated their ignorance rebelliously.

The census of 1850 shows that Georgia, with a white population of about half a million people, had thirteen "colleges," with a total of about 1500 students, nearly forty non-private libraries, with a total of over 30,000 volumes, twenty-two "literary and miscellaneous" and scientific publications, with a total circulation of almost 40,000,—the best showing of any state in the South. People wrote for the magazines, or at least talked about them, and had an interest in books, and in their dearth of books, for which they said there was no longer any good excuse. A critical attitude towards life was in way of showing itself, one loyal Georgian actually deprecating publicly the lack of what he termed independence in American journalism and criticism, and more particularly in these manifestations in the South.[1] Longstreet especially felt that it was no longer charitable or salutary to hide shortcomings that everybody knew about.[2]

Georgia lawyers had always been recognized as being among the best; there had also been good doctors and preachers. Now dawns the era Longstreet had so glowingly pictured in his Emory inaugural address, wherein Georgia writers and

---

[1] *Southern Field and Fireside*, 4 June, 1859.
[2] Longstreet, "Emory Inaugural," "Darby Anvil," "Sage Conversation."

scientists also were to win names for themselves and for the state. Besides himself and the literary tradition he had established, one could now find all sorts of writers,—poets everywhere one turned, and even poetesses, romancers, satirists, novel writers, literary critics, research workers, countless people who read with pleasure and discrimination and were concerned with the highest matters of the intellect. The two LeConte brothers, students at the University of Georgia, were already thinking upon a background of large intellectual liberalism.

But in much of the literature, in the very thought of the people, was a sickly morbidness—

> When thy soft round form was lying
> On the bed, where thou wert sighing

sings one of the poetasters describing the death of his beloved[1]—and a peculiar sensitiveness, that, once touched by suspicion of outside forces, might all too easily relapse into a defiant contempt of all outside forces whatever. Those times, like any other times, found it pleasanter to contemplate what was flattering than they did to contemplate what was irritating and portentous; they preferred to consider the number of colleges in Georgia, for instance, as compared with the number in Massachusetts, than they did to consider that Georgia, with about half as many people as Massachusetts, had in it over twenty times as many illiterate native white persons. The reverse side of the great seal of Georgia Civilization these people would not look at. "Beautiful and unique hedges," wrote a lady of the Old South describing the grounds of a typical pre-war mansion, "Beautiful and unique hedges hide from the eye every unpleasant object. . . ."[2]

To Longstreet, Oxford was delectable. Bishop Capers and Bishop Andrew, now President of the Emory Board of Trustees,[3] lived in the town, as did also many other persons intelligent enough to want their children educated, and ardent

---

[1] *Orion*, March–April, 1843, 370.

[2] Cook, *Ante Bellum Southern Life As It Was*, 45. U. S. Census 1850, 49, 56, 365, 376.

[3] Smith, *Andrew*, 9.

enough as Methodists to move to a Methodist college town to effect this meritorious end. Among his faculty members, the President found intellectual stimulus and personal affection; among his students he found adulation. He could talk about Horace here and not feel that he was taking time that should really have gone to a law case (it is actually in line with his business to read the Bible in Latin), could devote to the study of German enough time surely to learn much of its literature, and possibly to read it. With six other cultivated gentlemen, he formed a sort of secret organization called the Mystics, in which each member had to take a new name. Longstreet took "Bob Short." He could here carry on with more ease, likely, than in Augusta, extensive correspondences, bantering and whimsical, grave and wise, with all sorts of friends, notably with George McDuffie and with young George Pierce.[1]

And now his family relations were most interesting. He had a respectable square two-story house. His daughters, Fannie and Jennie, both of whom were very sensible and well read, were now getting into their teens, and his little son FitzRandolph, of whom he was inordinately proud (it was his great desire to leave a son to carry on his name), was getting to be very much of a boy, destined certainly to live till February, 1844,[2] though not much longer. For a while, the girls were sent to the excellent girls' school in Oxford, and later, to Wesleyan College in Macon, presided over by George Pierce; and, though neither of them finished the course at Wesleyan, Jennie at least stayed long enough to perform a charming chemical experiment upon the stage at commencement. She was unlucky in burning her hand in the process, but managed to conceal her pain until the business was over with.[3]

One could be proud of a daughter like that, and proud of belonging to a denomination and to a state supporting a school like that, especially proud if one is a Trustee of the school,[4] and if one's son, almost, is at the head of it. Could a man ever forget a Wesleyan Commencement,—the erudite exam-

---
[1] Smith, *Andrew*, 293.
[2] Fitzgerald, *Judge Longstreet*, 195.
[3] Mrs. A. L. Heiskell.
[4] Charles C. Jones, *Education in Georgia* (Washington, 1889), 95.

inations and exhibitions, the graduates, "beautiful as angels and dressed in white" with handkerchiefs spasmodically daubed to face during the grave baccalaureate, and then the "Fantasticals" who in all manner of ludicrous disguises would parade around the college, on horseback, in honor of the graduates,[1]—could one ever forget such a thing, having once enjoyed it?

Among the frequent visitors in Oxford, in this case a regular member of the household, was Longstreet's young nephew, James Longstreet, whose education the boy's widowed mother had turned over to the Judge to do with as he liked. James was in many ways exactly to his uncle's fancy, mischievous, fun loving, lovable in everything, and ambitious enough when you would give him free rein, but withal somewhat incorrigible, refusing to do his work after a fashion to justify his being kept in college.[2] Finally, the Judge helped get him into the Military Academy at West Point, writing to McDuffie and sending messages to Calhoun in Washington,—in general, the nephew said, acting towards him the part of one "more than a father."[3]

Occasionally the Judge would go off on a trip, and when he did, he was always, as he says, given "gratifying tokens of the people's confidence." "If large sums of money were to be borne from place to place whence and whither I was going, they were sure to be put in my hands, greatly to my discomfort. If wives and daughters were to be put in charge of anyone for long routes, I was sure to be first choice if I could be. This, always a pleasurable service (taking care of baggage always excepted), sometimes, I presume often, brought me into very flattering comparison with very honest upright neighbors of the world."[4] One incident in connection with his convoying these young ladies from caravanserai to caravanserai, the Judge always remembered and told with keen enjoyment. The young lady had heard of her guide before, but had never seen him. After she had been introduced to him, Longstreet over-

---

[1] Thompson, *Major Jones's Courtship*, Letter IV.
[2] James Longstreet, *Lee and Longstreet at High Tide*, 97-8.
[3] Fitzgerald, *Judge Longstreet*, 174.
[4] Fitzgerald, *Judge Longstreet*, 152.

heard her whisperingly inquire of her father as to whether or not he had really given her over to the right man. "Are you sure," she asked, "that that is Judge Longstreet? I don't think this man half so ugly as people are always picturing the Judge. Why this man isn't ugly at all!" The father reassured her.

Sometimes the Judge got as far as New York, and once, while there in 1846, he was ill, "as weak as an infant most of the time." On the way back from this visit he stopped in Philadelphia to see George McDuffie's daughter, who was there in school. "She's a sweet girl," he wrote to McDuffie, "far handsomer than I expected to find her; for in point of beauty she had nothing to hope for, at least on the paternal side, and yet she is decidedly good looking. Her voice is enrapturing, and, according to the best judgment that I could form upon a half-hour's acquaintance, she has an amiable disposition. Well, this is all that a father could ask in a daughter, and more than a father has a right to expect. . . . The sight of her tore open an old wound but it soon healed again. You remember that we used to talk of a match between her and my dear boy Torrance."[1]

It was to Augusta and to Athens, however, that the Judge's business called him oftenest. Longstreet was always glad of an excuse to go to Athens. It was a university town, at that time socially dominated by the university faculty, and as such it had considerable appeal for him. More than that, it was the home of many of his friends, particularly of his very intimate one, Henry Hull. Hull was eight years younger than Longstreet, and he was a doctor while Longstreet was a lawyer, but the two men had many points of congeniality; both were half-way farmers, both very high Methodists, both interested in the education of young Georgians, both advocates of a joke at any price. Longstreet often visited the Hulls, and always he was eagerly expected. The entire town seemed to love him, the young girls even keeping pages in their albums for him to fill when he should come again. In 1847, Hull decided to name his youngest baby Augustus Longstreet, because, he explained

---

[1] Fitzgerald, *Judge Longstreet*, 174.

to the delighted Judge, "it is such a humorous baby, and because too, you know, he is so unconscionably ugly. . . ." A little sharp this was, perhaps, but the Judge, the Doctor thought, deserved it. The Judge had had the joke on him many a time, and would have again; he was always laughing, for instance, about Athens' pretensions to being a city, writing jingles about the cows in the streets. Once Hull took Longstreet out to a farm of his near Athens and showed him, the Judge being given to inventions and such-like himself, a new gate-latch he had invented that permitted one to open the gate without getting out of his rockaway. The Judge was duly interested. That latch, he finally commented, would have been thought of only by a man who was lazy. The quip had just enough point for it to sting; that was not the first time people had said that Dr. Hull was not energetic.[1] Always these two men were very dear to one another. They corresponded with each other throughout their lives, and it was to Hull that Longstreet in 1859 dedicated his book *William Mitten*.

But it was always pleasant when these visits were over to get back to little Oxford. There at least, one could find a society not altogether unlike one's fanciful picture of that which Moses headed in the Wilderness. In Oxford, Mrs. Longstreet was happy with the happiness of living, if not in Greensboro again, in a place more like the Greensboro of her youth than Greensboro was now, perhaps, itself. When Bishop Andrew married the second time, he married a Greensboro woman, a circumstance which caused Mrs. Longstreet intense satisfaction. In the evenings when the Bishop and Mrs. Andrew would saunter down to her house it was fine beyond words, while the two dignitaries made their grave plans or chaffed each other, for Eliza and Leonora to talk about old times and scandals, and new obligations, and about the timeless love of God. They could all stop their talk, though, to shout in laughter with the Judge, to the Bishop's great discomfiture, over the prospect of the Bishop's writing a book on Family Government and on the Government of Servants! That was really too good!

---

[1] Miss America Carlton, Athens, Georgia.

Everybody knew that the Bishop's farming adventures were a farce![1] And in the evenings, as they would sit on their porch in the moonlight, they could hear Dr. Capers and the Capers girls across the street playing on the piano and singing—or merely singing without accompaniment—and they could occasionally see a dark figure among the trees, one of the Capers girls' sweethearts, listening to the music, a regular silent Romeo. This, too, the Judge thought a great joke, and would tease young Romeo about it interminably.

Here, too, better than in Augusta, perhaps, the Judge could exercise his skill in out-of-door activities acquired long ago in Edgefield. He was proud of his ability to swim and wrestle and ride horseback, to do odd carpentering, and to make prophecies concerning the weather (which he was vexed at, if it did not behave itself accordingly). He had various stories about weather prophecy, one he considered particularly amusing, about a man who always looked for rain when goats started their tails wagging. He was proud, too, of his ability to shoot accurately. The first fine imposed by the town of Oxford, the story goes, was one upon Longstreet for shooting down a squirrel from the top of a big oak. And here the man could go about his eternal tree-grafting. He had one apple tree, they say, that bore thirty varieties of apples! Mrs. Longstreet, for her part, looked upon all of this, and found it good. These somewhat boyish pursuits were unquestionably the very thing her husband most needed. His eyes had been troubling him, and in the early forties it seemed that he would actually lose his sight.[2] Riding, too, Mrs. Longstreet said, would be good for him. Accordingly the Judge rode much.

As for preaching, Longstreet had opportunity to hear enough to satisfy the most avid. In Oxford, as in Carcasonne, there were two bishops,—and any number of other preachers, "fifteen within sound of the college bell,"[3] including the pedago-ecclesiastics of the faculty. There were besides these, visitors, brethren of the church interested in the new college. Occasionally there would be polemical discussions (too often absurd

---

[1] Smith, *Andrew*, 338–92.
[2] *Magnolia*, December, 1842, 396.
[3] Fitzgerald, *Judge Longstreet*, 47.

and vulgar, and always tragic in the naïve faith with which they were listened to) held in the little wooden church between people of varying religious affiliations. These wrangles would attract great interest. Once there was a discussion "between a professed Universalist (who was in reality an infidel) and an old Methodist local preacher. . . ." In this discussion the Universalist was silly enough to compare the human soul to a bottle of smelling salts, and the Methodist cheap enough to confute the Universalist by the simple means of substituting for the word "soul," in a number of Biblical quotations he read, the phrase "smelling bottle." The audience, finding in this trick convincing rebuttal to all the Universalist had said, soon roared with laughter, whereupon the infidel, after "wincing" for a time, "fled from the field."[1] So were the ways of God justified to men.

Sundays frequently found the Judge preaching himself. He would go to the various neighboring villages,[2] and occasionally with Bishop Andrew and other members of the college community he would go off for several weeks and hold a meeting.[3] In 1847, with Bishop Andrew and Dr. Means he conducted in a warehouse the first revival ever held in Atlanta.[4] In August, 1841, somewhat in his capacity of minister and somewhat in that of old friend and former student of the University's dead President, he went to Athens and delivered before the alumni of the State University a very flatteringly received eulogy upon Dr. Waddel. Certainly it was conceived in the grand manner, but, however sincere a veneration the surviving fragments of it[5] may show for its subject, they manifest an inability on the part of the author to speak simply about his grief, and his admiration of Waddel, in terms not long crystallized and dead. But to his contemporaries the speech was ample.[6]

More in line with his training were the controversial and other articles he wrote for the church paper. Argumentation,

---

[1] Mayes, *L. Q. C. Lamar*, 31–2.
[2] Jackson, *Rev. Dr. Longstreet*, 23.
[3] Decatur, Ga., 1846. Mrs. Rebecca Latimer Felton, Letter, 7 February, 1922.
[4] Smith, *Andrew*, 20.
[5] Waddel, *Memorials*, 68–9.
[6] *Athens Banner*, 6 August, 1841.

obituaries,[1] letters to church magnates detailing the mortuary scenes of invalid women, with the women's parting attestations of orthodox Christianity,[2] all of these things he could do to please the most fastidious. It has been generally said that Longstreet contributed to the Methodist *Quarterly*, but the present writer has not been able to substantiate this claim.

Of the controversial articles the only series primarily concerned with church matters is the one which, running in the official church paper over the latter part of 1842, dealt with the propriety of introducing instrumental music into divine services. One of the visitors to the Emory commencement exercises of 1842 complained in the church paper that there was no music on the programme.[3] Evidently, this was the Judge's sore point. It was too ironical that he, who had just written an article justifying instrumental music in the church, should be so attacked. On the same day on which he received the paper publishing the complaint, Longstreet wrote a reply. Our not having any music, he said, was due to our "tenderness to the scruples of some of our brethren upon this subject, who, strange to tell, think it wrong to enliven such scenes with music—at least with instrumental music—and Oxford does not command a vocal corps. It is to be hoped that this notion will be abandoned before the next commencement."[4] Longstreet had for three or four years[5] been contemplating a defense of instrumental music as an entirely godly device, and had actually completed some of his vindication in time for one of the first sections of it already to have appeared in the church paper, before this complaint of the visitor had even been written.[6]

But the opponents of instrumental music were no less alert than its friends. A champion of its essential iniquity soon hastened into the field, and for a long time the battle went on. It is in following this indecent controversy in the old church periodicals that one's sympathy for Longstreet and one's disposition to palliate every shortcoming of his becomes most in-

---

[1] *Southern Christian Advocate*, 11 September, 1846.
[2] *Ibid.*, 6 May, 1842.
[3] *Southern Christian Advocate*, 29 July, 1842.
[4] *Ibid.*, 12 August, 1842.
[5] *Ibid.*, 16 September, 1842.
[6] *Ibid.*, 5 August, 1842.

sistent. Here was a man urbane and intellectually keen forced into contest with a person whose sincerity could only add to the effectiveness of his crudity and intellectual barbarism, a capable man of civilization having his feet shot at while he was made to dance by backwoodsmen whose weapons he disdained to use, but had nevertheless to keep clear of.

In this episode, in spite of the fact that his contention was finally accepted everywhere, Longstreet attains a tragic and almost heroic stature. He is frank and honest. Though a passionate advocate of his cause, he confessed that the researches he had been able to make had left him in doubt on some of the salient features of his argument. And though it is the desirability of instrumental music that he is advocating, he is prompt to concede that after all the business of praising God is not the work of "mere sounds, pipes or strings . . . no, nor hand nor knees nor eyes, nor voice, nor lips, nor tongue, but the heart's work, and the heart's only."[1] His conclusion hints at the methods of reasoning employed by his opponents. "I demand," he says, "that the texts and views which I have submitted be categorically answered; not that they all be disposed of by an answer to three or four of them, and a tirade upon 'fiddling Christians,' 'catgut scrapers' and 'piano thrumpers.' . . ."[2]

He did not get what he demanded. He got only gibing, contemptuous reference to his "researches" and information that his antagonist was too poor to educate *his* children [Longstreet's daughters were at college], but would beg, if necessary, the means to "educate them in *piety*";[3] he got the statement that instrumental music in the churches was evil, first because it would Judaize the church; and, "our second reason for our position," said his opponent, "is its uselessness." [Time evidently proved what the antagonist wrote but did not mean; that is, that *its* referred to *our position*.] Music, said this old soldier, should be held on the level of whiskey, whist, and polygamy, theaters, circuses, and dances,[4] which

---

[1] *Southern Christian Advocate*, 2 September, 1842.
[2] *Ibid.*, 9 September, 1842.
[3] *Ibid.*, 7 October, 1842.
[4] *Ibid.*, 16 September, 1842.

last, indeed, Longstreet was accused of having sanctioned.—
And then comes the scorn: "O for shame! O for power to
hide in a desert, where mortal eye could never see me again!
A good minister of Jesus Christ, to talk so unguardedly, about
music and dancing! We had thought that the demon had well
nigh been banished from these lands! But lo, he is to be invited back by a preacher . . . and a classical one at that!"
And then further and further does the old man pruriently drag
through the slough of personalities. "The other day, one of
the ministers of the town said to me, 'I was at the house of
A. B. L.'s pet—and saw the latest pieces of music—they were
dancing pieces—and Miss Ellsler at the top of all, in dancing
costume—and her skirt came down, a *little below* the *knee!*
Here is a sight for mixed company! And then next '*commencement*,' all the young men and young women are to be invited to attend a '*concert*' at the pet's—of course his daughters
must lead—and all the preachers daughters and *wives* that can
be got!! And then and there (as well as many times before)
see that '*dancing imp*,' hear dancing music. And a little sacred
music! And then close by prayer; by the Rev. Mr. ——.
And all go home!!! Yes; and as *good Christians*, as anybody!'"[1]

It was the college, of course, that consumed most of Longstreet's time and interest. Since 1789, the Methodists of
Georgia had been concerned in establishing a church school,
but all of their beginnings had turned out to be beginnings
only. There was always the matter of monetary considerations, and very often there was the suspicion that any official
connection the church might make with a school would prove
in the long run a weapon for the dangerous faction of the
church advocating trained intelligence as a qualification for the
ministry.[2] In 1829, the Virginia Conference had established
Randolph Macon College in Virginia, and the Tennessee Conference had established the La Grange College in Florence,
Alabama. Each of these institutions, out of regard for his
qualifications, and probably also with the idea of gaining for
itself the patronage of Georgia, had offered its presidency to

---
[1] Reply covers 16 September, 1842–6 January, 1843.
[2] Smith, *Georgia Methodism*, 376.

Stephen Olin. As a professor in the University of Georgia, Olin had lately quarreled with its president (like Olin, of New England origin), and determined to find a new place. The denominational schools guessed shrewdly; solicited by both of them for funds, the Georgia Conference of 1832 decided to give its patronage to whichever institution Olin should connect himself with.[1]

But under this plan the Georgians soon grew restive. The Georgia Baptists had a school and the Georgia Methodists wanted as much; the University of Georgia, they all conceded to the Presbyterians. And besides, there was the infectious idea of the manual labor school, carrying with it a degree of practical appeal that a good American could not resist even though he was a preacher. Not the most "subtle ingenuity," Longstreet commented, could "give a plausible reason why the youth who turns the sod two hours today may not turn the classic page four hours tomorrow."[2] There were such schools everywhere from New York downwards, and everywhere they were being hailed as a simple solution of some old problems. A Society for Promoting Manual Labor in Literary Institutions was formed in New York City in July, 1831, "its members being under conviction . . . that a reform in our seminaries of learning was greatly needed, both for the preservation of health, and for giving energy to the character by habits of useful and vigorous exercise." Ministers requested to deliver baccalaureate speeches found this new educational system a fit subject for their alloquies. One of them, at least, could show anybody by logic just how this was the only system that would at all serve. One must have physical exercise—the flaccidity of female character is an example of what lack of it leads to; "gymnastic exercises are both dangerous and frivolous." Ergo. . . . Fools and wayfaring men could read it.[3]

The manual labor system was not long in finding its way to Georgia. Such schools were evident in the early thirties. After a little there were small private schools of this nature

---

[1] *Quarterly Review, M. E. C. South,* January, 1859.
[2] Fitzgerald, *Judge Longstreet,* 81.
[3] E. F. Stanton, "Manual Labor Schools," in *Southern Literary Messenger,* March, 1836.

all over the state. In response to the national movement, as early as 1832, the Reverend Mr. Sherwood had led off for Georgia by setting in operation a school near Eatonton. He kept six or eight young men of from twelve to seventeen years of age through a three years' course in Agriculture, Mechanic Arts, Chemistry, Astronomy, and Natural Philosophy—all of this in return for the help of the young men on his farm, and for their tuition charges, which ranged from the first downwards to the third year, ninety, seventy-five and fifty dollars, a scale showing clearly in money just how great Mr. Sherwood considered the value of his training.[1]

The Presbyterians had a manual labor school in Lawrenceville; the Baptists, in Penfield. When the Methodists were offered a school already established in Culloden, and material inducements to locate a school in Covington,[2] the time for action could not in conscience be put off any longer. The Conference of 1835, though continuing to patronize Olin's school in Virginia, appointed a committee to decide between Covington and Culloden as proper sites for a manual labor school which should serve for all the Methodists in Georgia. This committee was to choose a location and then to organize the school. Dr. Alexander Means and Allen Turner (Longstreet's anti-music adversary) were sent to plead before the committee in favor of Covington, and Covington was selected. Means was named head of the new school, and Messrs. Round and Lane, both of them Northerners, were made assistants.

After a trip of investigation into the North, Means returned to Georgia and set the school going.[3] For four years this school was "eminently successful,"[4] the superintendent receiving applications for admission from six surrounding states, as well as from the territory of Florida. As the institution was primarily for Georgians, before 1839 nearly 500 prospective students from outside of the state had had to be denied admission.[5] People moved to Covington from neighboring

---

[1] *Augusta Chronicle*, 28 August, 1832.
[2] Smith, *Methodism in Georgia and Florida*, 500.
[3] *Ibid.*
[4] *Quarterly Review, M. E. C. South*, January, 1859.
[5] Smith, *Methodism in Georgia and Florida*, 501.

states and from all sections of Georgia so that their children might attend the new school.[1] "The labor was by no means arduous . . . three hours daily for five days in the week. Of the approximately 250 students who were in attendance, various sections relieved each other at work throughout the day. The boys were paid for their work a few cents an hour, the amounts being graduated, not according to the amount of labor done, but according to the size of the laborer."[2]

This arrangement worked so well that when the Baptists decided to turn their manual labor school into a college, the Methodist Conference, in view of the appeals of the Georgians sending their sons the inconvenient distance to Randolph Macon, and of the constant nagging of Dr. Ignatius Few, decided to outdo everybody by operating not simply a college, nor yet a college and a manual labor school, but a college to be conducted on the manual labor principle, and an elementary manual labor school in addition. The conference of December, 1836, appointed agents to collect funds and erect buildings for an institution to be situated near the school already existing, and to be known as Emory College, in honor of the second American Methodist Bishop.

In January, 1837, the college was incorporated;[3] in February, the Trustees met formally for the first time in Covington, and elected Dr. Few their President;[4] and during that spring, having bought for $14,000 a tract of 1400 acres, and having laid off upon this tract a campus and a town, they dedicated the newly commenced buildings. In December, 1837,[5] Few became President of the new institution, and was succeeded by Bishop Andrew in his office of President of the Board of Trustees.[6] In September, 1838, the first class was organized, "and from that time," writes an old brother who could not see much beyond finances, "the school began to decrease and eventually went down. . . . Nearly all that was expended upon it was lost, while the college never had enough funds for its wants.

---

[1] Mayes, *L. Q. C. Lamar*, 28.
[2] *Ibid.*, 28–9.
[3] Smith, *Georgia Methodism*, 378.
[4] Jones, *Education in Georgia*, 85.
[5] Smith, *Georgia Methodism*, 378.
[6] Jones, *Education in Georgia*, 85.

. . ."[1] These financial difficulties had not been anticipated and would not perhaps ever have arisen so disastrously had it not been for the fact that the subscriptions made for the maintenance of the college had been made when Georgia was on the crest of a wave of prosperity, which, by the time of the actual opening of the college, had turned into a fearful trough. The $100,000 that had been subscribed, "a marvellous sum for those days," writes 1859, could not be collected, but that did not prevent Few, although the money had been expressly subscribed for endowment purposes, from "borrowing" as much of it as he liked for purposes of building. Though the school was from the start saddled with debts made on the collateral of worthless subscriptions, its President did not stop throwing further weight into the saddle-bags. When the puny manual labor school began staggering under its engagements, the kind equerry transferred the whole mass of them over to the back of the big horse, the college. He had, says the *Methodist Quarterly*, no "financial talent whatever." His boldness and his faith were of the stripe that can win praise only when successful.

Dr. Few was bewildered. He had created a sort of beneficent but insatiably hungry Frankenstein monster. One guesses that he could hardly feel the resentment he should have felt against the general physical breakdown which in the nick of time overtook him during the summer of 1839. "My continued and increasing disease rendered it indispensable," he wrote in July of that year, "that I should retire at once. Judge Longstreet of Augusta has been elected in my stead and will enter upon his office at the commencement of the second session in January next."[2]

It was in January, 1840, then, that Longstreet removed to Oxford. On February 10, he delivered his inaugural address, a long composition on which he had evidently put much care and thought. Indeed the address is admirable. A reading of it leaves one impressed anew with the heroism and moral energy of its writer. He is here a practical American of the best sort, doggedly optimistic. Things have been bad, but

---

[1] *Quarterly M. E. C. S.*, January, 1859.
[2] Letter, 23 July, 1839, in *Advocate*, 2 August, 1839.

they are now in way of improving rapidly. Europe is ahead of us in some things, but in the essential things we are leaders. The address inspired personal following and enthusiasm; it was hailed as "beautiful and excellent, written in the author's usual happy style and characterized by valuable and practical views, sustaining the literary reputation of its author, and breathing the spirit of his well-known devotion to state and country."[1] Soon it was reprinted in many of the periodicals.

Longstreet had not said very much in his speech about how he was to finance his school, but it is certain that he had not accepted his new position without thinking of its requirement for a financier. In actual practice, when necessity arose, the Judge simply kept the school going out of his own pocket. He had come away from Augusta free of debt and with $13,000 saved up from his law practice, not to mention the amount received from the sale of his property. With this money he was enabled, he testified, to save the college "from death."[2] Nor was there ever a mention of his munificence made in any of the church papers; 1840 hardly knew what to say to Philanthropy when the two met each other in the road. It will be remembered, too, that Longstreet was a man who loved the consciousness of having money; in the midst of his religious ardor in the Augusta days, he had been unable to resist taking his chance in the gold rush; when he was offered a good price for his literary works he could never refrain from selling them, even though they were quite unfinished. He could, though, spend his money largely in the interest of a cause which he loved and believed worthy. . . .

The Methodist Church at this time was not of the radical trend of politics subscribed to by Longstreet, and there was some doubt as to how the President would acquit himself politically in his new office. He was not long in satisfying the curious. He taught state rights whenever he had opportunity. On the whole he was not blamed. The Methodists accepted him on account of his denomination, and it is possible that other people in the state, of the same political affiliations as Longstreet, were led to shift to him whatever influence they

---

[1] *Advocate*, 10 April, 1840.
[2] Fitzgerald, *Judge Longstreet*, 47.

would otherwise have given to the University of Georgia, necessarily, in politics, somewhat neutral. It is certain that in a few years he had made his college, as he himself stated, "the rival of the State University in reputation and patronage."[1] The University had graduated its first class in 1804, some thirty-seven years ahead of Emory, but during the five years of Longstreet's presidency, beginning with 1844, Emory always graduated about as many students as did the older institution in Athens.

Of course the popularity of its President was not the sole factor contributing to the school's prosperity. It was an era of denominationalism, of happy belief in the possibility that one might at any day, now, find absolute and definitive Truth. Georgia was democratic to the extent of indulging a hierarchy only in Heaven. Not the least of the counts upon which a state educational institution was suspect was the one that it fostered caste. Such an institution, wrote one of the commentators, "is, by itself, so inadequate to the wants of the population, and, through the prejudices of the people, is regarded as so aristocratic and exclusive, that the unlettered feel no interest in its operation or results, and therefore the collateral benefits are partial and restricted."[2] It took a suitable man, however, to develop for the suspicious citizenry an alternative that they were not afraid of. Longstreet did this notably well, possibly better than it could have been done by anyone else.

The outside world recognized the extent of his good work. The church paper in its editorials congratulated the Trustees from time to time on "having secured one so worthy, one who, to ripe and various learning, adds a genius of the first order, the popularity of an accomplished writer, the excellent virtues of a Christian minister, and the courtesy of a Southern gentleman of the old school." [How did one get to be such a gentleman,—by being born of New Jersey parents and educated in New England schools?] The paper further put itself on record as "confidently expecting for the country the happiest

---
[1] Fitzgerald, *Judge Longstreet*, 47.
[2] *Southern Christian Advocate*, 4 August, 1843.

results from the influence necessarily wielded by such a master spirit."[1]

When Longstreet came to the presidency of Emory, he found the college property to consist of four brick dormitories, a steward's hall, and a small wooden chapel.[2] His faculty consisted of four ministers, Mitchell, Lane, Means, and Myers, teaching respectively Moral Science and English Literature, Ancient Languages, Natural Science, and Mathematics.[3] Soon he added a Professor Haderman, who, as teacher of Modern Languages, was somewhat ostentatiously proclaimed a graduate of Leipsic and Paris.[4] This branch, however, was not in demand. After a year, Professor Haderman was dropped out as being too expensive an investment.[5] Also, during the course of Longstreet's administration, several young men, just graduated from the college, were engaged to work as teachers for their Alma Mater. With these younger men the Judge was most friendly, dispensing wisdom to them and dubbing them with nicknames, sometimes those of characters in *Georgia Scenes*.[6]

The dormitory and central-eating-plant ideal did not appeal to the instincts of a man who in spite of his Yale training persistently kept the habit of remembering Dr. Waddel every time he thought of education. Longstreet soon turned the Steward's Hall into class rooms, and proceeded to help sever from any official connection with the college the entire business of the students' boarding arrangements, by himself taking a number of boys to board in his family. The buildings of the original Manual Labor School, abandoned during 1840, he tore down and rebuilt near his own home, thus providing room for more students still.[7] In this way, much as had been the case at Willington, were the one hundred boys cared for.

The collegiate year was divided into two sessions, one beginning the last Monday in July, and the second on the second

---
[1] *Southern Christian Advocate*, 30 July, 1841.
[2] Smith, *Methodism in Georgia and Florida*, 607; *Emory Phoenix*, XX, 188–90.
[3] *Southern Christian Advocate*, 28 February, 1840; Minutes Annual Conference.
[4] *Advocate*, 25 June, 1841.
[5] *Ibid.*, 30 September, 1842.
[6] Authority, G. W. W. Stone, Oxford, Georgia.
[7] *Ibid.*

Monday in January. Tuition, room-rent, and fuel could be had for fifty dollars a year.[1] In private families, board including "eating, room, and washing," could be had at from nine to twelve dollars per month.[2] Classes were held on five days a week; and the manual labor programme was adhered to on the three-hours-a-day plan, until when, as the last step before it was completely abandoned, it was made one hour a day.[3] On Sundays, everybody was compelled to go to church twice. On week-days the half-ton bell on top of the Steward's Hall was rung four times daily: at dawn, at sunrise for prayers, at dark for study, and at nine o'clock for release from studies.[4] Prayers were held twice daily.[5] The Bible was taught throughout the course.[6] The young man who left this place "undevout," according to Bishop Fitzgerald, did so because of "ingrained and ineradicable tendencies beyond the reach of human agencies and influences."[7]

Commencement was the great event of the year. Held in July, after the crops were pretty well "laid by," these occasions were attended by people from all over the state,[8] made into regular carnivals. Who, witnessing this elevation of taste on the part of the people, could any longer doubt the superiority of Georgia civilization and taste to that of Europe? "In ancient Greece," said Alexander Stephens, speaking at Emory Commencement, July, 1852, "they had their gymnasia, and Olympic games. In Rome they had their saturnalia, and gladiatorial shows. In Spain, to this day they have their bull fights, and their carnivals. While, with the wild Indians of this continent, the green-corn dance and the ball play are as old as their legends. But with us (I speak now of Georgia) the great gala day in country, village, and town—the day when all business is suspended, and the whole people turn out to catch and enjoy

---

[1] *Southern Christian Advocate*, 25 February, 1842.
[2] *Ibid.*, 15 January, 1847.
[3] *Ibid.*, 30 July, 1841; 22 August, 1845.
[4] *Emory Phoenix*, XX, 188–90.
[5] *Southern Christian Advocate*, 22 August, 1845.
[6] *Southern Christian Advocate*, 22 August, 1845.
[7] Fitzgerald, *Judge Longstreet*, 72.
[8] *Southern Christian Advocate*, 28 July, 1848.

the prevailing spirit of the occasion—is the day of the school exhibition and the college commencement. . . ."[1]

How the people would crowd into the little village church and stand waiting outside at such times to hear the speeches,[2] speeches sometimes "outrageously" long and dull, but generally sufficiently trimmed by the President beforehand.[3] Sometimes a visitor complained that there were no speeches in Latin and Greek, but this complaint the President did not believe valid. "These exercises in our colleges are worthy," he said, "of the name Pedantry, and nothing more. Who understands a Greek or Latin speech? Not one in a thousand who attends Commencements. Why then tantalize an assembly with a form of words they do not understand?" And then he wound up by quoting St. Paul about the futility of speaking so that people could not tell what you were saying.[4] Once a visitor had complained that there had been no music in the exercises,[5] but that complaint, the President was, on the whole, thankful for. It helped him get that state of affairs changed; that was as distasteful to him as to anybody. Soon all of it was changed; before Longstreet left Emory, the papers in describing his commencements could chronicle that "at an early hour on Wednesday a procession led by a band of music formed at the college buildings and marched to the church."[6]

On Commencement Sunday there would be three sermons, and on other days addresses by distinguished visitors on such abstract subjects as "Power,"[7] and "Universal Peace,"[8] but the crowning glory of the season was the final night, when the young gentlemen would hold forth, and when Judge Longstreet would make them a pious baccalaureate, and when everybody could spend the evening hurrying in a most bewilderingly delightful way from tears to laughter. It was whispered that

---

[1] Henry Cleveland, *Alexander Stephens in Public and Private* (Philadelphia, 1866).
[2] Smith, *Methodism in Georgia and Florida*, 507.
[3] *Southern Christian Advocate*, 29 July, 1842.
[4] *Southern Christian Advocate*, 12 August, 1842.
[5] *Ibid.*, 24 July, 1842.
[6] *Ibid.*, 31 July, 1846.
[7] *Ibid.*
[8] *Ibid.*, 4 August, 1843.

the students very often reflected in their speeches the ideas of the President, and simple people listened to the performances of the young gentlemen with all the more unreserved faith.[1] Probably the titles of those old effusions may indicate what was chiefly in those days resting on President Longstreet's mind. Here is a list of them:[2] "Our Government Unfavorable to High Attainment in Literature"; "Government Patronage of Literary Institutions"; "I Must Come Into Notice"; "The Teacher's Value"; "Texas"; "Southern Literature"; "American Nationality"; "Themes for the Southern Poet"; "The Influence of Literary Institutions"; "Social Equality"; and also—

"Religion came, and where proud Science failed,
She bent her knee to earth, and over men prevailed."[3]

Occasionally there would be an address that everybody said had Judge Longstreet standing out all over it. Once a speech on "Modern Refinements" created a most pronounced sensation. "There were times during its delivery," wrote one of his listeners, "when the whole audience was convulsed from one end to the other, [sic] and yet all unmoved, and apparently unconscious of his own agency in producing it, the young speaker went on levelling shaft after shaft at the follies of the day, as if it was a matter of course business with him."

The addresses of the Judge were of course irreproachable, and to praise them would have seemed certainly to his contemporaries a very presumptuous painting of the lily.

"Any President of any College, in any country, might well be proud," wrote one of the old brethren, about his visit to Emory commencement, "of such a graduating class."[4] And good Georgians and Methodists would pass around among themselves information, coming from good authority, too, that "one who was present at the commencement of Yale College last year [said] that in point of interest and brilliancy, it was

---
[1] *Southern Christian Advocate.*
[2] *Ibid.*, 31 July, 1846, 30 July, 1847.
[3] *Ibid.*, 1 August, 1845.
[4] *Southern Christian Advocate*, 12 August, 1842.

not to be compared with this at Emory College."[1] Emory had that year a graduating class of sixteen; Yale of about sixty.

In theory, President Longstreet discountenanced utterly the idea that college boys must have their tricks; he disliked, he said, even the terms, "college boys" and "tricks of college boys"—thought them comparable to "veteran babes" and "follies of profound wisdom." The old conception of the authority to be exercised by a school executive was as severe upon the active agent as upon the passive. Dr. Waddel had felt it his duty to dole out money even to college students, and to administer official scoldings to boys who used "ugly" language.[2] In a very strict sense of the word Longstreet considered his duty toward his students "parental" in its nature.[3]

In spite, however, of that strict conception of his functions, Longstreet knew, and Dr. Waddel had known before him, that there is nothing so important in dealing with students, as with other people, as is the matter of having a way with you. He was profoundly and aggressively interested in the life of the young men under his charge and he brought into all of his dealings with them a sincerity that necessarily demanded respect from decently disposed youngsters. He had now transferred to the younger generation all the large hope for the future that he had once reposed in current politics, and the boys themselves, personally, he loved with much warmth. He knew perfectly by the simple expedient of consulting his own tastes just the things that young Georgians would accept in a man, and those they would not. He would be the personification, he probably determined, of the ideal which his boys would most readily, and should most properly, cherish. It was a good instinct. The behavior of the Emory students was irreproachable.[4]

Longstreet was of the very stuff of legend. To this day, they tell stories of him in Oxford, and to this day show visitors examples of his method. In front of the house he lived in, there is a gate so fastened to its supports as to prevent its being

---
[1] *Southern Christian Advocate*, 1 August, 1845.
[2] Waddel, Diary [Ms.], 8 March, 1826.
[3] Fitzgerald, *Judge Longstreet*, 76; W. C. Hutson, letter to author.
[4] *Southern Christian Advocate*, 9 October, 1840.

taken off. Mischievous boys roaming the streets at night looking for something to cause trouble are too often irresistibly led to people's front gates. The way to keep your gate from being tampered with is to make it tamper-proof. Of course the boys could cut it away from its hinges, but Longstreet knew the code too well to believe that possible. That sort of thing the Georgia conception of humor would not at all countenance. The story is that the President made this gate with his own turning lathe, and that the hinges, wherein lies the intricacy of the contrivance, were beaten by the blacksmith according to the inventor's explicit directions.

And there is the story of the boy who having been reproved once or twice for rowdyism confided to the Judge that he was at times the prey of an evil spirit which would give him no peace except under the spell of music. "Very well, sir," said the Judge, "if you will come to me when the demon troubles you next time, I shall do what I can on my flute and have my daughters to do what they can on the piano to get him appeased." It was winter. One cold morning at about two o'clock the Judge heard a knock on his front door. He went down to investigate, and found the student, declaring, as best he could through his chattering teeth, that the devil was upon him, and was fast becoming uncontrollable. Down then had to come Miss Jennie and Miss Fannie. Then in the cold bleak parlor, started the piano. Hour after hour until nearly daybreak the trio played away for the young man, who never did have the grace (Ned Brace that he was!) to declare himself set at rights. Finally the Judge ran him off still "possessed," warning him if he ever again let the devil get into the ascendancy, that things would go harder with him for his night's fun. But that was enough. According to the code Longstreet had come out of the episode at the big end of the horn. He had stuck up to his trade although doing so had made him smart.

Usually, however, he was able to turn the joke the other way. One afternoon, he overheard some of the boys planning to pull his carriage down an unfrequented roadway as soon as darkness came, and leave it concealed amid the trees. He said nothing, but that night when they got the carriage to the appointed place, the Judge was a secret passenger. Just as they were abandoning the vehicle, he rose up, and calmly looking out of the high carriage window, just long enough to thank the young men for the ride, requested them to pull him back home. Of course, they did so.

At another time, having discovered a plan among the boys to steal his chickens, he concealed himself, that night, close enough to the scene of the theft to overhear the entire transaction. Finally the brigands arrived. There were three of them. One hurriedly got up into the tree where the chickens were roosting, while the others remained at the foot of it to receive the chickens as they were handed down. "Here," said the boy in the tree as he handed down a rooster, "is the old Judge; here (handing down a hen) is Mrs. Longstreet, and here (handing down two pullets) are Miss Jennie and Miss Fannie." The Judge kept quiet, but he had recognized the boys' voices. The next day he casually invited those three boys to his house to dinner. They were very grateful for the invitation and accepted it without over-much suspicion. Finally they were all of them seated at the table, and the Judge was serving the plates. "Now, sir," said the host to one of his guests, as he held his great carving fork poised over a dish of chicken, "shall I help you to a piece of the old Judge, or would you prefer a nice portion of Mrs. Longstreet?" and then—"or perhaps you would prefer a piece of Miss Fannie or Miss Jennie."

At another time when one of the college Trustees was visiting the President, the boys slipped into the stable and cut off all of the hair on the tail of the Trustee's horse. Fortunately they let the hair lie where it fell. When the loss was discovered, the Judge contrived somehow, by some mucilage or glue, to get most of the hair temporarily back on its stub, and then so managed that, as soon as he could get the boys lined up for the Trustee's inspection, to have that functionary ride deliberately down the long line in front of them. As the great gentleman rode along, the horse switched his tail nervously, but all of the hair stuck. The boys were astounded. Such doings were past their understanding. Did any other school, they wanted to know, ever in this world have a president like theirs?

Bishop Fitzgerald says that it was as an educator that Longstreet did "the best work of his life, with the most enduring results," and doubtless in many regards he is right. Longstreet loved to teach. There are tales of his teaching geography to the little slaves around his home near Augusta by having them draw maps and scratch out letters and numbers in the sand, and of his repeating this service years later for the benefit of the little white children of one of the villages to which he "refugeed" during the Civil War.[1] He had a passion for uplifting and broadening humanity, and gloried in witnessing the effects of the expansion upon alert young minds.

He considered the position of a teacher "the most important, honorable, and sacred trust that can be confided to man in any country, but especially in this," believed "all that is dear to the Christian, the philanthropist, the patriot, and the statesman is involved in the moral and intellectual improvement of the people." A teacher, he conceived, puts his talent into a "more useful field of labor" than does the man aspiring for honors in the "forum or the Senate-house."

But education, according to his way of thinking, should never be considered anything more than the loyal handmaiden of religion; its processes of reasoning should be deductive so long as they do not touch matters of religious acceptation; when they reach these matters they must content themselves with being inductive. The ideal president of a college should be one "whose textbook in morals is the Bible, and whose lessons in physics all begin and end with its author."[2] If he thought, Longstreet averred, that "the self-sacrificing spirit of primitive Methodism" would suffer by being blended with the intellectual culture fostered by his college, he would wish the college "demolished immediately." The encroachments of nineteenth century science were to him increasingly abominable. Even the name "Nineteenth Century" he disliked as a title for a magazine, declaring it "unphilosophical" and "dangerously suggestive in this age of science and reform...."[3] Later he thought of the Civil War as essentially a struggle

---

[1] *Library Southern Literature*, 3243-4.
[2] Fitzgerald, *Judge Longstreet*, 76-9.
[3] Longstreet, "Old Things Become New," I, 846.

between a "Christ-taught band" and a "science-taught band."[1] "All science which puts God out of the world," he says, "or that makes Him the most inactive, inefficient being in all His vast dominion, by teaching that He wound up the machinery of the universe a hundred thousand years ago, set it going, and then seated Himself to look idly on its workings through eternity; all science which teaches that He made but one thing at first, a something like a thin cloud or mist, or white smoke, heated first very hot, and set it to rolling and flinging off hard, round ponderous worlds (or rather mist enough to make them, which went rolling in like manner but flinging off no little worlds); all science which teaches that one of these mist-made worlds cooled down to three-fourths water and one-fourth land, and that the water made the fishes, and the land made the bipeds and quadrupeds; all science which teaches that God has given no laws to man; that the Bible is a lie, and Jesus Christ an impostor and a liar: Get the ear of the yet uncorrupted, if you can, proclaim to them, and prove to them that all such teachings lead to incalculable misery on earth and immense agony in hell."[2] These words of Longstreet's, said James Jackson, one of his eulogists, should be "stereotyped in letters of gold upon fields of silver, and posted on the walls and the doors of every college in America."[3]

Longstreet thought that education would by the nicest adjustment increase a man's capacity for performance to the exact degree to which it would increase his responsibility to life. "God's exactions of us," he told one of his graduating classes, "are in direct proportion to our capabilities, and what would have satisfied his demands upon you, a few years ago, will not satisfy them now."[4] But the graduate was not to be distressed; since, indubitably, the young man who had been through a school like Emory was vastly better equipped to deal with the world than a mere untrained man could ever be, and since, likewise indubitably, "merit, like water, will find its level, though it may have to wind through many a loaming

---

[1] Fitzgerald, *Judge Longstreet*, 145.
[2] Longstreet, "Old Things Become New," I, 850.
[3] Jackson, *The Rev. Dr. Longstreet*, 27.
[4] *Southern Christian Advocate*, 6 August, 1841.

vale, and leap many a rugged precipice before it does so."[1] God's in his heaven; all's right with the world. And so forth, endlessly.

But Longstreet was as restless intellectually as he was physically—unbroken calm under the cool trees of little Oxford would not have suited his head any better than it did the rest of him. He was not the sort of man to be satisfied with intellectual victories won only over boys, whom he could be sure of subduing at any time merely by suffering them to remember his position. He was out in the world, against error wherever he saw it, ensconced or not ensconced, and he would lay into it whenever chance offered. Chance did offer, freely, in the summer of 1844; and it was answered freely.

---

[1] *Southern Christian Advocate*, 6 August, 1841.

XII

ECCLESIASTICAL CONTROVERSY OVER SLAVERY

There had always been a slight disposition on the part of the Methodist church to interfere with the institution of slavery, and in 1784 this movement had attained great strength.[1] But as the number of Methodists increased more rapidly in the South than it did in the North, the policy of the church toward slavery was gradually through the years 1786–1816[2] brought to accord with the Southern viewpoint.[3] From 1816–36 the question of slavery in church councils had been practically quiescent;[4] and as it was during these years that Longstreet had become interested in church policies he had probably not regarded slavery as in any way an affair for ecclesiastical adjudication.

In the early thirties, however, in response to Garrison's tom-tom, the New England Methodists again took up the question, and by June, 1835, some New England ministers had organized among themselves an anti-slavery society.[5] Soon afterwards the war of pamphlets, which preceded the great actual war of 1860–64, was already under way. The ministerial anti-slavery association having shortly after their origin published an *Appeal* were promptly replied to in a *Counter Appeal*, signed for the most part by Northern ministers. The appeal had stated that "no slave holder is truly awakened, and that no slave holder can rightly be permitted a place in the Christian church." To this indictment the counter appeal, after citing the primitive Church at Colosse, and much Scripture (Ephesians

---

[1] Gross Alexander, *History of the Methodist Episcopal Church South* (New York, 1894), 6.
[2] *Ibid.*, 7.
[3] W. W. Sweet, *The Methodist Episcopal Church and the Civil War* (Cincinnati, 1912), 16.
[4] Alexander, *Methodist Church*, 8.
[5] Sweet, *Methodist Church and Civil War*, 19.

VI, 5-9; Timothy V, 1-2, etc.), had replied that "slave holding is not, in all cases and invariably, sinful, that we may not say that no slave holder is truly awakened, and that it does not of itself form a ground of exclusion from the Christian Church."[1] Nor did they endorse "the position that slave holding should be universally and immediately abandoned."[2] In September of that year, two of the Bishops addressed to the New England conference upon the subject a letter of remonstrance in which they declared: "We have found no such excitement with any of [the conferences] except yours," and in which they pronounced the whole abolition movement "a deep political game," unfit for ministers to engage in or even to talk about, "from the pulpit or otherwise."[3] The Georgia Conference of 1837 and the South Carolina Conference of 1838 both took occasion to certify that the institution of slavery, not being a moral wrong, was out of the province of the Church.[4] The General Conference of 1840 marked the greatest concessions made to the slave holders. Indeed, these concessions were so great that in March, 1843, a large body of Methodists, having despaired of getting their church to go on record against slavery, withdrew from the old church and established a new one, known as the Wesleyan Methodist Church.[5] Conservatives were on the whole glad of the withdrawal and looked forward to a calm session of the General Conference to be held in New York City in May, 1844.[6]

But the ghost would not be laid. On reaching Baltimore in April, on his way to the Conference, Bishop Andrew learned to his surprise that a recent anti-slavery agitation, which had been in progress among the Maryland Methodists, had extended even to him. It was known that he was a slave owner only in a very restricted sense, but that knowledge had not, he was grieved to learn, prevented church members from feeling that he should either desist from the exercise of his func-

---

[1] Alexander, *Methodist Church*, 10; Matlock, *The Anti-Slavery Struggle* (New York, 1881), 87-8.
[2] Alexander, *Methodist Church*, 11.
[3] Sweet, *Methodist Church and Civil War*, 20; Matlock, *Anti-Slavery*, 90.
[4] Sweet, *Methodist Church and Civil War*, 20-1; Matlock, *Anti-Slavery*, 90.
[5] Alexander, *Methodist Church*, 13.
[6] *Ibid.*, 15.

tions as Bishop or get rid of his slaves. He determined to resign his position as soon as the Conference should convene in New York.[1]

On reaching New York, Andrew was not long in meeting the six men composing the Georgia delegation and apprising them of his distress. Longstreet, for one, assured the Bishop that there was little to apprehend; that the Northern Methodists were to be completely trusted to do what was just; that, above all things, he was not to think of resigning.[2]

Longstreet was typical of the best thought of the South toward the negro. As a child, he had learned from his mother that slaves were to be treated with humanity, and later he had had this viewpoint sanctified for him by his mother's Will, which expressly stated that her slave woman Leah was to be sold to a person of her own choosing.[3] . . . In selling his own slaves in Augusta he had taken care to dispose of them to a pious and kind master.[4] In defiance of state law,[5] he had taught some of his slaves to write. That he was personally kind and thoughtful is not to be doubted. Also, however, he was condescending and self-righteous in regard to slavery, with a condescension that time has made now almost inconceivable. While he would perhaps have been stayed by his humorous outlook from taking credit for "benevolence," as one man did, who, having found just where he had left some property for the supposed theft of which he had had a negro flogged, gave the negro five dollars and got himself praised therefor in the newspapers,—while Longstreet would have been saved from this, he did not think it unbecoming of him to complain when negro men and women whom he had more or less forcibly shoved into matrimonial alliances and then settled off in neat houses of their own, refused thereafter to live in those houses as they had originally been paired. Realist though he was, it simply did not occur to him that negroes had rights as imperative as anybody's. If a white person was cruel or inconsiderate

---

[1] Smith, *Andrew*, 340.
[2] *Ibid.*, 384.
[3] Mayes, *Genealogy*, 176.
[4] Fitzgerald, *Judge Longstreet*, 47.
[5] Prince, *Digest*, 804.

to negroes he would probably burn in hell for it, but there must be no thought of a negro's present retaliation. Practically, the Judge was right. That other could not exist. The system of slavery forbade the possibility of suggesting that such a course might at times become desirable. Longstreet thought, too, that there was no need of viewing the negro idealistically. It was well enough for a child to call an older negro "aunt" or "uncle," but for a married woman to keep that up—this seemed to him inexcusable.[1]

The attitude of the Southern Church had been parallel to that of Longstreet. Where whites and blacks lived in the same districts, they continued to worship in the same houses up to the period of the war, the negroes sitting in the balcony,[2] but in districts in which the black population was greatly preponderant, missions were established and conducted in a spirit of inspiring self-sacrifice. The Church officially declared that "the duty of giving the gospel to the slave population is binding on all, with the force of an indispensable obligation."[3] Capers had organized a negro mission as early as 1829. Bishop Andrew would spend the night at the home of a negro brother,[4] and Longstreet himself had contemplated the possibility of being sent to work on a negro mission.[5] By 1854, there were in South Carolina alone twenty-six colored missions, with thirty-two regular preachers, and 10,000 members.[6] But one had to acknowledge, however regretfully, that there was a slight social odium attached to such evangelists![7] Though the coöperation of the slave owners with the missionaries was reported "hearty"—that is, as soon as they became aware of the fact that the Methodists did not intend to incite insurrection, this heartiness was certainly not always of a very encouraging sort. "The people will not agree," one of the missionaries writes querulously to the church paper, "to have the negroes preached to on week days. Perhaps there are between two

---

[1] *Georgia Scenes*, 114.
[2] Smith, *Andrew*, 218.
[3] Alexander, *Methodist*, 48.
[4] Smith, *Andrew*, 47, 81.
[5] Williams, *Advice*, 110.
[6] Alexander, *Methodist*, 117.
[7] *Ibid.*, 118.

and three thousand blacks in the bounds of the mission; between two and three hundred attend my preaching. About one hundred are members of the Church . . . [we must make the plantation owners who are friendly to us] feel that they are accommodated, and not indeed that they accommodate us by letting us preach to their people."[1]

But more than this one complaint could not have broken the abiding unction and complacency of the upper classes in regard to slavery. Their shield of satisfaction with themselves, grown out of the old necessity for suppressing certain details, became daily more and more impenetrable. And what made things worse was that to the negroes neither condescension nor complacency was objectionable. They rather liked to be patronized. All they asked was kindness. So far as they cared, the giver might make his gift with any degree of personal sanctimoniousness he fancied. It was in this that certain old Southerners were chiefly right when they condemned slavery in their hearts and recognized, in spite of superficials, that it was more hazardous to master than to man.[2]

Bishop Andrew's connection with slavery, Longstreet knew like a book. The Bishop owned a negro boy named Jacob, whom he had inherited from his first wife, and a negro girl named Kitty, who had been left to him for rearing by a lady who had lived in Augusta. The slave property that had come to him through his marriage with his second wife he had secured to her by a deed of trust immediately after the marriage.[3]

Having come into the Andrew home when she was a young girl, Kitty had been reared by her guardians with a tenderness which she soon grew ardently to reciprocate. When the first Mrs. Andrew lay dying she sent for Kitty, and, after kissing her affectionately, extracted from the girl a promise to live righteously and strive for Heaven—held out to her for guerdon the possibility of meeting there at last her beloved mistress.[4] The scene had been most affecting. Longstreet himself had

---
[1] *Southern Christian Advocate*, 20 August, 1847.
[2] Alexander, *Methodist*, 34; Fitzgerald, *Life of McFerrin*, 269.
[3] *Journal*, General Conference, Methodist Church, 1844, 63–4.
[4] Smith, *Andrew*, 308.

witnessed it.[1] Another episode concerning Kitty he had witnessed in a capacity that was official. Upon Bishop Andrew's request, he and another member of the Emory faculty had undertaken to explain to the girl the provisions relative to her in the Will of her original owner. With his own hand, Longstreet had written down everything that happened at this meeting. According to the specifications of the Will, Kitty was to be offered the opportunity, when she was nineteen years old, either of going to Liberia, free, or of remaining a slave with Bishop Andrew. When the matter was explained to the child, she was naturally afraid. "I don't want to go to that country," she had said, "I know nobody there. It is a long ways, and I might die before I get there."[2] In a special sense, then, Longstreet was personally responsible in the matter of the Bishop's connection with slavery.

But he could not bring himself, with his lawyer's mind, to anticipate much trouble. Surely no body of intelligent men, it having been made clear to them how much of the property of the South was invested in slaves, could indorse any agitation threatening to throw that system over. It was, then, with anything but despondency that Longstreet with the other delegates from Georgia went to the opening session of the Conference held on May 1, at Green Street Church.

That was Wednesday. On Friday, some one moved that there be constituted a Committee on Slavery. Capers promptly moved that this resolution be tabled. The last motion lost and the committee was ordered.[3] Then, one after another, the New England brethren began presenting their anti-slavery memorials, all of which, one could be thankful, were turned over to the Committee. The next day, however, a man from the New Hampshire Conference asked that his memorial be read before the Conference. Longstreet thought this going too far. He moved that the reading be dispensed with. His motion was lost.[4] The situation looked bad. Perhaps there would be some help from Stephen Olin, a one-time Georgian, now

---
[1] *Southern Christian Advocate*, 6 May, 1842.
[2] Smith, *Andrew*, 311–13.
[3] *Journal*, Methodist Conference, 1844, 13.
[4] *Ibid.*, 23.

again a New Englander. But on the first test vote that came up Olin was, upon request, excused from voting, for the reason, he explained, that he had not heard all of the debate.[1] Hardly any sane man, one would guess, could have heard all of it. Here truly was a deluge of words, talk, talk, talk, mighty poorly guarded, most of it, serving chiefly to turn the passions of men hotter and hotter.

On May 22, the Committee on Episcopacy read before the conference Andrew's statement of his connection with the "peculiar institution." Then some one moved that the Bishop resign;[2] then some one offered a substitute motion that he desist from his work as a Bishop so long as he owned slaves.[3] The debate continued furiously, Longstreet participating, through June 1, when the substitute instead of the original motion was finally adopted.[4] Longstreet and Lovick Pierce had voted for the substitute, while the younger men from Georgia had demanded a cleaner issue.[5]

Two days later, on June 3, Capers introduced a motion that the Church divide into slave-holding and non-slave-holding branches,[6] and on June 5, Longstreet presented a memorial, signed by the delegates from the slave-holding states as well as from Missouri and one of the Illinois Conferences, to the effect that the further jurisdiction of the General Conference over those localities would be "inconsistent with the success of the ministry."[7]

On the whole, the Southerners seem to the present writer to have come out of this squabble with more cause for pride than the Northerners. They had on their side every technical right, and, in addition, the necessity for following the course they did follow, or seeing their church largely abandoned by its members. Churches apparently always find this consideration peremptory. It was well enough to say that the South,

---
[1] *Journal*, Methodist Conference, 34.
[2] *Ibid.*, 63–4.
[3] *Journal*, Methodist Conference, 1844, 66.
[4] *Ibid.*, 84.
[5] *Ibid.*, 73–4.
[6] *Debates*, Methodist Conference, 1844, 192.
[7] *Ibid.*, 200.

like the rich young man, was refusing to part, for Christ's sake, with the visible awards of earth, but it would have been hard—this is commonplace—for the North to give over a system as inextricably fixed in the tissues of its economic existence as slavery was in that of the South. And besides, the South did not believe slavery evil; it was clearly countenanced by the Bible, both Old and New Testaments. Bishop Andrew and the entire Southern delegation were disciples of passive resistance. They stood on their rights and were logical throughout. The Northerners, on the other hand, in their demands upon Andrew were altogether inconsistent, quite justifying McFerrin's comment upon their course as one counselling the Bishop as follows:

> You shall and you shan't,
> You will and you won't,
> You'll be damn'd if you do,
> You'll be damn'd if you don't.[1]

It is indeed disheartening to read a record of the debates at this conference. Unknowing persons, thinking that in such a body as a General Church Conference, if anywhere, they may look for justice, wisdom, and moderation, must needs turn away from a reading of these records in some despair about humanity. Both sides were often quite out of decent bounds, even so important and virtuous a man as George F. Pierce descending to uncouth rant and vulgar personal gibes.[2] Aside from Bishop Andrew himself, Olin and Longstreet preserved their respectability better than most of the participants. Though quiet when first called upon, Olin did not remain quiet. In the midst of the ugly wrangling he later spoke with dignity and power, unanswerably, it would seem, against the folly of driving the Southern delegates to underwrite a policy that their constituents would never support.[3]

Longstreet was before the body frequently, moving and counter-moving, explaining intricate legal points, reading protests, proceeding sometimes in a strain that one had to call

---
[1] *Debates*, 216.
[2] *Ibid.*, 122.
[3] *Ibid.*, 85.

caustic,[1] yet always dignified, always erudite and patently sincere, always rather curiously dominating the assembly, impressing the younger men as too "venerable and learned and talented" for them to challenge.[2] But his anger was none the less stirred. He had a certain aloofness and a disposition to make himself even more aloof, that struck the young men as almost weird. They were afraid of him. "Whether you stand bound together or not," he told the Conference, "to the best of my solemn convictions . . . I shall never mingle with you again."[3] And as time passed after the Conference was over, the Judge still became angrier and angrier. As he and Bishop Andrew were on the way to a conference in Petersburg, Virginia, two years later, he talked so unguardedly that the Bishop came to think of him as not believing there was a good Methodist in the whole North.[4]

* * * * * * *

During the forties Oxford was to a very considerable extent the intellectual capital not only of southeastern Methodism but of a good portion of the entire Georgia population. Its only rival in this latter regard was the state university, and that was laboring now under the difficulties of being held perhaps none too orthodox as regarded either Christianity or Simon-pure democracy; then, too, Middle Georgia could never altogether adjust itself to the Georgia dominated by Savannah, and Savannah continued to keep its hold upon the institution in Athens. Mercer University, it is true, was located in Middle Georgia, and ought to have done for the Baptists what Emory did for the Methodists. Somehow it did not. If you were a Middle Georgian and wanted some intellectual guidance more solid than that offered by lawyers, and you were too much of a localist to turn to a college often under the influence of a section other than your own, you turned then, unless you were an incorrigible Baptist, to Emory. Perhaps in this, more than in anything else, is shown Longstreet's ability as an organizer

---
[1] *Debates*, 115.
[2] *Ibid.*, 121.
[3] *Ibid.*, 113.
[4] Smith, *Andrew*, 384.

and executive. Mercer had every opportunity that Emory had except in the matter of its President.

Good Methodists looked eagerly now to Oxford to see what would come from it with reference to the late rupture in the Church; good Southerners of other religious persuasions looked as eagerly, knowing somehow that they were witnessing what might later happen on a grand scale in secular affairs.—Could the withdrawal—separation—secession, call it what you would, be effected amicably?—If you were a good Methodist and a good patriot combined, an acknowledged leader in the Church, and an intimate personal friend of Bishop Andrew's—in that case, you walked in these days very much on air. But if in addition to all of these things you were also a resident of Oxford, you found your neighbors walking so much in the same element that you could hardly recognize your own displacement.

On getting back to Oxford, Longstreet immediately began writing, setting down on paper thoughts that he had not been able to get out while in New York. He wrote a long letter to the editor of the ecclesiastical *New York Advocate and Journal*, and sent it to him before the middle of July, asking that it be published, over an assumed name, preferably, but over Longstreet's name if the editor thought necessary. He got not even a reply. Passing mention of the article was indeed made in the paper of July 24, but then nothing further was said. At this silence, Longstreet chafed fretfully, but kept his peace until about the first of October, when, in glancing over some controversial piece by the editor of the *Advocate and Journal*, he saw a statement by the editor of this paper "that he had received communications from Dr. Longstreet and Dr. Capers, which were very severe upon the senior editor, but that they would be published provided certain editors would give a pledge not to republish them without also publishing his rebuttal." In a later issue of the same paper, the Judge saw a reference he took as to himself about the editor's having received "pieces too severe to admit of publication!" There was now in Oxford a college president who was nothing short of furious. But "I am not satisfied," he wrote to the *Southern Advocate*, "to have it generally believed that I . . . addressed a Christian brother in language unworthy of a Christian Journal." All of this complication he wrote about in full to the *Southern Christian Advocate,* Charleston, which promptly published his letter, 25 October, 1844, requesting that the editors of the church papers in Richmond and Nashville do likewise.

The weary battle had just started. Writing over the names Elihu and Cleophas, throughout November and December, 1844, Longstreet regaled the clientele of the *Southern Christian Advocate* in three elaborate articles with much logical and Biblical justification of slavery. He did not mince words. "Abolition among Churchmen," he declares, "is a mania, a fanatical monster, an insatiable polyphemus, which will tear to pieces and devour everything sacred and all political and religious institutions."[1]

In the spring of 1845, he and the two Pierces and Dr. Few, with six other ministers constituting the Georgia delegation to a convention of Southern Methodists, went to Louisville, Kentucky, for the purpose of organizing a Southern Church.[2] He and Lovick Pierce served as the only Georgia members of the General Committee on Organization.[3]

It was probably at this time that Longstreet preached before the Louisville Y. M. C. A. his Sermon against Infidelity (now lost), which was so highly regarded by his contemporaries.

He was by now distinguished enough to be one of the "big" men of the gathering. He had all sorts of titles: President, Doctor, Judge, Reverend, and, gratuitously awarded, even Governor. He rather enjoyed this multiplicity of distinctions, was telling always as a joke on himself, about the confusion and embarrassment of the hotel authorities in Louisville upon being called upon to produce so many sorts of Longstreets.[4] . . .

The Louisville Convention having delegated Doctor Pierce to carry their fraternal greetings to the Convention of Northern Methodists shortly to be assembled in Pittsburg, that gentle-

---

[1] C. Elliott, *The Great Secession* (Cincinnati, 1855), 432.

[2] A. H. Redford, *History Organization Methodist Episcopal Church South* (Nashville, 1871), 623.

[3] *History Organization M. E. C. S., By order General Convention, Louisville* (Nashville, 1845).

[4] Fitzgerald, *Judge Longstreet,* 183.

man accordingly, while the other Georgians were returning homeward, set out for Pennsylvania. But his fraternal greetings were not received. The Pittsburg Conference "tendered him all personal courtesies, and invited him to attend their sessions," but did not, they said, "consider it proper to enter into fraternal relations with the Methodist Episcopal Church South."[1] Pierce was wounded and humiliated. With a grand gesture he shook the dust of that episode from him, and left the town, informing these cold brethren that the South had made its last advance; that the North could undertake to renew relations when it saw fit; as for the South, she had finished. All of this was not calculated to increase Longstreet's equanimity.

In April, 1845, H. B. Bascomb, President of the Southern Methodist Transylvania University, in Kentucky, had published a book called *Methodism and Slavery, with other matters in controversy between the North and South, Being a Review of . . . the case of Bishop Andrew.* John C. Calhoun, and Henry Clay himself, commended these letters heartily, but that did not prevent their being replied to at an early date by Dr. Peck of the Northern Church, in a pamphlet called *Slavery and the Episcopacy.*[2]

It was said tauntingly in Dr. Peck's book, that Bascomb confined his justification of slavery to a discussion of material things only—"counted upon nothing but food and raiment and lodging, or the like—never consider[ed] that the slave has no father, that marriage and all its holy influences are unknown to the slave code."[3] But the letters that Longstreet had sent North for publication in the *Advocate and Journal* had discussed the subject from a standpoint utterly religious.

Peck was one of the men to whom Longstreet had addressed his letters, as one who had particularly aroused his ire at the New York Convention. And the author's feelings had been further stirred in the matter of his letters by the shabby excuse that the editor of the *Advocate and Journal* had

---
[1] H. N. McTyeire, *History of Methodism* (Nashville, 1898), 467.
[2] Elliott, *Great Secession*, 518.
[3] *Ibid.*, 542.

given for not publishing them. He determined then to put the whole series into pamphlet form, thinking that they "might be serviceable to the cause, and to Southern Methodism in particular." "Some things in them," he admits in the preface to the book resulting from this resolution, "do not now suit the present state of the Methodist Church; but I preferred letting them remain, to taking the trouble that it would cost me to remove them, and accommodate the remainder to the change."

This pamphlet, published under the title *Letters on the Epistle of Paul to Philemon or the Connection of Apostolical Christianity with Slavery* (Charleston, 1845), consists of five letters, running altogether to about 17,000 words, all addressed to Drs. Durbin, Bangs, Peck and Elliott. Except for the evidence they give of the author's ability in careful research, for their vituperation, and for the tragic light they throw on the fallibility of sincere conviction, the letters are not of great interest.—"You of the North," they state, "believe slavery sinful; we believe it innocent. The only arbiter, therefore, is the Bible. If you will show us that the Bible condemns slavery, the most violent of us will yield readily. Will not some of you accept my ideas and then argue through the question on that basis, without taking recourse to the Declaration of Independence or throwing up a breastwork out of the long-forsaken rubbish of the Social Contract, or bewildering your pursuers in the mazes of metaphysical subtlety."[1] "We must meet this subject as we do every other involving duty; not with wire-drawn arguments from the laws of nature, but with honest arguments deduced from the word of God." Although Longstreet had put some effort into this series of letters, and had been fulsomely praised for writing them, he could somehow never be proud of them. Some ten or twelve years after they were published he wrote to his friend Dr. Winans that all of his efforts in connection with the church and slavery were the weakest of his life, and therefore to himself the most mortifying.[2]

Whatever else may have caused this weakness it is sure that

---

[1] Longstreet, *Letters on the Epistle of Paul to Philemon, or the Connection of Apostolic Christianity with Slavery* (Charleston, 1845), 7.
[2] Fitzgerald, *Judge Longstreet*, 119.

it was not caused by a sudden quiescence of spirit. In the *Southern Christian Advocate*, 12 December, 1845, Dr. Durbin of the Northern Church having taken it upon himself to remonstrate with Longstreet for the impetuosity and malignity of his writing, exhibited a grace and sweetness, it must be confessed, that made Longstreet's reply, published two weeks later, look very undeserving. Longstreet took Durbin's suavity for the most contemptible and maddening hypocrisy, and doubtless plumed himself on not being decoyed by it into gentleness. Possibly he was right, but the record is against him. "We of the South look upon you," he had written, "as a band of desperate fanatics alike reckless of the laws of God and man; shutting your eyes to the one code, that you may with quiet conscience violate the other. With us you are a tribe of self-infuriated madmen, rushing through the country with the Bible in one hand and a torch in the other; preaching peace, and scattering the flames of civil war; enjoining love, and arousing to butchery, lauding liberty, and firing liberty's last temple." To this Durbin protested in a letter throughout conciliatory in tone, that the object of the Northern Methodists had not been in any way "to assail the institution of domestic slavery."[1] Longstreet answered him only in the bitterest irony, and with the most trenchant down-rightness; "All of you Northern Methodists," he says, "invariably skip, forget, overleap, or dodge the Scriptural arguments which are urged. . . . None of your leaders are open and frank in your position. . . . [One of them demonstrably] has used the press to stifle truth and propagate error. . . . You are all, more or less, out of the line of your duty."[2]

In the North, says one of the men to whom the Paul-Philemon pamphlet had been addressed,[3] the *Letters* were not considered of such importance as to call for reply, but in the South they were received as very significant. A Charleston secular newspaper published about them an editorial column-and-a-half of praise, the Richmond Methodist *Advocate* thought that "in addition to its place in the Church controversy, the book is

---

[1] *Southern Christian Advocate*, 12 December, 1845.
[2] *Ibid.*, 26 December, 1845.
[3] Elliott, *Great Secession*, 522.

a valuable addition to the department of Biblical criticism to which it belongs, and will still increase the well-earned and extensive reputation of its already distinguished author."[1] The work was extensively bought by ministers attending the South Carolina and Georgia Conferences.[2] Longstreet was merely expressing the thought of his people. Even his rude reply to Dr. Durbin was spoken of approvingly in the *Southern Christian Advocate* as an example of his ability to maintain his doctrine, come what might.

The attitude of the Southern ministry towards slavery was well stated by Dr. Ross, of the Alabama Synod. "Let us then, North and South," he said in a speech delivered in Ohio, "bring our minds to comprehend *two ideas,* and to submit to their irresistible power. Let the Northern philanthropist learn from the Bible that the relation of master and slave is not sin *per se.* Let him learn that God says nowhere it is sin. Let him learn that sin is the transgression of the law; where there is no law there is no sin. . . . And let the Southern Christian—nay, the Southern man of every grade—comprehend that God never intended the relation of master and slave to be perpetual. . . . Let him believe that slavery, although not a sin, is a degraded condition,—the evil, the curse of the South,—yet having blessings in its time to the South and to the Union. Let him know that slavery is to pass away in the fullness of Providence. Let the South believe this, and prepare to obey the hand that moves their destiny."[3] Later in his speech, in comparing in a very amicable way the relative merits of North and South, the gentleman says that the South at least is not afflicted with women who frequent conventions, "convention ladies" who despise the Bible. "We of the South are afraid *of them,* and *for you.* When women despise the Bible, what next, *Paris,— then the city of the Great Salt Lake,—then Sodom,—before and after the Dead Sea.* Oh, sir, if slavery tends in any way to give the *honor of chivalry* of Southern young gentlemen towards ladies, and the exquisite delicacy and heavenly integrity

---
[1] Elliott, *Great Secession,* 540.
[2] *Ibid.*
[3] Fred A. Ross, *Slavery Ordained of God* (Philadelphia, 1857), 26–7.

and love to Southern maid and matron, it has then a glorious blessing with its curse."[1]

In April, 1846, Andrew and Longstreet went by way of Charleston to the Petersburg, Virginia, Convention where, particularly to the gratification of Longstreet, they saw the Southern Church definitely set on its way.[2] Here the Judge's activity was mainly in connection with the educational functions of the Church. Serving on the Educational Committee, he got through a resolution authorizing the Bishop to appoint a Methodist Chaplain to all educational institutions applying for one, even to those not under the jurisdiction of the Methodists.

When he got back to Oxford there was a new disquisition already well mapped out in the Judge's mind, this time a controversial essay, in which, through publication in the Baltimore *Western Continent*, edited by his friend W. T. Thompson,[3] he hoped to produce wider effects than had been possible for his Charleston-published *Letters on the Epistle of Paul to Philemon*. This, too, would be a series of "letters," addressed, in this case, from "Georgia" to her older sister "Massachusetts." Before it was concluded the series had reached eleven letters, nine from Georgia to Massachusetts, and two addressed by Georgia to her sister states in the South. At the beginning of each letter, the writer protests that this will be her last, but always before she stops she has thought of material for one more. This keeps up until the author has written about 35,000 words. In 1847, these letters were transcribed from the *Western Continent* and put into a book which proved so popular that by 1849 it ran through eight editions.[4] "They should," said the responsible *Southern Quarterly Review* in a critical notice, "be disseminated through the whole South, and read by every Southern man."[5]

In 1838, Rhett of South Carolina had suggested the desirability of disunion, and in 1844, statesmen throughout the South, under the influence of the objection of Massachusetts

---

[1] Fred A. Ross, *Slavery Ordained of God*, 20.
[2] Smith, *Andrew*, 384.
[3] *Southern Quarterly Review*, January, 1848.
[4] Ulrich B. Phillips, "Literary Movement for Secession" (in *W. A. Dunning, Studies in Southern History and Politics Inscribed to* (New York, 1914)), 35.
[5] *Southern Quarterly Review*, January, 1848.

to admitting Texas as a state, had written to their representatives in Washington urging that the issue between North and South be drawn immediately. A few of the irreconcilables had at that time been unable to keep themselves from issuing pamphlets.[1] During the fifties, controversial pamphlets became very frequent.[2] All of them, so far as they had good "Southrons" for authors, paraded the virtues of the South and condemned the vices of the North,—respectively exonerated and condemned the sections with regard to their volitional adherence to the Constitution,—defended the actual enslaving of negroes in the South as opposed to the virtual enslaving of white factory people in the North, or, for that matter, in England. Some of these articles appeared in the form of argumentative essays, some as novels,[3] some even as poetry.[4]

Longstreet's *Letters,* which were probably in advance of anything that had preceded them, presented the Southern viewpoint with great effectiveness, and, the introduction protests, with all harsh sentiments, carefully "expurgated." Often in them "Georgia" speaks with restrained indignation, and at times rises, or lapses, into an audacity of expression that must have proved ambrosial to Longstreet's co-partisans. The reader was told that though "Georgia" idolized the Union, she would not hesitate, should the Union prove the Golden Calf that it seemed much in way of proving, to crush it as remorselessly as Moses crushed the calf of Aaron[5]—was reminded that Massachusetts "by her lust had engendered a disease, which by her quackery, she had turned into a cancer"—was enheartened with the prediction that the South would be victorious in a test at arms[6]—was warned that military training should be introduced into the colleges and that the militia should be more adequately maintained. Through the whole series ran the

---

[1] Phillips, "Literary Movement for Secession," 44.
[2] *Ibid.*, Bibliography.
[3] Jeannette Reid Tandy, "Pro-Slavery Propaganda in American Fiction of the Fifties" (in *South Atlantic Quarterly,* January, 1922); *Ethel Somers, or the Fate of the Union,* by a Southerner (Augusta, Georgia, 1857).
[4] William J. Grayson, *The Hireling and the Slave* (Charleston, 1856).
[5] Longstreet, *A Voice from the South, Comprising Letters from Georgia to Massachusetts* (Baltimore, 1847), Letter 2.
[6] *Southern Quarterly Review,* January, 1848, 262.

theme that Massachusetts was supremely selfish, that she manifested evil characteristics which were obtrusive, contagious, and likely to become mortal to the body politic.[1] Weighted with this "satanic puritanism, puritanic satanicism, this Massachusettsia," the author says, "is responsible for most of the ills of an otherwise happy nation.[2]

In the South the *Letters* were acclaimed, but in the North, to the intense exasperation of the Southerners, they were hardly noticed. A number of the books having been sent by the publishers to a Northern bookseller were returned by the next mail.[3] This neglect was to the Southerners a cause of measureless discouragement. To them the matter dealt with in the letters was, whether primarily "political, religious, social or sectional," fast swallowing up all others under each and every of those heads.—Here was a book "respectful in tone, weighty in manner, and urgent in application," and the North refused to listen to it. If, says one of the old Southerners, the *North American Review*, instead of inquiring derisively "who reads a Southern book?" had asked "Who reads a Southern speech, remonstrance, argument or rebuke, addressed to the sense, the patriotism, the morality, the Christian forbearance and common humanity of the North?" the sneer would have been as true in its import as it was base in spirit, and disgraceful to the pompous pretenders who claim its benefit.[4]

In little Oxford events moved on quietly. The College was prospering. All together there were over a hundred students, and one-third of the senior class of nineteen members (1848) were to become preachers.[5] Bishop Andrew, it is true, would not be brought to recognize the desirability of political disunion, any more than Bishop Capers and the Pierces would, nor for that matter, the Methodists in general, but in their unwatchful moments many of them must have been brought to wonder if, after all, the Judge was not right. At any rate, they all of them loved him and respected him highly. One of his re-

---

[1] Longstreet, *Voice from South*, Letter 1.
[2] *Ibid.*
[3] *Southern Quarterly Review*, January, 1848, 527.
[4] *Southern Quarterly Review*, January, 1848, 527.
[5] *Southern Christian Advocate*, 8 October, 1847.

cent graduates, news came about now, loved him enough and thought highly enough of the prestige of his name to call a boarding school after him, "Longstreet Institute."[1]

In 1845, Longstreet's elder daughter, Frances Eliza, had married Dr. Henry R. Branham, a representative of a family long and affectionately known by all of the Longstreets, and for a long time prominently identified with Middle Georgia and the Methodist Church. On 15 July, 1847, the other daughter, Virginia Lafayette, had married L. Q. C. Lamar, who in addition to belonging to a family as much like the Longstreet's as the Branham family was, had the additional advantage over Dr. Branham, perhaps, in that he had only two years before been graduated from Emory College.[2] Soon there were grandchildren.[3] The Judge and his wife had every reason to believe they had at last settled where they would live out the rest of their lives. He was nearly sixty, and she about fifty.

---
[1] *Southern Christian Advocate*, 26 January, 1849.
[2] Mayes, *Genealogy*, 33.
[3] *Ibid.;* Fitzgerald, *Judge Longstreet*, 947.

XIII

COLLEGES TO THE WEST

But Destiny, after her old habit, though keeping her own counsel, was spinning her threads into a pattern no one was looking for. In the spring of 1848, Longstreet wrote, "I received letters from two of the Trustees of the University of Mississippi desiring to know if I would accept the presidency of that institution if elected, giving me strong assurance of the appointment. I was immediately impressed with the opinion that I could serve God and my country better at the head of a state institution than at the head of a sectarian institution. I submitted the matter to Bishop Andrew with these words: 'I am inclined to think that I ought to accept this appointment. Emory is now upon a firm basis. There are fifteen preachers within sound of the college bell, and therefore I am not needed here either as a preacher or a teacher. Take a little time to consider the matter and give me the light of your counsel upon it.' 'I don't want a moment's time to reflect upon it,' said he; 'you ought to go,' and gave his reasons. I immediately signified to the trustees my readiness to accept. The election did not come on till [later]."[1]

When the Emory Trustees met during Commencement, Longstreet gave in his resignation as President; and, in his baccalaureate of that year, took occasion to make a sort of valedictory. It was all very moving. "As Dr. Longstreet has yielded," wrote a correspondent to the church paper, "to what he and his friends consider a call of Providence, his baccalaureate terminated in an address to the friends of Emory College, calling upon them to rally around it with increased devotion, and, as they professed a warm regard for him, to manifest it by sustaining the institution which had been so long the cherished

---
[1] Fitzgerald, *Judge Longstreet*, 47-8.

object of his affections. I need not add the doctor's address produced a great effect—he leaves Emory with the deep regrets, though not complaints, of its friends. He takes charge (D. V.) of the Mississippi State University. . . ."[1] Young George Pierce was elected to succeed the Judge at Emory and everybody was glad beyond words to see the boat turned over to such a good pilot.

It was doubtless through John Newton Waddel, a son of Longstreet's old teacher, that the name of the President of Emory College had come before the Trustees in Mississippi. Born in 1812, and educated at the University of Georgia while his father was its President, young Waddel had by 1840 settled in Mississippi,[2] and bought a farm of 2500 acres.[3] On the way to Mississippi he had chanced to see in Mobile, Alabama, a newspaper account of some activities concerning the University of Mississippi, then just about to be established. He considered this chance Providential, and from that time on turned his attention to education as well as to farming. He was not long in establishing the "Montrose Academy," modelled apparently very much on the plan of the old academy at Willington.[4]

Waddel's educational activities caused him in 1844[5] to be appointed a trustee of the new University, and in April, 1847, he recorded, he went some 200 miles on horseback to a meeting[6] held in the town of Oxford, where the Trustees had been induced by land gifts to undertake the establishment of their school. In Jackson, in January, 1848, he had attended another meeting,[7] and it was after this that he and Jacob Thompson, likely, had written Longstreet asking him to accept the Presidency of the University.

"The best laid plans, according to Burns," reflects the erudite author of Yankee Hill's biography in commenting upon the undependability of circumstance, "are mice,"—and mice

---
[1] *Southern Christian Advocate*, 28 July, 1848.
[2] John N. Waddel, *Memorials*, 231.
[3] *Ibid.*, 235.
[4] John N. Waddel, *Memorials*, 240-3.
[5] *Ibid.*, 261.
[6] *Ibid.*, 249.
[7] *Ibid.*, 260.

indeed they proved in the case of Longstreet's new position. The Mississippi Trustees met according to plans in July, but they elected, only by one vote,[1] it is true, but none the less effectively, not Longstreet at all, but George Frederick Holmes, of Virginia, a man of foreign birth, then not yet thirty years old.[2] Waddel, assured that Longstreet would be elected, had resigned from the Board of Trustees in order himself to apply for a position as teacher of Ancient Languages. The meeting is said to have been a stormy one. There were seventeen applicants for the Presidency,[3] of whom Longstreet was not one, he having never formally applied.[4] But this had not kept his name from being long considered. His final defeat was due to the action of one of the Trustees who insisted that a minister should not be connected with a state educational institution,[5] and that no courses touching upon religious matters should be offered. The offending Trustee, overruled at least to the extent that Waddel was elected Professor, immediately resigned.[6] In sound, the teachers' duties were arduous. Waddel had as his assignment Greek, Latin, Hebrew, French, German, and Spanish, only the first two of which were known to him. At

---

[1] Fitzgerald, *Judge Longstreet*, 48; John Waddel, *Historical Discourse*, 72.

[2] George Frederick Holmes was born in Georgetown, Guiana, in 1820, and died in Charlottesville, Virginia, in 1897. Having been educated in England, Holmes came to America when he was seventeen, and taught school for several years thereafter in Virginia, South Carolina, and Georgia. Then he began to practice law in Charleston, but by 1846 he was back in Virginia, teaching Mathematics in a Baptist college in Richmond. He was no narrow specialist; the next year, he became Professor of Economy, Belles-Lettres, and History at William and Mary College, and in the summer of 1848, he accepted the presidency of the still unopened University of Mississippi, with the duty of teaching Mental and Moral Philosophy, Logic, Belles-Lettres, Political Economy, and International Law. In the spring of 1849, the young President left Mississppi for a visit to Virginia, but, due to sickness, and eye-trouble, and, most likely, to discouragement over the outlook in the West, he never returned. For nine years he lived in retirement with a relative in Virginia, farming, and writing when his eye-sight permitted. After 1857, until his death, except for the period of the War when he was Economic Adviser to the Confederate Government, he was Professor of History and Literature in the University of Virginia, impressing his students with his immeasurable erudition, but not, unfortunately, with the desirability of being always attentive to his display of it.

[3] John N. Waddel, *Memorials*, 252.

[4] *Ibid.*, 254.

[5] John N. Waddel, *Memorials*, 252.

[6] *Ibid.*, 253.

first he was considerably disconcerted by his shortcomings, but was reassured when told by the Trustees that in reality they meant to offer language courses in Greek and Latin only.[1]

But all of this did not give any better face to Longstreet's situation in Georgia. Having resigned his position at Emory with some flourish, and announced his destination, he suddenly found his destination now altogether withdrawn. He must have remembered with some sense of irony the "D. V." that the *Advocate* had used in speaking of his going westward. It was indeed lucky that he had enough money to live on. Fortunately, he was well-off, and was not obliged to fret himself about the condition of his family. "I was" [upon my resignation from the presidency of Emory], Longstreet wrote in a reminiscent letter late in life, "a gentleman at large, free to choose the mode of life that might seem to be the most agreeable to me. I entered the itinerancy without a circuit; and worked where I was most needed. My labors were greatly blessed, and, of course, so was I. Thus employed, the report of the Mississippi election found me. . . . I was so happy in my new vocation . . . that I rather rejoiced than repined at my defeat. The news of it had hardly had time to reach Louisiana before I received news that I had been unanimously elected by the Trustees of Centenary College, President of that institution. I accepted the appointment.

"Hitherto my changes of vocation and place had all been in Georgia, where from the mountains to the seaboard my wife and myself were well known and much esteemed. Now she was to journey to a far-off land, where neither she nor her husband knew a living soul. She accompanied me thither with the same equanimity and uncomplaining submission with which she accompanied me to Oxford, Georgia."[2] Now, in the first place, the truth probably is, Mrs. Longstreet knew that submission was a wife's part, and in the second place, it is likely, in spite of her duty as a lady wistfully to regret moving from one place to another, that she really somewhat enjoyed changing.

Centenary College was established in 1839, at a joint con-

---
[1] John N. Waddel, *Memorials*, 255.
[2] Fitzgerald, *Judge Longstreet*, 48.

ference of the Mississippi and Louisiana Conferences of the Methodist Church, and was opened with sixty students, in November, 1841, at Brandon Springs, Mississippi.[1] A year later the student body had grown to 175. In 1846, the Church bought the very adequate buildings of the defunct College of Louisiana, located at Jackson, Louisiana,[2] and transferred the College to that place, naming it "The Centenary College of Louisiana."[3] Even before it had come into possession of the new buildings the college was more pretentious than Emory. Its 1842–3 catalogue announced, for instance, that the college had six professors and 224 students. There was also an impressive list of "Schools,"—English Literature, Ancient Languages, Mathematics, Natural Sciences, Medicine, Law, Moral and Intellectual Sciences, and Sacred Literature.[4]

Among the Trustees of this institution was William Winans, a prominent Methodist preacher from Mississippi whom Longstreet had long known of and whom he had actually been thrown with when the two men championed the Southern cause at the New York Convention of 1844. Winans was only two years older than Longstreet, but he had by almost forty years preceded him in the Ministry. Having become a preacher in 1806, he had a few years later gone as a missionary to Mississippi, and there fallen into a position of leadership. Though not himself a man of collegiate training, Winans was a believer in the educational responsibility of the Church, and had done what he could to further denominational schools. It was only natural, when Centenary College found itself without a President at a time when one of the most distinguished ministers and educators of the Church found himself without a job, that the man and the position should be brought together. It was still, then, in theory, primarily as a minister that Longstreet went to Louisiana. At the Georgia Conference held in Augusta in January, 1849,[5] he was simply transferred from one jurisdiction of the Church to another.

---

[1] Rowland (*Encyclopedia of Mississippi*) says it was started at Clinton, Hinds County.
[2] Mayes, *Education in Mississippi*, 115–6.
[3] Edwin Whitfield Fay, *Education in Louisiana* (Washington, 1898), 139.
[4] *Southern Christian Advocate*, 6 October, 1843.
[5] Minutes Georgia Conference, I, 201.

In February or March, 1849, he took up his duties as President of Centenary. His reputation as a wit had preceded him; he was always having to tell jokes, and mimic the Georgians, always, without trying, he was collecting crowds of admiring listeners about him whenever he commenced talking.[1] But it is to be doubted whether he ever liked the place. The social and economic texture of the country there was different from the one he had been accustomed to; this Louisiana parish and the Georgia county he had left had each of them about 13,000 people, but while in Georgia there had been almost twice as many whites as there were negroes, in Louisiana there were more than twice as many negroes as there were whites.[2]

Jackson, it seemed, was peculiarly full of widows with sons to educate, who had come to live there with the idea of giving their offsprings at once the benefits of enlightment and circumspection under Methodistic influence. Specimens of this genus had also inhabited Oxford, but in Georgia, Longstreet had been able to dominate anything. Here the women would not turn the management of their boys over to him, but persistently interfered by excusing the boys[3] at all too frequent intervals from duties that the Judge thought indispensable for the youngsters' development. This interference on the part of parents was a thing which seemed to him, at its best, deplorable; not at its best, it was intolerable.

Another thing that must have disgusted the old gentleman was the system of student government which he found existing at Centenary when he took charge of it, and which he hardly dared destroy. Under this system, the executive and judiciary branches of government were indeed controlled by the faculty, but the legislative power was vested in two bodies, the first composed of members of the Board of Trustees and of the Board of Visitors, and the second, composed of twenty-one students who themselves had to be over seventeen years old, but who could be voted for by any student over fifteen.[4] This was quite contrary to Longstreet's notion. According to his

---

[1] Fitzgerald, *Judge Longstreet*, 169.
[2] Census 1850.
[3] Longstreet, *Mitten*, Introduction in *Southern Field and Fireside*, 28 May, 1854.
[4] Mayes, *Education in Mississippi*, 115-6.

idea, the Trustees, after framing a body of laws covering as nearly as possible every contingency that might arise, should publish those laws for the benefit of both students and faculty. The enforcement of them should then be left to the President.[1]

By April, Longstreet was already sadly discouraged. During that month he wrote for Sprague's *Annals of the American Pulpit* a sketch of Dr. Waddel, in which he included the following disillusioned, sinister paragraph: "The reputation of Dr. Waddel never suffered from change of time, place, or society, but bright at its rising, it grew brighter and broader at every move in its orbit. This certainly is a remarkable fact; for if there be any occupation in which merit is no guarantee of popularity, it is that of an instructor of youth: if there be anything in which age never confirms the views of youth, it is the direction and government of a school."[2]

At about this time also, the Judge began writing a book. "Two meritorious young men," he says in his account of this book's genesis, "established a Press in the village, and earnestly solicited contributions from my pen. In the hope of assisting them and of improving the over-indulgent mothers and unruly youth of the place, I commenced the story of Master Mitten,[3] with a design of teaching mothers the danger of allowing their affections for their children to interfere with their duty of exercising that parental discipline which is indispensable to the training of youth in industry, study, and moral conduct; and to set before youth of talents the evils of indolence and the rewards of industry and study in a manner which I thought most likely to stimulate them to a laudable ambition for literary distinction. I laid the scene in Georgia, that it might not be considered as a rebuke to the kind mothers of Jackson,"[4] and also "that it might thereby prove more interesting to Georgia friends should the book ever fall into their hands."[5]

Master William Mitten: or a Youth of Brilliant Talents Who Was Ruined by Bad Luck, the product of these benign

---
[1] South Carolina College, Minutes, 5 May, 1858.
[2] Sprague, *Annals*, IV, 63–7.
[3] *Southern Field and Fireside*, 28 May, 1859.
[4] Fitzgerald, *Judge Longstreet*, 167.
[5] Longstreet, *Mitten*, preface.

intentions, was doubtless, as the author says, written in a desire to help two meritorious young men, and to make good boys out of a countless number of bad ones, but incidentally it shows where the author had his heart while he was writing. His heart was in Middle Georgia, at the time in which he always remembered Middle Georgia most affectionately, during the first two decades of the century. The book ran in the weekly paper as far as five chapters,[1] until Centenary commencement, in fact, when Longstreet resigned[2] his office and set out as soon as he could for Georgia.

He had spent in Jackson, he says, "the five most tormenting" months of his life,[3]—adding, "How they came to be so, no matter." It is easy to guess the secret. "While packing up my things to return to Georgia," the Judge says, "I was informed that I had been unanimously elected President of the University of Mississippi." He accepted the place,[4] but proceeded, nevertheless, to Georgia. Professor Waddel was there before him, and glad enough certainly to redeem himself by telling the old Judge of the recent unanimous election. Whether in fun, or out of pure goodness, Longstreet let Waddel think that this was the first news he had had of his vindication. At any rate, Waddel died thinking he had been the first man to break the good news.[5]

The University of Mississippi had not prospered. Holmes, the young man who in July, 1848, had been elected in place of Longstreet, had opened the school in the early part of November. He had not, though, been able "to stand the racket." Under the perverse "mischief" of the boys, the carping demands of the Trustees, and the general distrust that the school labored under as a citadel of atheism, the young President broke down completely, and, taking his son with him, in April, 1849, returned to Virginia, professedly to recover his health. Mississippi never saw him again. Though it is said that he wrote back, and was actually contemplating a return,

---

[1] Longstreet, *Mitten*, introduction.
[2] Fitzgerald, *Judge Longstreet*, 48.
[3] *Ibid.*, 48.
[4] *Ibid.*, 48.
[5] John N. Waddel, *Memorials*, 273.

it is sure that neither he nor his letters ever arrived. The Trustees, when they met in July, very naturally declared their relations with the young man at an end, and having stipulated that he was to be paid no salary for time later than April 15, proceeded to elect a new President. Out of a board of at least thirteen there were but eight men[1] present on the day of the election,[2] but all of those present, in spite of the fact that he had never applied,[3] voted for Longstreet. They were eager enough for him to come. It was resolved that the secretary notify him of his unanimous election to the Presidency and *"urge upon him the acceptance of the same."*[4]

In September, 1849, Longstreet arrived in Oxford,[5] the seat of the Mississippi University, and began his work. Conditions there were in many ways probably as little to his fancy as they had been in Louisiana, but as he had at last got the place that he had left Emory for, it was necessary that he fight his battle and keep the faith. During the months the University had been without a President its reputation for poor discipline and for "infidelity" had grown rapidly; and in the first case, at least, the reputation seemed abundantly justified.[6] "Fidelity to my office as historian," says Mayes, "impels me to record that, in all probability, very rarely, if ever, was an institution attended by a body of students so disorderly and turbulent as the first students of the university, in mass, proved to be. It is true that among those early students were some of the first young men of the country; but in point of morals and intellectual advancement, the large body of the students were idle, uncultivated, and ungovernable."[7] There was much rowdiness and drunkenness, the students buying whiskey freely from the cotton wagons which rolled by constantly on the way to Memphis.[8]

The number of students, when Longstreet took charge, was

---

[1] John N. Waddel, *Memorials*, 261.
[2] Trustees Minutes, University Mississippi, 10-11 July, 1849.
[3] Waddel, *Memorials*, 273.
[4] Minutes, Trustees University Mississippi, 12 July, 1849.
[5] Mayes, *L. Q. C. Lamar*, 45; Fitzgerald, *Judge Longstreet*, 48.
[6] John N. Waddel, *Memorials*, 276.
[7] Mayes, *Education in Mississippi*, 138.
[8] John N. Waddel, *Memorials*, 269.

less than it had been the year previous; there were only seventy-six and there was dormitory space for two hundred. But conditions soon improved. By this "unoffensive vigilance," Longstreet soon "succeeded in impressing his students with the conviction that he was solicitous for their highest intellectual and moral advancement." Self-possessed, able to govern without any undue display of the machinery of government, endowed with a remarkable power of swaying masses of people under excitement, he soon had things going smoothly.[1] Nobody could now believe the University "infidel." The second year of Longstreet's administration it had 134 students, and after five years, 225.[2]

In addition to performing his duties as President, Longstreet taught Mental and Moral Philosophy, Rhetoric, Evidences of Christianity, Logic and Political Economy.[3] Under him were three teachers: Albert Taylor Bledsoe,[4] as Professor of Mathematics and Astronomy; John Millington, a former teacher at William and Mary College, as Professor of Chemistry and Natural Philosophy; and John Newton Waddel, as Professor of Ancient Languages.[5] Before a great while, Longstreet's son-in-law, Lamar,[6] became an assistant in the department of Mathematics. All of these men gave him all that they could give in the matter of loyal and intelligent coopera-

---

[1] John N. Waddel, *Memorials*, 276.
[2] *Ibid.*, 298-9.
[3] Minutes Trustees, University Mississippi, 25 February, 1848.
[4] Albert Taylor Bledsoe was born in Frankfort, Kentucky, in 1809 and died in Alexandria, Virginia, in 1877. His life refutes the adage about rolling stones. Two years after his graduation from West Point, he resigned from the Army to study law; he became, then, a teacher, an Episcopal rector, an army officer, a research worker, an editor, and, at last, a Methodist preacher. He was Professor of Mathematics at the University of Mississippi 1848-54, and at the University of Virginia from 1854 to the outbreak of the War, when, though he had always opposed secession, he entered the Confederate Army. In 1863, he went to England to collect material for a book which was to offer a constitutional justification of secession. Returning in 1866, and finding Jefferson Davis in prison, he made his book a plea for Davis's liberation, as well as a defence of the lost cause. Next he inaugurated a magazine in Baltimore, called *The Southern Review*, which, in 1870, became the official organ of the Southern Methodist Church, and so, perhaps, soon drew its now by no means reluctant editor once more into the fold of the ministry.
[5] John N. Waddel, *Memorials*, 254.
[6] Mayes, *L. Q. C. Lamar*, 46.

tion. In 1854, came Frederick A. P. Barnard, New Englander and graduate of Yale, lately a professor at the University of Alabama, bringing with him doubtless a troop of old Yale memories, certainly bringing with him an aggressiveness that must have made Longstreet and the other old-liners rub their eyes in amazement.[1] In January, 1855, Barnard's investigation of the state's debt to the University, made upon the President's request, caused great commotion all over the state, as indeed the announcement of a $900,000 incumbrance upon a state might be expected to do.[2]

At first, the President's salary was $2000 a year, and that of the Professors $1500, in both cases, plus the perquisites arising from tuition fees. After a while the President's salary became $2500.

The University was well equipped. "The campus, which was of great natural beauty, was located," writes Waddel, "in the center of a section of land [about a mile to the west of Oxford and] donated by the citizens of the town and of the county. Laid out in the form of a circle some two hundred yards in diameter, its circumference was occupied by dormitories, residences for faculty members, a chapel, and a Lyceum. The Lyceum, the most prominent building on the campus, occupied the central point of the circle at its highest elevation, with the other buildings on the right and left at successive points until the circle was complete. It was an imposing structure, three stories high, with a front portico supported by six large and handsome columns. . . . The dormitories were of a uniform height with the Lyceum. Adjacent to the dormitories were two double-tenement buildings also of three stories in height, built for the Professors."[3]

Oxford was agreeable enough to live in. Though too small to find a place in the Census of 1850, it was the residence of an unusually high grade of citizenry. Jacob Thompson, President of the Board of Trustees, and Secretary of the Interior in Buchanan's Cabinet, and members of the Board of Trustees

---

[1] *Barnard, Memoirs of*, 198–9.
[2] *Ibid.*, 199–200.
[3] John N. Waddel, *Memorials*, 263.

were residents.[1] Here, in addition to the University, was a school of some thirty pupils, known as the Oxford Female Academy, established in 1838 by a Northern lady, but now for a good while under the safe guidance of a Southern "reverend." In 1854, "moved by an impression very prevalent in the State at that period that a denominational connection was the only sure road to the achievement of a great career, an arrangement was made whereby the Female Academy was turned over to the Presbyterian Church.[2]

Lafayette County, Mississippi, the seat of the University, was in many ways parallel to Newton County, Georgia, the seat of Emory College. The population and the proportion of whites to blacks were about the same in both counties. Indeed, there had been for some years a sort of migration from old Newton to this new county in the West. "It is," wrote L. Q. C. Lamar, from Mississippi, in May, 1850, "a magnificent country for planters. There are men here who left Newton County poor and in debt eight and ten years ago, who now have a good plantation and fifteen to twenty hands, and are buying more every year. . . ."[3] As Longstreet's perceptibilities were always keen for making money, it cannot be thought that such opportunities were lost upon him. If the place had at first seemed unattractive, it did not long remain so.

The Judge was very much of a person for having his family close around him. Before he had been in Oxford two months he had persuaded his son-in-law, Lamar, to follow him. Lamar came in November, "making the trip overland in a rockaway and two wagons," bringing with him his wife, infant daughter, and servants. The Branhams (Mrs. Branham was Longstreet's other daughter) followed early in 1850.[4] Edward Mayes, who married one of the Lamar children and who was in consequence intimately associated with the entire Lamar family, writes delightfully of the almost phantasmal, idyllic nature of Longstreet's domestic life during those first years in Mississippi. The two daughters, he says, "were much alike in

---
[1] John N. Waddel, *Memorials*, 287–91.
[2] Mayes, *Education in Mississippi*, 93–5.
[3] Mayes, *L. Q. C. Lamar*, 45.
[4] *Ibid*

general appearance, rather above medium height, with very small and delicately cut and pleasing features (Mrs. Branham's being more like those of their father in outline), with remarkably fair complexions, black hair, and blue-gray eyes. Both were finely educated and accomplished. Notable housewives, they had all of the arts which go to make home delightful and to crown the lives of their family with a perfect happiness. Mrs. Branham had her father's wit, bright, sparkling and pungent, tempered by the kindest feeling; while Mrs. Lamar had her father's abounding and perennial humor, with his rare powers of mimicry, to which she occasionally gave rein in the retirement of her own home, to the great amusement of friends.

"Both had the cheerful disposition of their father. Mrs. Lamar, even while engaged in her household duties, effervesced and exhilarated. Her lively chatting from room to room with the various members of the family or with the servants, her audible little soliloquies, the mild hectoring in which the diligent but gentle and vivacious housewife indulged, were inspiring and often most amusing; and the whole was shot with snatches of song, now gay, and again devout. Mrs. Branham's cheerfulness, on the other hand, was of a more tranquil character, and she was much more given to serious and introspective musing than was her sister. Mrs. Lamar's heart was simply an unfailing spring of bright waters, and her brave eyes refused to fall before the glare of troubles. Mrs. Branham had a sober and more apprehensive temper. The trials which her sister ignored, she anticipated, recognized, brooded over, and either endured or conquered.

"The sisters were inseparable companions, in fact, were never during their lives separated, except for brief periods. They and their parents, their husbands and children, afforded a beautiful example of family unity and harmony. They all lived together much as one family, frequently in the same residence for long periods, and their children grew up calling each other 'brother' and 'sister.' "

Theirs was an absolute intimacy, and a continual understanding. "All of this," Mayes concludes, "sounds like a sketch of romance, but it is the simple statement of a truth, a feeble description of the personal relations that existed for years between loving, noble, and loyal souls."[1]

There is no doubting Longstreet's serene happiness. His sons-in-law he loved like his own children. "I am indebted to you," Lamar once wrote to him, "for ennobling influences from my boyhood up to middle age. I have doubtless often pained you, but for many years I have loved you as few sons love a father. . . . No applause of the public delights me so much as your declaration that I am unspeakably dear to you." Dr. Branham could not be too gracious to him. How the Judge expanded under such adulation! He could talk to Dr. Branham whenever he liked, about matters of business; and to Lamar he could always talk about law, or politics; with Mrs. Branham and Lamar, both of whom, like himself, were inveterate readers, he could talk whenever he chose to discuss books and reading.[2]

These three were always buying books and subscribing to magazines. They had a large library, especially rich in theology, in the Greek and Latin Classics, in the English Classics through Addison, and in various works on science and philosophy. To please Mrs. Longstreet there were the poems of Scott, Byron, Moore, Tennyson, and even Longfellow. All of the New England writers, however, the Judge thought too puerile for anything; he once derisively parodied the whole of *Hiawatha*.[3] And then, there was his collection of letters, enough of themselves, almost, to start a library, reaching back as they did into the 1820's, and representing correspondence carried on through all the time since with all manner of distinguished people, "statesmen, churchmen, classmates (North and South), and many friends."[4]

True to his fixed custom, Longstreet did not let slip any good chances of turning over an honest dollar. Before leaving Georgia he had purchased some Mississippi land owned by Asbury Hull, and since coming to Mississippi he had continued buying and selling real estate in both town and country. This

---
[1] Mayes, *L. Q. C. Lamar*, 42–4.
[2] Mrs. L. B. West, Jackson, Miss.
[3] Mrs. A. L. Heiskell, Memphis, Tenn., Letter, 12 January, 1922.
[4] Longstreet, "From Out the Fires," 545.

was his chief idea of financiering. He was most methodical in setting down in his little book every detail of his negotiations. Once a man to whom he sold some property would not take half of the roadway along the line between him and Longstreet as a part of his purchase. Over a small matter of this sort the Judge would, of course, not pick a quarrel. He let the niggling purchaser have his way, and went home marveling over men's cheapness. All of this he wrote down in his book, ending the story with the heavily underscored warning, "but remember, the whole road is mine." Having once been careless in a trade he moped over it through nine years until he could persuade himself that the Statute of Limitations having had time to become applicable, the affair could be considered "pretty safe." "How I came to take the Administrator's title," he says of this blunder, "without enquiring into his authority to sell, I don't know. I suppose it was from my confidence that he would not sell land *to me* without knowing that he was able to give good title." Even of his benefices to his two daughters the Judge kept strict account, this rather strangely since his business dealings with them consisted chiefly in his accepting from them in exchange for certain property, certain other property of which he had himself been the donor.[1] By dint of persistence and method the old gentleman was so firmly established before many years that even after the devastation of the Civil War it was found at his death in 1870, that he had left about $50,000, half in real estate, and half in cash.[2]

The attention that all of these activities had necessarily to consume, and the consequent implied neglect of University duties, did not escape the eyes of the watchful, nor fail of being duly proclaimed. During 1854, upon some complaint as to his management of the University, the President offered his resignation to the Trustees, and only upon their earnest solicitation did he withdraw it. But many people took his resignation for a bluff. "The trustees need not have fretted themselves," wrote a sour Oxford gentleman to his friend Governor McRae, "old Longstreet is making money too fast for him to be induced

---

[1] Longstreet, "History of My Land Purchases in Lafayette Co., Miss." [Ms.].
[2] Mrs. L. B. West.

to resign."[1] In truth he was engrossed. Friends in Georgia might write him as much as they would, but only a few of them ever got a reply. They found him "so occupied with his official duties," or so something else, that they could get not a solitary line from him.[2]

Longstreet still thought of himself essentially as a preacher, as a regular member of the Memphis Methodist Conference. He was always attending various church conventions, and visiting the sick whenever he felt that his character of minister demanded activities of that kind. This practice naturally entailed absences from the University, and the absences were objected to. The Board of Trustees passed a law requiring faculty members to render to it a report of their failures to meet classes. This Longstreet would not bear. "He insisted on resigning immediately unless the resolution was so explained, construed and understood as to allow him to attend the sick." . . . He announced his intention of resigning anyway when the Trustees should meet again.[3] But somehow he was placated, and the matter allowed to rest. At the 1855 Commencement, however, trouble was up again. On the grounds that this heinous law detracted from the dignity of the faculty and was a source of annoyance to them, Longstreet asked that the whole thing be annulled. Referred to a committee, his request got at length a great deal of discussion, but no definite compliance.

Things in general were going less and less to please the now veteran educator. Though in many respects Mississippi in 1850 was very similar to the Georgia of twenty or thirty years earlier, it was somehow of a different texture. In some indefinable way it suggested powerfully to Longstreet his old Georgia, but it was a Georgia come into being when the aristocratic restraint of the earliest years of the republic had become almost negligible. The difference was plainly perceptible. Some man, the author of a novel, who signs himself "A Georgia Huntsman," put the thing down clearly.

---

[1] State of Mississippi, *Governor's Letter Book*, J. M. Henry to Gov. J. J. McRae, Oxford, 1 May, 1854.
[2] Miller, *Bench and Bar*, II, 211.
[3] Mississippi, *Governor's Letter Book*, Henry to McRae, 1, 13 May, 1854.

"Rossius," he says, Rossius being a Georgian, "had not been long in New Orleans before he understood pretty well the western character, and that it was not congenial with his refined, cultivated, sensitive, sympathetic nature. . . . He was fully persuaded that the genius of the people and his own sensibilities had no affinity."[1] . . . Never, it seemed to Longstreet, had the students in Georgia been quite so persistent in their determination to snatch at a holiday. In Georgia they had been mischievous, and sometimes mischievous in a sharp sense of the word, but Georgia humor had known its bounds. In Mississippi, a student had from some hidden place thrown rocks at him.[2] . . . That was, to be sure, only an isolated case, only the thoughtlessness of a foolish boy who had afterwards so far deplored his folly as to confess it. . . . Nevertheless, the like had not happened in Georgia.

Political matters in Mississippi were going in a fashion not to suit an ex-nullifier; here, as in Georgia, the early fifties brought the state at times a Whig ascendency. Longstreet tried to whip things into line, but he was constantly getting tangled in his own lash. The activities of the Know-nothing Party seemed to him an instance of everything foolhardy, sensational, selfish, unscrupulous, and cowardly in politics; and he was no man to keep his opinions to himself. He began talking and writing, and the Know-nothings, of course, retaliated. During 1855, though his controversy with that party was, so far as Longstreet could see, not of his seeking, he had become the victim, he wrote, of "Know-nothing slanders, unmitigated and unrelenting—slanders which struck at my dearest interests and my most sacred relations. . . . I saw this 'political party' while protesting aloud against my teaching of politics in the University, whispering the students of my charge into its midnight gatherings, and there binding them by oath upon oath to everlasting fidelity to its own political creed. I now spoke out boldly in my own defence and against the party; not against its principles, but against its mode of propagating them. They assailed me from all sides and in all modes. Not one of them gravely answered my objections to the Know-noth-

---
[1] *Manolia*, 141–2.
[2] University of Mississippi, Trustees' Minutes, December, 1850.

ing discipline and dealings. They chose rather to assail me personally in language as unbecoming in them as it was undeserved by me. Even my literary *bagatelle*, the amusement of my idle hours five and twenty years ago, was held up to view as a test of my fitness morally and intellectually for the sacred office and responsible station to which I have been called.[1] I was called dotard, fool, likened to a clown, . . . charged with falsehood and turpitude. . . . nor have I ever been, in the course of my whole life, as much calumniated as I have been by Know-nothings and their champions in . . . nine months. Never did I see such an intolerant, arrogant, insolent, overbearing, inconsistent, vindictive party as this. It belies me into opposition to it, and then tells me that as a minister of the gospel I have no right to meddle with *politics*. I reply then that the hundreds of preachers who are in it should come out of it. It rejoins that it is *religious* in its character. I again respond that if it be religious I surely, as a religious man, have a right to discuss its orthodoxy, and to counsel my brethren who belong to it. And it again repeats that it is *political*. Its *religion* is reduced to one article. 'No office for Catholics.' "[2]

The whole base narrowness of the Know-nothing organization was to Longstreet totally repellent. He was no Romanist, but he could believe well of individual Romanists, and one of them, at least, Bishop John Barry, his friend since the old Augusta plague days, he loved profoundly. As for fearing the "Catholics," in the first place, they were numerically one of the weakest churches in the country, and in the second place, he felt about that as Mr. Wesley did. "Let all the Protestant Clergy," Mr. Wesley had said, "live like the apostles and preach like the apostles, the thing is done," that is, every Catholic will be converted. "Put Methodism and Romanism upon the field of fair argument," said Longstreet, "and I will stake my all upon the issue; but I am not such a coward as to flee the field of honorable warfare for savage ambush fighting, or such a fool as to believe that a man's religion is to be reformed by harassing his person."—But nearly three-fourths of

---

[1] Fitzgerald, *Judge Longstreet*, 117–8.
[2] *Ibid.*, 122–3.

the members of the Methodist Church had gone into this party.[1] Longstreet could not contemplate it patiently.

Sometime during the spring or summer of 1855 he addressed a letter, in two instalments, to the Methodist Church, South.[2] In this letter his method of discrediting the Know-nothings seems chiefly to have been to identify them with the Abolitionists.

A little later he became more specific in his appeal and addressed an essay to the Know-nothing preachers of his Church. This second essay was soon republished as a campaign document by the Democratic State Central Committee of Louisiana. The little book in which the politicians printed these argumentative epistles has sixteen pages, over half of which are given to *The Letters of President Longstreet;* the remainder are divided among The Alien and Sedition Laws of Virginia, the Kentucky Resolutions of 1798-9, and The Democratic Platform of 1852.

Here one finds still Longstreet's old graphic style, his tangibility and homeliness of figure, with just enough scholarly reference to make what he was saying vastly impressive to his audience. "You stand," he wrote to the Know-nothing ministers, "with one foot upon the platform of old Methodism and of Mr. Wesley, and the other upon the rickety structure of Know-nothingism, first reared by a criminal, if report be true, and miserably patched by un-Christian hands. I would have you withdraw the truant limb from this dangerous platform to its original position. You are, in short, straddling two stools." Then he quotes political economists, refers easily to the Census reports, giving sign of full acquaintance with the course of the world. One is not to condemn the religion of the immigrants, since many of them are Methodists; one is not to condemn the politics of the immigrants, since it is only in combining politically with them that one can put his hope of bringing to naught the iniquitous raging of the abolitionists. Immigration makes for the good of the South and for the confounding of the North,—and for the what, alas, of the Union? This, Longstreet had shown plainly, in the thirties, in his

---
[1] Fitzgerald, *Judge Longstreet*, 116-9.
[2] *Ibid.*, 116.

letter to President Lamar of Texas; but about the Union, and the Union's prosperity, he is now, in the fifties, quite silent. It is the South only that he is now concerned about. The Know-nothing party is twin-brother, or own child, one can hardly tell which, of the Abolition party. The earmarks of Northern origin are upon it, its candidates go "haranguing the multitude amidst thumps and screams and yells, firing at opposition and almost coming to blows, telling vulgar anecdotes, suppressing truth, encouraging, if not spreading, falsehood."[1]

The timid Know-nothing element of secretiveness also was out of Longstreet's comprehension, and seemed to him to spring only from a consciousness that recognized low expediency as its master.[2] Everywhere the organization was wholly unchristian. In spite, however, of these open facts, he says, though they do not exist in a corner, if any Bishop, any Elder, any Deacon, any Brother, any President of our Church has raised a warning voice against them, except my poor solitary self and one old brother more, I have yet to learn who, when, or where. From the holiest chamber of my soul I lift prayer to God to have mercy on us, and save our church from degradation and ruin. . . . "Brethren," he concludes his first letter, with an air of breathlessness, "I am not near done with you, but I must stop, my powers of calm discussion are suspended. My heart and my eyes take up the cause of my perilled Church in utterances which you might appreciate, but which I cannot expose to the ridicule of an unfeeling world." Longstreet was a life member of the persistent group who take every issue as the most momentous yet to assert itself. "It is always," grumbles one of the old Georgia lawyers, "the *great* issues of the day. Nobody ever heard of the small issues of the day in politics."[3]

Now, as the Whigs had looked upon Know-nothingism as a possible agent for breaking the Democratic supremacy, it is evident that the Methodist Whigs in Mississippi were disconcerted by Longstreet's "darts" against the people whom they

---

[1] Longstreet, *Letters from President Longstreet on Know Nothingism* (New Orleans, 1855), 3–4.
[2] Fitzgerald, *Judge Longstreet*, 121.
[3] Andrews, *Old Georgia Lawyer*, 82.

were putting most trust in. Soon William Winans, probably the most prominent Methodist in the state, though he had seen only one of the four letters published, and was aware, in fact, of the existence of only two of them, published in *The Natchez Courier*[1] a letter of rebuke to Longstreet, not for his active interest in politics (he himself was interested) but for his seeking to thrust the Church, as a Church, into secularism. [What else, Longstreet may have wondered, was the Church for?] He said further that Longstreet had permitted his intellect to be blinded by passion, that some of his suppositions were "ridiculously absurd," that the whole manifestation of the letters would be received with indifference by the Church and with hostile amazement by the world.

The Winans letter was published towards the middle of October, but it was two months before Longstreet answered it. In December, he published his answer in *The Memphis Appeal*.[2] Like Winans, he began his letter with endearment, but unlike Winans, to your increased respect for him, he had forgotten by the end of it to be even officially fraternal. This letter is sharp and bitter and reproachful. You are a professed Whig, he tells Winans, and doubtless you are one; doubtless, too, the appearance of your letter in a paper published some hundred and forty or fifty miles from your residence, edited by a Know-nothing Candidate for Congress, one of "my most wanton and implacable maligners, just in time to spread fully over the state before the elections, doubtless all of this was purely accidental. . . . You read my letter with no other design than to find in it grounds of censure and abuse." You answered it petulantly and without due consideration, you went off half-cocked. You had, in fact, not even taken trouble to read my letter through.—This reply is as arrogant as it is severe; meekness is no part of its author's programme either in his personal relations or in his conception of a desirable policy for the Church; he forgets meekness entirely. What he does not forget is his logical adroitness. He answers Winans completely on every point that Winans suggested. Winans had feared as much, had confessed himself persuaded, in chal-

---

[1] Fitzgerald, *Judge Longstreet*, 116.
[2] Fitzgerald, *Judge Longstreet*, 116 ff.

lenging Longstreet, that he was no equal match for him "with the pen."

Now a man who is financially independent, and who has as one of his earliest recollections a picture of his father withdrawing from a theater in which he found procedure not to his liking, such a man knows readily enough what to do when he is altogether too much harassed by the details of any position he may be occupying.—On 10 July, 1856, the Trustees of the University held a special meeting to consider President Longstreet's resignation. Many of them were doubtless glad of the chance of being rid of him, but when they looked back soberly upon the dismal months of Holmes's desertion and then upon the rapid development of the University under Longstreet, and then forward into a future that held evils perhaps they knew not of, they thought caution the best course. There was one wise thing to do. On July 14, they "unanimously resolved that it is the wish of the board that Dr. Longstreet should withdraw his resignation." On the sixteenth, while waiting for his answer, they conferred upon him, by way of a sop, the Degree of Doctor of Divinity. This proved no palliative. On the seventeenth he answered them finally that he would not continue as President any longer. In a diffuse and complimentary resolution, then, the President's last decision was declared accepted, regretfully but inevitably. A day later the Trustees made him their last bow by extending to him the free use of the library, "under the rules and regulations prescribed for faculty members." . . . And thus the Judge goes off the University minute-books, and thus, in fact, for a while, he went completely out of the University's life.

This was not what he had expected. Often and often had he talked with Professor Waddel, upon whom he considered the mantle of the presidency would fall next, about policies to be pursued in the future. In these plans, both as to his being next president, and as to University policy, Waddel acquiesced fully.[1] The rest of the faculty also took for granted the same plans. Waddel was Longstreet's candidate,[2] and the casual citizen naturally thought he would be elected. The casual

---
[1] John N. Waddel, *Memorials*, 325.
[2] Barnard, *Memoirs of*, 202.

citizen took at their face value all of the Trustees' resolutions about Longstreet's indispensability and his transcendent value. What the Trustees actually did was not to elect Waddel at all, but instead, to elect Barnard, the new New England professor of Mathematics, at the time away in Albany, New York, at a scientific meeting! Waddel promptly resigned even his professorship and went off to preside over a Presbyterian College in Tennessee.

In October, Longstreet severed his regular connection with the Methodist Conference, and was "located."[1] "I had now," he writes, "reached my sixty-sixth year, and felt no scruples at retiring from active service of Church or State. I felicitated my wife upon her having lived to see the end of my vagrant life."[2]

In the summer of 1852, Lamar had returned to Georgia to live and practice law in Covington.[3] Finding that he could not in connection with his law practice profitably employ there a number of slaves belonging to him, he had sent them back to Mississippi to be supervised by Judge Longstreet, who, the supposition went, would have no trouble in profitably employing them in connection with his duties as college president. It is one of life's contrarieties that this man who instinctively cared so little for farming was for so much of his existence engaged in it. He really did not like this occupation. His social instincts were too strong. He wanted to be with people, and to have somebody to talk to. He would tinker around with various things about the farm, examine some new intricate plowing device, for instance, invented by a Methodist preacher, and write a magnificent testimonial as to its worth,[4]—that sort of thing was in his line, he loved machinery, and loved to write testimonials,—but the steady application to a form of work that denied one association with his fellows,—he simply was not cut on that pattern. Furthermore, he did not like managing labor. He was overjoyed to turn the negroes back over to their owners when Lamar returned to Mississippi to live, in

---
[1] Minutes Methodist Episcopal Church South, I, 678-83.
[2] Fitzgerald, *Judge Longstreet*, 48.
[3] Mayes, *L. Q. C. Lamar*, 56.
[4] *Southern Christian Advocate*, 29 December, 1859.

October, 1855. The creatures persistently refused to live together as man and wife even after he had mated them with all the wisdom he could command, and after he had built such desirable houses for them.[1]

Though the Judge was now a private citizen, living in a remote village (he had retired to Abbeville, Mississippi, upon leaving the University), he was too conspicuous to be forgotten. In 1857, he was appointed, through the influence doubtless of his friend and Oxford neighbor, Jacob Thompson, then Secretary of the Interior, an honorary member of the Smithsonian Institution in Washington. The position meant little to him, most likely, except in its associating his name with that of his old teacher, now the eminent scientist, Benjamin Silliman, and with those of Washington Irving, and Jacob Thompson, the three persons beside himself who had been so honored.

This appointment was, of course, gratifying, but the deepest joy of the old gentleman's life was his association with his son-in-law, L. Q. C. Lamar. On returning from Georgia, Lamar had bought a farm of about 1100 acres, situated some twelve miles from Oxford, but only about two miles from the village of Abbeville. On this plantation, named Solitude, there was "an excellent dwelling with four rooms" in which the Lamars and, for most of the time, the Branhams also, all lived together during 1856 and part of 1857. But Lamar's farming operations were much like those of his father-in-law; that is, he devoted to them almost none of his time or thought. Somewhat remote from his dwelling house he had a small office to which he would go very, very often and study, sometimes for hours a day, law, politics, and philosophy,—"in the summer under a mosquito bar spread like a tent in the middle of the room."

Here in Abbeville, among their children and grandchildren, the Longstreets may be thought of as having typified much that was best in old Southern civilization when it was in its flower. Some idea of what that civilization was, as far as concerned all but its intellectual aspects, may be had from a description of life in the Lamar household given by Lamar's

---

[1] Mrs. L. B. West.

son-in-law and biographer, Edward Mayes. Here, "surrounded by his slaves," one is told, "to whom he was at once master, guardian, and friend, loved and petted by his women folk and his children, visited by cultivated and attractive friends for days and even weeks, and visiting them in turn, Lamar devoted his summers to the growing of cotton, and corn, and his winters to killing hogs, curing bacon sides and delicious hams, making sausages and trying out snowy lard. Over these latter functions, his wife, as was customary with even the most refined Southern ladies, presided. An ice house, which was a great curiosity in that neighborhood, and the stored treasures of which were a singular luxury at that period of slow transportation, had also to be filled."[1]

---

[1] Mayes, *L. Q. C. Lamar*, 60–1.

XIV

THE UNIVERSITY OF SOUTH CAROLINA

"Toward the close of 1857," writes Longstreet, "I received a letter from the Trustees of the University of South Carolina inquiring if I would accept the presidency of that institution if elected. 'Here,' said I, 'wife, you shall decide this matter. If the inquiry came from any other quarter, I would not hesitate a moment to answer in the negative; but South Carolina and Georgia have been twin nurses of me, and twin sisters in my affections; and if I could be tempted into the service of any state in the Union at this late day, it would be dear old South Carolina. But your word shall be law to me in this case, for I shall regard it as the suggestion of Providence.' She positively refused to decide the question. 'Well,' said I, 'I don't think it will be possible for my answer to reach the trustees in time for them to present my name to the Board before the election comes off. I will answer in the affirmative, and if it does not reach its destination in time, I shall conclude that I should not have accepted the place, and *vice versa*. It did reach its destination just in time, and that was all. I was elected." . . .[1]

It was James L. Petigru and the two Wardlaw brothers, friends of Longstreet's since the old days in Willington, who had inquired of him as to whether he would accept the position in South Carolina, but it was on the suggestion of a Methodist minister,[2] most likely, that these three, even before consulting their candidate, had presented his name for election. Before they actually urged their suggestion they, of course, waited to hear from him.[3] The election occurred November 25, and November 29, Petigru wrote to his friend confirming the official

---
[1] Fitzgerald, *Judge Longstreet*, 48-9. He calls it *University*, not *College*.
[2] *Ibid.*, 182.
[3] Laborde, *South Carolina College*, 441.

notice of the Secretary, which had been sent immediately after the election. "At the first ballot, without any preconcert," said Petigru, "you were chosen as the President of the College in a very full meeting of the Board of Trustees. It is an evidence of the high esteem which your life and character have created. . . . I am happy to say that the way in which our nomination has been received outside of the Board of Trustees is highly gratifying to your friends. . . . But I would not conceal from you that the task which you have undertaken is one of no ordinary difficulty. This College has never been remarkable for the docility of our youth to the restraints of authority. To maintain the cause of order in such a college requires the firmness of a strong hand tempered by the prudence of an enlightened discretion. . . . I assure you, my dear Longstreet, that not only on public grounds, but on those of long-cherished sentiments of early friendship, I feel the greatest solicitude for your success."[1]

At Emory and at the University of Mississippi, Longstreet had had the good fortune to come into the direction of colleges of which he was virtually the first president. At Centenary he had encountered a well-established tradition and had been unable or unwilling to adapt himself to it. The South Carolina College also was one of long standing—it had been in operation since 1804—but in many ways Longstreet here, too, as at the two Oxfords, found himself freed from encountering a set of conditions already established.

When James H. Thornwell in 1855 terminated his four years as President of the South Carolina College, he was succeeded by Charles F. McCay,[2] who had only recently become a

---

[1] Fitzgerald, *Judge Longstreet*, 197–8.

[2] Charles F. McCay was born in Pennsylvania, and died in Baltimore, Maryland. After studying in a Northern college he came South and in 1833 began teaching Mathematics at the University of Georgia. He was such a rigid disciplinarian that he won the dislike of many of his students, and was sometimes made the victim of their pranks. Once, after such an occasion, he was thwarted in his determination to have vengeance by the suspected young gentleman's flat denial of any connection with the crime. This was too much; McCay denied the denial, and the young gentleman's elder brother challenged the teacher to a duel. The duel was averted, but the teacher's usefulness at the University was manifestly at an end. This was in 1853. In the same year, McCay became connected with the South Carolina College at Columbia, and two years later, he became its President.

member of this faculty. A Professor Lieber who was in line for the position, in his chagrin, resigned immediately on learning of McCay's accession. McCay's administration was from the start a fiasco. Tin-pan serenades in front of his house, and riots between the students of the college and the citizens of Columbia, marked his term of office. In April, 1857, the students, accusing him of double-dealing in some matter of discipline, refused to attend any of his classes. A little later, he was virtually dismissed. From September to November, the College had no President at all. Truly, as Petigru wrote, the South Carolina youths had not been "remarkable for their docility to the restraints of authority."

The confused state of the college just prior to his taking control, probably worked in the long-run for the new President's benefit, but he could not have definitely augured to that effect, as he came eastward from Mississippi, during December. There was much about the new position which was not calculated to inspire confidence. Longstreet was in a complete sense a countryman, and while Columbia with its 6000 population was no bewildering metropolis, it was nevertheless more of a city than he had ever lived in. In Augusta, he had lived on his large farm several miles from the heart of town. So far as concerned his experience as a college president, he was a countryman through and through. The two Oxfords and Jackson could only by charity be called even villages. The idea of a college in or near a town of any size was to Longstreet totally repellent. In writing of Moses Waddel, he had commented with full approval that "the Doctor almost invaribaly established his school in some retired spot, which, while it brought his pupils night and day under his immediate supervision, removed them almost entirely from the temptations of vice."[1] The proximity of Columbia was undoubtedly to perturb the old gentleman greatly, but the administrative confusion in which he found the college was to aid him. Both

---

In 1857, the Trustees practically dismissed him. The unhorsed soldier went into business, first in Augusta, and later in Baltimore, becoming finally the leading insurance actuary in America. In 1877 he made a gift of $7,000 to the University of Georgia, providing that it be kept at compound interest for something like a hundred years. It is estimated that the sum will reach about $1,000,000.

[1] Longstreet, "Waddel" (in Sprague's *Annals*, IV, 63-7).

faculty and students were alive to the gravity of the crisis through which the institution had just passed and were prepared to behave themselves decorously under their' new executive.

Longstreet arrived in Columbia in January, 1858. On his faculty he found Maximilian Laborde, originally from Edgefield, and a contributor to the Temperance Campaign of the old *State Rights Sentinel,* and the two young LeConte brothers, both lately from a term of service at the University of Georgia.

The two hundred students were eagerly expecting him as the author of *Georgia Scenes;* everybody had recently got a copy of the book and re-read it.[1] They could not get into their heads the idea that the new President coming to them in 1858 was not precisely the same man he had been in 1833. They could not tell just where to place him. The new "refinement" that had taken hold of the country taught them that his book was decidedly coarse, that its vitality was obstreperous and unbecomingly hilarious. D. G. Mitchell noted at the last of the century that the taboo against robust realism had caused *Georgia Scenes* to be almost forgotten, but long before that, little girls, at least, in Georgia knew that this book was in the Index. To the young gentlemen in South Carolina, Longstreet, beside standing for this improbity, stood also for Georgia, and Georgia, everybody knew, was beyond the pale. Nothing else was needed to make him fascinating. The first night that the President got into his new quarters, the students gave him a grand serenade. He appeared at a window and responded graciously, telling the young men that he held himself towards them just as a parent would. But he made a very evil blunder. "I stand to you, young gentlemen," he said, using the Latin, *"in loco parentorum."* A hundred young gentlemen knew immediately that he had used the wrong form, and thought perhaps that they could not have expected much better from him. One of them could remember the incident vividly sixty-three years afterwards.[2] They began taking the new President a little lightly, a little jocularly, dubbing him "Ned Brace," some of them, others falling into the way of call-

---

[1] C. W. Hutson, "South Carolina College" (*Sewanee Review,* July, 1910), 337.
[2] Hutson, Letter to author, 5 November, 1921.

ing him "Old Bullet." The young men had much to learn, They had tackled at last a man stronger than any of them, or any combination of them, a man who could be as drastic as he could be persuasive, but above all a man who knew how to shatter mutiny before it could be set in motion by winning from his subordinates their truest and most affectionate loyalty.

Teaching, as such, the Judge no longer seemed to conceive of as his work. The subjects assigned to him, History, Political Philosophy, Political Economy, and Elocution, he took with something approaching nonchalance. "I have not," he told the Trustees near the completion of his first year's work, "carried a single class through a single text book, or delivered a tenth part of the lectures I usually deliver." He had supposed that he could complete his course at a rate of one lesson a week for each class, but had taken no account of the time necessary for examinations and reviews.[1] "In his class room," writes one of his students, "he read us long lectures to which we listened with no great ardor, and he was not well enough acquainted with individual members of the class to detect the cheat when one of us recited for another who happened to be absent."[2] How is any man of heroic proportions, forsooth, to keep himself to the business of being a drill-master? Students who were about to make speeches were bidden individually to the President's house to have them criticized. There they enjoyed themselves hugely, but nearly always they came away with more memory of the President's flute playing, of his regret for having published so frivolous a work as the *Scenes*, of his recollections of the Augusta plague in '39—with much more memory of these things than of any attention he had given their speeches.[3] "He was," says the historian of the University, "advanced in years, which perhaps accounts for his failure to make the impression of a successful teacher; he is said to have called on the students in his classes in a regu-

---

[1] Minutes, Trustees South Carolina College, 11 November, 1858.
[2] Hutson, "South Carolina College."
[3] *Ibid.*

lar order, thus enabling them to circumvent him and escape the duties of the class."[1]

The fact is that Longstreet probably felt that by now he was past the stage of habitually pleading with boys to make them study. He would offer them such pearls as he had, and if they cared to sleep rather than to gather up his offerings, that was not his lookout. His business was to make a great institution, brought nearly flat by an injudicious disciplinary programme in the past, function smoothly once more before an expectant constituency. His interest in politics, partly quiescent for a little period while he was living in Abbeville, had, once he was in South Carolina, again taken possession of him. A man whose work is in maintaining discipline and whose passion is in the large affairs of statecraft will not bother much because certain young gentlemen refuse to study hard enough of an evening to make their parents proud of them.

But his laxity as a teacher had no bearing upon his course as an executive. The students of the University were no ordinary group. They were, for the most part, consciously, embryonic grand gentlemen. Among them, "there was no thought at all of special training for business. In fact the student did not come there for that. He came for the education of the gentleman; and most of them did not look forward to making any professional use of what they learned." . . . What was the hurt in such a case, parents and Trustees alike seemed to wonder, if boys were out of school a day more or less? To Longstreet, this hurt was most palpable. "I have never known a college," he declared in a report to the Trustees, "in which the regular routine of business was so often interrupted by parental indulgence as in this. Since I became attached to it, I do not think a single day has passed in which some student has not been absent from it by permission of his parent or guardian." Whenever there was a Fair in town, parents wrote excuses enough to cause almost a temporary suspension of the college.

And then, too, there were other customs among the students, sanctioned by long usage, which the President could not be-

---
[1] Green, *University of South Carolina*, 66.

lieve helpful. He knew, however, that he could not be too sudden in his attack. The boys had a way of giving "slaminades," beating tin pans under the windows of anyone they had a grudge against; and another way they had of alarming the campus at night was to ride over it to and fro on horseback, shouting meantime like demons, and waving torches. These things, harmless in themselves perhaps, were none the less annoying. The difficulty was to stop them. People in general viewed them indifferently, or probably even revelled in the romantic secretiveness of them. And, after all, who was to tell these young lords where they must stop?—Certainly no ordinary man.

Of the amount of drinking that went on, Longstreet was probably ignorant. For his happiness it is good he was in the dark. Whiskey was drunk freely, especially among the freshmen, who gave constant "wine parties" in their rooms, with no effective let, it seems, except such as was occasionally exercised by the upper classmen.[1]

And withal there was a kind of sublimated cockiness that colored the students' entire outlook. This, on the whole, seemed to make for good more than for bad. If a gentleman would not permit his whim gainsaid, would he, then, offer even slightest valid grounds for his honor to be looked askance at? The possibility was not to be considered. An old student jingle shows admirably how things stood. After describing a night of carousal at the taven of one Billy Maybin, it proceeds to detail the consequences:

> "Next Monday morning surely, old Sheriff comes around,
> And you're up before the faculty, for going up the town,
> 'Did you go into an eating house, did you take a drink, or no?'
> 'Oh, yes, sirs, took a drink or two, at Billy Maybin's, O!' "[2]

There was no thought, apparently, of equivocation. One would even go out of his way to assert his adherence to this high code. Time and again a student had been known to give in his examination papers with some of the questions unanswered, the

---
[1] Hutson, "South Carolina College," 338.
[2] Green, *University of South Carolina*, 333–4.

blanks filled in only with "I cannot answer this question, as the answer was suggested to me,"—this, although his receiving the suggestion had been inadvertent.[1] Even when applying for readmission to college, an expelled student could have the hardihood to declare that though he was willing to abide by the new measure which had resulted in his expulsion, he did not feel that he could, rightfully, be compelled to.[2] In its highest reaches this romantic individualism among the students developed into a glorified *noblesse oblige* and gallantry which dominated all human relations. With the President, this state of affairs seemed most worshipful. One typical incident he thought fit to apprise the Trustees of in one of his reports. Two young men had been in intense rivalry for first honor. When the honor was finally awarded, the fortunate man insisted that it should not have come to him—he did not deserve it, while the unfortunate one insisted as earnestly that things had ranged themselves on the side of merit. . . . Longstreet fairly glowed in recounting this episode. "With two such men in the head of the leading class at the Institution," the President concluded his story, "you will not wonder that our report of the College is so flattering."[3]

But this sort of thing was the happier phase of what the President had to deal with—more often, his perplexities were commonplace and irksome. Before he had been at the College four months, he had run into unpleasantness, abruptly, more than once. What better trick, some of the students asked among themselves, could they play on Old Bullet than to "bar out" his teachers, just as he had, apparently with his endorsement, described the pupils' having done years before in Georgia?[4] To be done the trick needed only to be suggested. Curiosity was burning to see what would happen. Longstreet, for his part, knew all sorts of things they had better have tried. This maliciousness was not at all to be borne with. He knew that if the College was to be saved he had to do something peremptory and energetic. And his faculty knew with him.

---

[1] Hutson, "South Carolina College," 340.
[2] Hutson, Letter.
[3] Longstreet, South Carolina College, Trustees' Minutes, 30 November, 1859.
[4] *Ibid.*, 28 November, 1859.

After trying unsuccessfully to determine who were the culprits, he catechized the students in general. Half of them admitted that they were aware of everything, but refused to tell. Law, with all of its provisions as to what constitutes an accomplice to a crime, or at least contempt of Court, came to the old Judge's rescue. Every young gentleman who admitted that he knew about the offence, but refused to turn state's evidence, the President immediately expelled. This action, he was fully aware, put the College into the darkest hour of its existence, but he thought that it was only by some such policy that he could ever indicate to his game-cock students who was master. He guessed right. Soon most of the suspended young gentlemen sued for reinstatement upon Longstreet's terms, and, being admitted, took the tedious examinations required of them, covering the work done during their absence. He had won his victory. He could afford, as he did, to talk jocularly to the young men as they were agonizing over their papers.

One element of Longstreet's character that rendered him highly acceptable to the students was his ardent championship of the political principles dear to the entire South. In Mississippi the patriotic fire was burning as brightly as in Carolina. Immediately after the presidential election in 1859 Lamar wrote to his father-in-law that he was utterly dejected, had now only one hope, and that, in the resolution of South Carolina. "If South Carolina will only have the courage to go out," Lamar said, "all will be well. We will have a Southern Republic, or an amended Federal Constitution that will place our institutions beyond all attack in the future."[1] This letter probably reinforced Longstreet's already formed determination to speak on secession at the very next chance that came to him.

In his long baccalaureate address of 1857, the President stated the South's cause fervidly, with clear logic and impressive example. It was the old story. There was no hope of reconciliation left. In the North, even the Church was not scrupling at vulgarity and sacrilege if it might further the sectional policy of impudent interference. There was an incident

---

[1] Mayes, *L. Q. C. Lamar*, 86.

he could tell about the Reverend Mr. Ward Beecher's conduct in the old North Church at New Haven—endeared to him by ancient associations—that would disgust even the most callous. It was during the struggle that determined whether Kansas should be "free" or "slave." Mr. Beecher had finished his sermon and was making an appeal for funds with which to supply the anti-slavery pioneers with rifles. The pro-slavery pioneers, he announced, were "border ruffians" and needed shooting. While the collection was in progress, Longstreet declared, "His Worship amused himself, as the names of the contributors were called out, with punning upon their aptness to the service in which they were engaged. The name of a Mr. Killum was announced. 'Killum,' exclaimed Beecher, that's the name for a hater of 'border ruffians'! Could one imagine," the President wanted to know of his students, "how a more God-offending scene could ever be exhibited in a civilized community, by men of culture, refinement and professed loyalty to the Redeemer?"[1]

If this is typical of the Church, what could one hope from the politicians? The South is helpless to change its system and the North brutally intolerant. War will be the result, but we shall be victorious. The Bible justifies slavery unreservedly. Historically, too, our position is the more enviable. It is the North which was the aggressor in the slave trade; it is the North which is violating the Constitution. If the Northerners have a "higher law" than the Constitution, why, in accepting Federal offices, do they take the oath to support the Constitution? If they do not understand the oath definitely they surely understand that oaths are to be interpreted by the administrator and not by the man who takes them. The abolitionists are arch-criminals; their chief saint, John Brown, is "a living impersonation of hypocrisy, duplicity, treachery and falsehood . . . a ruthless monster, a night prowler, an alarmist of sleeping women and children, a vagrant husband, an unnatural father, a complotter with aliens against his countrymen, a robber, a traitor, a murderer, a shocking incarnation of all that is shocking in human nature and brazen in sin." If the

---

[1] Longstreet, "Old Things Become New," I.

South would withdraw from the Union in a body there would be no resistance—"I would stake everything I am worth upon this position." But even if there should be resistance we should stand a better chance of victory than the North would. "Away with this notion of whipping us into the Union, or whipping us at all!" If the North did not have its enmity to the South to keep it unified, it would soon split up into petty hostile confederacies. . . . I venture the prediction that in less than five years after the dissolution, rabid Massachusetts herself will be courting Southern commerce, as mute upon the subject of slavery as the Bunker Hill monument." With no moment's surcease this speech boiled through its long periods.

"Now, young gentlemen," it concludes, "you know your foe, your cause, and your power. Go forth, not to challenge a contest, not to fear it, not to strive for disunion, not to make a dishonorable surrender of the thousandth part of a mill more to save it. If the other States, with all the light of experience before them, will go on furnishing the means of their own oppression, if they are willing to barter away their rights, constitutional, commercial, and territorial, still further to save the Union—then I say, and would utter it with the trumpet's voice, let South Carolina put her cause in the hand of God and take her stand alone. . . . And do you, young gentlemen, acquit yourselves as nobly in her cause as you have in her college, and you will have an enviable fame. In the field, imitate your Butler, who like his own Palmetto when ball-struck, showed no outward sign of injury while life remained; and if compelled by overwhelming numbers to give way, let your flight be like that of the eagle in the storm, that rides in proud defiance before the blast that it cannot resist, and strikes with strong wing the angry elements which hurry it away."[1]

This was the voice of South Carolina. One man, however, demurred. That was Petigru. In spite of his close friendship for Longstreet, Petigru wrote him in some heat, blaming the speech as an unconsidered "diatribe," and counselling against its repetition, hinting that the Trustees would not look favorably upon a President rushing into politics, and especially

---

[1] Fitzgerald, *Judge Longstreet*, 105–6.

upon one given to such indiscretion. But this warning Longstreet answered explicitly, saying that the speech was an exact and deliberate expression of his opinion, and that he was ready to stand upon it; as for his participation in politics, he must reserve the right to talk politics whenever he thought proper.[1] Petigru might bluster as he would; that meant little to the state at large, and even less to the students. The students—what but enthusiastic worship were a group of young gentlemen to feel for a college president like this, one speaking so eloquently the very firmest canons of their thought? What mattered to them the fact that they had never seen an eagle beating his strong wings against the elements, any more, doubtless, than the President himself had ever seen one, what mattered the fact, since they were ignorant of it, that the same eagle had beaten his wings now, in Longstreet's speeches for at least twenty years?—What sentiment besides one even stronger than enthusiastic worship are they to have towards a president who, before the universal world, would declare the indubitable and eternal superiority of the white man to the negro and the equally indubitable and eternal superiority of America (God bless her!) to all creation?

Something of this sort Longstreet did in the summer of 1860. He had been sent to London as the only American delegate to the International Statistical Congress which was to convene there in July. On the day of the first meeting, just after an opening address by Prince Albert, old Lord Brougham had taken it upon himself formally to call the attention of the American Minister to England, George Mifflin Dallas, an ex-officio member of the convention, to the fact that there was present a negro delegate, a Doctor Delany, a native of the United States, but then a citizen of Canada. Then Brougham sat down. The delegates, hardly knowing what else to do, after the spurting way of delegates, applauded wildly, and Delany got up and said that he thanked Lord Brougham and wished to assure the delegates that he was a man.—Longstreet, taking all this for a deliberate reflection upon both him and his government, from that contaminate assemblage withdrew

---

[1] Fitzgerald, *Judge Longstreet*, 106–7.

his presence. Brougham's action, he reported to the Secretary of the Treasury, had constituted "an all-timed assault upon our country, a wanton indignity offered to our minister, and a pointed insult offered to me." There was great commotion. Lord Brougham publicly expressed the hope that he had not offended Mr. Dallas's feelings, and Longstreet was unofficially urged to return. But he was resolute. On the grounds that it was the way in which Brougham's affront had been received more than it was the substance of the affront that had caused his withdrawal, he refused ever again to enter the Congress which had so incensed him. To his friend, Howell Cobb, then Secretary of the Treasury, under whose commission he had gone to Europe, he wrote a long letter officially explaining the cause of his action; also he sent Cobb a voluminous "piece" which he had written for the London *Morning Chronicle,* and, to accompany the "piece," an introductory epistle almost a third as long.[1]

In these communications, Longstreet spoke for the United States as a slave-holding country against the rest of the world as free countries, and in so doing naturally pursued the same methods that he was so familiar with through his defences of the slave-holding South against the free North. There is the same violent emphasis upon the social imperfections of his antagonists, and upon the inconsistency of their criticizing his country while they continue to traffic with it. Denunciation of slavery, coming from the British, who look to slave-made cotton as one of their chief sources of wealth, was, he said, like the abuse for bleeding that one heaps on a man whom one has stabbed, and whose blood one catches to make up into puddings. There was the old logical ingenuity: The sin of the South, he said, was not in making slaves but in failing to alter the condition of people who were slaves before they ever came South.—There was the old insistence on Biblical justification of slavery. Paul and Philemon and Onesimus were made to walk beside Abraham, Isaac, and Jacob to prove its righteousness.—There was the old annoying disposition of the man to send his writings out only half finished. He was always

---

[1] For the two letters and the "Piece," see *Life of Delany,* 103–15.

hurrying; with him, there was always, just ahead, something to do much more important than the thing now in hand. He had gone to Europe to represent the American nation. That was his business. He felt bound, then, to write out an explanation of his impulsive though unregretted withdrawal. Was he to blame if after he had finished writing it somebody brought forth some additional matters that might have affected his explanation, had he known about them soon enough? In a way, of course, he was. He knew that the entire explanation should be rewritten. Life, however, was short, and there were countless tasks to be trimmed before night. What should a man do? Should one work over again, in one's own careful handwriting, the whole long tiresome essay? . . . Longstreet did not touch it. "I have neither time nor patience," he wrote, "to remodel it, much less to rewrite it. I am called away today. I should have been off from London before."[1] But whatever may be the faults of this "piece," it has also its merits; welding the whole thing together are the old grand manner that Longstreet knew so well how to strike, and the old passionate, sincere love of country. Defending his America there in London, Longstreet must have thought of himself as in some manner a symbol of forces more large and solemn than one can be identified with levitously, must have thought inevitably of those brave days before 1816, when the mere remembrance that he was an American citizen had been enough to make his humblest paths seem leading to the loftiest peaks of moral elevation.

The British newspapers took up the Longstreet withdrawal for what it was worth, some of them glorying in the exposure of the American Minister and promising themselves, in a manner suggestive of Ransy Sniffle, a rich treat when the President should realize in what contempt his Minister was held by the superior English. The American newspapers took it up, too, pronouncing, most of them, from Boston to Charleston,[2] that Dallas had been "made a spectacle of" and that Longstreet had saved the face of the government. Mrs. Longstreet, from the Lamar-Branham home in Mississippi, wrote to her

---

[1] *Life of Delany*, 106–7.
[2] Fitzgerald, *Judge Longstreet*, 202–3.

husband that as they had all known immediately on reading of the affront offered him that he would be compelled to do something decisive, they were none of them suprised when they learned later that he had withdrawn with such emphasis.

The old gentleman burned with impatience to return home. He had planned to spend the entire summer abroad, but now the whole alien Continent was offensive to him. He went hurriedly to Paris, walked for a little up and down the streets, observed with displeasure that the people did not speak English, bought himself a silver-mounted glass flute, and then thankfully turned his back on Europe with the complacent air of one who has done his full duty.

Returning quickly to London, he took one last look "at her wonders," bade good-bye to a few friends he had made,[1] the Admiral McHardy family in Chelmsford, and a Mrs. McCulloch, the wife of a member of Parliament, who having introduced herself to him as loving America because she had several kinsmen there, had got her remark and herself duly commended: "That's natural," he had commented, "that's womanlike—God bless her—and God bless the family in which she said it!" From London he went to Liverpool, which he liked better than London, and from Liverpool, after "another benefice to the Cunard line," he came home. "Farewell to Europe," he wrote, "forever and ever." It was a long adieu. Mrs. Longstreet, for her part, was slightly upset on hearing of it. Secretly she had cherished an idea that perhaps during the next year she herself might go traveling there, and she was now half-way in chagrin to learn of her husband's determination never to go back. "I was sorry," she wrote to him wistfully, "you made that vow before you took me on to see the marvelous wonders, beauties and curiosities to be met with in that distant region. But if my kind heavenly Father will vouchsafe a sure and favorable return for you, I will be perfectly satisfied with the measure of his goodness allotted to me."[2]

Longstreet's reception on his reaching South Carolina was more favorable than it had ever been. He had done what the

---
[1] Fitzgerald, *Judge Longstreet*, 199.
[2] Fitzgerald, *Judge Longstreet*, 203.

whole country could understand, and, even at that agitated period, generously approve of. The South, of course, applauded without stint. To one reviewing the old Judge's conduct as an ambassador, it is evident that a consideration of his training and environment establishes something very much like palliation for his narrowness in connection with Delany. But even leaving those considerations aside, it is vastly easier to think ill of him as a diplomat, in this connection, than as a flesh-and-blood mortal.

Delany was an objectionable and absurd mountebank, boasting of his unparalleled jet blackness and of his royal African ancestors,[1] considering, in the extremity of his recognition of racial backwardness, that no white man was so good as he was.[2] Before authority, he was fawning,[3] and in authority he was arrogant.[4] He was presumptuous in his demands,—beseeching Lincoln to make him a Major General[5]—and ridiculous in his suggestions,—canvassing the country, after Lincoln's assasination, to get the negroes to erect in Lincoln's honor a monument for the building of which he himself volunteered directions. The statue of Lincoln which he proposed should be erected, should have at the south base of it, he said, an idealized "African—very African" woman, kneeling by an urn filled with tears, and "distinct tear drops, passing down the face . . . were to be so arranged as to represent the figures 4,000,000 (four million) which would be emblematical of the number of contributors.[6] . . ." Born in 1812, this scion of black royalty had for some years before 1860 been editing a newspaper in the United States and Canada. He had championed John Brown, and it is probable that Longstreet knew immediately who he was when he was introduced at the Congress. The thing to speculate upon is what Longstreet would have done had he known then what time soon made manifest, that is, that inside of five or six years this Delany was to be a United States Army officer in practical control of Charleston, holding it under his

[1] *Delany, Life of*, 18–22.
[2] *Ibid.*, 20.
[3] *Ibid.*, 119.
[4] *Ibid.*, 217.
[5] *Ibid.*, 142.
[6] *Ibid.*, 211.

foot, revelling in his enjoyment of newly gained authority. That is the thing to guess about.

Longstreet would not long let himself be held even within the wide limits of pedagogy and high politics. He was still a preacher, after a fashion, and he was always a business man and a litterateur and a grand gentleman.

In the fall of 1857, he was contemplating a "new, revised, and enlarged edition of *Georgia Scenes*,"[1] and for much of his life he was hoping at some early time to redeem the levity of his *magnum opus* by writing another *Georgia Scenes* of a character chiefly religious.[2] Then, too, he had to answer the normal requests for biographical and personal matter naturally visited upon men of distinction. At Simms's request, during this time, he wrote a biography of himself, which had in it so much information about his father, William Longstreet, that Simms took the liberty of forwarding it to the Appletons, for whom he had solicited it, as two articles instead of one.[3]

In the spring of 1859, one James Gardiner had got together several gentlemen for the editorial staff of a new periodical to be issued weekly from Augusta, and known as the *Southern Field and Fireside*. There were three editors, one agricultural, one horticultural, and one literary. The literary editor was W. W. Mann, Longstreet's close friend and one-time law partner, now just returned from several years spent in Paris as an American newspaper and magazine correspondent.

"Too long," the prospectus of the *Field and Fireside* announced, "the Southern people have been content to look to Northern periodicals for instruction in agricultural matters and to Northern literary papers, for mental recreation. There is, however, a growing spirit of independence and of self-reliance in the South. Our people are awakening to the conviction that we have the elements of success in the experience, knowledge, and scientific investigation of the dwellers in our Southern homes. The truth is gleaming upon us that we have literary resources of our own worthy to be fostered—that among Southern writers should be divided some portion of that vast stream

---

[1] *Southern Field and Fireside*, 8 October, 1859.
[2] Fitzgerald, *Judge Longstreet*, 183.
[3] *Ibid.*, 199.

of Southern money that flows perpetually Northward to sustain Northern literature. . . . [By this paper] much latent talent will be brought to light, which will furnish some agreeable surprises to Southern people. 'Full many a gem of purest ray serene,' will flash before their admiring eyes, and cause a generous glow of pride in Southern Genius."[1]

A periodical actuated by motives of that kind could get Longstreet's support by merely hinting for it, and with his old friend Mann as one of its editors, it could of course so much the more readily secure him as one of its contributors. Indeed, the paper seems to have been a final rallying point for the persistent efforts of the pre-war South to establish for itself some standard literary publication. When Mann resigned in the spring of 1860, after carrying the paper through its first year, it was in favor of John R. Thompson, who had been for years editor of the *Southern Literary Messenger*. "The most distinguished Southern writers," one of the *Field and Fireside* announcements had said, "will adorn these columns, constituting an unrivalled galaxy of talent. Longstreet, Simms, Kennedy, Cooke, Turner, Thompson, Ingraham, Hayne—also, especially, many lady writers of established literary reputation, will contribute. . . . Judge Longstreet will furnish a series of *Georgia Scenes* never before published."[2]

The paper appeared first, 28 May, 1859, and continued regularly until November, 1864, when it was transferred to Raleigh, N. C., and merged with the *Illustrated Mercury*. The most notable of its publications perhaps were William W. Turner's "Jack Hopeton and His Friends; or, The Autobiography of a Georgian," and Longstreet's "Master William Mitten, or, A Youth of Brilliant Talents Who was Ruined by Bad Luck." Insensitiveness alone could read through the old files of this magazine and have no twinge of sadness, no suggestion of the futility that, in the long run, all too often stamps everything that intelligence and faithful, unselfish effort can accomplish. In its war issues, the paper is perhaps most disconcerting. There one can to exhaustion find the South vindicated and the North condemned. There are essays proving

---
[1] *Southern Field and Fireside*, 3 September, 1859.
[2] *Ibid.*, index to second six months' issues, May, 1860.

the unvarying superiority of Southern races, and, taken from some English paper, there is one article declaring that since the Confederate officials took better portraits than the Union officials, the Southerners were therefore inherently of better stock. The advertisements, too, have their significance; one of these calls for "fifty active intelligent young men, of good address and industrious business habits to canvass for . . . Pro-Slavery Arguments."[1]

The first issue carried Longstreet's story in a conspicuous place on the front page. An editorial note appeared just at the head of it: "It is with great pleasure that we offer in the first number of the *Southern Field and Fireside,* the first chapter of a new story by the very distinguished and very popular author of *Georgia Scenes.* This gentleman, so widely and well known, personally in all the Southern States, and by reputation throughout the country, assures us, by letter from his new residence—Columbia, S. C.,—that we may count with confidence upon frequent contributions from his pen. Our readers, we know, will share in the gratification which this promise has afforded." Then follows the story, which, published at the rate of a chapter a week, ran from 28 May–19 November, 1859.

The first five chapters of this book had been written and published in Louisiana in 1849, while Longstreet was President of Centenary College. Approaching seventy, the Judge was about the same man that he had been approaching sixty. He now took up the story where he had left off with it, without any shift of his original purpose in writing, which by announcement had been to teach good behavior to preternaturally bad young men. He had no illusions about his book's merit. "I very much doubted," he said, "whether the intelligent editors would admit it into their columns. They did so, however, and by those who saw the aim of it, it was well received."[2]

The scene of "William Mitten" is laid in Georgia in about 1815, and some of the minor characters are actually named, though not drawn, the author qualified, after important

---
[1] *Southern Field and Fireside,* 25 February, 1860.
[2] Fitzgerald, *Judge Longstreet,* 167.

Georgia people. A rich and pious Georgia widow, who, over her brother's objection, is unduly indulgent to her son, is recompensed for her folly by discovering when it is too late to mend matters, that her son does all sorts of things no proper young man should even know about. By way of violent protest, she departs this life, to be followed soon by her broken, though not unrepentant, not unconverted son. Around this story is a vast deal of valuable social history, much Longstreet autobiography, and a full mine of information for any one concerned with an evangelically religious concept of life. You get throughout the book an unmistakable impression of reality, of accurate observation, and of courage to transcribe faithfully. You sense the deep sincerity of a good and effective man, and the expansive breadth of universal and helpful sympathy. So far, the story is all right. As a work of art it is all wrong. In some ways the method is "romantic" and in some not. The author tells his story straight along without digressions, and takes occasion to express his disapproval of interrupting the movement of a narrative even by passages devoted to character development.[1] As a result of this literary taboo, or possibly rather of the fact that there are persons enough in the book to average two or three to the page, the characterization is worthless. Bad grammar abounds, even on the tongues of Princeton teachers, while lapses into dialogue form, whenever that method of expression became the simplest one, and other manifestations of unwillingness to stick at one thing until it was done well, show that Longstreet was still at his old tricks.

The book was moderately popular in the *Field and Fireside*, and caused some comment from its readers[2]—in general, people who had themselves lived under the circumstances portrayed in it. It has been popular since with ministers and historians; with persons who have been ministers and historians combined, as George G. Smith was, it has been extremely popular; but to the ordinary run of men, unacquainted with the particular environment through which Master Mitten moves, the book has never been interesting. In Longstreet's lifetime it was a dis-

---
[1] Longstreet, *Mitten*, 141.
[2] *Southern Field and Fireside*, 8 October, 1859.

appointment to the million, looking for a rehash of *Georgia Scenes*,[1] and an abomination to critics, looking for some rational method of presentation. One contemporary Southern critic, certainly, could find no breath of praise for it. "The author made his too-frequent mistake," says he, "of sacrificing too much—in this case nearly everything—to his idea of moral lesson. In attempting to adorn a moral, he has spoiled a tale; not much of a one, it is true, but still,—a tale. Poor Mitten has a time bad enough in all conscience, but scarcely worse than he will have who attempts to read through (without skipping) his dreary string of adventures. To say that *Master William Mitten* is a failure might mislead those who have no idea how terrible a failure it is. It is the author's Moscow."[2]

The story was put into book form and published in Macon, Georgia, in 1864 and again in 1889, the publisher there, as a staunch Methodist and one of Longstreet's friends and admirers, having been unwilling to see the work lie neglected in the files of the Augusta periodical. The book was dedicated to Dr. Henry Hull of Athens.

* * * * * * *

South Carolina in the late fifties was too lordly and high a place for whoever was at the head of its state college to live in any way but one of magnificence. Longstreet was a man with some property, and with many rich and prominent friends. He was enabled, therefore, to cut such a figure before the South Carolinians as suited their ideas of propriety, not always the ideas of the most punctilious Charlestonians, perhaps, but on the whole a figure as conforming as they could hope for in face of the increasing influence of the people "up-state." The Longstreets fell short for the Charlestonians in precisely those points that rendered them more typical of the American ideal in the nineteenth century. The ladies of Charleston could admire Mrs. Longstreet's familiarity with the poets, and could sigh almost covetously over her piety and her physical frailties, but they were not bound to admire her habit of making herself so much of an active major-domo. They were not pre-

---
[1] Fitzgerald, *Judge Longstreet*, 167.
[2] Davidson, *Living Writers*, 339.

pared to esteem moral solidarity at base so transcendent to all other virtues that it mattered little whether or not the possessor of that quality gave his time to quoting Mrs. Sigourney or to scalding pig-feet; to them it was perhaps more desirable to have some high clarity of intellect, some gaiety, some romance, some detestation for the real, and some insatiate yearning for the things they knew well could never come to them. The Longstreets, like most of their compatriots, believed that the emphasis should go elsewhere.

By that they were so much the more notables. There was a fine house for the President to live in, and there were countless invitations for the President to participate in all manner of social activities. Fine horses were in the stables, one pair of them, white horses named for two European sovereigns, "Vic" and "Gene," especially fine. Fine curtains were hanging in the parlor windows, curtains made originally for President Buchanan, in Germany, to go into the White House, but refused by him on account of their costliness, and bought by Congressman Lamar as a present for his mother-in-law. Fine plate and fine china there were for the table; and even imported wines;[1] Longstreet's "teetotalism," it seems, was declared against distilled liquors only.

"There was a charm about the house," writes a preacher who was often a guest there, but who apparently had seen no reprehensible intoxicants. "The table smiled. The quiet atmosphere was redolent of love. The lady was a queen in manners. Nothing was commanded, yet everyone owned the supremacy of a subtle power. . . . Milton, Shakespeare, Longfellow, Keats . . . she had put in her memory, and the sublime passages of these masters of poetry rolled from her bewitching tongue in colloquial eloquence. . . . [Here were] . . . no noisy show, no hollow flattery, nor nodding plumes hiding the worm that was gnawing at the heart, no gilded vanity and smooth and facile courtesy and sarcastic epigram; but a home of real joy. . . . Nor was this a house of idleness. Those delicious biscuits and smoking rolls and the aromatic coffee

---

[1] Hutson, Letter, 5 November, 1921.

told the story of a dutiful housewife. The table was hospitable, and from that board went food into the mouth of the poor."[1]

Mere students did not perceive Mrs. Longstreet's elusive fascination. To some boys who called at the house early in 1860, she was "a very pleasant old soul" who entreated one to stay a while and have a talk. The Judge shone brighter. "He got his pipe," one of these students wrote home, "and fell to smoking, and we all chatted together until the arrival of another visitor. This was Mr. Timrod, the young Charleston poet, quite a nice-looking, but a very little man. He behaved himself very well. During the conversation he spoke of a peculiarly sweet and plaintive Indian air, which he had heard the Judge played, whereupon that gentleman very obligingly got up and fetched his flute (an elegant glass one), and played the air for us. It was really beautiful. He then played some bugle notes upon the flute, the imitation being perfect, and afterwards gave us a number of the sweetest of the Scotch airs."[2]

At the President's house there were constant visitations from people distinguished and obscure, from friends, and from the friends of friends. "Your drafts on my hospitality," Longstreet wrote to Henry Hull, "even in favor of strangers, will ever be honored."[3] Frequently one made visits back to Mississippi, up to North Carolina, down to Georgia, or to Charleston, even to watering places, and wherever one went there was a sort of "progress," an almost triumphant celebration.

Contacts other than those of actual physical nearness also came up at times with great force. In April, 1859, during a Baptist convention held at Columbus, Georgia, a town settled largely by Greensboro people, a former Greensboro woman resident of the little village entertained at a grand dinner for a number of Greensboro patriarchs then in attendance at the

---

[1] Fitzgerald, *Judge Longstreet*, 185–7.

[2] Green, *University of South Carolina*, 358. This flute may be seen in the Smithsonian Institution in Washington. With it is a card bearing this inscription: "Glass flute.—Made by Lourent of Paris, France, and presented to Judge A. B. Longstreet, of Georgia, President of the University of South Carolina, and author of *Georgia Scenes and Characters*. Lent by H. P. Branham."

[3] Letter, 2 August, 1858. MS. in possession of Mrs. A. L. Heiskell, Memphis, Tenn.

Convention. Longstreet saw an account of the dinner, and wrote a letter about it for the *Southern Field and Fireside*.[1] "I would rather have been at it," he said, "than at a festival of as many Emperors, all doing me reverence. The tears roll down my cheeks while I write about it." He was deeply touched by the reawakening of old associations. It seemed to him peculiarly a matter for weeping. "Here my tears gush," he said, "and my eyes scarcely see the pen which traces these lines." He feels himself almost forsaken in the loneliness of age; nearly all of his friends are dead. But old age is still not without its joys: those friends who remain are increasingly dear to him; he has nothing to worry about for the future; he loves his children and his grandchildren; he could not attend the Columbus reunion, but he looks forward "calmly waiting" to being a guest soon "at *the marriage supper of the Lamb*."

"Calmly waiting" was a thing that he might fancy himself as doing, but one that he never did actually. He was always going to do that, as soon as he could hurry through what he was then engaged in and finish the one other thing next in line. Now there seemed less occasion than ever for dawdling. The old gentleman was burdened in these days as he had not been before with a realization of time's brevity. "A year," he wrote, "is a long time in the life of a man who has nearly seen his three score and ten."[2] He had "reached that period of life," he said, "when the wisdom of age begins to give place to its weaknesses."[3]

In November, 1859, "looking forward with deep interest to retirement," he offered to the Trustees his resignation from the Presidency, to take place the next May, but when May came round he reported as usual to the Trustees, and said nothing about resignation. That summer he was at the Statistical Congress in London. In November, 1860, his Report was most tranquil. "The college is doing . . . a little better than ever before. I have no improvements to suggest, nothing to ask." So far as the records show, the next mention the President made of resigning was in May, 1861, when he gave notice

---

[1] *Southern Field and Fireside*, 2 July, 1860.
[2] Longstreet, Minutes South Carolina Trustees, 30 November, 1859.
[3] Fitzgerald, *Judge Longstreet*, 128.

that if the Trustees would permit, he had decided, out of deference to the wishes of his students, to remain through November. The Trustees were always importunate in their protests against his leaving, and life was simply too full for him to persuade himself to any aggressive break.

XV

THE WAR

In December, 1860, South Carolina seceded; Georgia, Alabama, Mississippi, and Louisiana followed her in the next four months. At all of this, Longstreet rejoiced, but at the prospect of war, he now absolutely quailed. Lamar also was less confident than he had been formerly. Towards the middle of December, 1860, he resigned his seat in Congress and left Washington, he thought, for good, but the day before, he wrote Longstreet, inclosing in his letter an article setting forth his ideas about secession and the formation of a new Confederacy. "You will," he said in closing his letter, "doubtless deem my article too subdued in tone. What I know will happen in the next year has taken all the 'high-faluting' out of me. God bless you, my darling old father."[1]

The early spring of 1861 found the Judge in Charleston, appalled over the approach of the holocaust which up to that moment he had done nothing but further. A man can talk war freely enough, but when he is president of a school full of young men whom he feels himself father to, it takes good sternness to look unperturbed upon the hideous dragon of war as it in very fact comes nearer and nearer upon his charges.

Longstreet was about frantic. The self-appointed advance-guard against the Yankees turns now violently to push back his followers from the conflict he had helped precipitate. Impetuously he tore into print with a pamphlet, *Shall South Carolina Begin the War?* "I pray the authorities and people of South Carolina," he said in his pamphlet, "to put aside passion and hear patiently and thoughtfully. . . . Every man with whom I have conversed shows manifest excitement—the poorest accompaniment of reason and argument. . . . When I

---
[1] Mayes, *L. Q. C. Lamar*, 89.

think of the probability [of South Carolina's becoming the aggressor in this war] my soul is so heavily burdened with the awful responsibilities of the act that I can hardly bring my thoughts to decent order, or my pen to decent style. . . . Republican hirelings. *Hirelings!* Ay, when the war opens, it is to be between the bright and gallant sons of South Carolina and these hirelings. Woe to the people who bring on such a conflict but from dire necessity. Is it necessary? No, no, no! It is not only bootless, desperate, but wholly unnecessary. The Black Republicans mean to collect the revenues. This . . . is war in disguise, but practically it is harmless. . . . The revenues will be collected out at sea. Be it so; let them have them. [Soon] France and England will enter into treaties of commerce and open a glorious traffic with us. Thus by a little delay, and the forfeiture of the customs for a few months, we gain everything we desire without the loss of one drop of blood, without spoiling our harbors, and without interrupting our commerce for a single hour. . . . If you mean to hold Fort Moultrie, I implore you to let the first shot come from the enemy. *Burn that precept into your hearts if you despise all else that I have written.* But I would abandon it now, putting it just as Anderson left it. 'But no; it must be held, desperate as is the tenure, or we shall be called cowards.' Fools may so call you, no wise man will. 'It must end in war,' says one, 'and we'd as well bring it on at once.' It never will end in war if the South will be prudent, and we must let no Southern State begin it. . . ."[1] Strange talk this of prudence and expediency from a man who only a little while before had counselled his students so drastically! What were young gentlemen in the South Carolina College to think of such a man?

There was hardly time to think anything. New states were hurrying into the Confederacy. In April, Sumter fell and Baltimore declared itself Southern in sentiment; in July the Yankees were gloriously defeated at Bull Run; in November, stupidly, thank heaven, they let themselves become involved in the Trent affair. The students for the most part behaved themselves with surprising calmness, attending college straight

---

[1] Fitzgerald, *Judge Longstreet*, 128–34.

on through November, 1861. In April, truly, during the Fort Sumter excitement, most of them had, over the President's refusal, entered the army of the state and gone to Charleston. Longstreet had refused to recognize their absence, directing his professors, if necessary, to lecture before empty benches. This curious procedure went on for the three weeks during which the students were absent.[1] With the Governor, the President of the college probably thought "the war would be of short duration and the Government needed statesmen more than soldiers."[2] Upon being discharged from state service "most of the students," says Longstreet's report, "resumed their places in the college, as soldiers, their praises on all lips." The real break came in November, 1861, just after the fall of Port Royal. That news had "no sooner reached here," the President officially reported, "than Fripp, Rhett and Haywood, of the Sophomore class, craved permission to go home, as they resided in or about Beaufort. I refused peremptorily: whereupon they went without permission. Some ten or twelve others, I understood, followed their examples. The next day the students met *en masse* (without permission) and resolved (the Governor favoring) to leave for the scene of war. At a call meeting of the Faculty . . . we resolved unanimously that we had no authority to disband the college. The students, however, left in a body. Finding they were about to be off, I went to the Governor's office . . . to crave his assistance in persuading the students to postpone their departure. . . . [But] he had furnished their outfit, [and] secured their passage."[3] The only thing that such a foiled President could do was to go to the train and bid his boys "a pleasant farewell and God-speed,"[4] and then, as fast as ever he could, to get out of his cruel office altogether. Two days after making his report to the Trustees, the President had already left for Mississippi;[5] there Mrs. Longstreet had been for some time ill at the home

---

[1] Green, *University South Carolina*, 368.
[2] *Ibid.*, 369.
[3] Trustees' Minutes, University South Carolina, 27 November, 1861.
[4] Green, *University of South Carolina*, 366.
[5] Trustees, University South Carolina, 29 November, 1861.

of her daughter, and it was to be with her that the bewildered old Judge was now longing for most desperately.[1]

It is a trite thing to say of any old-time Southerner that in yielding himself completely to the cause of his section he did only what he felt was morally imperative. For Longstreet to have done otherwise would have seemed to him, if he had ever faintly considered it, both perfidious and shameful. It is not useless to recall, however, the pitch to which good Southerners had wrought themselves. The pulpit, throughout the war, was, after its habit, as strong as the next institution in proclaiming the virtues of the political system under which it existed.

On the outbreak of the war, all of the preachers had their say about the fearful tragedy, many of them chanting battle runes that have in them only too much of exultancy. Abolition was dominating the North, it was said, and abolition was at once "atheistic" and ultra democratic. "We defend the cause," said one curate in New Orleans, "of God and religion. The abolition spirit is undeniably atheistic. . . . It is alleged . . . that the President Elect has been chosen by a fair majority, under prescribed forms. But need I say to those who have read history, that no despotism is more absolute than that of an unprincipled democracy?"[2] "We are fighting," said another in Savannah, "for great principles, for sacred objects—principles which must not be compromised, objects which must not be abandoned. We are fighting to prevent ourselves from being transferred from American republicanism to French democracy. . . . We are fighting to drive away . . . the infidel rationalistic principles which are sweeping over the land."[3]

Christianity, many of these pastors told their already too complacent flocks, is nowhere out of accord with slavery. Formerly, said one of them, "many of us doubted whether we could religiously hold our servant. . . . But the question has been sifted to its very foundation [How much had Longstreet's *Paul to Philemon* helped in this sifting?] and we now feel our-

---

[1] Green, *University South Carolina*, 72.

[2] B. M. Palmer, 28 November, 1860 (in Frank Moore's *Spirit of the Pulpit* (New York, 1861)), 56.

[3] Stephen Elliott, 13 June, 1861, Moore, *Spirit of Pulpit*, 137-8.

selves safe, we now feel that as Christians we can hold them.
... We are willing to meet our adversaries, not only on Constitutional grounds, but on reason, on religion, on expediency, and dare them to their face to dislodge us from our position."[1]

Wherever slavery should prove unreligious, why, there, said Longstreet's predecessor as President of the South Carolina College speaking in Columbia, there, the South accepts full moral responsibility.[2] But whatever the outcome, all of these preachers imply, as one of them in fact says, "Whatever be the fortunes of the South, I accept them for my own. . . . She is in every sense my mother. I shall die upon her bosom; she shall know no peril, but it is my peril—no conflict, but it is my conflict—and no abyss of ruin into which I shall not share her fall. May the Lord God cover her head in this her day of battle!"

A little later, the ministerial order of the day was more hysterical. "Come then, my countrymen," said a combination preacher and teacher of belles-lettres, delivering a set homily before the Georgia Legislature, "let us behold the desolation. What emotion does it excite? What passion does it stimulate? To what action does it prompt? Indignation at the fanaticism, folly, and sin of those who brought it all about. Rage at the authors of our ruin. Retaliation! To arms! To arms! Let us kill! Let us destroy! Let us exterminate the miscreants from the earth. Up with the black flag! They deserve no quarter! They alone are to blame for this horror of horrors. We had no hand in bringing it on. We asked for nothing but our rights. Our desire was for peace. . . . I will not continue to give expression to thoughts which, alas, have already taken too deep hold on us all. . . ."[3] Most of the ministry went the same way. Even Bishop Andrew, who had through his whole long life been an ardent lover of the Union,[4] was very sure when war started as to whose side God worked with. He hoped, he wrote to a friend, God would disappoint the "un-

---

[1] W. T. Leacock, "Thanksgiving, 1860," Moore, *Spirit of the Pulpit*, 52.
[2] I. H. Thornwell, 21 November, 1860, *Spirit of the Pulpit*, 64.
[3] Henry H. Tucker, "God in the War," sermon before Legislature of Georgia, 15 November, 1861. It must be said that Tucker deplores this attitude.
[4] Smith, *Andrew*, 436.

scrupulous, persevering, ingenious foe" then seeking control of our territory.[1]

Longstreet had been heart and soul in the war from the minute he perceived that it was inevitable. He simply could not stay around Columbia, but found himself constantly impelled to the theater of Charleston. There he had been during the bombardment of Sumter, and there he was again during the early part of November, just before he left for Mississippi. A scheme had come to him by which he meant to destroy, at one time, a great part of the Yankee fleet lying off the Carolina coast. As soon as he heard of the Yankee ships' trafficking with the slaves, the whole thing became clear to him. He would get himself a small boat like those used by the slave hawkers, and, in the disguise of a negro—he could mimic the dialect faultlessly—he would, with six of his students similarly disguised, gain access to the great ships. Once on board, he would leave on every ship a charge of lighted dynamite. Having confided this plan to a Charleston lady whom he had known since her girlhood, he set out to lay the matter before Lee, then in command of the Southern defences around Charleston. To Lee the plan seemed impracticable, and too hazardous, he was courteous enough to say, of the life of a man whom the South could not sacrifice. It was a pleasant speech, that last part of it, but Longstreet was not any the more convinced of its wisdom. He came back to Charleston disheartened over the General's lack of "push, energy and aggressiveness," saying he should "use the gun more and the spade less," and wishing for his part that Nephew James might have control of everything.[2]

Before this venture, he had written the Governor of Georgia expressing his regret at being too old, at this time of peril to his native state, to enter upon any active participation in her defence; he would, though, offer some suggestions,[3] which he hoped might prove useful; and also, he would insofar as he could, if the Governor wished, preach to the Georgia troops whenever he was needed. Upon this offer the Governor made

---
[1] Smith, *Andrew*, 490.
[2] Williams, *Advice*, 112-3.
[3] Fitzgerald, *Judge Longstreet*, 204.

him chaplain in the Georgia Militia,[1] a position which entailed upon the old man some slight pleasant activity. There was always a degree of religious interest among the soldiers, revivals, prayer meetings, and so forth,[2] occurring with regularity and frequency; and often during the time in connection with his chaplaincy, Longstreet was in correspondence with such functionaries (among others, T. R. R. Cobb) as his prominence gave him access to. For the most part, those gentlemen were extremely reassuring about the spiritual state of all soldiers on the Southern side.[3]

On reaching Mississippi at the close of 1861, the Judge found himself in the very midst of the commotion. His son-in-law Lamar, at whose house he was living, had lately, as a member of the State Convention, himself drafted the Mississippi Ordinance of Secession.[4] Then in swift succession Lamar was member of the Confederate Congress, Colonel of a Mississippi regiment, Confederate envoy to Russia, and semi-official Confederate visitor to France and England. In September, 1862, Lamar's young brother, whom all of Longstreet's family loved very tenderly, was killed while conducting himself with romantic heroism on the field of battle. By November, 1862, it was evident that Mississippi was falling into the hands of the enemy. Longstreet was momentarily discouraged. "My dear Lucius," he wrote about then to his prominent son-in-law, "we are in a peck of troubles. Your plantation will soon be a battle-field. We shall be whipped on it, and the Yankees will make a desert of it. Mac is ready to move off the hands, but where to, he knows not, and I know not how to advise him. . . . Your plantation . . . will have neither stock nor provisions in the spring. Of course Oxford falls into the hands of the Yankees. . . . My wife will stay here and meet them, Virginia and children will go to Oxford or Covington, Georgia, and I will skulk about the country here somewhere. I say we shall be whipped, for I consider this about as certain as we fight. . . . The prospect before us is awful. . . . I am look-

---

[1] Williams, *Advice*, 114.
[2] Alexander, *History M. E. C. South*, 72–4.
[3] Smith, *Andrew*, 438.
[4] Mayes, *L. Q. C. Lamar*, 91.

ing daily for the advance of the enemy. Henry [Branham] will hold on to his place."[1]

When the Federals actually reached Oxford in December, 1862, it was General Grant who, in command of the troops, made his headquarters in the buildings of the University. Longstreet's house was burnt down, set fire to deliberately, in sheer wantonness, he believed, ignited with a torch which he knew was made of his treasured private papers, comprising a correspondence of forty years.[2] Contrary to their plans, the whole Longstreet connection now retired eastward before the advancing Yankees. The old man's heart must have been as nearly broken during this hegira as hearts get, but he managed in spite of everything to keep his spirit. As the carriage horses would be flying along through the woods, heartily, from the high front seat where he sat with the driver, he would shout out at the passing world. "Here we come!" the old man would shout, while bewildered and timorous folk looked on wonderingly at the splendid equipage, and at the fine passengers. "Here we come!" And laughing boisterously the old man would pass on.—One must have relief somewhere.

The Branhams stopped in Greensboro, Alabama, and the Lamars and Longstreets went on to Oxford, in Georgia. They reached there in January. Here they stayed some while, happy in renewing old friendships. Mrs. Longstreet's loveliness of character here, too, left its records in the testimonials of the discerning. These people saw her as a lady of "refinement and finished cultivation, of pure soul and tender heart, a serious but cheerful person, one rarely well in body, but chastened by affliction, having grown in grace until she looked like an angel." "Her matronly beauty" at this time, "her quiet unobtrusive demeanor, the sweet spirit that looked out from her expressive eyes, and the kind regard she manifested for the welfare and happiness of others, captured the heart at first sight and kept it."[3]

---
[1] Fitzgerald, *Judge Longstreet*, 198–9.
[2] Longstreet, "From Out the Fires," 545. (It is not certain that this burning occurred at this time. It may have occurred in September, 1864, when Oxford was shamefully dealt with by the Federals. See James Wilford Garner, *Reconstruction in Mississippi*, 18.)
[3] Fitzgerald, *Judge Longstreet*, 43–4.

THE WAR

From Oxford the old Judge went nearly everywhere. For a while he was back in Charleston establishing a Sunday school for white children and for negroes, praying and preaching whenever and wherever he could get opportunity, but most particularly preaching at Trinity Church, and praying there for the Confederate cause.[1] Once, for several months, apparently, he visited friends and relatives in the little village of Enon, Alabama, not far across the line from Columbus. Here he began an elementary school for little children who in the excitement of war were growing up without much schooling of one sort or another. It was a unique school, conducted out of doors with a sand pile for a blackboard, attended indifferently by white children and black. "He had some pet arithmetical theories and methods which he thus put into practice, much to his own satisfaction and to the delight of his little pupils." Bishop Fitzgerald observes that for one to be a strong pro-slavery man and at the same time a true friend to the negro race is a "paradox hard to be reconciled by those who look at the question from a distance, but readily understood by those who inherited the institution of slavery and were brought up in the midst of its peculiar conditions. The ex-President of the University of South Carolina teaching little negro children the rudiments of learning almost within hearing of the bugles of the Yankee cavalry then raiding the vicinity is a picture that tells its own story."[2]

But most of the two years that Longstreet spent "refugeeing" in Georgia, he was in Columbus. There, with Mrs. Longstreet, he visited for an indefinite time at the home of a lady whom, before her marriage, as a little girl, he had known in Middle Georgia. She was the daughter of his old friend Josiah Flournoy, one of his closest associates in the long past days of the Georgia Temperance Society. Flournoy had been a rich man, and his only child and heir had married a man richer than herself. It was accordingly in his accustomed upper level of material life that Longstreet lived while in Columbus. Always he was to be found visiting in this social class, more often there found, in fact, for a preacher, than a less generous age than

---
[1] Williams, *Advice*, 114. Possibly this was in 1861.
[2] Fitzgerald, *Judge Longstreet*, 172–3.

his own is always glad to hear of. Economic opportunity was so free in those times that most people considered failure to progress upward as indicating always some real discernible ineffectiveness on the part of the individual, and regarded a man's financial status as indicating no more or less than the result of his own deliberate and self-determined programme. Merit, according to Longstreet, invariably finds its reward,— and certainly all men have merit if they will only foster it. It was complacency of this sort that gave the old preachers moral sanction for numbering their associates so exclusively among persons of established position in society.

From Columbus, Longstreet looked upon the world, and indulged in his reflections. He recognized, as everybody else did, the horrors of the Andersonville prison, and fretted over them, but did not know how to make things better. There was some grim satisfaction in wondering how Grant would account in the future for his ruthlessness in refusing to exchange prisoners according to the Confederate suggestion. He did not think that this barbarism would go unpunished even should the North prove victorious.[1] The newspapers at least were of the opinion that despite all losses the South should really bless the war unendingly. It had aroused the South to a new life—manufacturers, for instance, were coming into their own, and there was also a changed concept of happiness, at least for the men, who one knew now, thanks to the war, should every one of them "have a calling, a *business*, a *place* in which he can be useful to others, and procure for himself an honorable support. . . . Our ladies—God bless them—they should be the models of all that is lovely and excellent in female character—walking in light and love—surpassing the 'virtuous woman' of ancient time in feminine gracefulness, matronly dignity, and the skillful management of every department of domestic industry and economy."[2] However all of this stood, about most things the Judge was at no loss whatever. About military affairs he was particularly confident. As Johnston kept retreating before Sherman, "all the knowing ones of Columbus . . . saw in it a master stroke of generalship [but]

---

[1] Longstreet, "From Out the Fires," 548.
[2] *Columbus Enquirer*, 6 May, 1864.

I," said Longstreet, writing later, "opposed it, and I have yet to learn the wisdom or the worth of it."[1] The disasters that would be visited on his state, should the prisoners at Andersonville be released, the old gentleman simply would not consider.

But he did not indulge merely his thoughts. He indulged also his love of giving directions. With his nephew, General James Longstreet, and with his son-in-law, Lamar, both high in the cause of the Confederacy, he corresponded vigorously. During the summer of 1863 he wrote his nephew explicit suggestions about the campaign into the North,[2] and a year later he was still telling him how to conduct the war in Tennessee.[3] To Lamar he wrote vehemently complaining that Jefferson Davis was deceitful, and that he was never just to Cousin James, who, if people only knew it, was the best hope left.[3]

Nor did he limit his activities to correspondence. Some time about now, late in 1863 or early in 1864, this venerable Chaplain published for the soldiers of the Confederate States a series of "Valuable Suggestions." "I do not know," he begins, "that the attempt has ever been made to improve soldiers by an address to their reason and understanding. I propose to try the experiment." As satisfactorily, then, as men can be reasoned into anything totally at odds with nature the Southern armies are in this article reasoned into a complete disdain of fear. All sources of danger in war are categorically examined and minimized by a logic calling to its support the long past days of country life in Edgefield, a minute acquaintance with the campaigns of Napoleon, accurate and broad contemporary observation, and finally, overwhelmingly, this dilemma—that if inferiority of numbers be a *hopeless* disadvantage, why does the Confederacy keep on at war? There is still at work here a stalwart and independent mind. Constantly the reader is caught up by the old man's boldness,—it was sheer cowardice that for thirty years kept the South from seceding; the better class of Southerners enlisted first after war was declared, and fought better than their inferiors who

---

[1] Longstreet, "From Out the Fires," 548.
[2] James Longstreet, *Lee and Longstreet at High Tide*, 64–5.
[3] Ms. Letter, Longstreet to L. Q. C. Lamar, 14 May, 1864.

enlisted later; to hope is the best thing that one can do for Johnston's wisdom (possibly before the war ends, soldiers, you may get under a General who will command you to pursue a routed foe). In these four thousand words there is not one to indicate the ecclesiastical character of their author. Whether the omission was due to the author's complete absorption in his subject, or to an instinct that his character of minister did not accord with the bloody counsellings of his address, one cannot know.—But the silence is there, grimly; one trusts, designedly.[1]

During the spring of 1864 he published a book, now apparently altogether vanished from the earth. It is only in one of the Judge's letters to Lamar, 14 May, 1864, that any reference to it remains: "I complete my book on Brown's extra session early next week. I published as I wrote. Gaither & Burton Harrison & Henry Branham have all the chapters but the one which appears today. I did not send them to you because I doubted whether they would find you in Oxford. . . ." As this "book" does not seem to have appeared in the Columbus newspapers, it is probable that it was published piecemeal, in pamphlets. A faithful search for it has not revealed even a fragment.

---

[1] Longstreet, "Valuable Suggestions" (in Frank Moore [ed.], *Rebellion Record*, VIII), 433–7.

XVI

HOME

Toward the first of 1865, the Longstreets left Columbus and went back to Mississippi, there to wait for the cruel end that everybody saw could not be much longer held off. The universal, grinding humiliation of reconstruction times bore upon the defeated Southerners in much the degree, obviously, to which they had been concerned in public affairs before the war. It had always been Longstreet's conviction, as it was in general the conviction of his class, that good men owe the public the best there is in them. "He who devotes himself ably, patriotically, unflinchingly and untiringly," wrote one of his old friends, "in the higher . . . spheres of service to the cause of his country's salvation . . . merits the homage of mankind."[1] Such was these men's creed. In an endeavor to abide by it, Longstreet had spent a long life devoted actively and sincerely to the uplift of his fellows. As a reward, he sees now the dearest holdings of his soul, his most absolute conceptions of practical expediency and moral righteousness, turned to plain nothing in the hands of what he believed a ruthless and pharisaical enemy. The privilege of exercising political adroitness and wisdom, the one sphere in which the South was supreme and universally alert, the last refuge which might, one could hope, in some degree mitigate the terrors of defeat,—this, too, the Yankees, ingenious in their foul inventions of browbeating, now snatch utterly away.

How often in those days must the old man have wondered to himself whether or not the South would have fared better had she forced the issue at the time of the Nullification controversy! How inevitably it must have presented itself to him that she indeed would have fared far better! How he must

---
[1] Chappel, *Miscellanies*, I, 30.

have been brought to marvel at Calhoun's presageful death-words: "The South, the South, God knows what will become of her!" Years before in contemplating the possibility of such wrack he had found comfort, in fancy, in the confidence that history at last would pronounce the South morally more worthy of victory, even though she had in fact been annihilated. But what he had counted upon then was annihilation, not slow inanition and proscription of effort to help one's self. This last was quite unsupportable.

Looking about him, the old man could see repulsive measure after measure being written into the Constitution, could see the proud states that he had loved so ardently staggering daily less and less hopefully under yokes that seemed at last about to become too heavy for their bearing. To Charleston, as a crowning insult, they had sent Delany as a Federal official—Delany who by his own statement regarded Charleston "with feelings of the utmost abhorrence," and looked not unjoyfully upon the ruins of what he termed "the once stately but now deserted edifices of the proud and supercilious occupants."[1] In Mississippi, they were ordering, *ordering* preachers to pray in their pulpits for the despicable officials of the Black Republican Government. One incident people were telling about, could rejoice the heart. It was about a Methodist preacher in Alabama, who, being so ordered by a little Yankee Captain, prayed for the President and his allies with a terrible effectiveness; he had asked God to bless the Yankees by bettering them, asked that the Lord "would take out of them the hearts of beasts and put in them the hearts of men, or remove them from office."[2]

Looking about him, the old Judge could see occasional Southerners moving North, or moving abroad, frightened by the long prospect of Southern poverty. With him and his house, praise God! there was no such cowardice. Lamar had stated that definitely. At Appomattox, when one of Lee's officers had suggested some such course to Lamar, he had met the suggestion with an immediate refusal to consider it. "I shall

---

[1] *Delany, Life of*, 187–8.
[2] Walter L. Fleming, *Documentary History of Reconstruction* (Cleveland, 1907), II, 222, 228.

stay with my people," he had said, "and share their fate. I feel it to be my duty to devote my life to the alleviation, so far as in my power lies, of the sufferings this day's disaster will entail upon them."[1]

In Oxford, the raw scars of battle obtruded themselves everywhere. Half of the innocent little town was burnt to ashes. The University buildings had done service as a military hospital during the war, and now the approaches to the village wound often among countless new graves. Griefs of inexpressible magnitude were weighing down relentlessly wherever one looked. Longstreet's old friend Jacob Thompson was away in prison at the North, accused calumniously of the most hideous war atrocities.

In God alone could men now repose any trust; all else had proved vain. On Sundays the dejected people in Oxford would often ask the old man to preach for them, and he in sad pleasure at their loyalty, would comply as best he could. At times during his sermon he would grow weak and sit down to continue, and everyone, somehow, would be uncontrollably affected. At last, they were all one in the South now, all one, all glad enough in this undependable world, in this too troublous time, to fall back upon the sure Refuge, and to surrender up to that Refuge all care and all necessity for planning. . . . "We used to have Universalists before the war," the old man observed, "now they are all gone."[2] Ah, they had learned in catastrophe, those people, that somewhere God must square life to accord with justice, lest otherwise, it prove unthinkable.

"Time," the Doctor had told Judge Longstreet back in Greensboro when the Judge was near breaking under his grief at the death of his son, "time, Judge, will prove your best doctor." It was a platitude the Doctor had spoken, but his prediction did not prove any the less accurate.

After a while, life became brighter even in Oxford. Through the influence of Barnard, now in New York, President of Columbia University, the Oxford University buildings had been spared by the Federal troops, and in the fall of 1865 the insti-

---

[1] Mayes, *L. Q. C. Lamar*, 115.
[2] Fitzgerald, *Judge Longstreet*, 146.

tution was re-opened with nearly two hundred students.[1] Waddel was at last President, the same Waddel whom the Trustees had repudiated in 1856, as being perhaps a little too old-fashioned in his politics. Where there had been divergence of opinion there was now no divergence. Know-nothing, Whig, and Democrat, all decent men were swept into one party, just as George McDuffie used so often to say would finally have to happen for the South ever to prosper. Perhaps here at last was something to be grateful for. "When I think of you and Toombs as you are now," Longstreet wrote to Alexander H. Stephens, "and as you were twelve or fourteen years ago, I feel like *killing the fatted calf, and waking up music and dancing.* . . . I considered you clean gone from the faith of your fathers. Hence my rejoicing when I found you both . . . defending [it] with arms invincible. Well, as Ransey Sniffle says, 'We are all friends now.' "[2] All friends. No disparity of opinion anywhere. Fixed conservatism at last had its seat.

Longstreet came out of the war with almost no money,— "his estate," he wrote, "had been made sad havoc of,"[3]—but he still had enough to live on. He had property, but it brought no income. During 1865–6 Lamar spent his days between an unlucrative law practice and an almost sterile farm, doing various small chores about the plantation—mending fences and gates, feeding stock, and cutting wood.[4] But the Longstreet connection was better off, even then, than many of their neighbors, and altogether they managed to keep in fair spirits. Mrs. Longstreet particularly met the new situation with high fortitude.

The Judge had a substantial four-room cottage with great oaks in front of it, and the Buchanan curtains hanging grandly in the windows; and the Branhams and Lamars (Lamar having come to teach in the University September, 1866) lived not far away. In fact, under some pretext or other the three families were generally living in the same house—the house of

---

[1] Mayes, *Education in Mississippi*, 159.
[2] Fitzgerald, *Judge Longstreet*, 194.
[3] Sherwood, *Memoir*, 350-1.
[4] Mayes, *L. Q. C. Lamar*, 124.

one of them was under repair—or the head of the household was away—always there was something. Always the house was merry with grandchildren, little citizens knowing the Judge for a man to be highly revered, and left alone when busy, but knowing him also, at times, for the best playmate to be found anywhere. These grandchildren the old Judge enjoyed mightily, reading Mother Goose with them, taking his flute to pieces for them and screwing it together again, blowing smoke rings with his pipe, teaching them odd bits of information, telling them of old times in Georgia, and of the Indians. . . . At night one could play euchre, a game which the old Judge relished greatly, but was content, in view of his ecclesiastical position, not to indulge in, or to acknowledge his fondness for, outside of his own family.[1] In one's own family, he explained, he did not believe the game harmful, but that belief would not do to give out. People as a rule had so little discretion. And one could read till one's eyes were dim—none too long at that—and then impress the young people into reading aloud to one, like little notaries. Magazines chiefly one read, and anything having to do with the South. Then there were letters to be written to old friends inquiring after their state under the new dispensation, and reminiscent letters to hero-worshipping young relatives.[2]

And there were constant visitors. In the summer of 1867, General James Longstreet came up from his new home in New Orleans. He had a letter with him that he was about to publish, he told the Judge, advising the Southern people to reconcile themselves to the results of war, and get to work as cheerfully and as speedily as they could. The old gentleman read the letter over, and thought there was much wisdom in it, but believed its expression too direct, perhaps, certainly too direct for the time. "It will ruin you, son, if you publish it. We are not ready yet to hear such hard counselling."—And then the General went away and published it anyhow,[3] raising such a storm of censure over his head as men do not often live through.

---

[1] The Reverend Mr. W. R. Branham II, Oxford, Georgia, Conversation, 28 October, 1921.
[2] Sherwood, *Memoir*, 350-1; Fitzgerald, *Judge Longstreet*, 45-9.
[3] Mrs. L. B. West.

Dr. Branham, for his part, thought every bit of the censure quite just, and made bold one day to say so at the dinner table. The old Judge did not mean to have his blood kin spoken ill of in his presence. He thrummed his long fingers nervously, warningly on the table, but Dr. Branham in his heat would not be silenced. The Judge had a recourse. He beat his fingers again on the table, pushed back his chair, and, steadying himself by the table, rose up to his full great height. "Gentlemen," he said, "I withdraw my presence from this table." His voice was tight with suppressed emotion, and he stalked off with all the grandeur of indignant venerableness. Here at least the recourse of protest by withdrawal, so long a method of his, had effects as overwhelming as he could wish.

In March, 1867, Mr. and Mrs. Longstreet celebrated the fiftieth anniversary of their wedding. Old Dr. Pierce, who had married them so long before in Greensboro, was living then in Columbus, Georgia, and there had been some plans to have him come out to Mississippi to perform the ceremony all over again, amid great festivities. The family insisted somewhat upon this arrangement, but Mrs. Longstreet was old, and the Judge and Doctor Pierce still older. They would be happier, they said, and all of them would love one another just as much, if they could pass the time more serenely. In October, 1868, Mrs. Longstreet died. This was the supreme blow of Longstreet's life. He had loved his wife romantically and she had been a part of his existence for so long, he knew that if it were not for the definite assurance he had of being reunited with her he could not at all bear the separation. But he had that assurance, gloriously, as the realest of all the things he knew. Wishing to leave a solemn token to the world of his undivided love for her, and his sense of oneness with her, he fell upon the device of putting a eulogy to her into the epitaph which must now before long be carved for him. He wrote, then, his own epitaph, and in it stated with arresting beauty the deep spiritual passion he bore his dead wife. "He sleeps," one can read now on his grave in the little cemetery, "by the side of his wife, of whom he never thought himself worthy, and who never thought herself worthy of her husband. In every innocent movement of his life she went hand in hand and heart in heart with him for over fifty-one years. Death was a kind visitor to them both."[1] Religion was an unfailing solace to him in these months, and the tender love of his family must have been most grateful.

In spite of himself almost the old man was waking to a new hope. There had come into his acquaintance a man named Edward Mayes, a young veteran of the Confederate Army, who since the close of the war had been a student at the University of Mississippi. Mayes was courting Longstreet's oldest granddaughter, Frances Eliza Lamar. He was only twenty-three years old when he and the Judge's granddaughter finally married in 1869, but he was already a vigorous and original thinker, and personally a most lovable young gentleman. Longstreet grew to esteem him highly, and listened always earnestly to his opinions. This young man had the most definite idea that the time for Southern repining had gone by, and that not all of the theoretical vindication one could wish for its past course would rehabilitate the section half so satisfactorily as would its becoming wealthy and populous. The freeing of the slaves he thought possibly the best thing that the South had ever had happen to it; with them free, he hoped that his section could foster industrialism to an extent which had been forbidden so long as slavery existed. "Glorious revolution of the labor system!" Mayes wrote at about this time. "Dear old land of Dixie, how have thine enemies blest thee when most they sought to wound! Short-sighted race of mortals that we are, how we clung to that institution whose abolition has unlocked the riches hidden in the earth's bosom to the poor man as well as the rich, and may yet make our loved land flourish and bloom as never she did before."[2] James Longstreet had announced himself as feeling much as Mayes did. Lamar was thinking already in terms which were to find expression in the Sumner Eulogy of 1874. Henry Branham alone held out resolute, and wished to eat fire whenever he thought of Yankees. It was Branham who, early in 1860, had brought up charges against Barnard in connection with his administration of the University. That was no time, Dr. Bran-

---
[1] Their graves are in Oxford, Mississippi.
[2] Mayes, "Possible Future of South" (*XIX Cent. Mag.*, Jan.–Feb., 1870).

ham evidently thought, for a Yankee to be running a Southern college.[1] Longstreet himself had not always escaped being called a fire-eater. His grudge against the Yankees was of long standing and he could blame them now with fresh and inexhaustible rancor. Nevertheless, he was at heart practical. There was nothing, he gives you to understand, in which William Mitten so clearly showed his incalculable folly as in his disposition to kick against the pricks. And besides, the South generally was coming to the viewpoint of Mayes and of James Longstreet. The people of Oxford had already met and decided that on religious grounds as well as on grounds of "policy and interest—the least elevated form of argument"—the negroes should be educated. If it could be done, the old Judge, for his part, meant to look at once with Branham to the past, and with young Mayes to the future.[2]

The end of the war found Longstreet still vigorous in mind and body. Tall and thin of frame, with his clean-shaved, rugged face and pale blue eyes, his large, firm mouth and well-preserved teeth, his thick gray hair cropped short and standing up in a pompadour, he gave an impression of undiminished strength and haleness. As a pseudonym for his occasional newspaper articles of this period, he selected "Vim," not "Senex."[3] His new associates in optimism had made him feel that after all now effort on his part might be of some avail for the South. He set to work, and, once started, kept at it in fierce earnest. He had a room full of great volumes, which the children would come in and look at wonderingly, calling them with accidental pointedness, "law bibles." And in this room there was a writing table which in winter was drawn up in front of a big wood fire. Here the Judge worked. Often one of the little granddaughters was seated across from him at the table, but she always knew that she must not talk. At intervals the old man would lay down his pen, fill up his pipe, and lean over for a fire coal to light it with. Then, invariably, in rising he would bump his head slightly, and as if accidentally, on the mantelpiece—so much for the amusement of his granddaughter. How

---

[1] *Barnard Memoir*, 204 ff.
[2] Fleming, *Reconstruction*, I, 179.
[3] Fitzgerald, *Judge Longstreet*, 204.

ruefully he would look across the table, rubbing his head! What a fine joke the whole business was between him and his little partner![1] In the nights, sometimes he would get up at all kinds of hours and go to his writing. A little negro boy named Prince slept in the room with him, and it was Prince's business whenever he was called to get up, light the lamp, and build a fire. Then he could go back to sleep.—Longstreet had a great way, as did all of the educated Southerners of his day, of dragging Shakespeare into everything. Often in those still nights, as he dismissed little black Prince, whom he called with affectionate humor, Pretty, he must have thought of Roman Brutus dismissing his little Lucius. In truth, in more ways than this one do Longstreet and Roman Brutus suggest each other.

To Longstreet, with his clear protestant conviction, the Bible had always been the nucleus and soul of Christianity, and yet he knew, even from his slight experience in Biblical research, that the version in which the Bible is best known contained some apparently slight but possibly (since every word of it was manifestly fraught with vast meaning) very hazardous errors. Heaven knows it was not his purpose to twist it into any new meaning. What he wanted was the old meaning, divested of all the "interpretations" and "implications" that humanity had endowed it with. From his acquaintance with the history of the American Constitution, he knew how easily such shifts of meaning could be accomplished. The Bible had stood much longer than the Constitution; and it had gone through the unsettling process of translation. At first, it had undoubtedly been as simple and as clear as it was morally perfect. God would not have dictated it otherwise—Longstreet's desire was to get back to the original. Latin he was master of, and Greek he could read well enough to follow the commentators. Hebrew, however, he knew not at all, and yet he was obliged to know it before he could speak with great authority as a Bible scholar. That he could not evade. As old as he was, then, he got a book and began studying, learning much Hebrew before even setting out seriously on his criticism.

---

[1] Mrs. A. L. Heiskell, Memphis, Tenn.

Soon he was fully under way. The resulting composition, known as *A Correction of the Canonized Errors in Biblical Interpretation*,[1] was completed in 1870, only shortly before Longstreet's death. After his death, along with other of his manuscripts, it was, in accord with his directions, entrusted to his literary executor, Edward Mayes, and in Mayes's house, with the house, in fact, it was burned, before it could be published. Mayes speaks of it as "a small work on Biblical interpretation, a revision and correction of several errors which have crept into the accepted version of the Scriptures."[2] Beyond Mayes's statement, the only other available source of light on the *Correction* is a New Testament, which, having been used by the author in the preparation of his work, exhibits some of his pencil-made marginal notes. These notes make it clear that Longstreet, working in the late 1860's, was already aware of many of the discrepancies later adjusted in the American Revised Version of the Bible, first issued in 1881, and make it clear too, somewhat surprisingly, that he had access to and had consulted, at second hand, of course, all of the latest Biblical manuscripts, even those discovered only a few years before he wrote.

Soon after the war there were established a number of Southern magazines, *The Land We Love* (later *The Eclectic*), *The Southern Review, The Southern Metropolitan*, and *The Nineteenth Century*.[3] Of these *The Nineteenth Century*, begun in Charleston, promised most favorably. Like most other magazines published in the South its main purpose was to provide an organ for a distinctly Southern expression of life. Longstreet was as usual appealed to to contribute, and he of course acceded to the request. This magazine was both brave and pathetic. Simms is seen in it constantly, and Alexander H. Stephens and Governor Perry of South Carolina. Young Edward Mayes is there, too, and young Walter B. Hill and Sidney Lanier from Georgia. The range of reading matter is very broad. There are articles telling what invalid ladies

---

[1] Fitzgerald, *Judge Longstreet*, 191.
[2] Mayes, "Letter" (*Nineteenth Century*, August, 1870), 267.
[3] Longstreet, "From Out the Fires," 543.

read during the war (mostly Scott, the Brontës, and Adelaide Proctor), articles on The Status and Prospects of the Negro, The Morality of Round Dancing, The Morality of Second Marriages, and one article by a keen observer showing a recognition of the increased interest which the war had brought about in literature.[1] In connection with the prospect of some plays, being given in the Charleston Academy of Music, there springs up a controversy over The Morality of Attending Theatrical Performances. The editors of the magazine are "disposed," they say, to let the Academy "vindicate its claims and prove its merit, wishing it every success in elevating and refining a noble people, over burdened and oppressed by the weighty and bitter things of life."[2] There are hortatory poems, "Keep heart, brave Southrons" or "The Truth Is Mighty and It Will Prevail" (in Latin). And through every issue run harangues on the importance of developing Southern letters. The Northern periodicals, complain the editors of this Southern magazine, are continually publishing the works of British authors;—and why? "Are English writers superior to our own? For our own section we return an emphatic *no*."[3]

Now Longstreet felt the most definite responsibility for offering an explanation of the South's course in the late war. In felicitating Alexander Stephens upon the publication of some work of his defending the South, Longstreet wrote him September, 1869, "You have relieved me, in my old age, from the arduous labor of a work upon the same subject which I had commenced, but which I am sure I could not live to finish, by anticipating me in nearly all that I could have said in that work. . . . Still I have some views on State sovereignty which have never occurred to anybody else so far as I know, and which seem to me to be of very great force."[4] The Southern people, he felt, were looking to him as their interpreter; he was to be, they said, "a pilot to our literary bark, and prevent its being put on a dangerous track by inexperienced writers . . .

---

[1] M. Elizabeth Smith, "Recreations of an Invalid," *Nineteenth Century*, February, 1870.
[2] *Nineteenth Century*, December, 1869, 563.
[3] *Ibid.*, April, 1870, 1894.
[4] Fitzgerald, *Judge Longstreet*, 194.

he is to elevate the standard of literary excellence, and diffuse the principles of correct taste. . . ."[1] It is easy to see then how eagerly the old gentleman would welcome any opportunity for expressing his ideas. This vindication of the South, apart from his religious essays, constituted the sum of his late work.

"Were all of the new Southern magazines suppressed tomorrow," says the first published of Longstreet's after-the-war writings,[2] enough would already have been published in them to enable our descendants "to institute a just comparison between their sires and their sires' conquerors, as statesmen, warriors, Christians and gentlemen. . . . The Federals in the late war [were distinguished] from all other belligerents that ever went before them, in point of cruelty and inhumanity." He knows some specific instances which he feels should be recorded for the future happiness of the South and shame of the North. When the Northerners of the future are searching the sources of history for their fathers' doings in the war, "let it be that when they come to our records, they shall find, the deeper the search, the deeper the infamy."[3] And then he displays his full exhibit of atrocities. He would advise all true ex-Confederates to have Grant's reasons for not exchanging prisoners printed "in golden letters upon lustrous satin, and pasted securely in their family Bibles; for never has there been and never will there be compressed into so small a compass, from a source so lofty, such a flattering eulogy upon the authorities and soldiers of the Confederate States, and such a biting sarcasm upon the authorities and soldiers of the United States. . . ."[4] This is the kind of thing the old Judge now delighted in.

But vituperation was unfortunately not limited to one section. In the North, people were talking as truly and as foolishly. "Every possible atrocity," said the *New York Times*, 17 April, 1865, "appertains to this Rebellion. There is nothing whatever that its leaders have scrupled at,—wholesale

---

[1] A. W. Dillard, "William Gilmore Simms and A. B. Longstreet," 425.
[2] Longstreet, "From Out the Fires," 543.
[3] *Ibid.*, 545.
[4] Longstreet, "From Out the Fires," 549.

massacres and torturings, wholesale starvation of prisoners, firing of great cities, piracies of the cruellest kind, persecutions of the most hideous character and vast extent, and finally, assassination in high places,—whatever is inhuman, whatever is brutal, whatever is fiendish, these men have resorted to. They will leave behind names so black, and the memory of deeds so infamous that the execration of this slave-holders' rebellion will be eternal."[1]

Governor Perry of South Carolina, in connection with some reminiscences of his, published in the March number of *The Land We Love,* and in the November *Nineteenth Century,* an article on John C. Calhoun.[2] There, though he praised Calhoun personally, he took issue with his politics, and declared that Calhoun's religious views were not orthodox. The mere statements were enough to rouse Longstreet's anger, but when he remembered who Perry was, a Southerner, in league with the North against his own people, seated in office by Northern power and administering Northern-made laws, when he remembered this, the old man was stirred to a state nothing short of rage. In the January, 1870, issue of the *Nineteenth Century* he published a review mordantly attacking Perry's honesty and intelligence. "The in-governor of the (reconstructed) State," he said, was an incompetent witness to the facts to which he had testified. "I am disposed to give to these cosey governors all the credit due them,[3] but Mr. Perry reminds me of nothing so much as of a "phoenix, risen from the ashes [of Columbia] and, borne on Northern breezes, perching himself proudly upon the dead palmetto."[4] "False, monstrous, remarkable only for their suicidal recoil," it seemed to him, were many of the phrases that bobbed up on page after page of Perry's article. "Oh! Land of Laurens, Rutledge, Sumter, Moultrie and Marion," the old Judge catalogues and apostrophizes both at once, "endeared to me by a thousand tender associations, what hast thou done to merit thy present deep, dark, tearful humiliation? Let her alone, Mr. Perry, for

---
[1] *New York Nation,* 19 October, 1918.
[2] Longstreet, "Review of Perry's Calhoun."
[3] Longstreet, "From Out the Fires," 619.
[4] *Ibid.,* 624.

your own sake, let her alone in her agony! Allow her at least and at last, the poor privilege of bewailing her fate undisturbed by your hail among the halls, and your howl among the tombs of her mighty dead!" Throughout the article Calhoun is fulgently praised, and cautiously announced as having been a good Christian, and Mr. Perry is bitterly and fiercely taken to task.

This article, according to the February number of the magazine, "greatly stirred the public mind." Longstreet's attack on Perry was made the excuse for many others. "Surely," a lady wrote, "I may be pardoned for my strictures since the Honorable A. B. Longstreet, of reputation beyond the reach of envy, both in South Carolina and Georgia, has entered his." Perry himself answered the month following, in an article headed "Judge Longstreet and His Malignantly False Criticisms." It must be admitted that Perry's article is written in better spirit than Longstreet's, and that it shows better sense. In it he demonstrates that Longstreet was always prone to hasty judgments, and adduces several instances in which the Calhoun "Review" was inaccurate. But after all, this was hardly a just tourney; Longstreet was seventy-nine years old, Perry not yet sixty.

In April, 1870, the *Nineteenth Century* published a rambling Longstreet article called "Old Things Become New," a sort of autobiography with emphasis on the author's political activities up to when he was about fifty, when he became a minister, and on his spiritual interests for the time subsequent. "Now, reader," this article concludes, "did you ever follow a writer through such a discursive, heterogeneous, incoherent piece of patch-work as this since you were born? 'It is the wanderings of a waning mind,' say you. Not so. Paul says to the Corinthians 'Being crafty, I caught you with guile' (a bait). When I first read these words from the apostle, I was startled, amazed and pained. Now I believe I have given, unintentionally, an exact illustration of Paul's meaning. I wished to bring before the public the matters herein contained, believing them highly instructive to all classes of readers, and to secure the reading of them, if possible, by all classes of persons. How can this be done, thought I. Separate the subjects and put one in one paper or journal and another in another? I may as well throw them in the fire for all the good they will do. . . . I must mix them together . . . and so mould them that what offends one class of readers shall please another, and link them together so that a man cannot read one part without reading the whole." His aim here as always was to vindicate the South, to further the Christian religion, and to confound the enemies of both. . . . "By what device will you link your discordant materials together so that each shall seem to come naturally in its place? Write your biography and bring them up in their order of time as incidents in it. Thus, being crafty, I have caught you, readers, with guile."[1]

In his effort at allurement, the writer failed; nothing would be easier than to separate the secular and religious elements of this essay. At times, truly, his religion finds a passionate utterance that seduces the imagination. His Christianity is of the sort, that, if it could prevail among all mankind, would leave no "use for legislators and courts of justice, for jails and penitentiaries, for ships or implements of war, for forts, arsenals and military schools; no locks, no bolts, nor bars, as means of security."[2] There is in Christianity, to him, he says, something "so fraternizing, so sin-restraining, sorrow-soothing, hope-uplifting, and soul-exalting, that it would be measureless cruelty [this in scorn to the 'scientist'] to me to disenchant me of my delusion."[3]

But on the whole, it is evident throughout this article that the author does not retain now his old keen power of discrimination. He is intolerably discursive and wandering, and more than that, he is illogical; if you will sincerely and on your knees, he keeps saying, ask God to convince you of his existance, if indeed He exists, you will be so convinced. Truly it was a hard irony that made the old gentleman state so explicitly in this writing that he was not the subject of diminishing powers of intellect. If he had not protested his continued vigor, by some vague possibility someone might have failed to

---

[1] Longstreet, "Old Things Become New," I, 839–51.
[2] *Ibid.*, 848, April, 1870.
[3] *Ibid.*, 845.

note the tragic diminution of it. As it is, the result is almost harrowing.

In its July issue, in reply to "Old Things Become New," the magazine published an article by one Charles Reemelin of Ohio, a German gentleman who was given to writing in the Cincinnati *Commoner*.[1] Immediately following this communication comes Longstreet's reply. The two articles make up over 12,000 words (the Judge's alone nearly 10,000), and the editors were uneasily conscious of this great length, but they felt that the interest evoked by Longstreet's first article warranted the space. "That article," they stated, to parry criticisms in advance, "attracted wide attention and received literary and critical notices almost innumerable. Among the number was a dignified and able review by Mr. Charles Reemelin of Cincinnati, in the *Commoner Journal*. . . . Our readers will not thank us for apologizing for the length of the paper, when we quote for them the following paragraph from Judge Longstreet's letter: 'Your patrons will excuse you for it (the publication of the paper), and many thank you. *I desire all my writings of a religious character to be collected in one magazine, and yours that one.*' "[2] The Judge evidently had no thought of stopping. As Reemelin was a believer in state rights, he accorded with Longstreet nicely, but as he was an avowed free thinker in religious matters, the distance between the two men became immeasurable. All that Longstreet had said for the South and against the North, Reemelin freely granted, but everything that he had said for orthodoxy and against free thinking, Reemelin with a heavy hand attacked. Longstreet's reply was consequently more concerned with religion than with politics.

Reemelin had begun with compliments all the more pleasing because of their discrimination. "Judge Longstreet's strength and his weakness," he had said, "lie in this: his intensification in all things. The first, because he espouses every cause with sincere fervor; the second because his zeal obscures his vision, so that he sees both too much and too little of any subject

---

[1] Mayes, *L. Q. C. Lamar*, 138.
[2] Longstreet, "Old Things Become New," II (in *Nineteenth Century*, July, 1870), 97.

which, for the time being, engages his mind. And to his friends it is really difficult to decide whether to love him most for his vigor or his softness." Having so spoken he had proceeded to his thesis which is that the aggression of the North was the result of its being politically goaded by the Northern churches, that the entire recent war was as truly religious in its essentials as was the Thirty Years' War in Europe. "It is the fatal words of Christ 'Go ye into the world and preach the gospel,' spoken by Christ in all innocence, we admit," says Reemelin, "that, causing people to arrogate to themselves the right of controlling the destinies of others, have cost the people of Europe rivers of blood." Throughout his entire article Reemelin is the apostle of a sweet reasonableness, and of as complacent a degree of optimism concerning the future state of the world as any early pseudo-Darwinist ever took for shibboleth.

These were the lines of thought Longstreet had before him to rebut. He took up his work wilfully. Unfortunately some of the things Reemelin had said about the Northern churches seemed to him all too sadly true. Let us, however, he says on this score, give even the devil his dues; the Northern churches after all are no more to blame than the Northern scientists, though, in passing, it must be conceded that the churches were "the most man-astounding, God-offending foes that we had." But pure Christianity is not always to be associated with the churches. "In the whole of Christianity, there is not one word calculated to stir an angry passion." On reviewing the inconsistency of Christians parading their silly quarrels before a hostile world, the old preacher is most indignant. "You point," he says to Reemelin, "to the hypocrites in the church in proof of the baseness of its religion. True, there are many, more and worse, in this country, at least, I believe, than there ever were before, and more in the Methodist Church North, than in all the other churches North put together."[1] . . . And on and on winds this long harangue, condemning "infidels," and flaying their foolhardiness, lauding Christianity both in its aims and accomplishments,—violent for a while, ecstatic for a while,

---

[1] "Old Things Become New," II, 108. This statement Bishop Fitzgerald carefully omits; see his version of this article in *Judge Longstreet*, 151.

for a while placidly reminiscent and autobiographical. This was the last of Longstreet's writings published during his life.

Youth and youth's strength and resiliency had by now at last left the old Judge almost desolate,—but much of his mental keenness stood by with all persistence. In how much, he must have wondered, in these days, as he looked back over his long life,—Augusta and Willington, New England, Greensboro, *Georgia Scenes,* Emory, Mississippi, South Carolina, back to Georgia again at the six graves of his little children,— reflecting on the harsh denial to him of his fond wish for a son,—in how much, on the whole, this old Roman must have wondered, had he conquered life, and in how much had life conquered him? He had had more capacity for work than is given to most men, and more intelligence, and he had been as honest as a man could be. In how much now had his own life illustrated the principle that he had so confidently enunciated years ago to his students at Emory, the principle that virtue must have its reward, and lack of virtue its mockery? Aside from his personal affairs he had had two main interests: the spiritual grace and social welfare of his country. Both of these he saw now, alas, under the control of utterly subversive powers. He had conquered life, he had to confess it,—born fighter that he was,—only in so far as he had evaded it. Only in the contemplation of otherwordliness and of God could he find now any true and lasting joy. There it was absolute.

His last days were both peaceful and stormy. In the records that one can gather of him from books and from personal recollections, he is seen nearly always at work, sometimes assertive, shrewd, and independent, sometimes wistfully despondent, sometimes idyllically pleased with the offerings of simple things like trees and starlight and with the music of unregardful birds.

In the summer of 1870, Lamar, feeling that Mississippi had become too wholly the prey of evil politics[1] for him any longer to remain in it and prosper, inquired of the Judge if he would like to move back to Georgia and become head of a law school in Macon. Nobody knew just how the Judge *would* like it. He loved Georgia with the passion of griefs both old and new.

---

[1] Mayes, *L. Q. C. Lamar,* 128.

He would be delighted. . . . He would take on a second youth there. . . . His contact with the fresh young manhood of Georgia, their bright hopes and budding aspirations, their reverential attachment to him as their preceptor (such they had manifested towards him at Emory years ago—had even wept when he had shaken hands with them for farewell at commencement), the interest that they would take in his lectures, all of these would enliven and illumine the evening of his life as nothing else of an earthly nature could. . . . But at last Lamar did not go; they continued to live in Oxford.

Longstreet knew that in the nature of things he could not hold on much longer, but he disdained idle waiting and repining. He kept at his old habit of grafting fruit trees. "Tell me, Judge," a tactful friend is reported to have asked him, "do you ever expect to eat any apples off that twig you are working with?" "Hardly—not hardly," the old man responded,—and then, remembering his chance to get in a lesson, "but somebody else will."

One night in summer, a student returning to his room, heard in the darkness as he passed the grove near Judge Longstreet's cottage a strange murmuring sound that he could not account for. Walking towards it, he at length found the venerable Judge himself, lying on a bench, looking straight upward, counting almost mechanically the intermittent callings of a whippoorwill. The boy hardly knew what to say or do. Was this man of such inexhaustible action reduced then to counting bird cries, like a child?—Yes, the Judge explained, that was what he was doing, counting bird cries. And then on he counted.[1] "Good-night, Judge," the boy said as he turned away, "Good-night, sir."—And still the Judge went on with his monotonous counting, how far the boy never could tell. But what should a man like Judge Longstreet be doing at these trivial ways, or were they trivial ways, after all,—if they were, would a wise man be following them? What, anyhow, is the measure of importance? Do such questions then peer out of life at one, as well as out of poetry books?—Or can it be simply that the old Judge in his great age has lost himself,

---

[1] Letter, Judge J. P. Young, Memphis, Tennessee, 13 January, 1922.

fancying now bird calls, perhaps, no less paramount than battle sounds, conceiving the faint light of stars, perhaps, no less material than statesmanship? Does all transcendent faculty at last then wane into dotage? What should a young man think of these things?

Towards the last of June the Judge had some slight fever, not serious, but enough in his physical state to do him up pretty sadly. It could not keep him down long. On July 6 he got up and dressed, and spent some time writing. Tomorrow, he declared that night, he would sit up all day. He never had been a man for lying abed, and he would not now take up a foolish habit he had so long avoided. But early the next morning he was seized with chills, so violent that there was no hope of moving. He knew soon that he had got up for his last time. The old enemy had put his shoulder on the ground, and no manner of shouting "calf-rope," as the boys had shouted in Georgia years ago, years, years ago,—would by any chance persuade this impassive enemy to release him. There was no pain, it was just that one was fastened quite down.

Except for normal intervals of sleep, the old man was conscious all day Thursday, Friday, and Saturday up till four in the afternoon.[1] He knew perfectly what was happening. This was no enemy, though, after all.—This is simply God's emissary. That much, and the new land he will take one to, and the blessed conditions that obtain there—all of that, one knows with absolute precision.—When he rouses himself, someone asks him about his ideas of eternity. It is a most lovely text, but one cannot now talk very much, one can only whisper —"not a cloud, not a cloud," whisper reassuringly at times, like a refrain, through the slow hours, "not a cloud."

But the method of Death's taking one—how intriguing it is! How does the body feel just as the spirit goes from it? What does the spirit know first in its new consciousness? Or is there any lapse? If one could only know. There is nothing that would prove more entertaining or instructive.

He puts his fingers on his pulse and counts it. Around his bed he observes his family, Fannie Branham and Jennie

---

[1] This was the time of his death, 9 July, 1870. Letter, Edward Mayes, *Nineteenth Century*, August, 1870.

Lamar, his daughters, and their husbands and children, all very, very dear to him. He thinks of their dead mother. His fingers slip away from his pulse, and he tries to replace them but he is too weak. Someone replaces them for him and he is grateful. It beats dimly and slowly, not so rapidly even as a whippoorwill calls in the woods, when it is night. It will not beat much longer.

Over the old man's face slowly now the awestruck bystanders saw coming a marvelous transformation. Weariness faded into peace, and peace became transmuted into living hope; wonder and illumination now again lent that old visage its ancient look of mastery, rapture burnt those pale eyes back into light.—"Look, Jennie, look," Mr. Lamar said to his wife.[1] Could one hold this thing quite earthly? "Not a cloud," the old man whispers again, "not a cloud."—Ah, is it wholly of this earth, after all?—The old face beams now with a light these people have never before seen; they are all of them aghast, knowing themselves in the presence of forces too great for reckoning. Only the Judge can look before him with all kingliness. "Look, Jennie, look," he calls to his daughter—"look, Jennie!"

---

[1] Mayes, *L. Q. C. Lamar*, 126.

AUGUSTUS BALDWIN LONGSTREET:
A BIBLIOGRAPHY

ABBOTT, JOHN S. C., *South and North.* New York, 1860.
ADAMS, NEHEMIAH, *South-side View of Slavery.* Boston, 1854.
ALDERMAN, EDWIN ANDERSON, and HARRIS, JOEL CHANDLER, *Library of Southern Literature.* Atlanta, 1909.
ALEXANDER, GROSS, *History Methodist Episcopal Church South.* New York, 1894.
ANDERSON, WILBERT LEE, *The Country Town.* New York, 1914.
ANDREWS, GARNETT, *Reminiscences of an Old Georgia Lawyer.* Atlanta, 1870.
ANONYMOUS, *Ethel Somers, or the Fate of the Union.* Augusta, 1857.
ANONYMOUS (A Georgia Huntsman), *Manolia, or the Vale of Tallulah.* Augusta, 1854.
ANONYMOUS (A Presbyterian Minister), *Pamphlets for the People.* Philadelphia, 1854.
ANONYMOUS, *Way Marks in the Life of a Wanderer.* Philadelphia, 1851.
ANSLEY, MRS. J. J., *Georgia W. C. T. U.* Columbus, 1914.
ANTHONY, J. D., *Life and Times of Rev. J. D. Anthony.* Atlanta, 1896.
Athens Banner, 1830's.
AUGUSTA, GEORGIA—*Handbook of Augusta,* compiled by J. L. MAXWELL, P. A. STOVALL, T. R. GIBSON. Augusta, 1878.—*Memorial History of Augusta,* C. C. JONES and SALEM DUTCHER. Syracuse, N. Y., 1890.
Augusta Chronicle, 1785–1870.
Augusta Constitutionalist, 1830's.
AVARY, MYRTA LOCKETT (ed.), *Recollections: Alexander H. Stephens.* New York, 1910.
BALDWIN, JOSEPH GLOVER, *The Flush Times of Alabama and Mississippi.* 1853.
Barnard, Frederick A. P., Memoirs of, by John Fulton. New York, 1896.
BASCOMB, HENRY BIDLEMAN, *Methodism and Slavery.* Frankfort, Ky., 1845.
BASKERVILLE, W. M., *Southern Writers.* Nashville, 1898–1903.
BELL, HIRAM P., *Men and Things.* Atlanta, 1907.
Bleckley, Logan Edwin, A Memorial of, by Georgia Bar Association. Macon, Georgia, 1909.
BLEDSOE, ALBERT TAYLOR, *Essay on Liberty and Slavery.* Philadelphia, 1856.—*Is Davis a Traitor, or Was Secession a Constitutional Right Previous to 1861?* Richmond, 1866.
BOYKIN, S., *History of the Baptist Denomination in Georgia.* Atlanta, 1881.

BOB SHORT [pseud.], *The Olio.* New York, 1823.—*Patriotic Effusions.* New York, 1819.
BRACKENRIDGE, HUGH HENRY, *Modern Chivalry* (6 vols.). Philadelphia, 1793–1805.
BROWNLOW, WILLIAM G., *The Great Iron Wheel Examined, or Its False Spokes Extracted, and An Exhibition of Elder Graves.* Nashville, 1856.
BROOKS, ROBERT PRESTON, *History of Georgia.* Chicago, 1913.
BROWN, WILLIAM GARROTT, *The Lower South in American History.* New York, 1902.
BRUCE, PHILIP ALEXANDER, *Centennial History of the University of Virginia* (5 vols.). New York, 1920.
BUTLER, J. C., *Historical Record of Macon and Central Georgia.* Macon, 1879.
CALHOUN, JOHN C., *Correspondence,* Edited by J. Franklin Jameson. Washington, 1900.
CANDLER, ALLEN D., *Georgia* (3 vols.). Atlanta, 1906.—*Memoirs of Georgia* (2 vols.). Atlanta, 1895.
Capers, William, Life of, by Wm. M. Wightman. Nashville, 1859.
CASSELS, SAMUEL J., *Providence and Other Poems.* Macon, 1838.
CHAPMAN, JOHN A., *History of Edgefield County.* Newberry, S. C., 1897.
CHARLTON, ROBERT M., and THOMAS J., *Poems.* Boston, 1842.
CHARLTON, ROBERT M., *Reports of Decisions.* Savannah, 1838.
CHARLTON, THOMAS U. P., *Reports of the Cases Argued and Determined in the Superior Courts of the State of Georgia.* New York, 1824.
CHIVERS, THOMAS HOLLEY, *The Lost Pleiad and Other Poems.* New York, 1845.
CLARK, RICHARD H., *Memoirs.* Atlanta, 1898.
COBB, HOWELL, *Scripture Examination of Slavery.* Perry, Ga., 1856.
COBB, JOSEPH B., *Leisure Labors.* New York, 1858.
COBB, T. R. R., *Historical Sketch Southern Slavery.* Philadelphia, 1858.
Columbus Daily Enquirer, 1860's.
COOK, MRS. MARY LOUISE REDD, *Antebellum Southern Life as It Was.* Philadelphia, 1868.
COTTER, WILLIAM JASPER, *Autobiography.* Nashville, 1917.
COULTER, E. MERTON, "Nullification Movement in Georgia." *Georgia Historical Quarterly,* March, 1921.
CROCKETT, DAVID, *Narrative of the Life of David Crockett.* Baltimore, 1834.—*Account of Col. Crockett's Tour to the North and Down East.* Baltimore, 1835.—*Col. Crockett's Exploits and Adventures in Texas.* London and New York, 1837.—*Life.* Philadelphia, 1860.
DAVIDSON, JAMES WOOD, *The Living Writers of the South.* New York, 1869.
DAVIS, CHARLES AUGUSTUS, *Letters of Jack Downing.* 1834.—*Jack Downing's Song Book.* Providence, 1836.—*Jack Downing's Letters.*

Philadelphia, 1845.—*May-Day in New York.* 1845.—*Labor, or Productive Industry.* 1849.
Delany, Martin R., *Life and Public Services of,* by Frank A. Rollin, Boston, 1883.
Desmond, Humphrey J., *The Know-Nothing Party.* Washington, 1905.
Dillard, A. W., "William Gilmore Simms and A. B. Longstreet," *Nineteenth Centure Magazine.* October, 1870.
Dugas, L., *Psychology of Laughter.*
Dunning, William Archibald, *Studies in Southern History and Politics* inscribed to. New York, 1914.
Duyckincks' *Cyclopedia of American Literature* (2 vols.). New York, 1856.
Eastman, Max, *Sense of Humor.* New York, 1821.
Elliott, C., *The Great Secession.* Cincinnati, 1855.
Emory College, *Phoenix* (A Student Magazine).
Evans, Clement A., Scrap Books, University of Georgia Library.
Evans, Lawton B., *History of Georgia.* New York, 1906.
Fay, Edwin Whitfield, *History of Education in Louisiana.* Washington, 1898.
Felton, Rebecca Latimer, *Country Life in Georgia in the Days of My Youth.* Atlanta, 1919.—*Memories of Georgia Politics.* Atlanta, 1911.
Fitzgerald, Oscar Penn, *Judge Longstreet, A Life Sketch.* Nashville, 1891.—*Life of McFerrin.* Nashville.
Fleming, Walter L., *Documentary History Reconstruction* (2 vols.). Cleveland, 1907.
Forrest, Mary, *Women of the South Distinguished in Literature.* New York, 1866.
Freud, Sigmund, *Psychoanalysis,* A. A. Brill's Summary. Philadelphia, 1914. (Freud's philosophy of humor.)
Fulton, John, *Memoirs of Frederick A. P. Barnard.* New York, 1896.
Garner, James Wilford, *Reconstruction in Mississippi.* New York, 1901.
Gault, Joseph, *A Coat of Many Colors* (fifth edition). Americus, Ga., 1902.
Georgia, State of—*Journal* House of Representatives. 1821.—*Minutes,* Executive Department. Governor's *Letter Book.*—*Code of Laws,* L. Q. C. Lamar, I. Augusta, 1821.—*Digest of Laws,* O. H. Prince. Athens, 1837.
Georgia, University of—Trustees' *Minutes.*—*Georgia University Magazine,* 1849.
Gildersleeve, Basil L., *The Creed of the Old South.* Baltimore, 1915.
Gilman, Caroline, *Recollections of A Southern Matron.* New York, 1838.
Gilmer, George Rockingham, *Sketches of Some of the First Settlers of Upper Georgia.* New York, 1855.—*The Literary Progress of Georgia.* Speech at University of Georgia. August 7, 1851

GORDON, JOHN B., *Reminiscences of the Civil War.* New York, 1903, 1905.
GORDON, WILLIAM W., "Georgia's Debt to Monmouth County, New Jersey," in *Georgia Historical Quarterly,* June, 1923.
GOULDING, FRANCIS R., *The Young Marooners.* 1852.
GRAVES, J. R., *The Great Iron Wheel, or Republicanism Backwards and Christianity Reversed.* Nashville, 1855.
GRAYSON, WM. J., *The Hireling and the Slave.* Charleston, 1856.—*James Louis Petigru: A Biographical Sketch.* Charleston, 1866.
GREEN, EDWIN L., *History of the University of South Carolina.* Columbia, 1916.
GREENE COUNTY, GEORGIA—Court Records.
HALL, ROBERT PLEASANTS, *Poems by a South Carolinian.* Charleston, 1848. (See Miller, *Bench and Bar,* II, 76.)
HARDEN, E. J., *George McIntosh Troup.* Savannah, 1859.
Harris, Joel Chandler, By Julia Collier Harris. Boston, 1918.
HARRIS, GEORGE WASHINGTON, *Sut Lovingood's Yarns.* 1867.
HARRISON, W. P., *Gospel Among the Slaves.* 1893.
HART, ALBERT BUSHNELL, *Formation of the Union.* New York, 1842.—*The Southern South.* New York, 1910.
Hayne, Robert Y., Life of, By Theodore D. Jervey. New York, 1909.
HELPER, HINTON ROWAN, *Nojoque* [Deportation of Negroes]. New York, 1868.
HENDERSON, ARCHIBALD, *Conquest of the Old South West.* New York, 1920.
HENNEMAN, JOHN BELL, *The South in the Building of the Nation.* Richmond, 1909.
HERRING, J. L., *Saturday Night Sketches, Stories of Old Wiregrass Georgia.* Boston, 1918.
Hill, "Yankee," Life and Recollections of. New York, 1850.
HODGSON, JOSEPH, *Cradle of the Confederacy.* Mobile, 1876.
HOOPER, JOHNSON JONES, *Some Adventures of Captain Simion Suggs.* Philadelphia, 1845.—*Widow Rugby's Husband . . . and Other Tales of Alabama.* Philadelphia, 1845.—*Dog and Gun;—A Few Loose Chapters on Shooting.* 1856.
HOUSTON, DAVID FRANKLIN, *A Study of Nullification in South Carolina.* New York, 1896.
HULL, AUGUSTUS LONGSTREET, *Annals of Athens, Georgia, 1801-1901.* Athens, 1906.
HULL, HENRY, *Sketches from the Early History of Athens, Georgia, 1801–25.*
HUNDLEY, D. R., *Social Relations in Our Southern States.* New York, 1860.
HUTSON, CHARLES WOODWARD, "The South Carolina College in the Late Fifties," in *Sewanee Review.* July, 1910.
INGRAHAM, J. H., *The Sunny South, or the Southerner at Home.* Philadelphia, 1860.

BIBLIOGRAPHY

JACKSON, HENRY R., "Politics—Literature," *Mirror*, 14. November, 1840.
—*Tallulah and Other Poems*. Savannah, 1850.
JACKSON, JAMES, "Life and Character of Rev. Dr. A. B. Longstreet, an Address Delivered at Oxford, Georgia, July 18, 1871" (in *In Memoriam, Rev. Bishop James Osgood Andrew, D.D.; Rev. Augustus B. Longstreet, D.D., LL.D.; Rev. William A. Smith, D.D.;* Wm. T. Smithson, editor and compiler. New York, 1871.)
JOHNSTON, RICHARD MALCOLM, *Autobiography* [Second ed.]. Washington, 1901.—*Dukesborough Tales*. Baltimore, 1871, 1874; New York, 1883, 1892.—*Early Educational Life in Middle Georgia*. Report Commissioner Education. 1895.—*Georgia Sketches*. Augusta, Ga., 1864. *Mr. Absolom Billingslea and Other Georgia Folk*. 1888.—*Mr. Billy Downs and His Likes*. 1892.—*Mr. Fortner's Marital Claims*. 1892.—*Ogeechee Cross Firing*. 1889.—*Old Mark Langston*. 1884.—*Old Times in Middle Georgia*. 1897.—*Pierce Amerson's Will*. Chicago, 1898.—*The Primes and Their Neighbors*. 1891.—*Two Gay Tourists*. Baltimore, 1885; New York, 1893.—*Widow Guthrie*. 1890.
JONES, CHARLES C., *Religious Instruction of the Negroes*. Savannah, 1842.
JONES, CHARLES C. JR., *Commodore Josiah Tatnall*. Savannah, 1878.—*Education in Georgia*. Washington, 1889.—*Memorial History of Augusta, Georgia*. Syracuse, N. Y., 1890.
KELL, JOHN MCINTOSH, *Recollections of a Naval Life*. Washington, 1900.
KILBOURNE, DWIGHT C., *The Bench and Bar of Litchfield 1709–1909*. Litchfield, Conn., 1909.
KNIGHT, LUCIAN LAMAR, *Georgia and Georgians* (6 vols.). Chicago, 1917.—*Georgia Landmarks, Memorials and Legends* (2 vols.). Atlanta, 1907.—*Reminiscences of Famous Georgians* (2 vols.). Atlanta, 1907.
LA BORDE, MAXIMILIAN, *History of the South Carolina College*. Charleston, 1874.
LaFayette In America in 1824, or *Journal of a Voyage* (2 vols.), by A. Levasseur. Philadelphia, 1829.
LAMAR, JOHN B., *Polly Peablossom's Wedding*. Philadelphia, 1851.
LAMAR, JOSEPH L., *Recollections of Pioneer Days in Georgia* (privately printed).
Lamar, Mirabeau Buonaparte, *Papers of* (ed. Charles Adams Gulic, Katherine Elliott; published Texas State Library, 2 vols.). Austin, Texas, 1922.—*Verse Memorials*, 1857.
LATROBE, CHARLES JOSEPH, *The Rambler in North America* (2 vols.). New York, 1835.
LENNOX, MARY [pseud.]. See Cook, Mrs. M. L. R.
LEONARD, O. B., *The Fitz Randolphs of Massachusetts and New Jersey* (pamphlet, privately printed).
LONGSTREET, JAMES, *From Manassas to Appomattox*. Philadelphia, 1896.

378   AUGUSTUS BALDWIN LONGSTREET

LONGSTREET, JAMES and HELEN D., *Lee and Longstreet at High Tide.* Gainesville, Ga., 1905, printed Philadelphia.

LONGSTREET, AUGUSTUS B., "Darby Anvil," *Southern Literary Messenger,* January, 1844; Fitzgerald, *Judge Longstreet; Stories with a Moral* —"From Out the Fires," *Nineteenth Century,* December, 1869.— *Georgia Scenes* (serially, in Newspapers—See "Table" at end of this bibliography); (in book form)—Augusta, 1835; New York, 1840, '42, '46, '50, '54, '57, '58, '60, '84, '97; Quitman, Georgia, 1894 (The references to *Georgia Scenes* in this book are to the Quitman, Ga., edition).—Hymn, "Glory" (detached newspaper clipping).— "Gnatville Gem," *Magnolia.* June, 1843.—Letter to Henry Hull, 2 Aug. 1858. [Ms.]—Letter to L. Q. C. Lamar, date Columbus, Ga., 14 May, 1864. [Ms.]—Letter published *Macon Telegraph,* 23 February, 1867, signed "Vim." (See Fitzgerald, *Judge Longstreet,* 204.)—Letter to Mirabeau Buonaparte Lamar, date about 1837, published in *Papers of Mirabeau Buonaparte Lamar,* II, 1-5.—History of My Land Purchases in Lafayette Co., Miss. [Ms.]—*Letters on the Epistle of Paul to Philemon or the Connection of Apostolical Christianity With Slavery,* Charleston, 1845.—*Letters from President Longstreet* [on Know Nothingism] *to the Know Nothing Preachers of the Methodist Church South, in Campaign Document No. 2* issued by the Democratic State Central Committee of Louisiana, 1855.—*Master William Mitten* (by the author of Georgia Scenes), Macon, 1864. (By Rev. Augustus B. Longstreet, D. D., LL.D., author of *Georgia Scenes*), Macon, 1889.—"Old Things Become New," I, *Nineteenth Century Magazine.* April, 1870. "Old Things Become New," II, (Reply to Reemelin), *Nineteenth Century Magazine.* July, 1870.—*Review of the Decision of the U. S. Supreme Court in the Case of McCulloch vs. the State of Maryland* (Lost).—"Review of Gov. Perry's Article on John C. Calhoun," *Nineteenth Century Magazine.* January, 1870.—*State Rights Sentinel,* Augusta, 9 January, 1834-3 January, 1837.—Statistical Congress, London, Correspondence relative to. See Life of Delany.— *Stories with a Moral.* Philadelphia, 1912.—"Valuable Suggestions, Addressed to the Soldiers of the Confederate States." (In Frank Moore's *Rebellion Record,* VIII, 433-7.)—*A Voice from the South. Comprising Letters from Georgia to Massachusetts.* Baltimore, 1847.

MCGEHEE, JOHN B., *Autobiography.* Blakeley, Ga., 1917.

MCDUFFIE, GEORGE, *Defence of a Liberal Construction of the Powers of Congress.* Philadelphia, 1831.

MCPHERSON, JOHN HANSON THOMAS, *History of Liberia.* Baltimore, 1891.

MCTEIRE, H. N., *History of Methodism.* Nashville, 1898.

MACKIE, J. MILTON, *From Cape Cod to Dixie and the Tropics.* New York, 1812.

Magnolia Monthly Magazine. Savannah, 1841-2; Charleston, 1842-3.

MEEK, ALEX B., *Americanism in Literature.* Charleston, 1844.

BIBLIOGRAPHY 379

Meigs, Josiah, Life of, by Wm. M. Meigs. Philadelphia, 1887.
MELISH, JOHN, *Travels in the United States of America* (2 vols.). New York, 1812.
Mell, Patrick Hues, Life of, by P. H. Mell, jr. Louisville, 1895.
MENCKEN, HENRY LOUIS, *Prejudices,* Series II. New York, 1821.
Mercer, Elder Jesse, Memoirs of, by C. D. Mallory. New York, 1844.
MESICK, JANE LOUISE, *British Travellers in the United States, 1785-1835.* New York, 1922.
METHODISTS (see also, this bibliography)—Anthony, Alexander, Bascomb, Brownlow, Boykin, Capers, Cotter, Elliott, Fitzgerald, Graves, Harrison, Longstreet, A. B.; McGehee, McTyeire, Matlock, Olin, Quillian, Redford, Richardson, Smith, George G.; *Southern Christian Advocate, Southwestern Advocate,* Sweet, Wilson, J. W.
METHODIST EPISCOPAL CHURCH—*History Organization M. E. C. S.* Nashville, 1845.
METHODIST EPISCOPAL CHURCH—*Journal and Debates Gen. Conference.* 1844.
METHODIST EPISCOPAL CHURCH—*Property Case.* 1851.
METHODIST EPISCOPAL CHURCH—*Quarterly Review of.* New York, 1840-1860.
METHODIST EPISCOPAL CHURCH and M. E. C. South—M. E. C., *Minutes of the Annual Conferences,* Vol. II, 1829-39; Vol. III, 1839-45; M. E. C. S., Vol. I., 1845-57; Vol. II, 1858-65; Vol. III, 1866-73.
METHODISTS—*Minutes Miss. Conference,* 1849, 1857-76. (Lent by A. F. Watkins, Millsaps College.)
MILLER, STEPHEN F., *Bench and Bar of Georgia* (2 vols.). Philadelphia, 1858.
Mirror (ed. Thompson). Augusta, Ga., 1838-42.
MISSISSIPPI, STATE OF—Governor's *Letter Book.*
MISSISSIPPI, UNIVERSITY OF—Trustees' *Minutes.*
MITCHELL, DONALD GRANT, *American Lands and Letters.* New York, 1897-9.
MOORE, FRANK (ed.), *The Rebellion Record,* Vol. VIII. New York, 1865. *Spirit of the Pulpit, A Collection of Sermons by Distinguished Divines, North and South.* New York, 1861.
MORGAN COUNTY, GEORGIA—Court Records.
Niles' Register—Baltimore, Washington, Philadelphia, 1811-49.
Nineteenth Century Magazine—Charleston, 1869-1871.
NORTHERN, WILLIAM J., *Men of Mark in Georgia.* Atlanta, 1907-12.
OLIN, STEPHEN, *Life and Letters.* New York, 1853.
OLMSTED, F. L., *A Journey in the Seaboard Slave States.* New York, 1856.—*A Journey in the Black Country.* New York, 1860.—*The Cotton Kingdom.* New York, 1861.
Orion, PENFIELD, GEORGIA. March, 1842-February, 1844.
OZANNE, THE REVEREND T. D., *The South As It Is.* London, 1863.
PAGE, J. W., *Uncle Robin in His Cabin in Virginia and Tom Without One in Boston.*

PATTON, JULIA, *The English Village.* New York, 1919.
PASCAL, GEORGE W., *Ninety-four Years, Agnes Pascal.* Washington, 1871.
PATTEE, F. L., *American Literature Since 1870.* New York, 1915.
PENDLETON, LOUIS, *Alexander H. Stephens.* Philadelphia, 1907.
PERRY, BLISS, *The American Mind.* Boston, 1912.
PERRY, BENJAMIN FRANKLIN, "Judge Longstreet and His Malignantly False Criticisms," *Nineteenth Century.* February, 1870.—*Biographical Sketches of Eminent American Statesmen.* Philadelphia, 1887.
PHILLIPS, ULRICH BONNEL, *American Negro Slavery.* New York, 1918.—*Correspondence Toombs, Stephens, Howell Cobb.* New York, 1911.—"Literary Movement for Secession" in *William L. Dunning, Studies in Southern History and Politics.* New York, 1914.—*Plantation and Frontier, 1649–1863.* Cleveland, 1909.—*Transportation in Eastern Cotton Belt.* New York, 1908.
PRINCE, OLIVER HILLHOUSE, *Digest Georgia Laws.* Athens, 1837.
PRINGLE, E. W. A., *Chicora Wood.* N. Y., 1922.—*Woman Rice Planter.* N. Y., 1914.
QUILLIAN, WILLIAM E., *Life and Sermons.* Atlanta, 1907.
RAMSAY, DAVID, *The History of South Carolina* (2 volumes). Charleston, 1809.
RAVENEL, MRS. ST. J., *Charleston, the Place and the People.* New York, 1906.—*Eliza Pinckney.* New York, 1896.
REDFORD, A. H., *History of the Organization, Methodist Episcopal Church South.* Nashville, 1900.
RICHARDSON, SIMON PETER, *Lights and Shadows of Itinerant Life.* Nashville, 1900.
RICHMOND COUNTY, GEORGIA—*Court Records.*
ROATH, D., *Zara, A Romance.* Athens, 1851.
ROWLAND, DUNBAR, *Encyclopaedia of Mississippi.* Madison, Wisconsin, 1907.
ROSS, FRED A., *Slavery Ordained of God.* Philadelphia, 1857.
RUSSELL, WILLIAM HOWARD, *My Diary North and South.* New York, 1863.—*Pictures of Southern Life.* New York, 1861.
RUTHERFORD, MILDRED, *South in History and Literature.* Atlanta, 1907.
SALTER, *History of Monmouth and Ocean Counties, New Jersey.* Bayonne, N. J., 1890.
SCOMP, HENRY A., *King Alcohol on the Realm of King Cotton, 1733–1887.* Blakely, Ga., 1888.
SCOTT, REV. W. J., *Seventy-one Years in Georgia.* Atlanta, 1898 (?).
Sherwood, Adiel, *Memoir of,* Written by his Daughter. Philadelphia, 1884.
SHIPP, J. E. D., *William H. Crawford.* Americus, Georgia, 1909.
"SHORT, BOB" (pseud.), *Olio, The.* New York, 1823.—*Patriotic Effusions.* New York, 1819.
SIMMS, WILLIAM GILMORE, *As Good as a Comedy.* New York, 1852.—*Guy Rivers,* New York, 1834.
SMITH, CHARLES H., *A School History of Georgia.* Boston, 1896.

BIBLIOGRAPHY

SMITH, EMMA EVE, *Our Family History.* Mss. in possession of Mr. Paul E. Carmichael, Augusta.
SMITH, GEORGE G., JR., *History of Georgia Methodism.* 1786–1866, Atlanta, 1913.—*History of Methodism in Georgia and Florida, 1785–1865.* Macon, 1877.—*A Hundred Years of Methodism in Augusta.* Augusta, 1898.—*Life and Letters of James Osgood Andrew.* Nashville, 1883.—*Life and Times of George Foster Pierce.* Sparta, Ga., 1888.—"Some Overlooked Georgians: A B. Longstreet, Jurist, Wit, Divine, Scholar, Teacher, Editor." (Detached newspaper clipping.)—*Story of Georgia and the Georgia People.* Atlanta, 1900.
SMITH, M. ELIZABETH, "Recreations of an Invalid." *Nineteenth Century.* February, 1870.
SMITH, SEBA, *Life and Writing of Major Jack Downing.* Portland, 1833, Boston, 1833, 1834.—*Select Letters.* Philadelphia, 1834.—*Letters, Written during the President's Tour.* Cincinnati, 1833.—*John Smith's Letters.* 1839.—*Powhatan, a Metrical Romance.* 1841.—*The Religion and the Superstitions of the North American Indians.* 1864.—*Dew Drops of the Nineteenth Century.* [Anthology, 1846.]—*New Elements of Geometry.* 1850.—*Way Down East, or Portraitures of Yankee Life.* 1854–59.—*My Thirty Years Out of the Senate.* 1859.—*Speeches of John Smith, Esquire, not Delivered at Smithville.* 1864.
SOUTH CAROLINA, UNIVERSITY OF—*Trustees' Minutes.*
Southern Christian Advocate. Charleston, 1830 through 1850.
Southern Field and Fireside. Augusta, Georgia, 28 May, 1859; absorbed November, 1864, by Raleigh, N. C., *Illustrated Mercury.*
Southern Ladies' Book. Macon, Georgia, January, 1840–October, 1840.
Southern Literature, Library of. Atlanta, 1909–13.
Southern Literary Gazette. Athens, Ga., 1848.
Southern Literary Journal. Charleston, S. C., 1835–1839.
Southern Literary Messenger. Richmond, Va., 1834–1865.
Southern Quarterly Review. New Orleans, January–April, 1842; Charleston, July, 1842–55; Columbia, S. C., 1856.
Southern Recorder. Milledgeville, Georgia, 1830–36.
Southwestern Christian Advocate. Nashville, Tenn., November, 1842–October, 1844.
SPARKS, W. H., "Dosing a Patient." Clipping from *Atlanta Constitution* in Clement A. Evans' Scrap Book, University of Georgia Library.—*The Memories of Fifty Years* [3rd ed.]. Philadelphia and Macon, 1872.
SPRAGUE, WM. B., *Annals of the American Pulpit.* New York, 1857.
STANTON, Rev. E. F., "Manual Labor Schools," *Southern Literary Messenger.* March, 1836.
State Rights Sentinel. Augusta, 9 January, 1834–3 January, 1837.
STEDMAN-HUTCHINSON, *Library American Literature..* New York, 1888.
Stephens, Alexander (in public and private), by Henry Cleveland. Philadelphia, 1866.

Stephens, Linton, Biographical Sketch of, by James D. Waddel. Atlanta, 1877.

STILES, C. W., *Soil Pollution as Cause of Ground Itch and Hookworm*. Washington, 1910. (Publications of Rockefeller Sanitary Commission.)

STIRLING, JAMES, *Letters from the Slave States*. London, 1857.

STOVALL, P. A., with J. L. Maxwell and T. R. Gibson, *Handbook of Augusta*. Augusta, 1878.—*Robert Toombs*. New York, 1892.

SWEET, W. W., *The Methodist Episcopal Church and the Civil War*. Cincinnati, 1912.

STRAUS, OSCAR S., *Under Four Administrations*, Boston and New York, 1922.

TANDY, JEANNETTE REID, "Pro-Slavery Propaganda in American Fiction," *South Atlantic Quarterly*. January, 1922.

THOMPSON, WILLIAM TAPPAN, *Major Jones' Courtship*. Philadelphia, 1840.—*Major Jones' Chronicles of Pineville, embracing Sketches of Georgia*. Philadelphia, 1843. As *Georgia Scenes*. 1880.—*Major Jones' Sketches of Travel*. Philadelphia, 1848.—*Mirror*. Augusta, Ga., 1838–42. *The Slaveholder Abroad*. Philadelphia, 1860.—*Ransy Cotton's Courtship*. Philadelphia [1879].—*Western Continent*. Baltimore, 1845–50.—*John's Alive, or, the Bride of a Ghost, and other Sketches*. [Collected by Thompson's daughter, Mrs. May A. Wade.] Philadelphia, 1883.

TRENT, WILLIAM P., "Retrospect of American Humor," *Century Magazine* [New York], November, 1901.—*Southern Statesmen of the Old Régime*. New York, 1897.

Troup, George McIntosh, Life of, E. J. Harden. Savannah, 1859.

TROWBRIDGE, J. T., *The South; A Tour*. Hartford, Conn., 1866.

TUCKER, HENRY H., "*God in the War*," a sermon delivered before the Legislature of Georgia in the Capitol at Milledgeville, Friday, 15 November, 1861. Milledgeville, 1861. In Volume of *Public Documents*, University of Georgia Library.

TURNER, FREDERICK JACKSON, *The Frontier in American History*. New York, 1920.

TURNER, J. A., "American Literature," *Southern Field and Fireside*. 4 June, 1859.

TURNER, WILLIAM W., *Jack Hopeton*. New York, 1860.

United States, Supreme Court of—Docket.

VANDERPOOL, EMILY NOYES [Compiler], BARNEY, ELIZABETH C. [Editor]. *Chronicles of a Pioneer School*. Cambridge, 1903.

WADE, JOHN DONALD, "The Authorship of David Crockett's 'Autobiography,'" in *Georgia Historical Quarterly*. September, 1922.

WADDEL, JOHN NEWTON, *Historical Discourse* delivered Quarter-Centennial University of Mississippi. Oxford, 1873.—*Memorials of Academic Life*. Richmond, 1891.

BIBLIOGRAPHY

WADDEL, MOSES, *Diary of.* 7 September, 1824–25 May, 1826 [Ms.].
  Memoirs of the Life of Miss Caroline Elizabeth Smelt, New York, Liverpool, 1819.
WALLACE, DAVID DUNCAN, *Life of Henry Laurens*, New York, 1915.
Watterson, Henry, The Editorials of. [Edited by Arthur Krock.] New York, 1923.
WEEKS, STEPHEN B., "Anti-Slavery Sentiment in the South," *Publication Southern Historical Association*, II, 2.
Western Continent. Baltimore, 1845–50.
WHITE, GEORGE, *Statistics of the State of Georgia.* Savannah, 1849.—
  Historical Collections of Georgia. New York, 1854.
WHITE, ROBERT A., *The Georgia Home Gazette.* Augusta, 1851.
WILDE, RICHARD HENRY, *Conjectures and Researches Concerning Torquanto Tasso*, 1842.
WILLIAMS, GEORGE W., *Advice to Young Men, and Nacoochee and its Surroundings.* Charleston, S. C., 1899.
WILSON, ADELAIDE, *Historical and Picturesque Savannah.* Boston, 1889.
WILSON, JOHN S., *The Dead of the Synod of Georgia.* Atlanta, 1868.
WILSON, WOODROW, *Division and Reunion.* New York, 1893.
WIRT, WILLIAM, *Letters of a British Spy.* Richmond, 1803.
WYLLY, CHARLES SPALDING, *The Seed that Was Sown in the Colony of Georgia.* New York, 1910.
Yale Biographies, Sketches and Annals. Sixth Series. New York, 1907. Longstreet, 580–83.
Yale—Catalogues.
Yale College—A Sketch of Its History. New York, 1879.
Yale Records of Alumni—"Reunion Class of 1813 at New Haven, 1843."
"*Yankee Hill*," *Life of.* New York, 1850.
YOUNG, E., *The Lady Lillian and other Poems.* Lexington, Ga., 1859.

TABLE SHOWING FIRST APPEARANCE OF GEORGIA SCENES

Title	Publication	Date
The Ball*	*Southern Recorder*, Milledgeville.	1832
The Character of a Native Georgian	*Southern Recorder*, Milledgeville.	Jan. 1, 8, 1834
The Charming Creature as a Wife	*State Rights Sentinel*, Augusta...	Apr. 14, 1834
The Dance	*Southern Recorder*, Milledgeville.	Oct. 30, 1833
Darby Anvil	*Mirror*, Augusta	1839
The Debating Society	*State Rights Sentinel*, Augusta...	Mar. 5, 1835
Dropping to Sleep	*State Rights Sentinel*, Augusta...	Feb. 26, 1835
Family Government	*Mirror*, Augusta	1838
A Family Picture	*Mirror*, Augusta	1838
The Fight	*Southern Recorder*, Milledgeville.	Nov. 27, 1833
The Fox Hunt	*State Rights Sentinel*, Augusta..	Feb. 12, 1835
The Gander Pulling	*Southern Recorder*, Milledgeville.	Jan. 15, 1834
Georgia Theatrics*	*Southern Recorder*, Milledgeville.	1833
The Gnatville Gem	*Magnolia*, Charleston	June, 1843
The Horse Swap	*Southern Recorder*, Milledgeville.	Nov. 13, 1833
The India Rubber Story		
An Interesting Interview*	*Southern Recorder*, Milledgeville.	1834
John Bull Story*	*Magnolia* (Reference to in), Charleston	1843
Julia and Clarissa	*Magnolia*, Charleston	Sept.-Oct., 1843
Little Ben	*Mirror*, Augusta	
Militia Drill	*State Rights Sentinel*, Augusta...	May 15, 1834
The Mother and Her Child	*State Rights Sentinel*, Augusta...	June 2, 1834
The Old Soldiers	*Magnolia*, Charleston	Mar., 1843
A Sage Conversation	*State Rights Sentinel*, Augusta...	Mar. 17, 1835
The Shooting Match*	*State Rights Sentinel*, Augusta...	Mar. 17, 1836
The Song	*Southern Recorder*, Milledgeville.	Nov. 6, 1833
The Turf	*Southern Recorder*, Milledgeville.	Nov. 20, 1833
The Turn Out	*Southern Recorder*, Milledgeville.	Dec. 11, 1833
The Wax Works	*State Rights Sentinel*, Augusta...	Feb. 19, 1835

* Dates given by Fitz R. Longstreet, Letter, Gainesville, Georgia, 23 January, 1922. Mr. Longstreet himself saw these publications in files since destroyed by fire.

INDEX

Adams, J. Q., caste system in South, 60; music in America, 69.
Addison, Joseph, 76; comparison of *Spectator* with *Georgia Scenes*, 157–160.
Andersonville Prison, 348, 349, 362.
Andrew, Bishop J. O., prayer, 107; visits Greensboro, 109; revival in Milledgeville, 111; becomes pastor in Augusta, 221, 222; exhorts to seriousness, 225; invites Longstreet to lecture on hymn reading, 226; President Emory Board of Trustees, 244, 256; second marriage, plans two books, 248; object anti-slavery agitation, 271, 277, 281; Church conference, Petersburg, Va., 285; state education more important than sectarian, 289.
Andrews, Garnett, 237.
Annals of American Pulpit, Longstreet writes for, 295.
Appleton Publishers, 330.
Art, 68, 146, 147, 209.
Asbury, Bishop, 105.
As Good as a Comedy, 177.
Atlanta, 250.
Augusta, early 19th century, 14–17; 112; Lafayette's visit, 113–114; cotton center, 116, 117; Longstreet purchases residence, 118; intellectual atmosphere, 119; yellow fever, 232–234, 318; Longstreet abandons, 235; commercial decline, 240.
Augusta Chronicle, 17, 126, 132, 137, 138.

Bacon, Edmund, 75; Longstreet writes epitaph, 90–91; original of "Ned Brace," 170–171.
Baldwin, Abraham, 150.
Baldwin, J. G., 166.
"Ball," 149, 177.
Bangs, Rev. Mr., 282.

Bar, avenue to "success," 53, 192; 73–85; religion, 89; 95; 119–121 (see Politics).
Barlow, James, 37.
Barnard, F. A. P., 36 38, 299, 311, 353, 357.
Barry, John, Bishop, 233–234, 306.
Bascomb, H. B., 280.
Beecher, Ward, 42, 323.
Benjamin, Parke, 195.
Berrien, J. M., 75, 237.
Bethlehem Moravian Seminary, 7.
Bibb, W. W., 33.
"Blacksmith of Mountain Pass," 166.
Bledsoe, A. T., 298.
"Bob Short," Poet, 89–90; Newspaper politician, 136; not "Temperance" fanatic, 141; "Mystic," 245.
Branham, Frances Eliza Longstreet, 97, 245, 265, 288, 300–301, 346, 354, 370.
Branham, H. R., 288, 300, 302, 346, 350, 356, 357.
Brougham, Lord, 121, 325–326.
Brown, John, 323, 329.
Brown, Joseph E., 343, 350.
Bryant, W. C., 134.
Buchanan, James, 335, 354.

Calhoun Family, 21, 23, 29, 32, 60.
Calhoun, John C., at Waddel's School, 26, 33–36; at Yale and Litchfield, 39, 41, 44; religion, 51; Social Philosophy, 60; Nullification, 121–124; procures honorary degree for Longstreet, 156; helps James Longstreet appointment U. S. Military Academy, 246; Death-words, 352.
Campbell, D. G., 75.
Capers, Bishop William, 244, 273, 276, 279.
Cassells, S. J., 187, 192–193, 214.

INDEX

Centenary College, Longstreet President, 292-296, 315, 333.
Chaplain, Confederate Army, 344-345, 349.
Chappell, A. H., 71-72.
"Character of a Native Georgian," 149, 170-172.
Charleston, 16, 198, 211, 285.
Charlton, R. M., 197.
Charlton, T. U. P., 187.
"Charming Creature as a Wife," 149, 175-176.
Christian Index, 135, 188.
Church, Alonzo, 197.
Cincinnati Commoner, 366.
"Clara," 197.
Clark, R. H., 180.
Clark, John, 93, 96.
Clay, Henry, 281.
Clayton, Augustin S., association with David Crockett, 75-76, 167; speaks before George Washington, 75, 78; host to Longstreet, 112, 124; *Mysterious Picture*, 164, 187-188; religion, 223; on oratory, 237-238; procures honorary degree for Longstreet, U. of Ga., 96.
"Climbing the Greasy Pole," 200.
Cobb, Howell, 237, 326.
Cobb, T. R. R., 345.
Colquitt, W. T., 197.
Columbiad, 37.
Columbus, Ga., 336; Longstreet "refugees," 347, 350; 351.
Commencement, at Doctor Waddel's, 32-34; at Wesleyan, 245-246; Alexander Stephens at Emory, 261-262; 253. (See Georgia University.)
Connecticut, 56-57.
Conquest of Canaan, 37.
Cooke, John E., 331.
Cooper, J. F., 143.
"Coquettes," 200.
"Corn Shucking," 200.
Correction Canonized Errors in Biblical Interpretation, 359.
Cotton Gin, 10-11.
Countryman, 212.
Crawford, Wm. H., 26, 33, 75, 124.
Critical Spirit, active in early Georgia, 73, 150-151, 164, 188-194, 214-217, 219-220, 243-244; suppressed later, 180-181, 211, 244, 353-357, 367 (note).
Crockett, David, 62; association with Clayton, 76, 167; curiosity, 109, 185; "Georgia Theatrics," 169-170; a shooting match, 183-185; in Texas, 205.
Curiosity, 109, 146, 185.

Dallas, G. M., 325.
"Dance," 149, 170, 361.
"Darby Anvil," 162, 199, 204.
"Darby the Politician," 204.
Davidson, J. W., 45, 148, 166.
Davis, Jefferson, 349.
Dawson, Wm. C., 75.
Day, Jeremiah, 37, 156.
"Debating Society," 31, 149, 177-178.
Delany, M. F., 325, 328, 352.
Denominationalism, 102-106; 109; method of Baptism, 110, 189, 196; cohesiveness, 103, 133, 211; Longstreet transcends, 231-234; 254; 256.
Dirt eating, 172-175.
Dooley, John M., 75-76, 78, 80, 96.
"Dropping to Sleep," 149, 185-186.
Duels, McDuffie, 21; Longstreet opposes, 137; McCay at U. of Ga., 315.
Durbin, Rev. Mr., 282-284.
Duyckincks, 153.
Dwight, Timothy, 37.

Eclectic, 360.
Education, female, 7, 41, 195, 252 (see Wesleyan College); methods, 17, 175; Longstreet's, 23-47; lack of interest, 65-66, 68; secular-denominational, 103, 231, 259, 285, 289, 300; colleges, 189, 243-244; (see also Georgia University, Emory College, Mercer University, Wesleyan College, Centenary College, Mississippi University, South Carolina University, "Science.")
Elliott, Rev. Dr., 282.
Ellsler, Fannie, 253.
Emory College, 45, 89, 90, 133, 231, 234, 241-269, 289, 315, 369.
Enon, Ala., Longstreet "refugees," 346.

Family Companion, 195, 208, 210.
Family Government, 205.

INDEX 387

"Family Picture," 199, 205.
Fantasticals, 246.
Few, I. A., 197, 241, 256–257, 280.
"Fight," 149, 172–175.
Fitzgerald, Bishop O. P., 114; *Georgia Scenes*, 157; 204; 228; 261; 347; 367 (note).
Flournoy, Josiah, 140, 347.
Flush Times in Alabama and Mississippi, 166.
Forsyth, John, 7, 75, 125, 130, 232.
"Fox Hunt," 139, 182.
Franklin, Benj., 143.
Frederick, James D., 141.
"From Out the Fires," 362.

"Gander Pulling," 61, 149, 176.
Gardiner, James, 330.
Garrison, Wm. L., 270.
Georgia Academician and Southern Journal of Education, 135, 212.
Georgia Cracker, 150.
Georgia Home Gazette, 205, 212.
"Georgia Huntsman," 304.
Georgia Illustrated, 208.
Georgia to Massachusetts, 285–287.
Georgia Scenes, 114, 134; 136; "demand" for *Georgia Scenes*, 143–149; newspaper origin, 149; reception in the South, 150–155, 157, 317, 334; editions, 151, 156; illustrations, 156; reception in the North, 156; compared with *Spectator*, 157–164; historical source-book, 164, 213; historical position in American literature, 164–168, comment—*scene* by *scene*, 169–186; indiscreet?, 213–214, 306, 317, 318, 330; unpublished, 199, 200, 331; uncollected, 199–218.
"Georgia Theatrics," 149, 169–170.
Georgia University, 178, 216, 217, 227, 237, 244, 316; Dr. Waddel, 25, 26, 250; politics, 36, 124, 132, 259; neglect, 68; confers degree on Longstreet, 96; denominationalism, 103, 231; "Temperance," 141; Magazine, 167, 202; New England, 56, 254; aristocratic, 259, 278.
Gifford, C. H., 180.
Gilmer, G. R., 26, 62, 119, 170.
"Gnatville Gem," 207, 208.
Grant, U. S., 348.

Great Iron Wheel, 103.
Greeley, Horace, 135.
Greensboro, 83, 92, 114, 183, 248, 336, 353; Longstreet's residence, 86–89, 112, 117; plantation system, 94–95; Methodists, 108, 111.
Griffin, Sarah Lawrence, 195.
Guy Rivers, 508.

Hall, Lyman, 150.
Halleck, Fitz Greene, 56.
Hardy, Thomas, 179–180.
Harris, G. W., 166.
Harris, Joel C., 62, 167.
Harrison, Burton, 350.
Harte, Bret, 168.
Hartford Convention, 38.
Harvard University, 156.
Hayne, P. H., 211, 331.
Hawthorne, Nathaniel, 143.
Heraldry, 41.
Hill, Walter B., 360.
"Hill, Yankee," 165, 290.
History, Wars French Revolution, 180.
Holmes, G. F., 291, 296, 310.
Hooper, J. J., 166.
Horace, 181, 202, 245.
"Horse Swap," 149, 170.
Hotels, 67, 79–81.
Howard, John, 111.
Hull, A. L., 247–248.
Hull, Henry, friendship with Longstreet, 112, 247–248, 336; *Mitten*, 334.
Humor on the Frontier, 28, 40, 76–81, 83, 88, 148, 165–166, 171, 208, 265, 305.
Hyde, E. H., 156.

Illustrations *Georgia Scenes*, 156.
Immigration, Longstreet disapproves, 139; Longstreet approves, 307–308.
"India Rubber Story," 199.
Indians, 27, 53, 72, 355; music, 82, 336.
Ingersoll Family, 38, 147.
Ingraham, J. H., 331.
"Interesting Interview," 149, 182.
Irving, Washington, 312.

Jackson, Andrew, 122, 124, 156.
Jackson, H. R., 189, 192.
Jackson, James, 137, 153, 229, 268.

INDEX

Jenkins, C. J., 118.
"John Bull's Trip to the Gold Mines," 199.
Johnston, J. E., 348, 350.
Johnston, R. M., 55, 56, 167–168, 174; not a professional writer, 201.
"Julia and Clarissa," 199, 207.

Kennedy, J. P., 331.
Kitty, 274.
Know Nothing Party, 173, 305–309.
King, Y. P., 96.

LaBorde, Maximilian, 141, 154, 316.
La Fayette, visits Augusta, 112–114; rides Longstreet's horse, 116.
La Grange College, 253.
Lamar, L. Q. C., member of Longstreet family, 57, 86, 169, 288, 302, 311–313, 335, 350, 354, 369–370; secession, 322, 339; Mississippi, 300, 311–313, 354, 369; the War, 345, 349, 357.
Lamar, J. B., 166.
Lamar, M. B., Longstreet's suggestions concerning Texas, 138, 202, 308.
Lamar, Virginia La Fayette Longstreet, 300–301, 371; birth, 97, 113; Wesleyan College, 245; marries L. Q. C. Lamar, 288.
Land We Love, 360, 363.
Lane, George, 255.
Lanier, Sidney, 360.
Le Conte Brothers, 244, 317.
Legare, H. S., 26.
Lee, M. E., 198.
Letters on the Epistle of Paul to Philemon, 282–284, 287, 342.
Letters from Georgia to Massachusetts, 285–287.
Liberia, 275.
Lieber, Frances, 315.
Linton, A. B., 28.
Litchfield (see Reeves and Gould).
Literary Associations, 87, 95, 210.
"Little Ben," 199, 202–204.
Living Writers of the South (see Davidson, J. W.).
London, 129, 325–328.
Longfellow, H. W., 91.
Longstreet, Augustus Baldwin, birth, 2; genealogy, 2–4; boyhood in Augusta, 12–18, 20–22; boyhood in S. C., 18–19; preparatory school, 23–34; Yale, 36–40; law school, 39–46; handwriting, 45–46, 100, 327; personality, 48–52; appearance, 53, 358; lawyer, 74, 119–121; marries, 83; poet, 89–92; financier, 53, 98, 115, 141, 217–218, 258, 302–303, 354; judge, 81, 97; politician, 89–100, 122–132, 137, 214–220, 305–309, 319–329; publishes *Georgia Scenes*, 156; not a professional author, 151–152, 201–202; newspaper editor, 132–138; "Temperance," 139; Minister, 221, 226–230, 250, 304, 311; Emory College, 234–289; Centenary College, 292–296; Mississippi University, 297–310; South Carolina University, 314, 342; the War, 342–350; magazine articles, 362–368; honorary degrees, 96, 156, 310; death, 370.
Longstreet, Frances Eliza Parke, 85–86, 89, 97, 248, 292, 334, 335–336, 346, 347, 354; as wife of Longstreet, 83–85, 98, 100, 101–102, 111, 112, 222, 223, 238, 248, 249, 292, 314, 327–328, 356–357; children, 97, 223.
Longstreet, Hannah Randolph, 3–9, 20, 235, 239, 272.
Longstreet, James, 344–345, 349, 357–358; Longstreet sponsors, 246; Reconciliation after War, 355.
Longstreet, William, 3–4, 9–14, 47–48, 53, 114, 128–129, 330; inventions, 9–13.
Loring, C. H., 43.
Lumpkin, J. H., 73, 140, 197.
Lumpkin, Wilson, 132.
Lynching, 58.

McCay, C. F., 315–316.
"McCulloch vs. Maryland," 92.
McDuffie, George, 21–22; 29–32; 34–35; 177, 245–247; Longstreet names child for, 97; politics, 121–123, speaks at Georgia University, 132; appoints James Longstreet to U. S. Military Academy, 246; political unanimity of South, 354.
McFerrin, J. P., 277.
McFingall, 37.
McRae, Gov., 303.

INDEX

Macon, Ga., no school teachers in 1831, 65; residence O. H. Prince, 178; 195, 334; Lamar contemplates removal to, 368.
Macon Telegraph, 148, 195, 334.
Magazines, 187, 193–198, 208–212, 330–332, 360.
Magnolia, 198, Longstreet's contributions, 199, 201, 206, 212.
"Major Jones" (see Thompson, W. T.).
"Major Jack Downing," 165.
Mann, Wm. W., 118, 127, 221, 330.
Manolia, or The Vale of Tallulah, 145, 146, 304–305.
Manual Labor Schools, 254–257.
Mark Twain, 168, 183.
"Match Maker," 206.
Master William Mitten (see *William Mitten*).
Mayes, Edward, 57, 90, 297, 357, 358, 359, 360.
Means, A., 197, 249, 255.
Medical Institute of Georgia, 236.
Meek, A. B., 197, 216.
Meigs, Josiah, 35, 217.
Mencken, H. L., 58.
Mercer, Jesse, 104; *Christian Index*, 135, 188; *Cluster*, 187.
Mercer University, 208, 278, 279.
Methodist (see Religion, Denominationalism).
Methodist Quarterly Review, 251, 257.
Migration, William Longstreet to Georgia, 4; "Canetuck," 5; Virginia and North Carolina in Georgia, 17, 53–55, 205; New England in Georgia, 55–56; crime as a motive, 205; Georgia deserted, 73, 239, 300.
Military, political advancement, 81–82, 135, 178, 204, 220, 286; religion, 345.
"Militia Drill," 81, 82, 149, 178–180.
Milledgeville Southern Recorder, 149.
Miller, S. F., 154, 190.
Mirror, 166, 194–196, 208–210; Longstreet's contributions, 199, 202, 204, 205.
Miscellany, 165, 195.
Mississippi Scenes, 167.
Mississippi University, Longstreet preaches, 229; Andrew advises Longstreet to accept Presidency, 289; J. N. Waddel, 290; G. F. Holmes, 291, 296; Longstreet President, 297–310; honorary degree to Longstreet, 310; Barnard, 299, 311; Edward Mayes, 357, 290–292, 296, 311, 315, 353.
Mitchell, D. G., 317.
"Mother and her Child," 149, 177.
Music, Longstreet's taste, 52, 175; Church, 64–65, 69, 231, 251–253; flute, 82, 140, 318, 328, 336.
Myers, Prof., 260.
Mysterious Picture, 76.
"Mystics," 245.

Nesbit, E. A., 197.
New England in Georgia, 53–58, 165, 183, 254, 323.
New York Advocate and Journal, 279.
New York Times, 362.
"Night at College," 200.
Niles's Register, 56, 148.
Nineteenth Century, 360, 361, 363–364.
North American Gazette, 133.
North American Review, 287.
Note Book (Longstreet's), 45–46.
Nullification, 121–132, 136, 138 (see Secession).

"Old Soldiers," 199, 200, 207.
"Old Things Become New," 364–368.
Olin, Stephen, Georgia, 56, 109, 111; Randolph-Macon, 254; Slavery and the Church, 276.
Olio, 90.
Oratory, 31; best means of spreading information, 63, 73, 140–141; 136–138, 225–226.
Orion, 208–211.

Paul to Philemon (see *Letters on Epistle of Paul to Philemon*).
Pace, Dredzel, 171–172.
Patriotic Effusions, 89–90.
Patriotism, 207, 325, 327; Mission of the Republic, 16, 42–43, 47, 108; Georgia, 69–73, 197–198, 330–332, La Fayette, 112–115; Georgia civilization superior to European, 261; decline, 220, 307–308; the South, 361–363.
Peck, Rev. Dr., 281–282.
Pendleton, P. C., 196–198.

390 INDEX

Perry, B. F., 360, 363-364.
Petigru, J. L., 26, 30, 114, 314-315, 324-325.
Pierce, George F., 46, *Southern Ladies Book*, 196, 198; minister, 222, 245, 280; Church and slavery, 277; President of Emory College, 290; President of Wesleyan College, 245.
Pierce, Lovick, 20, 108-109, 110, 111, 356; "music, drawing and painting," 69; Longstreet's marriage, 88-89; Church and slavery, 276, 280, 281.
Pierce's (Miss) School for Young Ladies, 41.
Prince, O. H., 75, 76, 78, 82, 178.
Princeton University, 4, 7, 35, 36, 333.
Poe, Edgar Allan, 152, 153, 170, 177, 189.
Politics, State Rights—Federalist, 36, 46-47, 138; only avenue to distinction, 84-85, 191, 192, 194; Longstreet, 93, 96, 98-100, 108, 125, 137-138, 305, 309, 319-329; Nullification, 121-132; methods, 125, 209, 219, 220; Know-Nothings, 305-309; secession, 319, 329.

Race Relations, 63, 98, 117-118, 135, 171, 345, 347, 358-359; prejudice a social expedient, 54; slavery and caste, 59-60, 61; white complacency, 76, 145, 242, 272-273, 311-312; slavery and intellectual advancement, 217, 267, 272; Church and slavery, 222-223, 232, 270-288, 342-343; slavery and chivalry, 67, 284-285; Delany, 325-327, 329.
Racing, in Georgia, 15-16, 61, 180; none in New England, 40; morality, 181-182.
Ramsay, David, 27.
Randolph-Macon College, 253, 255, 256.
Reading, 312, 335, 361; Latin classics, 31; "bad form," 66, 192-193; frontier, 68, 73; Literary Associations, 87, 95, 210; circulation libraries, 135; early publications in Georgia, 187; indifference, 191-193, 196-198, 214-217, 221, 331; libraries, 243, 302 (see Magazines).
Recreation, country store as center, 61; *Georgia Scenes*, 176-178, 180-185; 203-204; leisure, 188-189, 193-194, 313, 335; "Muster," 204, 178-179.
Reemelin, Charles, 366.
Reeves and Gould Law School, 34, 39-46, 82, 146, 165, 171.
Religion, Longstreet, 32, 51, 89, 91, 100-112, 219-240, 367; social force in early Georgia, 63-65, 100-112; Church and slavery, 270-288, 342-343; Confederate soldiers, 345 (see Denominationalism; "Science").
Richards, T. A., 208.
Richards, W. C., 208-212.
Richmond Academy, 13, 14-15, 17, 20, 22, 24, 171.
Ross, F. A., 284.
Rutherford, Mildred L., 180.

"Sage Conversation," 149, 183.
Savannah, 16, 170, 198, 278.
School Fellow, 211.
"Science," 267-268, 342, 365, 367.
Secession, 46, 48, 121, 127, 130, 132, 136, 138, 202, 323-324, 339-340, 349, 351; Methodist division, 270-288; literature of secession, 285-286; (see Nullification).
Shall S. C. Begin the War?, 339, 340.
Sherman, W. T., 348.
Sherwood, Adiel, 56, 111, 112, 139, 151; 189; Methodists "unscriptural," 110, manual labor schools, 255.
"Shooting Match," 149, 183-185.
Sigourney, Mrs., 335.
Silliman, Benjamin, 37-38, 312.
Sims, W. G., 55, 58, 177, 197, 206, 215, 225, 330, 331, 360.
"Simon Suggs," 166.
Smelt, Miss, Memoir of, 181, 187, 295.
Smith, George G., 228, 333.
Smithsonian Institution, 312.
"Snakebite," 200.
Social Structure, Georgia, 53-69, 73, 95, 114-115, 143-151, 167-168, 180-181, 201, 205, 208, 239, 242-244, 259, 278; Louisiana, 294; Mississippi, 300, 304-305, 312-313; South Carolina, 319-321, 334-335.
Somerville, 181.
"Song," 149, 175.
South Carolina University, 35, 314-325, 334-341.

INDEX

Southern Christian Advocate, 251–253, 259, 280, 283.
Southern Field and Fireside, publishes *William Mitten*, 31–34; 118, 212, 221, 337.
Southern Ladies Book, 196–198, 208–211.
Southern Literary Gazette, 109, 211.
Southern Literary Journal, 152, 174.
Southern Literary Messenger, 146–147, 151, 154, 166, 170, 202, 204, 211, 221, 331.
Southern Quarterly Review, 285.
Southern Review, 360.
Sparks, Jared, 134.
Sparks, Wm. H., 77–80, 82.
Spectator, 157.
Speeches, political, 126–128, 322–325; educational, 257–258, 262–264; religious, 226–230, 280.
Sprague, W. B., *Annals of the American Pulpit*, 295.
"Squirrel Hunt," 199.
State Rights Sentinel, 113, 132–138, 149, 151, 317.
Statistical Congress, 325–328.
Stephens, A. H., 93, 119, 197, 227, 261, 354, 360, 361.
Stephens, Linton, 227.
Stories with a Moral, 204–207.
Stowe, Harriet Beecher, 42.
Student Government, 294–295.
Sumner Eulogy, 357.
Supreme Court, 92, 120.
"Sut Lovingood," 166.

Talmage, Benjamin, 42.
Taine, H.-A., 162.
Taylor Select Female School, 175.
"Temperance," drinking, 61, 66, 89, 95, 320; Longstreet, 95, 134, 139–142, 158, 182, 317, 335, 347; organized, 106, 139–142.
Texas, 138–139, 202, 205, 307–308.
Theater, Augusta, 12–13, 15, 16; immoral, 106, 361.
Thompson, Jacob, 290, 299, 312, 352.
Thompson, J. R., 331.
Thompson, W. T., 151, 165–167, 239–240; art critic, 68; "yankee" and "cracker" related, 165; *Mirror*, 194–196, 204, 208; Longstreet's *Paul to Philemon*, 285.
Thornwell, J. H., 315, 343.
Timrod, Henry, 82, 336.
Toombs, Robert, 354.
Torrance, Ebenezer, 85, 101, 109.
Transportation, 7, 19, 36, 56, 113, 114, 116, 137, 235, 246–247, 300, 346.
Trent, W. P., 57, 70, 115, 180.
Troop, G. M., 75, 96.
Trumble, Horace, 37.
Trumpet Major, 179–180.
Tucker, Beverley, 144.
"Turf," 149, 180, 181.
Turner, Allen, 231, 252, 255.
Turner, W. W., 140, 215, 331.
"Turn Out," 149, 175.

"Valuable Suggestions," 349.
"Village Editor," 207.
Virginian, 170.
Voice from the South, 285–287.

Waddel, J. P., 197.
Waddel, J. N., 290, 296, 298, 299, 310–311, 353, 354.
Waddel, Moses, 112, 295, 316; school at Willington, 23–34, 41, 61, 82, 171, 177, 260, 316; racing, 181; *Memoir of Miss Smelt*, 187; Longstreet eulogy, 250; Georgia University, 25, 264, 290.
Walker, Freeman, 78.
Wardlaw Brothers, 314.
Washington, George, 42, 75, 88, 113, 134, 171.
"Wax Works," 149, 183.
Waymarks in the Life of a Wanderer, 144–145.
Waynesboro, 183, 195.
Weems, Mason Lock, 187.
Wesleyan College, 245–246.
Western Continent, 195, 285.
"Westover," 118.
Whitney, Eli, 11.
Whyte, R. A., 205.
Wilde, R. H., theater, 15; Tasso, 16, 75, 190, 221; "My Life is like the Summer Rose," 187.
William Mitten, 36, 358; Waddel, 26–27, 32; autobiography, 207; Henry Hull, 248, 334; begun in Louisiana,

295–296; completed in South Carolina, 331–334.
Williams, A. F., 173.
Willington Academy (see Waddel, Moses).
Winans, Wm., 293, 309.
Wirt, Wm., 134, 157.
Wister, Owen, 170.
Women, frontier, 5–9, 66–67, 177, 183; intelligence, 67, 197, 302, 331, 334–335; "chivalry," 68, 175–176, 253, 284–285, 348; independence, 97–98, 117, 178, 195, 223, 292, 314, 364; education, 201, 245–246, 300; housekeeping, 313, 334–335; large families, 223.

Yale, 23, 34, 35, 36–40, 143; confers honorary degree, 156; 260, 261, 264.
Yazoo Land Act, 12, 36, 73.
Yellow Fever, 233, 318.
Young Men's Christian Association, 280.

www.ingramcontent.com/pod-product-compliance
Lightning Source LLC
Chambersburg PA
CBHW031958220426
43664CB00005B/67